Music, Sensation, and Sensuality

Music, Sensation, and Sensuality

Edited by
Linda Phyllis Austern

CRITICAL AND CULTURAL MUSICOLOGY
Volume 5

ROUTLEDGE
NEW YORK AND LONDON

Published in 2002 by
Routledge
29 West 35th Street
New York, New York 10001

Published in Great Britain by
Routledge
11 New Fetter Lane
London EC4P 4EE

Routledge is an imprint of the Taylor and Francis Group.

Printed on acid-free, 250-year-life paper.
Manufactured in the United States of America.
10 9 8 7 6 5 4 3 2 1

Design and typography: Jack Donner

The publisher wishes to thank the School of Music at Northwestern University for helping to underwrite the publication of this book.

Library of Congress Cataloging-in-Publication Data is available from the Library of Congress.

Music, Sensation, and Sensuality/ edited by Linda Phyllis Austern
ISBN 0-8153-3421-4

*To the memory of my father,
who took me folk-dancing, to many sorts of concerts,
and walked me to my violin lessons*

CONTENTS

Representation Touching Hearing

Noise and Science

SERIES EDITOR'S FOREWORD
General Introduction to
Critical and Cultural Musicology
Martha Feldman

Musicology has undergone a seachange in recent years. Where once the discipline knew its limits, today its boundaries seem all but limitless. Its subjects have expanded from the great composers, patronage, manuscripts, and genre formations to include race, sexuality, jazz, and rock; its methods from textual criticism, formal analysis, paleography, narrative history, and archival studies to deconstruction, narrativity, postcolonial analysis, phenomenology, and performance studies. These categories point to deeper shifts in the discipline that have led musicologists to explore phenomena which previously had little or no place in musicology. Such shifts have changed our principles of evidence while urging new understandings of existing ones. They have transformed prevailing notions of musical texts, created new analytic strategies, recast our sense of subjectivity, and produced new archives of data. In the process they have also destabilized canons of scholarly value.

The implications of these changes remain challenging in a field whose intellectual ground has shifted so quickly. In response to them, this series offers essay collections that give thematic focus to new critical and cultural perspectives in musicology. Most of the essays contained herein pursue their projects through sustained research on specific musical practices and contexts. They aim to put strategies of scholarship that have developed recently in the discipline into meaningful exchanges with one another while also helping to construct fresh approaches. At the same time they try to reconcile these new approaches with older methods, building on the traditional achievements of musicology in helping to forge new disciplinary idioms. In both ventures, volumes in this series also attempt to press new associations among fields outside of musicology, making aspects of what has often seemed an inaccessible field intelligible to scholars in other disciplines.

In keeping with this agenda, topics treated in forthcoming volumes of the series include music and the cultures of print; music, art, and synesthesia in nineteenth-century Europe; music in the African diaspora; relations between opera and cinema; and music in the cultural sensorium. Through enterprises like these, the series hopes to facilitate new disciplinary directions and dialogues, challenging the boundaries of musicology and helping to refine its critical and cultural methods.

Introduction

Linda Phyllis Austern

We never cease living in the world of perception, but we bypass it in critical thought[.]

—Maurice Merleau-Ponty, *"Un inédit de Maurice Merleau-Ponty"*

The scholar and the critic have been taught to reduce the savory stew of experience to the texture of words on paper. Convention demands silence of the "musical examples" at the core of a learned journal article and discrete fragmentation of the orgiastic experience of a rock concert in a review. How can those who labor in the pristine world of the intellect return to the rich sensorium of music? How can those who work with words as theorists or critics of perceptible experience re-member an embodied art? The varied essays in this collection, written by scholars from across the arts and human sciences, begin to address these questions. They bring us from modern Hungary to colonial Mexico, from Enlightenment France to the Bolivian Andes over two centuries later. They speak of the artifice of museum display and the manic pace of dance video; of the scientific study of acoustics and the impact of noise; of love, death, tears, and the classification of knowledge. But they never abandon the kaleidoscopic world of perception. This book is an attempt to gather together some of the many ways in which manufactured sound can be perceived as part of the corporeal world of human culture and contemplation.

The experience of music remains firmly rooted in the senses. The production of ordered sound involves not only the intellect, but, depending on the medium, also touch, taste, sight, and smell as well as hearing. Advertising executives and purveyors of goods and services toy with our sensory expectations, particularly as one pleasure suggests the intoxication

of another. "Sleep-inducing piano compositions that are as soothing as a
warm tub soak before slipping between cotton sheets," proclaims the
advertisement for a compact disc packaged in soft, glowing colors. A famous
billboard image suggests the ancient synaesthetic pleasures of musical notes
and alcohol every Christmas in North America. One French master-
perfumer likens her art to symphonic composition, while a major-label
recording offers "a romantic Italian feast for your ears." Behind the counter
of an upscale cookware and gourmet shop, "Sunday Brunch" is served as an
audio disc. Across the way, "Harmony," "Music," "Rhapsody," and
"Whisper" are proffered as tiny pots of rich color and luxurious texture at
a Swedish cosmetic boutique. The list is endless, yet the phenomenon
escapes serious critical attention.

On any given evening in any large Western city, the symphony patron
moves across smooth marble and plush carpeting whose contrasting textures
and colors invite the caress of eye or hand. Moving through a sea of bodies
whose attire has been selected to draw the gaze and suggest pleasure to the
other senses, she passes stalls purveying aperitifs and dainty foods. As she
sinks into a cushioned seat covered with sumptuous fabric, she becomes
aware of the carved and glittering architectural details of the hall before
being plunged into darkness designed to draw the vision toward the stage
and accentuate the sense of hearing: crystal chandeliers, velvet draperies,
gilded coats of arms, voluptuous plaster nymphs, and sirens. Not many
blocks away, the club-goer gyrates in an equal darkness punctuated by
flashes of vivid light in a haze of smoke and the mingled scent of alcohol,
human sweat, and fragrances meant to allure. Amplified music, selected by
a headphone-crowned disc-jockey isolated in a soundproof booth, vibrates
through the bodies of dancers, drinkers, and auditors alike, drawing them
together in communion. Scattered across town stand still, silent houses of
worship awaiting the canonical hours at which the faithful will join in
celebrations which link music to the objects of the other senses in an effort
to contemplate the otherworldly. Yet the scholars and critics who consider
these musics—or those of the cinema, theater, passing automobile, or other
venues that incorporate the art across time and space—tend to isolate them
from their full sensory complement.

> To return the word to the flesh. To make knowledge carnal again; not by
> deduction, but by immediate perception or sense at once; the bodily senses
>
> —Norman O. Brown, *Love's Body*

The last two decades of the twentieth century witnessed an explosion of
popular and scholarly works about the senses. Shifting between the poles
of philosophy and social science, or cognition and culture, the common

point of these reconsiderations has been a return to an epistemology of embodiment.[1] "When a person becomes ill, he is likely to become aware of it through his own senses," begins one of the *Cambridge Texts in the Physiological Sciences* (1982). Gravely pronouncing a fundamental truth to "a medical student in the second or third year of a preclinical course," the passage continues:

> If the condition progresses to the point where he seeks help, his advisor, even while *listening* [italics mine] to the patient's story, will use his own senses to pick up what he can of the cause of illness, and in very many cases what he sees, hears, feels, and smells will be enough for him to diagnose the condition. . . . Of course it is not just in sickness that the senses tell one about one's own body. . . .
>
> Thus the senses are the bodily mechanisms for gathering up-to-date information, and as such it is hard to exaggerate their importance.[2]

Hard to exaggerate, indeed. In a bold new study from the end of the twentieth century, George Lakoff and Mark Johnson, representing a radical branch of cognitive science, overthrow at least 2,500 years of Western assumptions about the link between mind and body. Using the sort of lush language most often banished from philosophical and clinical studies of the intellect, they conclude that:

> The embodied mind is part of the living body and is dependent on the body for its existence. The properties of mind are not purely mental: They are shaped in crucial ways by the body and brain and how the body can function in everyday life. The embodied mind is thus very much of this world. Our flesh is inseparable from what Merleau-Ponty called the "flesh of the world" and what David Abram refers to as "the more-than-human world." Our body is intimately tied to what we walk on, sit on, touch, taste, smell, see, breathe, and move within. Our corporeality is part of the corporeality of the world. . . . The mind is not merely corporeal but also passionate, desiring, and social. It has a culture and cannot exist culture-free.[3]

It can hardly be coincidental that the same twenty years of theoretical re-emphasis on the senses also marked the rise of the music video worldwide, and a sharp increase in the Western marketing of music to accompany an ever-expanding array of routine physical tasks. From exercise to shopping, from public travel to waiting for service, even the most mundane ventures are now regularly enhanced by commercially designed mood-altering soundtracks. Music scholars and critics have nonetheless been as slow to join their multidisciplinary colleagues in the investigation of bodily modes of knowing, as others have been to recognize the full impact of music on the human sensorium and its cultural extensions.[4]

The senses clearly help to mediate consciousness and communication. There has, however, been little agreement about their nature, value, or even number across human time and geography. Are they valid or invalid means to recognize the self and the world? How are they linked to each other and to which additional cognitive faculties? Are they shared with other entities, visible or invisible? Are their data trustworthy? In what ways are they linked to the arts and sciences, to morality, emotion, or social structures? Even the five senses of common Western parlance owe their categorical foundation to Aristotle and are far from universal. Their definition and order have been seriously questioned by many experts from our own culture, let alone from others that evaluate them differently.[5]

For over two millennia, even Western intellectual inquiry has been torn between rationalist and empiricist models of the human processing of sense-data, roughly based on the Aristotelian idea that knowledge was ultimately derived from information gathered by five discrete senses, and its Platonic opposite that found sense-data as a distraction from true wisdom.[6] For the past century, especially its final quarter, perceptual modalities and the very conditions of sensory experience have undergone rapid and unprecedented transformation as new technologies and new forms of intellectual inquiry have emerged.[7] We belong to an overtly visual age in which less "pristine" senses are sometimes underestimated, an age of passive reception of artificially created sense-data. Ours is an era in which machines from seismographs to televisions enhance and transmit sense-data before it reaches us. How easy it has become to surrender our sensory consciousness, to let others feel and think for us: how easy and how dangerous. For sensation, as concept or process, is far from simple.

One of the most vexing questions has long been the relationship between emotion, intellect, and the senses. Is there a higher form of contemplation that stands divorced from physical stimuli and bestial desires? How and when does bodily perception contribute to the cognitive process, visceral reaction, or aesthetic judgment? Through what processes do sensory responses become part of narrative, ritual, or creative vision? In an intellectual culture that has traditionally divorced subject from object and fact from feeling, Western thinkers have tended to separate perceived from perceiver, to create separate faculties for processing things sensed and things known.[8] "Man communicates with his whole body, and yet the word is his primary medium," writes Walter Ong, "and communication, like knowledge itself, flowers in speech."[9] Nowhere is this attitude more strongly reinforced than in scientific studies of the sensory process or its objects, especially in their pristine publication as silenced speech. "Sensing is to knowing as a cry is to words," adds medical doctor Erwin Straus, "A cry reaches only him who hears it, here and now; but words abide, they can reach everyone when and where ever they may be. In sensing, everything is for me. But knowing seeks the 'in itself' of things."[10] However, "to sense" is not merely "to feel." It is to become aware of the hidden meaning of something, to be affected, concerned, pleased, or displeased, or aroused by it. Sensibility is both perception and apprehension by sense. It is only a short step from sensation to metaphor, from sense to symbol, or from bodily sensation to intellection and back again.[11] One of the results of recent inquiry into the nature of sensation and its relationship to thought has been a recognition that, in spite of the traditional opposition between reason and sensation in Western culture and aesthetics, any human faculty of thought is ultimately inseparable from bodily experience. "The perceiving mind is an incarnated mind," wrote Merleau-Ponty some forty years ago.[12] Music, with its physical origin and paradoxical intangibility, with its beginning in the mind and end in the imagination or memory between mind and body, must necessarily occupy a complicated place in any scheme linking corporeality and contemplation. The essays in this book barely begin to intimate just how complicated it can be.

Music is most immediately rooted in the perception of sound. Sound, through which music becomes inextricably tangled with language, communication, and bodily ways of locating the self in culture and in space, reaches outward toward the other senses, and toward the senses of others. "Sound is literally disembodiment, an emanation from the bodies producing it that leaves their materiality and concentrated localization behind," writes David L. Burrows in a pioneering study of sound, speech, and music:

> The singers themselves have the sensation of expanding, in attenuating form, into surrounding space, and filling it, and when their listeners close their eyes, the whole auditorium becomes their music. What expands outward from them in every direction presses in on the audience from all sides, neutralizing the normally charged issue of here and there.
>
> All of this takes place without any overt activity on the part of the listeners. Looking is an outwardly active process, involving as it does active movements of the eyes, head, trunk, and body to achieve favorable orientation and focus. . . . [I]nwardly, listening may be just as active as looking, but outwardly we often arrest movement and wait for the sound to come clear. Seeing is like touching, hearing like being touched; except that the touch of sound does not stop at the skin. It seems to reach inside and to attenuate . . . the biologically still more basic one between within and without.[13]

No wonder those medieval and early modern thinkers who retained more than a slight suspicion of the power of music over the body likened its effect to the rape of the ear, or the forcible theft of the soul.[14] And no wonder so many rituals that draw together multiple senses and multiple bodies from across multiple dimensions feature music at their very centers.

If sound itself may be likened to a disembodied emanation, its "grain," its uniqueness, its individually identifying factors come from and refer back to the materiality of the producing body. Sound unites its listeners communally within the orbit of its motion even as it dissolves the bounds between the senses of its performer.[15] From infancy, children learn their place in the world and the overlapping powers of their senses through the production of sound:

> [S]ound, a medium of communication since the child's first cry, manifests new potential of meaning as the child passes through the lalling stage, where he constructs around himself a vast bubble of sound, burbling, gurgling, playing with his diversifying vocal powers— and with his lips at the same time, for sound, both in speaking and in hearing, is closely linked with touch and kinaesthesia. One "mouths" words quite literally, and our hearing is partly feeling.[16]

Hearing begins in the womb and helps the newborn identify his mother and the warm nourishment she provides. From this primal sensory coccoon, the female body has easily been refigured in sound or remembered as an ear.[17] Perhaps for this reason, as Adshead-Lansdale's and Tolbert's essays in this collection particularly make clear, the music-language knot has often been tied with gendered strings and copious strands from Nature instead of Artifice. Perhaps this is a contributory factor to the many forms of opposition between (manly) restraint and emotional response to music that Christensen, Craig-McFeely, Kramer, and McIver present in such different manifestations. Likewise, absence of the rich, vibrant texture of living sound is often read or figured as a metaphor for death or the dehumanization of the landscape, as Grover Friedlander and Kassler remind us quite differently in their essays.[18]

Western thinkers have traditionally positioned music somewhere in the shifting space between mathematical abstraction and corporeality, between reasoned creation and emotive response. To contemplate, study, or compose enduring music is to be intellectually active; to abandon oneself entirely to the pleasures of listening (or even performing) has become the passive partner in a potentially damaging physical entanglement. "Pure" taste and the aesthetics that provides its basis, even in scholarship, has been founded on a refusal of "impure" taste and the simple, primitive delights of sensation.[19] The discipline of music theory has long emphasized the clinical relationships between notes with the ultimate goal of preserving such interplay as printed text, proceeding through what Roland Barthes refers to as the "toilette of the dead."[20]

Psychoacoustical studies of the phenomenon have tended to be based on the physics of sound and hearing, on the clean reception into the ear (and thence summarily to the brain) of waves of motion, on sound as an element of itself; Amy Graziano's historical summary in the present collection illuminates this long-standing tendency even through its very language. "A musical note is just pulsating air stimulating the organs in our ears," proclaims Diane Ackerman in her *Natural History of the Senses*.[21] Nonetheless, there is always a tacit understanding that, somewhere at the basis of these manipulations and these abstract studies, lies pulsating, affective embodied music, received by the senses through physical and cultural filters.[22] "The score of a Bach fugue cannot be understood in the complete absence of mathematics; nor can it be understood with mathematics alone," says Straus of even the silent skeleton of a piece of music, awaiting the stroke of a hand to give it sonic flesh.[23] "We listen with our bodies," concludes Ackerman.[24]

Even the most erudite discussions of music from beyond the narrow confines of traditional academic musicology and theory have tended to dissolve the boundaries between sensations, between action and passive reception. Orphic legend and the myths of the sirens and of similar beings worldwide emphasize the overwhelming admixture of sensation and desire in attentive listening. St. Augustine's famously lachrymose account of his baptism conjoins music, water, tears, and overwhelming passion into a powerful unity that appears again and again in Western thought, as in Kramer's article in the present volume.[25] William Barley invited the would-be purchaser of his Elizabethan book of lute tabliture "to have a taste of so ravishing a sweet science as music" with a deliciously synaesthetic metaphor.[26] Over three-and-a-half centuries later, the German physician Erwin Straus evoked multisensory images of intoxication, addiction, and erotic fulfillment in an anachronistic flight of fancy triggered by echoes of Bach, birds, and Roma violins:

> The gypsy, like the bird, knows only surrender to the individual tone: a sometimes stormy, sometimes tarrying progression from one resting point to the next, a rhapsodic outpouring and an intoxicated dilatoriness. . . . His music-making is Dionysiac; his slow relishing of individual sounds and moods is drunkenness. . . . Classical music is strict, strictly exact in measurement and laws. . . . the listener, too, may be carried away into dreams of landscape; or he can become an attentive listener who understands the language of music and who perceives its manifest expression.

Let us once more recall the intoxicated addict. They all long for the space of landscape; they find their fulfillment in the Dionysiac lingering by their dreams, intoxications, ecstasies, by turning from the bright waking world of the day to the night, to sleep and to that music of which the gypsy is the master. The tavern is the sympathetic landscape of the drinker and his center of life.[27]

In an interview conducted by Hector Biancotti and published in December of 1973, French critic Roland Barthes drew on a multisensory vocabulary to describe the unique qualities of Gundula Janowitz's voice in a performance of Mozart's *Le nozze di Figaro*: "To describe [Janowitz's vocal] grain, I find images of milkweed acidity, of a nacreous vibration situated at the exquisite and dangerous limit of the toneless."[28] Through hearing, through an engagement with the performing body, Barthes's senses of sight, taste, touch, and smell became aroused in auditory-linguistic imagination. These are, in turn, transmitted to the interviewer through the sound of his words and transformed into verbal images of pearly luster and the smoothness of milkweed. It was also Barthes who, in 1970, famously divided practical music, bodily music, and fully sensed music into "the music one listens to, [and] the music one plays," music received through the ear and music engaging the entire body.[29] Finally, at the end of the twentieth century, it has been recognized that the music of the theater and the cinema, unfolding in darkness along with narrative and visual stimulation, permits public indulgence in private fantasy and forbidden emotional release.[30]

The eighteen essays in this book share a number of common themes. They reinforce each other even as each raises new issues from contrasting perspectives. I have organized them not according to specific sense, culture, or historical epoch, but by the questions they raise and the manner in which they raise them. Each one is unique, self-contained, and can also be read in any order at the reader's own pace. The collection begins with Descartes as do many studies in the philosophy of mind or history of cognition. But here Van Orden reevaluates the synthetic work of a youthful scholar, which draws on over a millenium's worth of information about music and on early-modern developments in mathematics, experimental science, and applied kinaesthetics. Like the other two essays with which it is grouped, it shows some of the dynamic tensions inherent in any attempt to categorize and delimit particular effects of music on the body physical and the body social from which it cannot be separated. Christensen also brings us into a world in which sounding music merges with theory, philosophy, prescriptive action, and premodern Western medicine conjoined to physics. Here, it is the sense of touch that circumscribes all others. Musicians surrender aspects of the rational mind to pure corporeal instinct and tonal sensibility before improvising a keyboard prelude. It is with this blend of music and overflowing affect that Kramer's article opens, considering the German Romantic cultural conjunction of tears, song, and sympathy. Tears, so often linked to the primal, prelinguistic utterance at the boundary between sensation and rationality, are conjoined through a varied musical vocabulary to sublimation and erotic longing, to hidden truth and vivid pain expressed through voice and keyboard.

The next section includes four essays that feature contrasting forms of sensory overload, excess, and transgression from one sense to another through the use of music. Tolbert's essay begins in the same primal realm of emotive sensuality as Kramer's. She draws on cultural criticism, semiotics, and gender theory to shed new light on the tangled reception of music as standing somewhere between the natural cries of animals and the pure "manly" rationality of language. Stobart begins with the complexities of the subjectivity and embodiment of the musical voice with which Tolbert ends. He takes the reader through the multisensory landscape of Andean music with its cultural and calendrical oscillation between excess and austerity, and its numerous links to evident and hidden energies. Adshead-Lansdale unifies the strains of sensory intoxication and the powerfully feminine capacities of embodied music raised respectively in the two preceeding essays. Her reading of a multimedia piece of performance art from the end of the twentieth century adds the dimension of dance to the linguistic argument articulated by Tolbert, and returns to the cusp between the physical and metaphysical worlds where music is so often located. Here, primal myth, sound, light, and movement work together through the body and the camera to reinforce a deeply rooted misogynist vision. Gordon-Seifert's paper also works with the multimedia retelling of mythological material through the highly gendered and sexualized body in performance. In this case, parody, scatology, politics, and erotica serve as a focal point for exposing the foibles of a royal court that favored unlikely narrative romances full of stock male and female character archetypes; and for the experience, through music, of a powerful sexual energy that ran counter to the culture's didactic images of men and women in control of their passions.

The next three essays focus on the evident transcendence of this world of sensuous excess. In them, music takes its place of ontological mystery by spanning the distance between things physical and metaphysical. Wagstaff and Wilkinson present contrasting rituals of mourning, death, and burial, in which objects of many senses and many sorts of formal gesture blend together and help to create different senses of community. Wagstaff demonstrates how music mixed with other sensory stimuli not only to bridge the temporal and the eternal, the living and the dead, but reinforce a sense of colonial power and concomitant cultural hierarchy in sixteenth-century Mexico. Kertész Wilkinson outlines the funereal and mourning rites of the minority Vlach Roma people of present-day Hungary against the rich sensory texture of their lives. Instead of strengthening an external cultural hierarchy, the music and associated ritual coalesce into a unifying signifier of community, a hedge against the perceived impurity of the majority people. Grover-Friedlander presents a mid-twentieth century opera that raises questions of vocality, embodiment, and death through the metaphor of the telephone, a machine that displaces the rich sensuality of the (operatic) voice. Her reading of the work emphasizes death as an outcome of vocal excess—a topos as old as the myth of Orpheus. Consequently she begins to raise vital questions about the fragmentation of voice and body in the machine age.

The next three essays continue the theme of multisensory fragmentation and synechdotal refiguration of the body as one or more of its senses. In each one, mechanical dominance of the sensorium becomes a creative media triumph instead of a loss, an artificial resurrection of the displaced performing body of Grover-Friedlander's piece. The potentially over-whelming power and danger of music as heard and felt has been replaced. Here, for the final part of the twentieth century, sound has been subjugated to sight. And the senses of touch, movement, and involuntary physical response so closely linked to music have been obliterated or ceded to the camera's or curator's eye, or to the absent director's or technician's hand. Citron discusses a production of Mozart's *Così fan tutte* not only translated from the medium of theater to that of television, but from a late-eighteenth-century setting to a late twentieth. Through such techniques of dissolving boundaries, and a set of slangy English subtitles sharply juxtaposed with the elegant Italian sung on the recorded soundtrack, the work distances the viewer/listener in ways that raise questions about art, culture, history, and the packaging of older representational works for new "media-savvy" audiences. Dodds, like Adshead-Lansdale, presents a multimedia form conceived and born in an age of enhanced production, and not incidentally, consumerism. Her essay raises questions about the relationship between sound and image in music video and video dance in terms of the performing body captured by the camera, and of the watcher/listener for whom the works are created. Zecher gives us a completely different take on anachronism, media update, commercialism, and the manipulated musical body. Her essay literally presents older musics as museum pieces, with sound utterly severed from the other senses so necessary to full participation in the art. Instruments in glass cases are literally silenced and left to lie untouched in sterile surroundings. Meanwhile, visitors hear disjunct recorded sound through headphones that isolate them not only from the musical bodies they are meant to hear, but from other members of the "audience." Where now is the *jouissance*, the communal experience of embodied music?

The next three essays also consider sound displaced by sight, but to the opposite end. Here, in "old master" paintings, visual images are meant to stir the other senses, and through such imaginary stimulation to lead to cogitation. We learn of the cultural position of music and musical activity through these works, and of music's position as an object of embodied listening and performance in relation to other sensory-intellectual stimuli. Minamino brings us into the richly sensuous world of late-medieval Netherlandish painting, in which imaged sound is as vibrantly textured as the shapes and colors of the landscape. He shows us how much of the social and cultural world of the musician is given by the painterly hand and eye, from which point it may be further corroborated by extant music and documents, and by biography. McIver returns the reader to the allegorical world and to the figurations of women featured in several previous essays, but this time with a visual focus. Her work presents the multisensory message of sixteenth-century Italian images that unite eroticism and objects of bodily pleasure against a didactic background. Craig-McFeely follows up by locating verbal and visual evocations of early modern female musicians at the permeable boundary between the aural, the visual, and the tactile. She reminds us of how easily voice and body have been refigured as musical instruments, which themselves have taken on animate and even erotic qualities in metaphor.

The collection closes as it had begun, with considerations of sound and the listening process as they extend to the entire body, cognition, and consciousness; and to the acoustic culture within which the body is located. Kassler raises questions about noise, sonic overload, and psycho-physical response to extreme stimulation of the human auditory mechanism, as well as their history and need for future multidisciplinary study. Graziano also gives us a phenomenological history with a crossdisciplinary intellectual future. Her essay raises provocative questions about an empirical study of human sound reception that arises from a science that had all but ignored the richly sensual dimensions of the musical experience.

Notes

1. Among scholarly studies, see, for example, David Abram, *The Spell of the Sensuous: Perception and Language in a More-Than-Human World* (New York: Pantheon Books, 1996); Diane Ackerman, *A Natural History of the Senses* (New York: Random House, 1990); H. B. Barlow and J. D. Mollon, eds., *The Senses* (Cambridge: Cambridge University Press, 1982); David Chidester, *Word and Light: Seeing, Hearing and Religious Discourse* (Urbana: University of Illinois Press, 1992); F. Gonzalez-Crussi, *The Five Senses* (New York: Harcourt, Brace Jovanovich, 1989); David Howes, ed., *The Varieties of Sensory Experience: A Sourcebook in the Anthropology of the Senses* (Toronto: University of Toronto Press, 1991); Mark Johnson, *The Body in the Mind: The Bodily Basis of Meaning, Imagination, and Reason* (Chicago: University of Chicago Press, 1987); Alphonso Lingis, "The Sensuality and the Sensitivity," in Richard A. Cohen, ed., *Face*

to Face with Levinas (Albany: State University of New York Press, 1986), 219–30; Jillyn Smith, *Senses and Sensibilities* (New York: John Wiley, 1989); Paul Stoller, *The Taste of Ethnographic Things: The Senses in Anthropology* (Philadelphia: University of Pennsylvania Press, 1989); Gary Taylor, "Feeling Bodies," in Jonathan Bate, Jill L. Levenson, and Dieter Mehl, eds., *Shakespeare and the Twentieth Century: The Selected Proceedings of the International Shakespeare Association World Congress[,] Los Angeles, 1996* (Newark: University of Delaware Press, 1998); and Charles Wegener, *The Discipline of Taste and Feeling* (Chicago: University of Chicago Press, 1992). Of course, the serious investigation of the senses is far older, although the emphasis was more often on historical changes or the internal processing of data than the input of signals through bodily receptors; for an idea of the range of mid-twentieth century studies see, for example, Edwin G. Boring, *Sensation and Perception in the History of Experimental Psychology* (New York: Apleton-Century-Crofts, 1942); Frank A. Geldard, *The Human Senses*, 2nd ed. (London: John Wiley and Sons, 1972); D. W. Hamlyn, *Sensation and Perception: A History of the Philosophy of Perception* (London: Routledge and Kegan Paul, 1961); Maurice Mandelbaum, *Philosophy, Science, and Sense Perception: Historical and Critical Studies* (Baltimore: Johns Hopkins University Press, 1964); Maurice Merleau-Ponty, *Phenomenology of Perception*, trans. Colin Smith (London: Routledge and Kegan Paul, 1962); Merleau-Ponty, *The Primacy of Perception*, ed. James M. Edie (Evanston: Northwestern Unviersity Press, 1964); and Erwin Straus, MD, *The Primary World of Senses: A Vindication of Sensory Experience*, trans. by Jacob Needleman (London: Collier-Macmillan Ltd., 1963).

2. H. B. Barlow and J. D. Mollon, eds., *The Senses* (Cambridge: Cambridge University Press, 1982), p. 1.

3. George Lakoff and Mark Johnson, *Philosophy in the Flesh: The Embodied Mind and Its Challenge to Western Thought* (New York: Basic Books, 1999), 565. For an outline of the complete development of this thesis, see 551–68.

4. Tia DeNora's recent study of the social uses of music in Great Britain and the United States, *Music in Everyday Life* (Cambridge: Cambridge University Press, 2000), begins to raise important issues of the relationship between music, social institutions, and the body, especially 75–108. On the current widespread use of background music to alter mood, see Joseph Lanza, *Elevator Music: A Surreal History of Muzak, Easy-Listening, and Other Moodsong* (New York: St. Martin's Press, 1994).

5. See Ackerman, *Natural History of the Senses*, xv; Pierre Bourdieu, *Distinction: A Social Critique of the Judgment of Taste*, trans. Richard Nice (Cambridge: Harvard University Press, 1984), 486–88; Chidester, *Word and Light: Seeing, Hearing and Religious Discourse*, pp. 1–24; Constance Classen, *The Color of Angels: Cosmology, Gender and the Aesthetic Imagination* (London and New York: Routledge, 1998), 13–35; Jonathan Crary, *Suspensions of Perception: Attention, Spectacle and Modern Culture* (Cambridge, 1999), 1–10; Geldard, *The Human Senses*, 258–59; David Howes, "Sensory Anthropology," in Howes, ed., *The Variety of Sensory Experience: A Sourcebook in the Anthropology of the Senses*, 167–91; Hamlyn, *Sensation and Perception: A History of the Philosophy of Perception*; Merleau-Ponty, *Phenomenology of Perception*, 2–12; Walter J. Ong, "The Shifting Sensorium," *The Variety of Sensory Experience*, 25; Straus, *The Primary World of Senses: A Vindication of Sensory Experience*, 373; and Anthony Synnott, *The Body Social: Symbolism, Self, and Society* (London: Routledge, 1993), 128–49.

6. See Morris Berman, *The Reenchantment of the World* (Ithaca and London: Cornell University Press, 1981), 27. For a succinct summary of traditional Western insights concerning the senses, particularly from an anthropological perspective, see Anthony Synnott, "Puzzling Over the Senses: From Plato to Marx," in Howes, ed., *The Variety of Sensory Experience*, 61–78.

7. See Berman, *The Reenchantment of the World*, 16–17; Crary, *Suspensions of Perception*, 1–10; 13, and 46–48; Johnson, *The Body in the Mind*, 141–72; and Lakoff and Johnson, *Philosophy in the Flesh*, 3.

8. See Bourdieu, *Distinction*, 486–88; Johnson, *Body in the Mind*, 139–40; Lakoff and

Johnson, *Philosophy in the Flesh*, 16–44; Alphonso Lingis, "The Sensuality and the Sensitivity," in *Face to Face with Levinas*, ed. Richard A. Cohen (Albany: State University of New York Press, 1986), 220; Merleau-Ponty, *Phenomenology of Perception*, 207; Aaron Ridley, *Music, Value and the Passions* (Ithaca: Cornell University Press, 1995), 19–28; Leone Vivante, *Essays on Art and Ontology*, trans. Arturo Vivante (Salt Lake City: University of Utah Press, 1980), 58; and Charles Wegener, *The Discipline of Taste and Feeling* (Chicago: University of Chicago Press, 1992), 37–38.

9. Ong, "Shifting Sensorium," 25. See also Abram, *Spell of the Sensuous*, 73–76; Ackerman, *Natural History of the Senses*, 213–14; Roland Barthes, *The Grain of the Voice: Interviews 1962–1980*, trans. Linda Coverdale (New York: Hill and Wang, 1985), 3–7; and Vivante, *Essays on Art and Ontology*, 63.

10. Straus, *Primary World of Senses*, 312–13. Shakespeare scholar Gary Taylor has pointed out the paradoxical gap between the study of narrative and representational art and the work itself, reminding his readers that even the academic act of live presentation of material is a staid reading of a written text, cleansed of sensual and emotive content, "Feeling Bodies," 258–59.

11. See Chidester, *Word and Light*, 25–50; Classen, *Color of Angels*, 13–35; Lakoff and Johnson, *Philosophy in the Flesh*, 564–65; Lingis, "Sensuality and Sensitivity," 219; and Vivante, *Essays in Art and Ontology*, 58–59.

12. Merleau-Ponty, *The Primacy of Perception*, 3–11. See also Bourdieu, *Distinction*, 488; Crary, *Suspensions of Perception*, 11–79; Johnson, *The Body in the Mind*, 166–70; Lakoff and Johnson, *Philosophy in the Flesh*, 3 and 16–44.

13. David L. Burrows, *Sound, Speech and Music* (Amherst: University of Massachusetts Press, 1990), 20–21. See also Barthes, *Grain of the Voice*, 183–84; and Barthes, *Image, Music, Text*, 188–89.

14. See Linda Phyllis Austern, *Music in English Intellectual Culture, 1550–1650* (forthcoming).

15. See Abram, *Spell of the Sensuous*, 73–76; Ackerman, *Natural History of the Senses*, 175–80; Barthes, *Image, Music, Text*, 182; Straus, *Primary World of the Senses*, 378; and Vivante, *Essays on Art and Ontology*, 63.

16. Ong, "Shifting Sensorium," 25. See also Abram, *Spell of the Sensuous*, 74–75.

17. See Burrows, *Sound, Speech and Music*, 17–18; Henry Alden Bunker, Jr., "The Voice as Female Phallus," in *The Psychoanalytic Quarterly* 3 (1934), 392; Chantal Chawaf, "Linguistic Flesh," trans. Yvonne Rochette-Ozello, in Elaine Marks and Isabelle de Courtivron, eds., *New French Feminisms* (Amherst: University of Massachusetts Press, 1980), 177–78; Luce Irigaray, "The Fecundity of the Caress," in Richard A. Cohen, ed., *Face to Face with Levinas*, 249–51; and Thomas Pavel, "In Praise of the Ear (Gloss's Glosses)," in Susan Rubin Sulieman, ed., *The Female Body in Western Culture: Contemporary Perspectives* (Cambridge: Harvard University Press, 1986), 46–51.

18. For further information on this topos, see Burrows, *Sound, Speech and Music*, 22–23; and for the connection between music that ceases and death, see Carl Dalhaus, *Esthetics of Music*, trans. William Austin (Cambridge: Cambridge University Press, 1982), 11, as well as several of the essays in this collection.

19. See Bourdieu, *Distinction*, 486–87; and Lydia Goehr, *The Imaginary Museum of Musical Works: An Essay in the Philosophy of Music* (Oxford: Clarendon Press, 1992), 155–57.

20. Barthes, *Grain of the Voice*, 3.

21. Ackerman, *A Natural History of the Senses*, 212.

22. See, for example, Carl E. Seashore, *Psychology of Music* (New York: McGraw-Hill, 1938; reprint ed., New York: Dover Books, 1967), 1–2; and Mary Louise Serafine, *Music as Cognition: The Development of Thought in Sound* (New York: Columbia University Press, 1988), 35–36. Even in the pre-modern period of the glorification of musical abstraction there were dissenting thinkers who followed the Epicurean idea that the beauty of music should be judged not by its mimetic or referential qualities, but by the pleasurable and passionate responses it triggered through sensation; see Goehr, *Imaginary Museum of Musical Works*, 138, 141–47, and 154–57.

23. Straus, *Primary World of Senses*, 324.
24. Ackerman, *A Natural History of the Senses*, 212.
25. Saint Augustine, *Confessions*, trans. R. S. Pine-Coffin (London: Penguin Books, 1961), Book IX, Chapter 6, 190. Michel Poizat notes that tears and shivers, the usual sign of bereavement and suffering, are the outward manifestation of overwhelming musical pleasure, *The Angel's Cry: Beyond the Pleasure Principle in Opera*, trans. Arthur Denner (Ithaca: Cornell University Press, 1992), 3–4.
26. William Barley, *A New Book of Tabliture* (London: William Barley, 1596), sig. A2v.
27. Straus, *Primary World of Senses*, 324.
28. Barthes, *Grain of the Voice*, 184.
29. Barthes, *Image, Music, Text*, 149–50.
30. See Simon Frith, *Music for Pleasure: Essays on the Sociology of Pop* (Oxford: Polity Press, 1988), 129; and Poizat, *Angel's Cry*, 3–8.

Minding
Affect

I

Descartes
on Musical Training and the Body

Kate van Orden

The object of [Musick] is a Sound. The *end*; to delight,
and move various Affections in us.[1]

These are the opening lines of René Descartes's first treatise, the
Compendium Musicae (1618). Sound, delight, the passions. It would seem that
Descartes began his philosophical career in the body, a body craving sensual
delight and pleasure. The world of the *Compendium*—to recall its own
examples—is one where thunder and cannon fire offend the ear, where
animals dance to music, where duple meter excites "gentle and sluggish
motions, such as a kind of Languor, Sadnesse, Fear, Pride, and other heavy
and dull Passions," where antipathy causes a drum made of wolf skin to
silence one made of sheepskin.[2] It is a world still far from the philosopher's
celebrated dislocation of mind and body, even while the intellectual method
by which he would arrive there is very much on the horizon.

The *Compendium* is vexed, superficial in places, and occasionally
contradictory; as such, it is perhaps justifiably ignored by many historians
of philosophy. After all, Descartes never revised it for publication. It was a
private gift for his newfound friend, Isaac Beeckman, a manuscript for the
latter to tuck away in his library, far from the judgment of others. As for the
choice of subject matter, we know from Beeckman's journals that he was
interested in music himself, making it easy to suppose that Descartes hoped
only to please his friend by writing on music.[3] Music historians, for their
part, have quickly spotted Descartes's reliance on Zarlino's *Istituzioni
harmoniche* (1558), a comparison that shows up the *Compendium*'s lack of
theoretical novelty.[4] Rehearsing the work of earlier writers, its treatment of
rhythm, consonance, dissonance, degrees, counterpoint, vocal ranges, and
modes reaches few new conclusions, even though the path by which
Descartes comes to them is rather unusual.

My own interest in the *Compendium* lies somewhat outside the history of music theory and the history of philosophy, in the messy stuff of cultural history. It lies in the real world, so to speak, in the world often invoked by Descartes in the *Compendium*, where living, breathing, dancing, hearing beings sought the pleasure of music. Beginning here, in the body, grates against the usual interpretation of the *Compendium* as pure math, a tendency nicely summed up by H. Floris Cohen's quip that the *Compendium* is "Zarlino, *more geometrico*."[5] With this Cohen claims that Descartes only furthered Zarlino's urge to explain music geometrically.[6] But Descartes' geometry in no way negates the phenomenological orientation of his musical science. On the contrary, geometry proved a humane alternative to arithmetic precisely because it proceeds in terms that can be verified by sight and—in those cases where lines represent string lengths—by hearing. Indeed, the first two "ground rules" Descartes establishes at the outset of the *Compendium* make clear that his will be a study of sounding music, of music as heard:

1. Each Sense is capable of some Delectation.
2. To this Delectation is required a certain proportion of the object to the sense.[7]

For Descartes, the appeal of simple geometrical figures rested in one's ability to perceive their proportions directly with the senses. Hence even the geometry in the *Compendium* invites the reader to *see* the beauty in music, building a visual analog to the beauty one hears. The math does become slightly abstract in Descartes's chapter on degrees, in which arbitrary numbers are assigned to each pitch, making middle C [c'] = 180, c = 360, and c'' = 90, the whole representing string lengths with numbers that allow him to avoid fractions; but Descartes always works into math from the sensible. The "anecdotes" threaded throughout the treatise should be taken quite seriously for this reason, because they too fix Descartes's musical analysis in the body, bidding the reader to feel the shock of cannon fire, hear a leaping bass line as an aggressive counter to an attractive soprano line, and take physical delight in an evaded cadence as it denies the listener satisfaction and rest.

The *Compendium* was not written for the small circle of polyphonists, music theorists, and Aristotelians that formed the usual audience for music theory treatises at the time. It was written in the first instance for Beeckman, of course, but it also speaks to a general public with an inclusiveness that invites the broad reading I propose. Only good sense is required to understand its arguments, and just as Descartes would begin the *Discours de la méthode* (Leiden, 1637) by stating that "good sense or reason is by nature equal in all men," so too the *Compendium* asks nothing more of its readers than sound mind and senses.[8] Descartes disregards ancient and Renaissance authorities (there is no prerequisite reading for his course); intellectual, professional, social, and moral hierarchies are largely banished; and even the class distinctions implicit in the elevated status of vocal polyphony crumble when he heaps praise on the simplest music around: namely military drumming.[9] Armed with good sense, he cuts through the prevailing labyrinth of harmonic theory and its elaborate calculations to find a more direct and rational explanation of how music brings delight and moves "various Affections" in listeners.[10]

Already in his preliminary remarks, Descartes strips the cosmos of its philosophical mysteries, laying it bare with his example of an astrolabe (Figure 1.1). Looking upon such an object, he remarks, the viewer takes pleasure in the simple proportions of its net (the fretwork cut from a sheet of metal that rotates over its face), but not in the complex proportions of its mother (the circles of altitude and azimuth engraved in its face). We will turn to the exact nature of proportions and their action on the senses subsequently; what we should remark here is the significance of the astrolabe as a tool of contact with the heavens and why Descartes may have chosen it as an example at the outset of his treatise. Astronomers used astrolabes to measure the altitude of stars, and navigators, so equipped, used them to determine their position at sea. These were fairly precious instruments, part of the expensive technical equipment prospectors paid for when financing exploratory ventures such as the Magellan voyage, and sumptuous enough to offer as gifts to suitably wealthy patrons.[11] Since they were certainly not commonplace at the time of Descartes's writing (though Beeckman would have been familiar with them), they had special significance as a device whereby man might solve problems in positional astronomy. Engraved with the houses of the zodiac and the major constellations, the astrolabe appears to be a mobile model of celestial gyrations, a toy version of the cosmos to be held in the hand and manipulated at whim.[12] Whereas music treatises traditionally paid homage to the idea that the celestial spheres produced divine music as they spun in their orbits, Descartes offers up this cosmos for human inspection, implying that the senses are capable of judging heavenly truths.

By choosing music as the object of his first scientific essay, Descartes struck at the very heart of the musical cosmology favored by Renaissance philosophers. Music enabled him to interrogate the order of the world through a subject that, since the time of Pythagoras and Plato, had explained the coherence of terrestrial and heavenly matter in the mathematical language of harmonic proportions. What distinguishes the *Compendium* from prior thought is its method, which—in addition to its well-noted mathematics—enlists the senses in sizing up this order, heightening the tension in a treatise marked by the dualism of rational inquiry and bodily perception. I examine his method in the following section *Mathesis Universalis* and the Senses.

Figure 1.1. Brass Astrolabe by George Hartmann (1558). Courtesy of the Science &
Society Picture Library, London.

Why make the senses arbiters of proportion and, by implication, of beauty?[13] Why limit mathematical order to the blunt ratios that can be seen and heard? Not only must we acknowledge the importance of the body in Descartes's early work on music, we must assess the way Descartes construed the body and its senses to learn more about the cultural office of music at the time. For in the end, the *Compendium* is a cultural document, and Descartes was a witness to, participant in, and commentator on a set of deeply imbedded practices regulating the body's proper form and conduct. This physical discourse of civility or manners operated on the assumption that the visible language of the face and limbs and hands signaled a person's inner virtue and moral relationship with the world at large. As we shall see, music remained the touchstone of goodness as Renaissance thought gave way to rationalism, but did so only after the body was reconstructed and the senses retooled to be able to judge beauty more assuredly. This is the subject of the last section of my essay Music, Measure, and the Body.

Mathesis Universalis and the Senses

At the time Descartes wrote the *Compendium*, his methods were largely scientific, and his motives were characterized by a yearning to measure the physical world with the yardstick of mathematics. According to Stephen Gaukroger, Descartes's early work strove to give a naturalistic account of perceptual cognition, and it does appear to be in the spirit of natural philosophy that we find him studying sympathetic vibration by plucking lute strings tuned an octave apart and blowing on a flute to study the physical production of octaves on wind instruments.[14] This is observational science at its purest—the science of acoustics—which Descartes pursued in order to explain human perception in terms of basic mechanical actions. Music was the perfect object for a study of the senses because its sounds could be rationalized in terms of simple mathematical formulae: consonances please the ear because of their basic proportions (octaves stand in a 1:2 ratio, fifths 2:3, and fourths 3:4, all of which can be observed by dividing a string in parts), and we like duple and triple meter because they are based on the simple proportions 1:2 and 1:3.[15] But we should not see in Descartes's rationalization of string divisions a move toward mathematical abstraction. For Descartes, string divisions were actual sounding parts, hence the extraordinary opening line of the treatise: the object of music is sound. When manipulating string divisions, he is actually adding and subtracting sounds, which is unprecedented in the canonic tradition.[16] Early theory centered around the monochord, a scientific instrument strung with one length of string and fixed with moveable bridges that theorists used to divide the string according to simple proportions. But whereas Descartes used the monochord to manipulate sounds, early monochord theorists employed the instrument primarily as a calculator, or tool for compounding continuous ratios.[17] Although number theory and music theory intersected—particularly in precisely this domain of representing physical relationships in terms of proportionalities—Descartes made sound, rather than number, his primary object.

Descartes performed many of his experiments in the company of Beeckman, who recorded their first encounters in his journal.[18] Their mutual interest in combining physics and mathematics unfolded in meetings and letters, and Beeckman described them as two rare "Physico-mathematicians" in search of a method that could explain natural order with the language of mathematics.[19] The *Compendium Musicae* was but the first result of this project, which later included essays in dioptrics, meteors, and geometry. All of these treatises are, of course, related to the new method of reasoning Descartes began to develop in 1619, a method treating problems in the natural sciences by reducing them to their mathematical core and solving them rationally. Indeed, Descartes's entire science tended to understand fundamental physical concepts such as motion (which will interest us shortly) as the object of pure mathematics.[20] This explains why he appended the *Dioptrics* and *Meteors* to the first edition of his *Discours de la méthode*, for their scientific examples helped to corroborate *la méthode*. Although Descartes did not include the *Compendium* along with these other essays, it would have fit with them quite nicely. In fact, one of the first commentators of the *Compendium*, Père Nicolas Poisson, did issue the music treatise with the other supporting essays in his edition of the *Discours de la méthode* from 1668.[21] As Descartes said in *Regulae ad directionem ingenii* (in a section of it composed in 1619), "The exclusive concern of mathematics is with questions of order or measure and . . . it is irrelevant whether the measure in question involves numbers, shapes, stars, sounds, or any other object whatever. This made me realize that there must be a general science which explains all the points that can be raised concerning order and measure, irrespective of subject matter."[22] The point of this rule and, indeed, of the mathematical project underlying the *Compendium*, is to deny the Aristotelian distinction between pure mathematics (arithmetic and geometry, glossed here as numbers and figures) and mixed mathematics (astronomy, harmonics, optics, mechanics, glossed here as stars, sound, or some other object).[23] By showing that a general science of quantity or *mathesis universalis* applied equally to the concrete objects of mixed mathematics and the abstractions of pure mathematics, Descartes drew the sensible world of stars, sound, and other things to the same level as numbers and figures in all their perfection. Music in this way proved a bridge between pure and mixed mathematics, and the *Compendium* the first glimmer of Descartes's interest in *mathesis universalis*, the search for a set of operations and intellectual procedures proper to all mathematics—whatever the sort of quantity—that would, in the *Discourse*, be expanded to include the whole of knowledge.[24]

Descartes and Beeckman were hardly alone in their quest to find a mathematical key to the physical world. Their experiments were, in fact, symptomatic of an epistemological shift affecting many disciplines. In *The Order of Things*, Michel Foucault described this shift as a reordering of knowledge that occurred as intellectuals slowly shirked off a Renaissance episteme based on similitude, correspondence, and resemblance in favor of a new episteme based on analysis and representation.[25]

> The empirical domain which sixteenth-century man saw as a complex of kinships, resemblances, and affinities, and in which language and things were endlessly interwoven—this whole vast field was to take on a new configuration. This new configuration may, I suppose, be called "rationalism"; one might say, if one's mind is filled with ready-made concepts, that the seventeenth century marks the disappearance of the old superstitious or magical beliefs and the entry of nature, at long last, into the scientific order.[26]

At the center of the new episteme stood *mathesis*, the universal science of measurement and order, which replaced the magical ordering of the world that had structured knowledge in earlier times.[27] Despite the "capriciousness," as Gary Tomlinson has put it, of Foucault's totalizing description of Renaissance and Classical systems of knowledge, his notion of magical and rational epistemes rightfully draws our attention to the period around the year 1600 when "the order of things" did indeed seem to shudder and shift slowly through all levels of society.[28]

Here we should be clear that it was not mathematical developments per se that created the conditions for the new episteme—many areas of mathematics had achieved a state of rarefaction in the ancient world that Renaissance mathematics hardly surpassed. Rather, in ancient Greece, the speculative science of mathematics and the practical science of measurement remained distinct, whereas during the course of the sixteenth century the development of tools of measurement brought these two sciences firmly into relation with one another. In the period between the years 1250 and 1600, Western Europe experienced a "measurement" revolution that would set the stage for the mathematization of empirical knowledge to follow.[29] Daily life saw the rise of quantification as ordinary folk began to measure out their days to the chime of church clocks, merchants replaced finger reckoning with the abacus and began to employ double-entry bookkeeping, carpenters sized up the world with plumb lines and T-squares, soldiers calculated the trajectory of cannon fire, and generals deployed massive troops in geometrical formations that cast them into "the large sea of Algebra & numbers."[30] In the realm of exploration, quadrants, polyhedral sundials, and elaborate torqueta enabled sailors to circumnavigate the globe and astronomers to map the heavens. The nature and motion of the heavens became a highly political topic in both positive and negative ways: long before Galileo suffered condemnation for his empirical verification of Copernicus's heliocentric model of the universe, his *perspicillum* (spyglass) helped him discover the moons of Jupiter, which he sagely named for the Medicis in hope of gaining Grand Duke Cosimo II de' Medici as a patron.[31] He subsequently gave the grand duke a copy of the book in which he published his discovery, the *Sidereus nuncius* (Venice, 1610), along with a telescope, gifts rewarded with the position of "Filosofo e Matematico Primario." The case of Galileo—another scientist, by the way, who dabbled in musical experiments—illustrates the politicization of science as court astronomers turned from calculating horoscopes to investigating the natural order of the universe and, implicitly, the political and religious orders modeled upon it. Galileo incurred the wrath of Aristotelian philosophers when he criticized their syllogisms based on sympathy, correspondences, and occult properties, a critique echoed by Descartes, who likewise reasoned using measure and number rather than language.[32] Nonetheless, Descartes took Galileo's condemnation in 1633 as a warning to temper his "physico-mathematical" method with a spiritual component, and he ultimately grafted a metaphysical dimension onto his natural philosophy to save it and himself from the Inquisition.[33] In sum, the measuring devices that allowed man to size up the world flooded domains of knowledge formerly comprehensible only through numerical abstraction with conflicting data. Measurement created new conditions of possibility for knowledge; indeed, it forced intellectuals into a painful empirical reevaluation of the universe.

Music, as Descartes well knew, was a traditional hinge between the magical and the mathematical.[34] Some philosophers—most notably neo-Platonists—still accepted the Pythagorean description of universal order with its basis in the ratios of musical harmony; in this musical cosmos, the spheres in which the sun, planets, and stars were fixed turned according to celestial proportions, producing a music—the music of the spheres—of untold beauty and perfection.[35] Poets paid regular lip service to cosmic harmony in court fête and lyric poetry, and magi such as Marsilio Ficino attempted to harness beneficent heavenly influxes with magical songs.[36] And of course, Johannes Kepler even attempted to measure celestial harmonies and their ratios in his *Harmonices mundi libri quinque* (1619). For some, the entire mathematical domain dealing with ratios and the proportions between them was conceptually bound to music and the method of compounding ratios developed by mathematicians using monochords.[37] Even Isaac Newton limited himself to this "musical" terminology in the first edition of his *Principia mathematica* (1687), a work that, incidentally, began as a proof of the relations governing celestial motions based on Kepler's Third Law of elliptical orbits and was originally titled *De Motu Corporum*, or *On the Motions of Bodies in Orbit*.[38] The music of the spheres was the subject of everything from well-worn poetic metaphors to mathematical inquiries in Descartes's day.

We have already noted how the example of the astrolabe at the outset of the *Compendium* replaces and negates the standard *laus musicae* recognizing the divinity of music. Descartes's math, too, attacks the complex calculations employed in the study of proportion. The preliminary remarks of the treatise, for example, advance the theory that simple proportions are the most pleasing, specifying that an object bearing arithmetical proportions among its parts is more pleasing than one structured according to geometrical proportions. The point is illustrated by two sets of three lines, the first set bearing the lengths 2, 3, 4 and the second set the lengths 2, √8, 4. The middle line of the first set, of the length 3, is derived by taking the arithmetic mean of 2 and 4, whereas the middle line of the second set, √8, is derived using the geometric mean. Descartes argues that the relationship governing the second set of lines is too difficult to perceive with the senses, even though it can be worked out in (almost) rational numbers with a bit of arithmetical tinkering (see Figure 1.2).

Here the reader pauses to wonder what will become of the harmonic mean so beloved of musical mathematicians, and with good reason, for Descartes dismisses it, going on in the central portion of the treatise to derive all of the consonant intervals of harmony using only the simple arithmetic mean and stopping with the terms of Zarlino's famous *senario*.[39] "I can subdivide the line into 4, or 5, or 6 parts, but no further; because such is the imbecillity of the Ears, as that they cannot distinguish, without so much labour as must drown the pleasure, any more Differences of

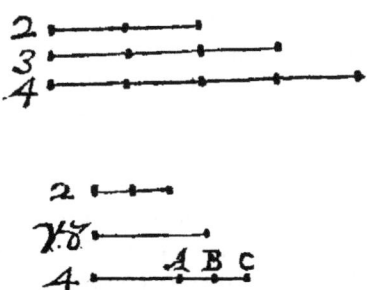

Figure 1.2 Descartes, *Compendium Musicae*, AT 10: 91–92.

Sounds."[40] Working outward from the sensible, then, Descartes finds a way to explain the delightful sounds of harmony based on perceptible mathematical structures. What has changed with Descartes—and perhaps this is the most important point to make about his choice of musical subject matter—is not the quest for an overarching *mathesis* structuring the universe or the search for it in musical terms. Late Renaissance musical mathematics are still very much in place—"numbers, figures, stars, and sound" all exhibit order and measure. What has changed instead is the need to draw the mathematical abstractions upon which so much earlier thought was based down into the sensible realm, to judge the proportional scheme ordering matter and motion with the senses.

Music, Measure, and the Body

Music drew Descartes's attention not only outward to the stars, but inward as well, to the hidden parts of the body and the gray matter of its soul, for the senses he enjoined in his study mediated between the outer and inner worlds. The senses operated as conduits of stimulation, and their effects on the inside of the body required a deepened *mathesis* that could include the physics of this internal microcosm.

Before Descartes's time, research into the body's passions, their seats in the heart and liver, and the motions they caused in the soul engaged intellectuals from disciplines as diverse as humoral medicine and astrology to magic.[41] Music was commonly accepted as a strong force upon the passions. But while doctors might recommend music to cure this ill and that—its warming effect could help counteract the black bile of melancholy, for instance—the most intense site of research into music and the passions in Renaissance France was the neo-Platonic Academy of Poetry and Music, formed in Paris in 1570 by Jean-Antoine de Baïf. Although the Academy lasted only a few years, its goal to create a morally uplifting art form survived in France for many years, just as the measured music and poetry developed there continued to influence French song styles, as evidenced by the compositions of Claude Le Jeune and Jacques Mauduit.

Modern scholars have thus been understandably keen to situate Descartes within this sphere of influence, and some improbable claims have been advanced in order to place him in Paris in the company of Marin Mersenne and Mauduit in the period just before he wrote the *Compendium*. But evidence that Descartes spent any portion of the years 1616 to 1618 in Paris is circumstantial at best, and in any case, he did not get to know Mersenne until around 1622.[42] As for the secrets of the Academy, a number of its musical scores and neo-Platonic texts on music were eventually published, and we know that they had some currency in the early seventeenth century because Mersenne, who was fascinated by the Academy, speaks of them with admiration. But forcing Descartes into the mold of an Academic disciple before 1618 is tricky indeed.[43] Admittedly, Descartes's parable of two drums, in which one headed with wolf skin silences another made of sheepskin, introduces the doctrine of sympathy and antipathy into the *Compendium*, rupturing the scientific tone of the rest of the treatise and suggesting a latent neo-Platonism.[44] But there are other places, such as the chapter on modes, where Descartes could easily have indulged in retelling fables of sympathy and antipathy but does not. The famous story of Timothy and Alexander remains untold, nor is there a breath of Orpheus, Amphion, natural magic, or demonic seizure of listeners by song.

Descartes does take up contemporary discourse on the nature of the body, its senses, and the effect of music on them, but not in the narrow terms of French neo-Platonism. Rather, the elitist projects of the Academy might themselves best be construed as part of a more general trend in which Europeans paid increasing attention to the body and to how the presentation of it mirrored and molded the moral lives of individuals. It is this broader discourse of civility and manners, it seems to me, that textures the *Compendium*.

Training the body and regulating its natural impulses obsessed the French following the civil wars of the sixteenth century. From the wreckage of those protracted disturbances, which wiped out the cultural academies of the Valois, shut down the University of Paris, and virtually destroyed the *collèges*, a new France was erected by Henry IV. Henry drew up his blueprint for the kingdom with one overwhelming concern: to centralize control in the hands of the monarch in such a way that civil war would be unlikely to come again. Largely constructive in nature, Henry's project depended on the establishment of royalist educational institutions designed to train a new breed of nobleman and bureaucrat: he restructured the University, opened a state military academy for nobles in Paris, and, after a brief expulsion of the Jesuits in 1595, he invited the fathers back to France in 1603, establishing the College of Nobles at La Flèche in one of his family chateaux. So close were the ties between Henry and La Flèche that he asked for his heart to be buried there when he died; following his assassination in 1610, his heart was interred at the college in an elaborate ceremony that the fathers continued to commemorate annually. The Jesuits were thus quite literally close to the heart of the Bourbons, answering to them directly and fulfilling their educational aims. Descartes studied at La Flèche between 1607 and 1615, receiving a royalist education and no doubt witnessing the 1610 ceremony that made the relations between the college and the king so plain.

The Jesuits inculcated civility with a detailed *Ratio Studiorum* regulating all aspects of life in the colleges.[45] The hours of teaching, recreation, meals, and rest were strictly maintained, courses of study never varied, and even the games that could be played during free time were controlled. By setting up a system of student monitors (a highly desirable position), no action, no utterance, no moment of the day or night escaped surveillance, and it was in this way that Jesuit colleges achieved the heightened self-censorship that translated so marvelously into *courtoisie.*

At court itself, etiquette and politesse were the lifeblood of what Norbert Elias has termed "the civilizing process."[46] What had begun to a large extent with Erasmus's slight manual on manners for children, *De civilitate morum puerilium libellus* (Basel, 1530), had, by the early seventeenth century, grown into a vast discourse vesting gesture, bearing, and physical habit with social import.[47] From the well-thumbed vernacular translations of Erasmus collected by ordinary folk to the unspoken laws of conduct at the *chambre bleue* held in the Hôtel de Rambouillet by Catherine de Vivonne beginning in 1620, the expansion of etiquette created a discourse not of words but of action, movement, and practice that aimed to wipe away the brutish behavior of the war years. At court we can observe most clearly the connection between the explicit goal of the monarchy to achieve absolute power and the internal social machinery by which this goal was pursued.[48] For attention to manners promoted the insidious sort of self-censorship that kept subjects in check. By making nobles slaves to style, to politeness, and to the minutiae of self-fashioning, civility literally policed the nobility from the inside out (*policer* = to civilize). Thus when war proved an impossible means to rally or defeat the belligerent nobles who confronted the monarchy during the civil wars, the battle moved, in effect, into the private lives of individuals.

Good manners displayed inner virtue, and along with them, physical activities requiring balance and poise came to the fore as registers of moral uprightness.[49] Seventeenth-century France saw an upswing in corseting of the body, the refinement of social dance and its use for physical education, and the stylization of military skills such as fencing into artificial forms that forced the body to move within a geometrical grid of implied circles and squares. Dance achieved such a state of rarefaction that in 1623 François de Lauze called it an "eloquence muete" that "could fashion the young and render them deserving of civil conversation."[50] His *Apologie de la Danse* suggests that only through this "alphabet of the fingers and grammar of gestures"—to borrow an expression from Montaigne—might one enter successfully into polite society.[51] *Civilité* expanded the semiotics of nobility in such a way that dance and good carriage served as the meta-language for a class-bound notion of virtue. Controlling one's body was a visible sign of a well-regulated inner life. And dance displayed this self-control within the carefully constructed boundaries of an art form that made it possible for spectators to watch moving bodies and their sumptuous dress and for dancers to show themselves without the whole collapsing into voyeurism and ostentation. Ballet was in essence a sumptuary privilege.

The emphasis on proportion and measure in the civilizing process—and these were very much the buzzwords of *civilité*—drew music to the center of its programs, for music provided structures against which movement and even posture could be measured. A dancer's sensitivity to timing in making turns or his or her ability to balance on demi-point could all be checked against the music in a calculus figuring grace as a harmonic proportionality between body and musical measure. With little adjustment, apologists for dance freighted its very practical semiotics of harmony with metaphysical import, holding up the body as a microcosm of Pythagorean harmony in all of its perfection. With or without the accompaniment of a dance band, the body always moved according to musical structures. Thus it was possible for all those who worked in physical arts such as dance, fencing, tumbling, playing instruments (especially the viola da gamba, an instrument notable for the dance-like gestures it elicited from players), and even painting and sculpture to claim that harmony governed their work. Descartes chose well to begin his study of proportion and pleasure with music because proportion was so often glossed as harmony.

We know nothing of whether Descartes danced, though the students at La Flèche celebrated Twelfth Night, Carnival, and St. John's Night with dances, ballets, musical combats, and inoffensive masquerades, and Descartes himself wrote a ballet libretto at the end of his life.[52] The program of physical education there favored fencing sooner than dancing, for which La Flèche employed a permanent fencing instructor. We do know that Descartes fenced, beginning at La Flèche and continuing his studies in the Netherlands under a private instructor.[53] According to Charles Adam and Paul Tannery, he had quite a reputation as a fencer among his friends in Paris, and he wrote an *Art d'escrime* or fencing treatise (now lost) at some point between 1622 and 1629.[54]

But the discipline Descartes experienced at La Flèche, while it emphasized control of the body as a means to control the mind, tended to use manners and daily regime to accomplish its task. Only with his arrival in Breda in 1618 did Descartes enter into an institution designed to instill obedience at the muscular level without the liberal trimmings of college life. The army of Maurice of Nassau army functioned as something of a European finishing school for young nobles in the day, a place where they could experience firsthand the practical results of the military humanism preached by Justus Lipsius, whose perfect prince combined, in the words of Anthony Grafton and Lisa Jardine, "the self-control to endure religious war without despairing, the art of maintaining one's influence over subordinates, and technical mastery of the most vital craft of all, the soldier's."[55] Nassau established one of the first standing armies in Europe, an institution with its own codes of behavior, strict discipline and punishment, and daily routines of close-order drill, weapons drills, and physical labor including ditch-digging and the building of fortified camps. Nassau's military machine instilled corporeal discipline at a degree and on a scale theretofore unknown in Europe.

Drill proved key to Nassau's success, and it was this new technology that others swiftly copied as they reformed their own forces in the years around 1600.[56] Nassau and his cousin John realized that only with daily rehearsal could troops learn to load and fire their weapons in quick succession or to move effectively in tight formations. Pikemen, musketeers, and arquebusiers all drilled to drums, internalizing the synchronicity that would save them in battle. It is this practice, one Descartes would have been expected to learn and direct, that seems to have provided material evidence for several arguments he advances in the *Compendium*.

Descartes wrote his music treatise in the army's winter quarters at Breda, "in the midst of military ignorance" and "tumult."[57] Cannon fire, flutes, and military drums all resound in the text, and the visceral force of them seems to prompt his observation that "sound doth concusse, or shake all circumjacent bodies."[58] Descartes asserts that sound has the power to set things in motion through a physical process (left unexplained) that we might best think of as a pulse or concussion that travels through the ear to impact the passions, setting them in motion and stirring the body.[59] Unsurprisingly, Descartes presents this theory of concussion in the portion of the treatise devoted to rhythm, where it arises in the course of explaining why music with a strong beat makes us feel like dancing: "in Tunes at whose numbers we are wont to dance and leap," singers and instrumentalists communicate meter by accenting the beginning of each bar.[60] These beats strike the body, making it move. "For this Rule is there kept, that we may distinguish every stroke of the Musick with a single motion of our bodies; to the doing of which we are also naturally impelled by Musick."[61]

It is worth remarking here that Descartes's rather blunt characterization of dancing as a physical response to musical accent accords well with the aesthetic of French Renaissance dance, which employed a basic vocabulary of hops and leaps. Compared to the stillness of French Baroque dance, Renaissance movement was dramatic indeed, and it fit with the clearly accentuated beat patterns of dances such as the pavane, galliard, and branle in much more obvious ways than the steps of the minuet and gavotte, for instance, which work within a delightful aesthetic of rhythmic dissonance between body and musical meter.[62] Descartes was right to see in the dance of his era a direct correlation between beat and step.

Based on this evidence, his extremely mechanical scenario presents an unproblematized physiology of the senses, which respond to stimuli with automatic reflexes. Physical pulses strike the body with the same force and effect that they have on inanimate objects, setting off chain reactions of motion starting in the ear and moving to the passions and the limbs. What Descartes dispenses with is not the body and soul as they were construed by earlier thinkers, but the magical correspondences by which music was understood to push further into the soul and draw motion upward into its higher regions. In Neoplatonic theory, an individual with a "well-tuned" soul—read: virtuous, moral, noble, balanced—was especially sensitive to music.[63] Music set in motion a process by which the entire soul might realign itself with the perfect proportions of the world soul from which it came, achieving grace and bringing divine understanding to the listener. But Descartes untethers music from this sublime. Even more disturbing is the way his mechanistic theory of the senses does away with *sensibility*, leaving no possibility for one person to be moved by music that leaves another unaffected, leaving no room for taste or qualitative differences of experience. Indeed, the reflexes initiated by music—divorced as they are from divinity, virtue, and the residence of these qualities in the human soul—have, in Descartes's paradigm, the same effect on animals, whose base passions react in kind when struck by the strong beats of dance music:

> We may well affirm . . . by consequence [of music's concussing effect], that *Beasts* may dance to number, or keep time with their Feet, if they be taught and accustomed thereto; because to this, nothing more is required, then only a mere naturall *Impetus*, or pleasant violence."[64]

Descartes seems to deny the social benefits of dance and its use as a measure of inner virtue. After all, bears and horses dance in time from reflex, not sensitivity.[65] In *Le monde* (written 1629 to 1633) Descartes would go on to elaborate a mechanistic conception of matter and continue in *L'homme* (written 1632 to 1633) to describe the human body as a marvelously complex machine; we might therefore see in this remark from the *Compendium* a hint of his coming fascination with automata. But it may also be that Descartes responds here to a higher truth about the nature of physical education. For what dance and drill do so well is to train the body to react automatically to regular stimuli. The mechanism for these reflexes may be hard-wired into the body, but it is training that turns animals and men into automata.

Training is the repetitive impression of sensations on the brain and their concomitant reactions, which can be activated by the same stimuli. Well before Pavlov, Descartes supposed that "if a dog were whipped five or six times to the sound of a violin, as soon as it heard this music again it would begin to cry and run away," attributing to physical "training" an element of cognitive memory.[66] In man, the process worked the same, where sensory stimulation produced a cognitive process as well as an immediate motor response (this was a different process from a strictly reflexive motor response that did not involve any recognition whatsoever, such as recoiling from pain). Hence in the same letter just cited, Descartes remarks: "for those who have taken pleasure in dancing to a certain tune, the desire to dance returns when they hear the same music again."[67] But the human mind is not consciously engaged. This conditioned reflex works "as if the mind is elsewhere" in humans. In such cases, the mental impressions made by stimuli "cause our limbs to make various movements, although we are quite unaware of them. In such a case we too move just like automata."[68] Of course, the point of military drill was to get soldiers to relinquish their individual will and reason and simply to respond mechanically to commands. The repetition of regular motions to the sound of drums in daily drill did indeed produce a sort of mindlessness in conscripts even as it heightened esprit de corps and instilled courage. Thus it would seem that Descartes's comments on the "military ignorance" and "tumult" around him were not passing slights made by a young author hurrying to finish a New Year's gift for his friend, but an accurate reflection of precisely the goal and mode of Nassau's civilizing process, in which constant physical activity (tumult) prevented any time for trouble-making and suppressed independent volition in order to produce obedience (which one might gloss as military ignorance).[69]

It was music that imposed order on Nassau's troops. Each captain had a military drummer with a large side drum to relay commands to his squadron of a hundred men and to assist with daily drills.[70] In camp and in battle, drummers beat out their company's signature "tune" and soldiers internalized this acoustic badge of corporate identity. Descartes found military drumming so effective that he was even led to praise rhythm above harmony in the *Compendium*: "So great is the force of *Time* in Musick, as that it alone can of it selfe adfer a certain *Delectation*; as is experimented in that Military Instrument, the *Drum*, wherein nothing else is required then meerly measure of Time."[71] Harmony is nothing without time (rhythm), whereas rhythm alone can please the senses. As Nicolas Bergier (an older contemporary of Descartes's) put it, without rhythm, melody is "a body without form or soul."[72]

It should not surprise us that the *Compendium*'s chapter on rhythm contains the treatise's most embodied analyses. The way drums produce sound is very extroverted, after all—they are, in fact, the least occult members of the Renaissance instrumentarium—and the beats they produce can often be felt as well as heard. Drums emit a visceral sound that "doth concusse or shake all circumjacent bodies"; rhythm, in turn, is the most elemental component of music. As even the most ordinary sounds become regularized they take on "rhythm": the machines Descartes compares to the human body—ticking clocks and creaking windmills—all turned on gears and shafts that made themselves heard.[73]

Machines constrained those within earshot of them to move in time with their audible rhythms, to work by the hours chimed on clocks and at the pace dictated by mills. They also created political orders. Tellingly, the Valois erected an official "grande horloge" at the Louvre in the sixteenth century, a timepiece whose regulation of the hours kept by the court reached its apogee in the age of Louis XIV with the lengthy sequence of ceremonies centered around the king's daily routine. Internalizing the complex gearing of the court, social climbers showed themselves ready to enter smoothly into courtiership with ability in music and dance, the performance of which proved the most important theater for showing off the mechanistic etiquette, formulaic discourse, and prescribed gestures expected of those close to the king. Not unlike the rules of Maurice's army, *courtoisie* regulated social interaction with such attention to measure that civility itself could be called a *mathesis* of control, building its system of universal conformity on the demonstrable principles of a musical mathematics. Moreover, music remained for many the foundation of heavenly, divine, and *majestic* principles too, underpinning political theories of absolutism such as Jean Bodin's demonstration that absolutism deployed power in the French state according to the relationships of the harmonic mean.[74] "Juste proportion" was the going concern of most nobles in Descartes day, a virtue developed in the bodily codes of civility and the political order of absolutism. Music made the transition from a magic cosmology to a rationalized world without losing any of its power as an *instrumentum regni*.

In a culture where music made the world go 'round, where it made things tick, where it joined philosophical notions of harmony and governance to programs of physical education, where it trained individuals how to govern themselves and others, Descartes had good reason to begin his philosophical career with a study of music and the body. In 1618 the senses were instruments of control—receptors to be packed with edifying stimuli and tools of external domination. Not only did musical training prove to be one of the latest technologies of constraint in the army and at court, Neoplatonists still awarded pride of place in their sensorium to hearing, which conveyed divine knowledge to the soul. As Pierre Charron said in his *De la sagesse* (1601), "Science, Trueth, and Vertue have no other entrance into the Soule but by the Eare."[75] From the mechanistic dancing of animals to the joyful shudders of the soul, Descartes's science is in no way free of its cultural moment. Descartes wrote in a time when the senses charged numbers with qualities, civility trained the passions to lust for its measured ideal of beauty, and the concussions of music, as he reminds us, could make the most brutish animals dance.

Notes

1. The standard edition of Descartes's works is *Oeuvres de Descartes*, ed. Charles Adam and Paul Tannery, augmented new edition, 11 vols. (Paris: Vrin, 1974–1986), which I abbreviate AT. English translations of the *Compendium* are my own or from the first English edition *Renatus Descartes Excellent Compendium of Musick: with Necessary and Judicious Animadversions Thereupon by a Person of Honour*, trans. Lord William Brouncker (London: Thomas Harper for Humphrey Moseley, 1653), from which this passage is drawn (p. 1). I thank Frédéric de Buzon for sharing his copy of Brouncker's translation with me. For Descartes's Latin works, I cite both AT and the standard

English translation, *The Philosophical Writings of Descartes*, trans. John Cottingham, Robert Stoothoff, Dugald Murdoch, 3 vols. (Cambridge: Cambridge University Press, 1985–1991), which I abbreviate CSM. CSM does not include a translation of the *Compendium*. The best modern language translation broadly available is *Abrégé de musique, Compendium Musicae*, ed. and trans. Frédéric de Buzon (Paris: Presses Universitaires de France, 1987). Buzon's edition is keyed to AT.

A fuller version of many of these arguments will appear in my *Music and Military Virtue in Early Modern France* (Cambridge: Cambridge University Press, forthcoming). Among the many colleagues who shared their thoughts, special thanks go to Wye J. Allanbrook, Frédéric de Buzon, Thomas Christensen, Timothy Reiss, and Martha Feldman for their careful readings of my essay and thoughtful contributions to it.

2. For these examples see Descartes, *Compendium of Musick*, trans. Brouncker, 1–7, AT 10: 89–95.

3. *Journal tenu par Isaac Beeckman de 1604 à 1634*, ed. Cornelius de Waard, 4 vols. (The Hague: Martinus Nijhoff, 1939–1953); on Beeckman's theories see H. Floris Cohen, *Quantifying Music: The Science of Music at the First Stage of the Scientific Revolution, 1580–1650* (Dordrecht, Boston, and Lancaster: D. Reidel Publishing, 1984), 116–61.

4. See especially H. Floris Cohen, *Quantifying Music*, 161–66, and the introduction to Descartes, *Abrégé de musique, Compendium Musicae*, ed. and trans. Frédéric de Buzon.

5. H. F. Cohen, *Quantifying Music*, 163.

6. On Zarlino's geometrical impulse see Guido Mambella, "Corps sonore, géométrie et tempéraments chez Zarlino," forthcoming in proceedings of the conference "Musique et mathématique à la Renaissance," Centre d'Études Supérieures de la Renaissance, Tours, February, 2000, ed. Philippe Vendrix. I thank Dr. Mambella for sharing his paper with me in advance of its publication. For a salient example of Zarlino's geometrical investigations, consider his use of the mesolable or proportional compass to divide a string into equal semitones. Descartes employed the instrument in his *Géométrie*; Stephen Gaukroger believes that from those investigations, Descartes went on to see the whole problem of a *mathesis universalis* in terms of proportional relations. For an overview of Descartes, Zarlino, and the mesolabe compass see Gaukroger, *Descartes*, 95–99.

7. Descartes, *Compendium of Musick*, 2, AT 10: 91. Descartes calls ratios "proportions," a mistake made by Boethius and many after him. I follow Descartes's use of the term in my own text.

8. Michel de Montaigne made similar remarks in his *Essais*, ed. Pierre Villey, 3 vols. (Paris: Presses Universitaires de France, 1978), 1: 152, "La verité et la raison sont communes à un chacun, et ne sont non plus à qui les a dites premierement, qu'à qui les dict apres. Ce n'est non plus selon Platon que selon moy, puis que luy et moi l'entendons et voyons de mesme." And even more aptly, 2: 641, "On dit communément que le plus juste partage que nature nous aye fait de ses graces, c'est celuy du sens: car il n'est aucun qui ne se contente de ce qu'elle luy en a distribué."

9. AT 10: 95.

10. Frédéric de Buzon, in his unsurpassed commentary on the *Compendium*, finds this to be the most innovative aspect of the work. See his edition and translation of Descartes, *Abrégé de musique, Compendium Musicae*, 8.

11. On the social significance of astrolabes and other scientific instruments, see Lisa Jardine, *Worldly Goods: A New History of the Renaissance* (New York and London: W. W. Norton, 1996), 302–9.

12. The word "astrolabe" itself—from the Greek astron and lambaneir—means "the one who catches heavenly bodies."

13. Here it should be said that Descartes does not develop an aesthetic theory in the *Compendium*, even though his theory of proportions points toward one. See Frédéric de Buzon, "Descartes et le problème de l'Art," *Bulletin des amis du Musée Descartes 2* (1986): 11–19, and Timothy Reiss, *Knowledge, Discovery, and Imagination in Early Modern Europe: The Rise of Aesthetic Rationalism* (Cambridge: Cambridge University Press, 1997), esp. 195–96. Also see David Summers, *The Judgment of Sense: Renaissance Naturalism and the Rise of Aesthetics* (Cambridge: Cambridge University Press, 1987).

14. See Stephen Gaukroger, *Descartes: An Intellectual Biography* (Oxford and New York: Oxford University Press, 1995).

15. Descartes subsequently engaged in a revealing correspondence with Marin Mersenne over the "excellence" or "agreeableness" of intervals, in which he attempted to establish the difference between the former (produced by the coincidence of beats or vibrations and determinable by the traditional methods of *musica theorica*) and the latter (a sensualistic ranking determined by individual taste or the context of the piece). See Marin Mersenne *Correspondance du Père Marin Mersenne, Religieux Minime*, ed. Cornelius de Waard, R. Pintard, B. Rochot, and A. Baelieu, 17 vols. (Paris: Centre National de la Recherche Scientifique, 1932–1988), 2: 368–82, 392–405, 413–20, 3: 211–23, 8: 227–36. This rationalist-sensualist dualism in Descartes's interval evaluation exemplifies the dualism evident in his general epistemology.

16. An observation made by Thomas Christensen, whom I thank for his thoughtful reading of my work.

17. Oscar João Abdounur, "Ratios and Music in the Late Middle Ages: A Preliminary Survey," forthcoming in proceedings of the conference "Musique et mathématique à la Renaissance," Centre d'Études Supérieures de la Renaissance, Tours, February, 2000, ed. Philippe Vendrix. I thank Professor Abdounur for sharing his paper with me in advance of publication.

18. *Journal tenu par Isaac Beeckman*, see 1: 237 for their first meeting, and 1: 242 ff. for the experiments.

19. Ibid., 1: 244.

20. In addition to Gaukroger, *Descartes*, see Frédéric de Buzon, "Mathesis universalis," *La science classique, dictionnaire critique*, ed. Michel Blay and Robert Halleux (Paris: Flammarion, 1998), 610–21, and Daniel Garber, *Descartes's Metaphysical Physics* (Chicago and London: University of Chicago Press, 1992), 34–35, 319–23.

21. The full title of that edition is *Discours de la méthode pour bien conduire sa raison & chercher la verité dans les sciences. Plus la Dioptrique, les Météores, la Mechanique, et la Musique qui sont des essais de cette methode par René Descartes, avec des remarques et des éclaircissemens necessaires* (Paris: Ch. Angot, 1668).

22. AT 10: 377–78, CSM 1:19. For a summary and bibliography of the scholarship attempting to date the composition of the *Regulae*, Rule 4, see Gaukroger, *Descartes*, 111–12.

23. On the ordering of knowledge and the place of music among the disciplines, see Penelope Gouk, *Music, Science, and Natural Magic in Seventeenth-Century England* (New Haven and London: Yale University Press, 1999), esp. chapter 3.

24. See AT 10: 377–78, CSM 1:19, Frédéric de Buzon, "Mathesis universalis," and Stephen Gaukroger, *Descartes*, 100–06.

25. Michel Foucault, *The Order of Things: An Archaeology of the Human Sciences* (New York: Vintage Books, 1973). Also see Gary Tomlinson, *Music in Renaissance Magic: Toward a Historiography of Others* (Chicago and London: University of Chicago Press, 1993) for an interpretation of this shift in musical terms, and idem, *Metaphysical Song: An Essay on Opera* (Princeton: Princeton University Press, 1999), chapter 3.

26. Foucault, *The Order of Things*, 54.

27. Ibid., 56–58. The persistence of natural magic in the age of science and the importance of music in both traditions is discussed in Charles Webster, *From Paracelsus to Newton: Magic and the Making of Modern Science* (Cambridge: Cambridge University Press, 1982), and Penelope Gouk, *Music, Science, and Natural Magic*.

28. Gary Tomlinson, *Music in Renaissance Magic*, 52 ff. On Foucault's epistemes and music history also see Penelope Gouk, *Music, Science, and Natural Magic*, 14–15.

29. See Alfred W. Crosby, *The Measure of Reality: Quantification and Western Society, 1250–1600* (Cambridge: Cambridge University Press, 1997).

30. Quotation from Thomas Digges, *An Arithmeticall Militaire Treatise Named Stratioticos (London, 1571)* (Amsterdam: Da Capo Press, 1968), 70, cited in Alfred W. Crosby, *The Measure of Reality*, 7.

31. See Roger Chartier, "Princely Patronage and the Economy of Dedication," in *Forms*

and Meanings: Texts, Performances, and Audiences from Codex to Computer (Philadelphia: University of Pennsylvania Press, 1995), 25–42 and 35–37.

32. See Galileo Galilei, *Il saggiatore*, ed. Libero Sosio (Milan: Feltrinelli Editore, 1965) and Descartes, *Regulae ad directionem ingenii* (AT 10, CSM 1), esp. rules 2, 10, and 13. Also see Descartes, *Discours* (AT 6, CSM 1), esp. part 2. On the general turn away from language and logic and toward mathematics as the means of constructing and ordering knowledge, see Timothy Reiss, *Knowledge, Discovery, and Imagination*.

33. This metaphysical legitimatization of his natural philosophy has greatly complicated our understanding of Descartes's work, particularly the early treatises. My reading of the *Compendium*, following the recent conclusions of Stephen Gaukroger (see *Descartes*, esp. the overview of the problem on pp. 10–14), attempts to take his treatise on the terms established by his natural philosophy rather than reading it through later doctrines.

34. On the importance of music as a site of mathematical certainty, see Timothy Reiss, *Knowledge, Discovery, and Imagination*, a brilliant assessment of why music was the perfect bridge between the magical and rational epistemes. On the confluence of magic and rational thought, see Penelope Gouk, *Music, Science, and Natural Magic*.

35. Jamie Croy Kassler, "Music as a Model in Early Science," *History of Science* 20 (1982): 103–39.

36. On Ficino see Gary Tomlinson, *Music in Renaissance Magic*.

37. Oscar João Abdounur, "Ratios and Music in the Late Middle Ages."

38. On the "musical" mathematics of Newton's treatise, see ibid. and Edith Sylla, "Compounding Ratios: Bradwardine, Oresme, and the First Edition of Newton's *Principia*" in *Transformation and Tradition in the Sciences: Essays in Honor of I. Bernard Cohen*, ed. Everett Mendelsohn (Cambridge: Cambridge University Press, 1984), 11–45. On Newton and music in general see Penelope Gouk, *Music, Science, and Natural Magic*, chapter 7.

39. Frédéric de Buzon finds this to be one of the major originalities of the *Compendium* (Descartes, *Abrégé de musique, Compendium Musicae*, ed. and trans. Frédéric de Buzon, 11). One difference between Zarlino and Descartes is that the former espoused a *senario* (a static source of *harmonia*), while the latter used the senary series (a generative process and hierarchy of acoustical intervals).

40. Descartes, *Compendium of Musick*, 9, AT 10: 97–98.

41. See Gary Tomlinson, *Music in Renaissance Magic* and see Penelope Gouk, *Music, Science, and Natural Magic*.

42. For recent analyses of Descartes's youth and education, see the opening chapters of Geneviève Rodis-Lewis, *Descartes: His Life and Thought*, trans. by Jane Marie Todd (Ithaca and London: Cornell University Press, 1998) and Stephen Gaukroger, *Descartes*. Rodis-Lewis believes Descartes spent this period in Sucé at the home of his father's second wife based on the existence of two baptismal certificates Descartes signed at the end of 1617 in Sucé.

43. We can suppose that Descartes had some passing contact with Neoplatonism, though we would also do well to remember that the curriculum at La Flèche was primarily Aristotelian. A number of scholars have gone to some length to suggest a personal contact between Descartes and Jacque Mauduit, a member of the circle of Claude Le Jeune and Jean-Antoine de Baïf that was at the center of Neoplatonic musical experiments in France. The case for this association has been egregiously overstated, most recently by Pascal Dumont in his introduction to Descartes, *Abrégé de musique suivi des Éclaircissements physiques sur la musique de Descartes du R. P. Nicholas Poisson* (Paris: Méridiens Klincksieck, 1990), 26–28. The argument for Descartes's acquaintance with Mauduit is based on a letter from Descartes to Mersenne from April 1634 in which Descartes mentions a musician—"M. M"—with whom he had had personal contact before the latter died (see AT 1: 286 for the text of the letter. The letter may be from February 1634; see Marin Mersenne *Correspondance*, ed. Cornelius de Waard, 4: 51; on Mauduit, also see ibid., 1: 203, 541, 578). In a footnote to his *Descartes et la musique* ([Paris: Fischbacher, 1907], 16, n. 1), André Pirro hazards that "M. M." might be "Monsieur Mauduit" or Jacques Mauduit. This suggestion has been accepted as fact

and circulated by scholars such as Bertrand Augst, Pascal Dumont, and Geneviève Rodis-Lewis with no further substantiation. As for Descartes's early acquaintance with Mersenne (before 1618, that is), it is true that Mersenne was studying at La Flèche when Descartes first arrived there, though there is no reason to suppose that they got to know each other at that time, for Mersenne was some eight years Descartes's senior.

44. According to Adam and Tannery, the example of drums made from sheepskin and wolf skin can be found in the second book of Ambroise Paré, *Oeuvres*, in a chapter on the antipathy and sympathy of animals (chapter 21). Paré was one of the top royal surgeons and is commonly accepted as the father of modern surgery for having introduced the technique of suturing arteries instead of cauterizing them. His *Oeuvres* went into a seventh edition in 1614. See AT, 10: 90. For a fuller discussion of this passage, see Frédéric de Buzon, "Sympathie et antipathie dans le *Compendium Musicae*," *Archives de philosophie* 46 (1983): 647–53.

45. See Camille de Rochemonteix, *Le Collège Henri IV de La Flèche*, 2 vols. (Le Mans: Leguicheux, 1889), vol. 2, Aldo Scaglione, *The Liberal Arts and the Jesuit College System* (Amsterdam and Philadelphia: John Benjamins Publishing, 1986), and Stephen Gaukroger, *Descartes*, 38–45.

46. Norbert Elias, *The Civilizing Process: Sociogenetic and Psychogenetic Investigations*, trans. Edmund Jephcott, revised edition edited by Eric Dunning, Johan Goudsblom, and Stephen Mennell (Oxford: Blackwell Publishers, 2000).

47. On civility manuals, see Roger Chartier, "From Texts to Manners. A Concept and Its Books: *Civilité* between Aristocratic Distinction and Popular Appropriation," in *The Cultural Uses of Print in Early Modern France*, trans. Lydia G. Cochrane (Princeton: Princeton University Press, 1987), 71–109.

48. See the history of manners in Norbert Elias, *The Civilizing Process*, 1–182. For a deft overview of civility in early modern Europe see Jacques Revel, "The Uses of Civility," in *Passions of the Renaissance*, ed. Roger Chartier, trans. Arthur Goldhammer, vol. 3 of *A History of Private Life*, general eds. Philippe Ariès and Georges Duby (Cambridge and London: Belknap/Harvard University Press, 1989), 167–205.

49. See Georges Vigarello, "The Upward Training of the Body from the Age of Chivalry to Courtly Civility," in *Fragments for a History of the Human Body*, vol. 2, ed. Michel Feher with Ramona Naddaff and Nadia Tazi (New York: Zone Books, 1989), 149–99.

50. François de Lauze, *Apologie de la Danse et la parfaicte methode de l'enseigner tant aux Cavaliers qu'aux dames*, facsimile edition (Geneva: Minkoff Reprint, 1977), 15, 14.

51. Michel de Montaigne, *Essais*, ed. Pierre Villey, 2: 454.

52. On life at La Flèche, see Camille de Rochemonteix, *Le Collège Henri IV*, esp. 2: 47–48 and 2: 219–50.

53. Geneviéve Rodis-Lewis, *Descartes*, trans. Todd, 232–33 n. 19.

54. AT 10: 535–38.

55. On Lipsius and Prince Maurice see Anthony Grafton and Lisa Jardine, *From Humanism to the Humanities* (Cambridge: Harvard University Press, 1986), 197–99, Hans Delbrück, *The Dawn of Modern Warfare*, trans. Walter J. Renfroe, Jr. (Lincoln and London: University of Nebraska Press, 1990), 155–71, and Geoffrey Parker, *The Military Revolution: Military Innovation and the Rise of the West, 1500–1800*, second edition (Cambridge: Cambridge University Press, 1996), 18–22.

56. The drills were first published in Jacques de Gheyn, *Maniement d'armes, d'arquebuses, mousquetz, et piques* (The Hague, 1607), a book quickly translated and pirated by other printers.

57. Descartes, *Compendium of Musick*, AT 10: 141.

58. Ibid., 6; AT 10: 95.

59. Descartes's theory is not fundamentally at odds with Renaissance ideas of how music stirs the passions, though it reduces these operations to their basest level and leaves no room for the engagement of higher passions in the enjoyment of music. For more on earlier constructs of the body and soul as they relate to this question, see my "An Erotic Metaphysics of Hearing in Early Modern France," *The Musical Quarterly* 82 (1999): 678–91, and Gary Tomlinson, *Music in Renaissance Magic*.

60. Descartes, *Compendium of Musick*, 6; AT 10: 94. Some commentators on the *Com-*

pendium have ignored this passage when trying to situate Descartes's understanding of acoustics at the time relative to Beeckman's fairly advanced corpuscular theories and the subsequent theories of Mersenne. While it is true that acoustics turns on the study of pitch and not duration, Descartes's comments here suggest that he was thinking about sound as a physical phenomena, not, as H. Floris Cohen maintains in his *Quantifying Music*, strictly in terms of mathematics (161–66). Gaukroger (*Descartes*, 79–80) follows Cohen's interpretation, though Buzon's more nuanced interpretation acknowledges Descartes's discussion of sympathetic vibrations as one that makes an important distinction between Cartesian thought—even if less mechanistic than it was to become in 1633—and Zarlinian mathematics (Descartes, *Abrégé de musique, Compendium Musicae*, ed. and trans. Frédéric de Buzon, 12–16). Thus it is neither fair nor accurate to say, as Cohen has done, that Descartes is "Zarlino, *more geometrico*" (*Quantifying Music*, 163) (see Timothy Reiss, *Knowledge, Discovery, and Imagination*, 189). For a probing analysis of the rhythmic portion of the treatise and its nascent mechanism, see Bertrand Augst, "Descartes's Compendium on Music," *Journal of the History of Ideas* 26 (1965): 119–32, esp., 129–32.

61. Descartes, *Compendium of Musick*, 6, AT 10: 94–95.
62. Descartes specifically mentions the galliard in his letter to Mersenne of March 18, 1630 that I cite below (n. 66). See AT 1: 134.
63. See Gary Tomlinson, *Music in Renaissance Magic.*
64. Descartes, *Compendium of Musick*, 6, AT 10: 95.
65. Augst gives a "spirit of the times" explanation for Descartes's mechanism, in which he tries—despite the utter lack of biographical evidence to support such a claim—to link Descartes with the vestiges of Baïf's Neoplatonic Academy in France. On the body and memory in particular and the complexity of Descartes's understanding of the mind and body more generally, see Timothy J. Reiss, "Denying the Body? Memory and the Dilemmas of History in Descartes," *Journal of the History of Ideas* 57 (1996): 587–607.
66. Descartes, *Compendium of Musick*, AT 1: 134.
67. Ibid.
68. See the discussion of *L'homme* and of this letter to Plempius in Stephen Gaukroger, *Descartes*, 276–90. I cite Gaukroger's translation (282).
69. For a cross-cultural study of drill and its particular form of socialization, see William McNeill, *Keeping Together in Time: Dance and Drill in Human History* (Cambridge: Harvard University Press, 1995).
70. On the organization of Nassau's army see Johann Jacobus von Wallhausen, *L'art militaire pour l'infanterie* (Oppenheim: Uldrick Balck, 1615).
71. Descartes, *Compendium of Musick*, 7, AT 10: 95.
72. Nicolas Bergier, *La musique speculative*, ed. and trans. Ekkehard Jost (Cologne: Arno Volk Verlag, 1970), 98. See my "Calculating Absolute Power," forthcoming in proceedings of the conference "Musique et mathématique à la Renaissance," Centre d'Études Supérieures de la Renaissance, Tours, February, 2000, ed. Philippe Vendrix.
73. *L'homme*, AT 11: 120, 130–32, 165–66, 202. The other machines Descartes mentions in *L'homme* are artificial fountains and organs. The fountains may have been the ones in the Royal Gardens at Saint-Germain-en-Lay, which included a hydraulic mechanical organ and mechanical singing birds (see Stephen Gaukroger, *Descartes*, 63–64).
74. Jean Bodin, *Les six livres de la république*, ed. Christiane Frémont, Marie-Dominique Couzinet, Henri Rochais, 6 vols. (Paris: Fayard, 1986) or Bodin, *The Six Bookes of a Commonweale, A Facsimile Reprint of the English Translation of 1606*, trans. Richard Knolles, ed. Kenneth Douglas Mc Rae (Cambridge, Mass.: Harvard University Press, 1962).
75. Pierre Charron, *De la sagesse livres trois* (Bordeaux: Simon Millanges, 1601), translated as *Of wisdome three bookes written in French by Peter Charron* (London: Blount and Will, [1613]), Book 1, Chapter 11.

2

Bemetzrieder's Dream

Diderot and the Pathology of Tonal Sensibility in the *Leçons de clavecin*

Thomas Christensen

In 1771, a manual for learning to play the harpsichord was published in Paris by a virtually unknown music pedagogue and composer newly arrived from Alsace: the *Leçons de clavecin* by Anton Bemetzrieder.[1] While the appearance of yet another keyboard tutor would hardly merit much attention at this time, the *Leçons* were unusual in that they were cast as a series of witty dialogues between a teacher (*le Maître*) and his student (*l'Elève*), with periodic commentary from the student's sardonic father (*le Philosophe*), who it seems would occasionally sit in on the lessons. Never had the dry material of scale fingering, chordal realization, and harmonic theory been presented in catechism with such sparkling banter and urbane humor.

Reading the preface to the *Leçons* clarifies the mystery concerning Bemetzrieder's unexpected literary sophistication. It turns out that the great Encyclopedist Denis Diderot was in fact responsible for casting the "François Tudesque" of the German-speaking Bemetzrieder into polished dialogue (p. vii). Three years earlier, Bemetzrieder had begun instructing Diderot's sixteen-year-old daughter, Angélique, on the harpsichord. The *Leçons* purportedly represent a transcription of these lessons, though obviously embellished by Diderot's imaginative pen. Indeed, so obvious is Diderot's hand in the composition of this text that it is now accepted as a part of Diderot's literary canon.[2]

Yet one question remains largely unanswered by scholars; indeed, the question itself is rarely raised. And that is what in Bemetzrieder's oral lessons inspired the older Encyclopedist to translate them into such witty dialogue.[3] Given the effort this work must have cost, there was surely a motivation beyond mere gratitude for having instructed Angélique in her harpsichord lessons. I believe that one answer is that Diderot found in Bemetzrieder's keyboard pedagogy a theory of music that resonated strongly with several ideas that he had been recently developing on the subject of vitalistic materialism. Specifically, questions related to the nature of bodily sensibility that Diderot had explored in "La Rêve de d'Alembert" (written, we think, around 1769) receive surprisingly resonant exemplification in Bemetzrieder's pedagogy two years later.

Any reader acquainted with Diderot's writings will recognize a familiar pattern. Diderot was forever absorbing ideas from his contemporaries and developing them in his writings, testing and probing them in his own fertile imagination. Thus it should be no surprise to find Diderot taking a series of prosaic music lessons and uncovering in them a series of rich aesthetic and epistemological paradoxes that might seem to be completely foreign to the technical or pedagogical aims at hand. It would certainly not be the first time music theory would serve as such an intellectual stimulant for Diderot.[4]

Yet the reason for Diderot's attraction to Bemetzrieder's theory may not be obvious at first glance given its dry and pedantic tone. Bemetzrieder approaches the learning of keyboard skills in a rigidly mechanical and almost unremittingly abstract manner, with pages and pages of mind-numbing recitations of scales, fingerings, keys, and key signatures. When the subject of harmony is finally broached on page 122, things don't improve much. For the next two hundred pages, master and student are constantly cataloging the chromatic harmonies possible above a given scale degree, calculating their various permutations and hand positions, and generating dozens of derivative harmonies through various ad hoc manipulations. (One would be hard pressed to find another eighteenth-century document that better illustrates Foucault's classic episteme of Enlightenment *taxinomia*.)

While it is not my intention to offer a more elaborated analysis of Bemetzrieder's keyboard pedagogy, suffice to say that his method has to be considered a disaster. By learning harmonies in such isolation and in such a plodding, abstract manner, the student gains no understanding whatsoever of their connections, let alone how to create large-scale harmonic spans. Moreover, there is absolutely no consideration of melody given, thus depriving the student of any means of controlling the voicing and shaping of harmonic phrases. The few illustrations of actual harmonic progressions given are filled with such egregious voice-leading errors that it is simply unbelievable that any reader could ever get to the point of improvising and composing an intelligible, let alone satisfying, musical composition following these models.

Clearly, though, these were not the issues that concerned Diderot. Just as in his earlier collaboration with Rameau, where it is obvious that Diderot could not easily follow the composer into the intricacies of the *basse fondamentale*, something more was at stake than keyboard pedagogy per se. The issue that must have attracted Diderot comes up subtly at the beginning of the treatise, but emerges ever more explicitly as the dialogue proceeds. And that is the issue of tonal sensibility. It turns out that despite the pedantry of Bemetzrieder's pedagogy—or perhaps because of it—the student learns to play and connect chords through an innate sensitivity to tonality that is instinctive, almost visceral.[5] The worst approach to learning harmony, Bemetzrieder reminds the student again and again, is to approach it exclusively as a rational, mathematical science. This was the problem, he notes, with Rameau's theory of the fundamental bass (p. 352).

From the very beginning of the treatise where the instructor offers guidelines to the fingering of scales, the pupil is encouraged to develop a tactile sensitivity to the keys in relation to the scales being played (pp. 75–103). This is especially important in "sensing" certain notes of tonal instability: particularly the leading tone, and those points of semitone connection in all diatonic scales.[6] Again and again, the master exhorts the student to "feel" or "sense" what he is teaching here. "It is not something to be discussed," the student is admonished at one point, "it is something to be felt, just as in most unknown causes that exert such powerful effects in all events of daily usage" (p. 331).

Bemetzrieder's pedagogy is structured to cultivate this musical sensitivity in the student. The hundreds of chordal signatures that comprise eighteenth-century manuals of thorough-bass realization are presented not in any systematic, rationally ordered tabulation based on their interval construction. Rather, they are introduced *tout court* in the context of scale degrees, where Bemetzrieder feels the real dynamic and principle of tonality is located. Chords are taught as manifestations of the tonal dynamics inherent in a given mode by virtue of their position in the *basso continuo*. The student learns progressively basic scale harmonizations (the so-called *règle de l'octave*), circle-of-fifth progressions, and cadential progressions as harmonic models to memorize, transpose, and elaborate with various improvised diminutions or figurations (*batteries*). Likewise, modulations to related keys are taught as shifts of tonal orientation and are navigated as much by instinct as by rational intent. This is why the master spends so much time having the student think about the sound of each key and ways of connecting them through a hierarchy of common tones (*enchaînment de modulations*; pp. 103–11). Above all, the student is advised to embellish all of the prescribed harmonic progressions with a series of improvised diminutions.

It is probably not surprising, given this empirical pedagogy, that Bemetzrieder rejects Rameau's theory of the fundamental bass, which he considered to be "incoherent and indigestible" (p. 315), the product of a baleful theoretical "systematizer" (p. 352), and worshiped by its idolaters as some "revealed truth" (p. 357). This rejection of the fundamental bass was quite the exception for a music treatise written in France in 1771, given that virtually every other harmony teacher had adopted it by then in some form.[7] Bemetzrieder's diatribe against Rameau becomes so heated, in fact, that Diderot evidently felt compelled to defend it under the guise of the thoughtful philosophe (p. 115, and 353).[8]

Of course, Bemetzrieder was not entirely immune to Rameau's influence. He invoked Rameau's *corps sonore* to establish the tonal priority of the major triad. (The *corps sonore* was Rameau's term for any vibrating system sounding its first five harmonic partials, constituting the consonant major triad.) But the *corps sonore* did not enjoy quite the same ontological status for Bemetzrieder as it did in Rameau's theory. For one thing, Bemetzrieder did not worry as did Rameau about the theoretical/acoustical origins of the triad—let alone the problems of generating the minor triad. For him, chords and scales were simply empirical facts of nature to be accepted. Like Rousseau's innocent child of nature, the teacher disavows any rational understanding of their origin: "However that may be, it is the concern of Rameau and not mine. I came along and found seven sounds ordered like this, and that was enough for me" (p. 316).

In several of his later publications, Bemetzrieder offered a kind of epistemological reconstruction of the process by which early man might have discovered the diatonic scale. Mimicking the pseudo-anthropological fictions of writers like Condillac and Rousseau, Bemetzrieder suggested that a "musicien sauvage" would naturally have known and sung the notes of the *corps sonore* given to him by nature. By singing the natural triad, a primitive musician would have realized that there were gaps of differing sizes between the notes. Through experimentation and thoughtful reflection, our musician—now called an "apprentis theoricien"—would eventually have discovered the various notes of the full diatonic and chromatic scales and established their subordinate relation to the tonic triad.[9] (Presumably, too, the minor triad and its scales would have also been found in this way.)

By dispensing with Rameau's fundamental bass and starting only with tone relations afforded by the *corps sonore*, the student is forced to rely even more on a certain instinctual sensitivity to harmony because there is now no rationalized syntax by which chord successions can be modeled and taught. The notes comprising all harmonies are understood only as possessing various kinds of urges and tendencies ordered around the consonant tonic triad. Essentially, a tonic is felt as a place of rest or stability that "calls to" or "solicits" all non-tonic scale degrees to resolution; conversely, all of these non-tonic scale degrees are endowed with a certain instability and tension that is relieved only by their resolution to the tonic (normally by stepwise motion). As we see in Example 2.1, every note of the tonic C major triad (indicated by whole notes) may be embellished by upper or lower neighbor displacements (indicated by black notes), and these displacements are "called back" to the tonic triad by stepwise motion. Hence the sixth scale degree (*la*) possesses a tendency to resolve to the fifth scale degree of the tonic triad (*sol*), while the fourth scale degree (*fa*) may be heard as displacing either the fifth or the third of the tonic and the second scale degree (*re*) may displace either the third scale degree or the tonic. (Several of these displacements, it must be noted, would be highly unlikely in tonal practice, and indicate the kind of stultified pedantry one finds throughout Bemeztrieder's text for the sake of systematization.)

In a similar fashion, more than one note of a tonic chord may be displaced and this may give rise to a number of dependent harmonic functions, all of which point to the tonic as a place of rest. As shown in Example 2.2, the chain of three "consonant voices" comprising the submediant, subdominant, and dominant chords respectively, can be seen as a series of concatenated tonic solicitations.

This is Bemetzrieder's "law of appellation" (*loi des appels*). All tonic notes are labeled *appels* because they "call to" all non-tonic notes, which are themselves labeled as *appelés*, since they are "called to."[10] Even the four non-tonic diatonic scale degrees can be gathered together in the single harmony of the half-diminished seventh chord (*si, re, fa, la*), which Bemetzrieder calls "la grande dissonance," and this harmony possesses an almost irresistible tendency to resolve to the tonic triad.[11]

Of course, in practice, these four scale degrees do not always move directly to notes of the tonic triad. As shown in Example 2.3, the chord

Example 2.1. Illustration of "différens écarts du corps sonore, avec le retour de ce corps après chaque appel." *Leçons de clavecin*, 333.

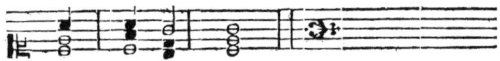

Example 2.2. "Exemple du corps sonore appellé par trois voix consonnantes." *Leçons de clavecin*, 336.

Example 2.3. Illustration of "le grand dissonance." *Leçons de clavecin*, 349.

possesses a number of possible resolutions depending on tonal context.[12] Sometimes, as we saw in Example 2.2, these resolutions are delayed by the introduction of other non-tonic harmonies, in which case a succession of *appels* is created (p. 348). Other times the diatonic notes can be altered chromatically, which has the result of "fortifying" the tendency toward resolution (p. 353). Such is the case with the augmented sixth chord. Unfortunately, Bemetzrieder fails to develop this theory in any pedagogically useful way because the conditions and contexts by which given notes or harmonies may move are never spelled out. He makes a feeble attempt at some systematization and hierarchy of attraction by distinguishing "classes" of closeness to the tonic based on the number of common tones (pp. 343–48).[13] Likewise, he tries to correlate the metrical placement of harmony with particular beats of the measure, reserving the final dominant "solicitation" to the upbeat and its resolution to the tonic triad on the downbeat (see p. 348; also the *Traité*, pp. 70–74). But, as already noted, there is no systematic tonal hierarchy given by which the student might learn to distinguish the various grades of non-tonic functions or to control these modulatory progressions and the voice-leading of individual chordal resolutions.[14]

As unsystematic as the theory of tonal appellation may be, it is clear what Bemetzrieder is trying to do. He is establishing tonal motion to the tonic triad—grounded by the *corps sonore*—as the supreme, governing principle of music. The tonic acts as a kind of home base toward which all other tonal materials gravitate. This might be at the level of a single note of suspension, or it might be an entire chord. Indeed, it accounts—in Bemetzrieder's view—even for entire modulations. The further any harmonic progression wanders from the tonic key, the stronger is its urge to return home again. All music, then, can be seen as a dynamic of movement away from and toward the tonic triad. In Bemetzrieder's world of binary tonality, every note has one of only two possible meanings: one of stability and rest on the tonic triad, or one of instability and tension on all other scale degrees.

While there is much more one could say critically about the details of Bemetzrieder's theory, this brief sketch may suffice for us to grasp what must have aroused Diderot's keen interest. Conceiving a musical piece as a conglomeration of vibrant, undulating tones possessing cyclical tendencies of attraction and repulsion parallels perfectly Diderot's own vitalistic metaphysics.

Since his earliest philosophical writings, Diderot largely identified with materialist vitalism as a preferable alternative to the rigid iatro-mechanism of the materialists or the dualist agnosticism of the Cartesians. The animal body, Diderot believed, was endowed with a vitalistic quality of *sensibilité* by which consciousness and thought were ultimately formed and united. As it turned out, music—and specifically the vibrating strings of musical instruments—offered one of the most striking metaphors for imagining these relations. In early works such as the *Lettre sur les sourds et muets* (1751), Diderot suggested that the human mind could be conceived of as a large harpsichord composed of countless strings that would "resonate" to the outside stimuli of the world. By transferring these resonances to the mind, complex capacities such as memory and feeling could be accounted for in a quasi-mechanistic manner.[15] This was a theme Diderot returned to in 1769 when composing his most ambitious dialogue on vitalistic materialism, *La rêve de d'Alembert*. Here Diderot specifically speaks of the human mind as a "living harpsichord":

> We humans are instruments gifted with sensation and memory. Our senses are merely keys that are struck by the natural world around us, keys that often strike themselves—and this, according to my way of thinking, is all that would take place in a harpsichord organized as you and I are organized. There is an impression that has its cause either inside or outside the instrument; from this impression a sensation is born, a sensation that persists, for it is impossible to suppose that a sensation can both arise and be extinguished in a single indivisible instant of time. Then a second impression follows the first, arising similarly out of an external or internal cause; then there occurs a second sensation. And these sensations all have tones—either natural or conventional sounds—that serve to identify them.[16]

Tactile sensibility—the "irritability of our nerve fibers"—becomes the quality to which all the senses can be reduced. Having absorbed much of the physiological theories of the so-called Montpellier physicians (of whom Théophile de Bordeu, the main protagonist in *D'Alembert's Dream*, was a leading member), Diderot became fascinated by the nervous constitution that endowed living creatures with their capacity of sensation.[17] Diderot surmised that all living objects possess such sensibility. Indeed, in a virtual parody of Spinoza, he wonders if the smallest material objects might contain a small spark of *anima sensitiva* that is simply reproduced epigenetically in larger life forms. The vivid image he describes of a swarm of bees, which becomes a significant metaphor in *La rêve* (again borrowed from Bordeu), suggests how any living being might be conceived of as a cluster of smaller elements that by themselves possess the capacity of sensibility. The smallest atom, Diderot goes on, might contain the same quality of irritability as do all animals.[18] These countless components that make up a living creature are connected to the mind by a network of sensitive fibers much like that of the threads of a spider's web, another of Diderot's favorite images.

Without explicating further Diderot's complex and shifting theories of sensibility, a few resonances with Bemetzrieder's theory should be obvious by now. To take the most original element first, we can see how the theory of *appel* can be interpreted as a quasi-vitalistic model of tonal behavior. Much as a living being could be understood as an aggregate of individual, sensitized components, so a musical piece was an analogous accretion of energized musical notes. Indeed, what more vivid image is there of an organic body made up of vitalized parts than that of a musical composition with its own swarms of vibrant tones, sensual chords, and volatile modulations?[19]

For Diderot, music was a percussive phenomenon comprising a *tourbillon* of animated notes colliding with the ear of the musician and conveying endless waves of undulating tendencies. The notes of a composition or an improvisation moving in a regular diastolic/systolic rhythm of attraction and repulsion in relation to the tonic triad is a perfect simulacrum of the physiological dynamic of antagonism the Montpellier physicians saw in the animal economy: the nerves of the body are in alternating states of stimulation and rest regulated by the respiratory rhythms of the diaphragm.[20] "What is a living creature?" Diderot has the dreaming d'Alembert ask, immediately answering his own question: "The sum of a certain number of tendencies. . . . Can it be that I myself am anything more than a tendency? . . . And life itself? . . . Life is a series of actions and reactions."[21] The result of any sensible individual to the constant agitation of the auditory nerves by music can lead to the most intense corporeal and even erotic stimulation. (It is no surprise, then, that one of the most overtly sexual seductions in Diderot's novel *La Religieuse* takes place when Suzanne is playing the harpsichord.) At the same time, this may offer one interpretation of Diderot's otherwise cryptic remark in *Le Neveu de Rameau* that music is the "most violent of the arts." In respect to its actual mechanics, music among all the arts might indeed be the most unremittingly stimulating, the most percussively violent agitation of our nervous system.

Still, Bemetzrieder is not able to make clear just *why* all tones project the appellative tendencies he posits. He offers both mechanistic and energetic metaphors to account for their behavior, models that are not entirely congruent. On the one hand, an "appel" is spoken of as an "impact" or "collision" (*choc*) and "deflection" (*écart*) from the consonant tones of the tonic triad:

> Melody and harmony unceasingly offer us only an concatenation [*enchaînement*] of deflections [*écarts*] of longer or shorter durations, a series of little collisions [*chocs*] more or less severe, a repetition of more or less intense calls [*appels*] to a natural state of [the *corps sonore*] which we regret leaving, and which we do only to return again with increased pleasure (pp. 331–32).[22]

The sense here is that the stable notes of the tonic triad are somehow mechanically displaced by adjacent diatonic or chromatic neighbors, and the subsequent sounds have a dissonant quality to them that causes the musician to return to the consonance of the tonic triad.[23] Bemetzrieder at one point offers an almost pathological description of an *appel*, calling it a kind of unpleasant irritation (p. 356) that provokes an involuntary contraction of or fatigue to the tonal body, and compels the tones to return to the *corps sonore* (p. 331).[24] This characterization of stimulus is nothing less than the principle of "irritability" that Diderot (following the Montpellier physicians) proposed as the "universal attribute of matter."[25] Just as any living creature responds to such irritable stimulus, the musical organism responds to the irritation of a dissonant note. The musician composing or playing an instrument is sensitive to this musical irritation through a kind of symbiotic resonance, desiring the dissonant note to be resolved in the composition or improvisation. Of course, too many *appels*—too much *dissonance fatiguent*—would be unbearable. Any overstimulation of the auditory nerves would essentially enervate the attractive appellation of the *corps sonore* "comme une douleur qui ôteroit la connoissance, ne laissant plus de comparaison entre la mal-aise et le bien-être" (p. 332).[26] But, just as clearly, a lack of stimulating, irritating *appels* would deprive music of precisely its animated and affective capacities.

Here we can perhaps make better sense of the image of the man caught in a labyrinth that is so often excerpted from the *Leçons* by scholars as one of the most characteristically "Diderotesque" passages of the text. Whereas the immediate context of the passage concerns modulatory progressions, we can also now understand it as a kind of parable of physiological determinism:

> If you have a little imagination, if you have feeling, if sounds captivate your soul, if you are endowed with an excitable disposition [*entrailles mobiles*], if you are naturally enthusiastic and can convey this enthusiasm to others, then what will have occurred to you? You will have seen a man who wakes up in the middle of a labyrinth. He searches left and right for a way out. For a moment, he thinks he has come to the end of his wandering. He stops short; then slowly and with trepidation he follows the path, treacherous perhaps, that opens before him. Now he is lost once again. He runs, rests, runs again. He climbs, he climbs. He glances around and recognizes the very spot where he awoke. Overcome with worry and distress, his laments echo throughout the labyrinth. What will become of him? With no way of knowing, he abandons himself to the destiny that offers him only false hopes of a way out. Having taken just a few steps, he is brought back to the place where he began (p. 327).

In one sense, this passage presents us with a harrowing image. The pitiful man is caught in an inescapable labyrinth within which he is driven almost like a mouse in some Pavlovian laboratory maze. Just as he searches desperately for an exit, a modulatory musical progression must also somehow make its way home to the tonic following the strict rules and inviolable constraints of harmonic theory. (Not by chance did the student at one point call the master's many rules and regulations a "catechism of musical Jansenism" [p. 342].) As Guy Poitry has suggested in a provocative article, the many "shocks" and "irritations" of his musical wanderings prod the musician onwards in almost hapless passivity to his final tonic destiny. The *loi des appels* thus becomes a metaphor for Diderot to illustrate the determinist laws of nature to which humans must submit. There can be no ultimate free will for men in nature, just as the musician must submit to the "imperious magnetic force of the harmonic system" even though this harmonic determinism might seem to be mollified by the "veil" of melodic creativity.[27]

But it would be wrong to overemphasize such mechanistic determinism in the case of harmonic modulation. A trip through a labyrinth can also be a pleasant and even playful experience. To begin with, the notion of a "labyrinth" to describe a harmonic progression is an old and venerable one in thorough-bass pedagogy, where many elaborate, chromatic chord successions received such designation. More importantly, though, the way through any harmonic labyrinth is never predetermined; there are inevitably multiple paths a musician might take. In most parts of Bemetzrieder's text, a migration through various keys is narrated more cheerfully as a "promenade" through the tonal landscape in which the animated performer turns this way and that way through various keys, choosing at times to linger in one that seems particularly pleasing, and just as abruptly leaving it (*écarter*) to jump to another, often through "magical" means like an enharmonic change of notation.[28] These tonal narratives bring to mind, of course, the more famous ones Diderot offered in his Salons, where the observer enters peripatetically *into* one of Vernet's canvases in order to stroll leisurely through its landscape and comment on its many parts.[29]

This points, then, to a second quality of *appel* mentioned earlier. An *appel* is not simply an iatro-mechanistic irritation to the tonal body condemning the musician to an inevitable harmonic response. There is a more vitalistic, energetic quality of attraction implied here that can only be called instinctive and volitional—but hardly mechanistic or fatalistic. We have earlier seen how Bemetzrieder describes the tonic triad as "calling forth" and "soliciting" its diatonic and chromatic neighbors, while conversely, those non-tonic tones themselves are "called by" and "drawn to" the *corps sonore*. Regardless of whether these non-tonic scale degrees are themselves harmonized with a consonant triad, there will be a desire for these tones to move by closest proximity to the tonic triad, a desire that the sensitive musicians and keyboardist will also feel. This homing instinct helps guide not only the individual voice-leading of particular chords but also entire chord progressions and chains of modulations, all of which will lead eventually back home. The important point is, though, that this way home is neither direct nor prescribed.

Thus the theory of *appel* becomes one of almost corporeal instinct: the musician groping and feeling his way through the tonal labyrinth. In order to navigate the web of distant key relations, a musician must not only use reason but also rely on a kind of visceral instinct and "enthusiasm" (Diderot calls it an "excitable disposition"—*entrailles mobiles*). The striking moment in the *Leçons* where Angélique improvises a prelude for her father offers just such a scene (pp. 302–06). The performance is set up by Diderot as a kind of dream sequence in which the student is a vessel for the notes somnambulistically controlled by the fingers. It is revealing that moments before Angélique's performance, she begins to shed tears as if to underscore her sensible condition before turning to the keyboard. Diderot reflects the mood linguistically by having the dialogue fracture into a serious of paratactic utterances, rhetorical questions, and disjointed commentary. Even the orthography of the page is striking for its multiple ellipses, as if Diderot were attempting to modulate his characters away from the preceding conscious state of rational discourse into a more passive state of sensory catalepsy (see Example 2.4).[30] The performance of the music is no longer entirely in her control, just as the dreaming d'Alembert no longer has mastery of his thoughts (or his hands!) but rather is taken over by the words implanted in his waking mind by the cunning Diderot, or just as Rameau's nephew pantomimes a virtuosic fugue imitating all the instruments of the orchestra in a semi-conscious state of manic possession. It is not without deeper meaning that the student at one point confesses to her teacher that it is not she who commands harmonies, but harmonies that govern her (p. 168). This is not to deny that some semblance of rational thought and study is necessary to prepare for such an improvisation. The student says as much at the end of her performance. (How could it not be given that she has chosen to play in the extraordinarily difficult key of G# major, containing eight sharps!) As Cynthia Verba has correctly pointed out, both inspiration and theory are essential components of Diderot's pedagogy.[31] But, just as clearly, the kind of study and theory Bemetzrieder is proposing in this pedagogy is one that seems to be cultivated as much by touch and enhanced sensibility as by any process of detached ratiocination.

In one sense, the *Leçons de clavecin* presents the most visceral, corporeal pedagogy of keyboard performance imaginable. It is first of all presented as a dialogue between individuals discussing music, individuals who are manifestly *sentient*. On almost every page, we find someone stopping and

302   L E Ç O N S
                                L' E L E V E.

Auparavant , permettez que je vous embraſſe.... Le Concert d'hier
fut le Bouquet commun de tous nos amis....

                          L E   P H I L O S O P H E.

Et le tien.

                                L' E L E V E.

Aſſurément ; mais voici celui de votre enfant... De cet enfant.....

                          L E   P H I L O S O P H E.

Qu'as-tu ? Tu pleures.

                                L' E L E V E.

C'eſt de plaiſir ; c'eſt de joie.... Je voudrois vous dire... Et voilà
que je ne ſçaurois parler.

                          L E   P H I L O S O P H E.

Tu n'as jamais mieux dit.... J'ai tout entendu.

                                L' E L E V E.

Excepté mon Prélude.... J'ai fait de mon mieux..., Je voudrois
qu'il vous plût ; je voudrois qu'il fût.....

                          L E   P H I L O S O P H E.

Il ſera bien..... Remets-toi... Joue.. J'écoute.

                                L E   M A î T R E.

Adagio... C'eſt un Adagio.... En majeur de *ſol* dieze.... Huit
diezes.

                          L E   P H I L O S O P H E.

Eſt-ce que vous ne le connoiſſez pas ?

                    L E   M A î T R E   E T   L' E L E V E.

Non, Monſieur.....   Non, mon Papa.

                          L E   P H I L O S O P H E.

Tant mieux.

                                L E   M A î T R E.

Vous tremblez.... Vous avez peur.

                                L' E L E V E.

Vous vous trompez , Monſieur. Ce n'eſt pas cela... Je n'y étois pas.
Il faut que je recommence.

Example 2.4. *Leçons de clavecin*, 302.

listening to some extraordinary modulation, commenting on specific chords or dissonances, and savoring some delectable chromatic progression or lively diminution. In short, Diderot brings the *body* into the text. And in classic dialectical fashion, he finds in the dynamic of the dialogue a means to offer temporal vitality to the material he is discussing. As Julie Hayes has put it: "In a profound sense, the *Leçons* stage the dissolution of the complex structural relationships constitutive of harmony, and harmony's reappropriation and reassimilation into a flexible, linear, discursive model—something rather like *chant*."[32]

For Downing Thomas, the implications of the *Leçons* is its "semiotic polyphony" with its multiple superposition of images to describe the representation and interpretation of musical affections. "[It] is less concerned with tracing the norms of a normative, referential, musical discourse as it is with a rhetoric of performance and reception. Diderot's text marks a shift from mimesis as content to mimesis as interpretive event."[33]

The dialogue captures some of the experience of music in its dynamic flow with its characters talking in counterpoint, disagreeing, coming and going, stopping themselves for digressions and commentary. In a remarkable example of mimetic prosody, the one point in the text when the master insists no one interrupt his monologue is precisely when he is expounding the theory of *appels* and its various *chocs* and *écarts* (pp. 314 ff.)!

This chapter of the text—we should note that it is the only one that is in any sense properly "theoretical"—was evidently added by Bemetzrieder with Diderot's encouragement (see note 19). As if to emphasize its alterity, the conversation moves from the parlor and keyboard where all the other lessons were given and instead takes place outside "à l'Etoile" after dinner and "une long promenade à pied." The three interlocutors sit under a tree whereupon the teacher agrees to offer a short discourse concerning his theory of *chocs* and *écarts* provided he is not interrupted by the student or the philosophe (pp. 314–15)—a contract that neither will be able to honor.

The periodic staccato intrusions of commentary and questions from both the student and philosophe are received by the exasperated teacher as irritating disruptions to the unity and flow of his presentation. This is a brilliant stroke by Diderot to provide for his readers palpable examples of disruptive *chocs* and *écarts*. It is a wonderful instance of a literary strategy perfected by Diderot that has been pointed out by Walter Rex: to bend prose mimetically such that it becomes itself a simulacrum of the very topic under discussion.[34]

One senses that Diderot's hopes were too high. The initial faith he placed in Bemetzrieder's theory as an alternative to Rameau's system was soon shaken when the two fell into heated dispute.[35] Ultimately, the *loi des appels* was not one sufficiently thorough and systematic to compete with Rameau's theory. While the general notion of music consisting of oscillating motions away from and toward the home tonic does capture the basic dynamic of Western harmonic tonality, the syntactic details of those movements are far more complex than the idea of harmonic "appel" allows. Ironically, it was Rameau's fundamental bass that ultimately offered a more compelling and successful model of this tonal dynamic. No other analytic notation was ever developed in the eighteenth century that better captures the temporal flow of musical motion, while at the same time measuring precisely the various degrees of deflection from the tonic and regulating the motion to and from tonic through various intermediary chords and keys. But by the time of the *Leçons*, Rameau's ideas were too contaminated for Diderot by the composer's increasingly aggressive metaphysical and occult speculations. Yet as problematic as the theory of *appel* may have been from the perspective of a discerning music theorist or seasoned keyboard teacher, for a brilliant philosophe fascinated by its *brouillement* of vitalistic and mechanistic resonances, it was difficult indeed to resist its attraction.

Notes

1. Anton Bemetzrieder, *Leçons de clavecin et principes d'harmonie* (Paris: Bluet, 1771); reprint edition by Broude Brothers (New York, 1966). All subsequent page references are to the pagination found in the original 1771 edition.
2. The *Leçons* are reprinted in *Diderot: Oeuvres Complètes*, vol. 19, ed. Jean Mayer and Pierre Citron (Paris: Herman, 1983), 61–387.
3. For example, Guy Buchman, "Une Oeuvre paradoxale de Bemetzrieder," in *Diderot, les Beaux-Arts et la musique* (Aix-en-Provence: Publications de l'université de Provence, 1986), 185–209; Guy Poitry, "*Les Leçons de clavecin et principes d'harmonie:* un ouvrage à plusieurs mains," Ibid., 209–20; Jean Gribenski, "A propos des *Leçons de clavecin* (1771): Diderot et Bemetzrieder," *Revue de musicologie* 60, no. 2 (1980): 15–78; Robert Niklaus, "Diderot and the *Leçons de clavecin*," *Modern Miscellany Presented to Eugene Vinauer* (Manchester: Manchester University Press, 1969), 180–94.
4. Almost twenty years earlier, Diderot undertook much the same kind of collaboration with another French music theorist, Jean-Philippe Rameau. In that instance, too, Diderot acted far more than a mere amanuensis for the distinguished composer. Epistemological and aesthetical ideas in which Diderot was then enthralled—particularly that of Lockian sensationalism and an informal aesthetic of "rapport"—found a wonderful and resonant exemplification in Rameau's generative harmonic principle of the "resonating body" (*corps sonore*). Diderot was likely responsible for the remarkable evolution in Rameau's harmonic theory in which these epistemological and aesthetic qualities were increasingly emphasized. See my "Diderot, Rameau and Resonating Strings: New Evidence of an Early Collaboration," *Studies on Voltaire and the Eighteenth Century*, vol. 323 (London: Oxford University Press, 1994), 131–66.
5. By "tonality," I refer narrowly to the nexus of tonal relations and functions that cluster hierarchically around the central tonic triad of the Western major/minor key system. Admittedly, the term "tonality" can be faulted as an anachronistic one in regard to any eighteenth-century music theory, as it was not used until the early nineteenth century

by writers such as Choron and Fétis. But as we will see, Bemetzrieder's theory closely anticipated (and influenced) the concept of *tonalité* as developed by these subsequent theorists, particularly Fétis.

6. Bemetzrieder recognizes three diatonic scales in music: the major, the harmonic minor, and a *mode mixte* that corresponds to a "phrygian" scale, the white notes of a keyboard beginning on E (p. 27). This "third mode" was the subject of considerable discussion and debate among French musicians in the later eighteenth century after its "rediscovery" and promotion by the composer Charles Blainville in 1751. Not surprisingly, though, Bemetzrieder makes no use of this scale in subsequent sections of his treatise.

7. See Cynthia Gessele, "The Institutionalization of Music Theory in France: 1764–1802" (Ph.D. Dissertation, Princeton University, 1989), pp. 77–86.

8. Diderot's attitude toward Rameau and the fundamental bass at this point of time is not simple to assess. While Diderot did offer several caustic comments about Rameau's theory in comparison to Bemetzrieder's (especially in the summary he wrote for Grimm; see *Oeuvres complétes*, 19, 405), I suspect his real bone of contention remained the excessive metaphysical speculations in which the elderly composer indulged at the end of his life (and which were lampooned so mercilessly in *Le Neveu de Rameau*). Still, even if Rameau had carried his speculative zeal too far, Diderot always seemed to hold a grudging respect for his theoretical accomplishments, as the comments of the *Philosophe* make clear at the end of the *Leçons* (p. 353).

9. Bemetzrieder's tale of the "musicien sauvage" is first proposed in his *Lettre de M. Bemetzrieder a MM. *** musiciens de profession: ou réponse a quelques objections qu'on a faites à sa méthode* (Paris: Pissot, 1771) published shortly after the appearance of the *Leçons* as a response to several criticisms that had been raised concerning his treatise. Bemetzrieder recycled the same material, as he frequently did, in many of his later publications; in the present case, the story of the "primitive musician" can be found in his *Traité de musique concernant les tons, les harmonies, les accords et le discours musical* (Paris: chez l'auteur, 1776) and the *Méthode et réflexions sur les leçons de musique* (Paris: chez l'auteur, 1778).

10. As far as I have been able to determine, the term "appel" applied to tonal dynamics originates with Bemetzrieder. Rameau, it is true, used similar gravitational rhetoric to discuss the attractive property of the tonic function in relation to its dominant and subdominant neighbors (see Thomas Christensen, *Rameau and Musical Thought in the Enlightenment* [Cambridge: Cambridge University Press, 1993], 185–90.) But I am not aware that Rameau ever explicitly used the term "appellation" to describe these attractive properties of tones.

11. The focus of Bemetzrieder on scale degree as a source of musical dynamic rather than harmony is an extraordinary change from the Rameauian paradigm and anticipates, as I suggested earlier, the theory of *tonalité* articulated by Francois-Joseph Fétis some seventy years later in his *Traité de l'harmonie* (Paris: M. Schlesinger, 1844). Not coincidentally, I think, Fétis referred to his dissonant scale degrees as "appelative." Typical of the arrogance of Fétis, however, he failed to acknowledge the contributions of Bemetzrieder, characterizing his theory simply as a "mishmash" of incoherent thinking and metaphysics. See Francois-Joseph Fétis, *Biographie universelle des musiciens* (Paris: Didot Frères, 1861), s.v. "Bemetzrieder."

12. Here we see Bemetzrieder illustrating a half-diminished chord on B resolving to four possible triads: its "normal" resolution on C major, but also cadences on A minor, E minor, and E major (p. 349). The resolution to A minor is particularly ungraceful, but typical of the harmonic parataxis found throughout the treatise.

13. This classification proves disastrous in practice. In the first class of such chords, containing two common tones and one note of suspension, Bemetzrieder includes (in the key of C major) the harmonies of A minor and E minor (p. 333)—or the submediant (vi) and mediant (iii) in modern functional nomenclature. Yet a direct move to the tonic I from these chords is not particularly stylistic in eighteenth-century music because neither chord projects easily any sense of tonal displacement characteristic of a

suspension. To make matters worse, Bemetzrieder excludes as faulty one of the few inversional possibilities by which the chords A minor and C might be coherently joined (vi-I6/3), and instead recommends a voicing that contains an egregious error of parallel octaves (vi-I6/4) only because the displaced note *la* resolves directly to the adjacent *sol* (p. 342). Similar problems plague the "second" class of appellatives, in which one note is held in common with the tonic (p. 344). In this class, we have grouped together as possessing the same "energy of appellation" the dominant triad (V) and the super-tonic seventh chord (ii7). The latter chord, as any first-year harmony student learns, normally does not move directly to the tonic without first moving through the dominant to which it is subordinate.

14. Bemetzrieder seems to have recognized this deficiency in the *Leçons*. In his later publications (particularly the *Traité de musique* of 1776 and the *Nouvelle Essai sur l'harmonie* [Paris: chex l'auteur, 1779]), he expands considerably the number of examples given illustrating chord successions and modulatory progressions. But again, he was not able to offer any coherent guidelines or systematic rules for these progressions, relying instead on students observing as many patterns as possible and relying on their instinct and good judgment.

15. Downing Thomas has pointed out that the metaphor of the harpsichord to model the mind's capacity for cognition and memory is one that predates Diderot's use, and can be found in the writings of Cartaud de la Vilate and Condillac. See Downing Thomas, *Music and the Origins of Language: Theories from the French Enlightenment* (Cambridge: Cambridge University Press, 1995), 158, n. 59.

16. "D'Alembert's Dream," translated by Jacques Barzun and Ralph H. Bowen in *Rameau's Nephew and Other Works* (Indianapolis: Bobbs-Merrill, 1964), 101. (I have slightly modified this translation.) It is interesting to compare this description with that of the "animated bell" in Diderot's *Lettre sur les sourds et muets* some twenty years earlier. Both rely on the notion of resonant strings to image the behavior of the human mind. For a thoughtful discussion of this image and its greater epistemological implications in Diderot's thought, see Wilda Anderson, *Diderot's Dream* (Baltimore: Johns Hopkins University Press, 1990), 11–41. Walter Rex offers a slightly different reading of this passage in *Diderot's Counterpoints: The Dynamics of Contrariety in His Major Works* (Oxford: Oxford University Press, 1998), 83–84.

17. For a helpful introduction to the Montpellier school of pathological vitalism, see Anne C. Vila, *Enlightenment and Pathology: Sensibility in the Literature and Medicine of Eighteenth-Century France* (Baltimore: Johns Hopkins University Press 1998), 43–79. For the influence of these physician-philosophers on Diderot's own thought, see pp. 152–81.

18. Properly speaking "sensibility" was not the same thing as "irritability." For Albrecht von Haller, the Swiss physician whose studies on sensibility and irritability were the most influential on the subsequent generation of Montpellier physicians, irritability was interpreted mechanistically, as a stimulation and subsequent contraction of the muscular tissue, while sensibility was a feeling associated with the nervous fibers (Vila, *Enlightenment and Pathology*, 14–15). But increasingly, such distinctions were being blurred by philosophers like Diderot who tended to subsume affective responses within a more materialist model of *sensibilité*.

19. The extraordinary congruence of Bemetzrieder's theory of appellation with tenets of Diderot's philosophy invites the intriguing speculation that Diderot might actually have played a role in encouraging the composer to develop further this aspect of his pedagogy. Such a possibility is raised in the excellent study by Jean Gribenski, who provides evidence that the last section of Bemetzrieder's treatise (containing the discussion of "appel") was added only after the preceding chapters were already developed and written, most likely due to the prodding and encouragement of Diderot ("A propos des *Leçons de clavecin* (1771): Diderot et Bemetzrieder," 136–37). It certainly seems that the theory of *appel* sketched out in the final pages of the dialogue

comes as something of an afterthought. Tellingly, too, it is Diderot (speaking as the *Philosophe*) who in the first reversion to third-person narrative reports having asked "M. Bemetz." why he had not structured his lessons more closely following these "speculative principles" (p. 357). Bemetzrieder confesses the reason being that the principle was not yet sufficiently developed in his mind. And in a subsequent writing, Bemetzrieder confesses that the theory of *appels* appearing at the end of the *Leçons* was not yet well worked out, and was included "malgré moi"—undoubtedly at the encouragement of Diderot (*Lettre de M. Bemetzrieder*, 29).

20. Vila, *Enlightenment and Pathology*, 49.

21. *D'Alembert's Dream*, 125.

22. The term "écart" is a particularly important one in Diderot's writings, especially in his narrative descriptions of his *Salons*. The word not only conveys a sense of deflection in a mechanical sense, but also that of a diversion or detour. Such a detour may be the result of error (like getting lost on a trip), but it also may be an intentional digression. (See Julie C. Hayes, "Sequence and Simultaneity in Diderot's *Promenade Vernet* and *Leçons de clavecin*," *Eighteenth-Century Studies* 29, no. 3 [1996]: 292–93.) This latter sense, of course, is more meaningful to a composer or performer who intentionally sets out to produce a series of modulatory progressions that "diverge" from the tonic triad and key. The English translation of the *Leçons* published in 1779 tends toward this meaning, with its poetic choice of "wanderings" as a translation for *écart*. *Music Made Easy to Every Capacity, in a Series of Dialogues*, 3 vols. (London: R. Ayre and G. Moore, 1778–79), part 3.

23. Were Bemetzrieder to have left his description of *appel* at that, his theory would have been surprisingly similar to that articulated by Rameau some fifty years earlier in his *Traité de l'harmonie* of 1722. There, Rameau had offered a fully mechanistic model of harmonic motion whereby the dissonant seventh is described as a kind of Cartesian causative impact (*choc*) impelling the harmonic motion forward until its ultimate resolution at the static, consonant triad. See my study, *Rameau and Musical Thought in the Enlightenment*, 103–13. The crucial difference, however, is that Rameau provided with his *basse fondamentale* a coherent syntax by which these various tonal "collisions" of the dissonant seventh were regulated, whereas Bemetzrieder, as already pointed out, lacked any semblance of such grammatical organization.

24. The English edition of the *Leçons* appropriately translates these as "painful shocks." *Music Made Easy*, part 3, p. 246.

25. *D'Alembert's Dream*, 103.

26. Again a comparison with Fétis is suggestive. Fétis argued that if the appellative character of *tonalité* was overexploited by composers, it would cross over into the genre of *omnitonique* music, and would soon result in a neutralization of all appellative qualities due to their overuse. See Thomas Christensen, "Fétis and Emerging Tonal Consciousness," *Music Theory in the Age of Romanticism*, ed. Ian Bent (Cambridge: Cambridge University Press, 1996), 37–56.

27. Guy Poitry, "Diderot et la 'loi des appels': La peur dans le labyrinthe," *Poetique* 92 (1992), 467–76.

28. For an example of such a narration by the instructor, see page 326. Bemetzrieder, we might note, repeats the same story of the labyrinth in one of his later publications, but in a far more elaborate and expanded version. Tellingly, Bemetzrieder ends the story on a positive, optimistic note. After the initial bout of fear and despair in the labyrinth, he tells us, the musician will finally arrive home full of pleasure, confidence, and hope (*Traité*, 209–10).

29. See Hayes, "Sequence and Simultaneity." This fascinating article suggests to me the parallel rhetorics Diderot uses to juxtapose a journey through the spatial canvas of the painter and the tonal space of a musical composition. In the former case, the static visual terrain of the painting is given temporal animation through the critic's narrative,

while in the later case, the phenomenological flow of the music is suspended in time through the critic's methodical analysis of the music's harmonic structure.

30. Tropes of parataxis, fractured syntax, and fragmented speech were commonly employed by writers in the eighteenth century to convey qualities of exacerbated sentimentality and pathos in their characters, particularly female characters. Indeed, it is a hallmark in Diderot's own bourgeois dramas (e.g., in *Le Fils naturel* and *Le Père de famille*).

31. Cynthia Verba, *Music and the French Enlightenment: Reconstruction of a Dialogue 1750–1764* (Oxford: Clarendon Press, 1993), 110–11.

32. Hayes, "Sequence and Simultaneity," 298.

33. Thomas, *Music and the Origins of Language*, 172.

34. Walter Rex, *Diderot's Counterpoints*.

35. The falling out between Diderot and Bemetzrieder is extensively covered in Gribenski, "A propos des *Leçons de clavecin*."

3

"Little Pearl Teardrops"

Schubert, Schumann, and the Tremulous Body of Romantic Song

Lawrence Kramer

Who will write the history of tears?
—Roland Barthes, *A Lover's Discourse*

The eyes, those windows of the soul, have traditionally been the place where the link between body and spirit most fully appears. When the eyes weep, however, the figure changes. Weeping is supposed to be a force of nature, the earliest and most spontaneous expression of overflowing feeling; "We came crying hither," says King Lear; "Thou knowest, the first time that we smell the air / We wawl and cry" (IV/iv, 185–87). As the symbolic implications of Lear's lines suggest, however, this most natural of acts is also one of the most social. Tears, seemingly so involuntary—forming a sign of feeling only in the "indexical" sense that blood is the sign of a wound—are actually one of the places where the essentially social character of the human body most fully appears. (And I do mean "essentially": except in extreme pain and mortal terror, the purely natural body emerges only as a fiction projected from the social one that is the vehicle of everyday life.) Tears are a social practice, highly regulated in regard to time, place, and person, and invested with an elaborate network of multiple meanings.[1]

Several of those meanings bear closely on the topic of this paper, which is the role played by tears at a pair of exemplary moments in the development of song, specifically of the German Lied, which I take to be (among other things) the nineteenth-century prototype of the popular love songs with which the twentieth century was saturated as by a soundtrack. These musical moments, torch songs *avant la lettre* by Schubert and Schumann, are particularly suggestive because they mark out a small turning point in the history of Western music. They go well beyond the traditional representation of tears by melodic "sob" figures (which, in fact, they do not use)[2] and concentrate on the material, bodily dimension of tears. And they do so at just about the time that philosophical aesthetics, continuing a project begun in the mid-eighteenth century, is detaching music from the body with ever-greater severity. In these songs, both of them famous canonical pieces, tears become a means of recapturing music for the body: for, that is to say, the social body, although it continually masquerades as the natural one.

The meanings in the background of this process all stem from the eighteenth-century cult of sensibility, which identifies exquisiteness of bodily feeling with social gentility and makes this pairing identifiable by means of certain physical signs that are written, so to speak, on the text of the body. As the foremost of these signs (which also include trembling, blushing or blanching, sighing or catching of breath, and involuntary gesturing), tears become a precious substance. They were often likened to pearls—"Perlentränentröpfchen" [little pearl teardrops] in Heinrich Heine's inimitably German coinage[3]—a metaphor exemplary in its union of the exquisite with the socially elevated.

The meanings, of course, continually overlap. First, tears indicate a paradoxical combination of sincerity, a natural quality, and refinement, a social one, especially in relation to a pair of phenomena that may seem unconnected, but that actually tend to intertwine during the period: music and human sympathy. The acme of both often seemed to lodge in the power of song to move a listener to tears in which empathy or pity is indistinguishable from musical pleasure:

> The tears fell upon her cheeks, while she sung a vesper hymn, so soft, and so solemn! and her voice trembled, as it were, and then she would stop a moment, and wipe away her tears, and go on again, lower than before. O! I had often listened to my lady, but never heard any thing so sweet as this; it made me cry, almost, to hear it.[4]

This novelistic passage is particularly telling for its intimation that the moral sensitivity of the singer, a noblewoman, communicates itself to the listener, a servant, who returns it in the form of sympathy.

Second, tears act as a symbolic substitute for sexual passion, up to and including orgasm. Like the older metaphor of dying, crying in this usage was readily understood and sometimes close to explicit. The two figures combine in a poem by Heine that Schumann set for use in his song cycle *Dichterliebe* [A Poet's Love, 1840] but ultimately withheld:

Lehn' deine Wang' an meine Wang',	Lay your cheek on my cheek
Dann fliessen die Tränen zusammen,	And our tears will flow together,
Und an mein Herz drück' fest dein Herz,	And press your heart fast to my heart

| Dann schlagen zusammen | And our flames will beat together. |
| die Flammen. | |

Und wenn in die grosse Flamme fliesst	And if in the great flames flows
Der Strom von unsern Tränen,	The river of our tears,
Und wenn dich mein Arm gewaltig	And if my arm forcefully clasps
umschliest,	you,
Sterb' ich vor Liebessehnen!	I'll die of yearning love![5]

Schumann's vocal line for the literal and figurative climax is a drooping melisma on "—sehnen" [yearning]; the piano follows with a swooning figure that swirls up from the depths of the bass and then sinks away to a greater depth. As with the singer of the vesper hymn, the tears evoke a low, throaty sound, resonant with the depths of the body, in which sensation and sentiment seem to fuse.[6]

Finally, tears form a barometer of what a later age would call mental health, understood as a firm and finely discriminated linkage between the social system and the nervous system. Eminent psychologists such as Philippe Pinel promoted the "healthy sentimentality" exemplified by generous tears as fundamental to the enlightened individual, as much on the basis of a reading of Rousseau as anything else. This eighteenth-century standpoint, however, would erode in the course of the nineteenth, by the end of which tears had been reinterpreted as a symptom of nervousness, emotional instability, and "feminine" overexcitement.[7] The exception to this rule (and its proverbial proof) lay in the aesthetic sphere, where the older signification of tears tended to persist, although only at the risk of seeming suspect even to some of its advocates. In the past fifty years or so, the problem has tended to play itself out at the movies and on TV in attitudes toward the genre of sentimental melodrama: the tearjerker. The genre renews itself by continually offering stronger reasons to shed a tear, but the underlying logic is the same as it was in the eighteenth century. Because tears are supposed to be the involuntary product of strong emotion, tears prompted by sensitivity or compassion give physical proof of the weeper's moral fineness. The result is both to fend off feelings of shame, embarrassment, or weakness and to turn crying into an intense physical pleasure.[8]

The cultivation of tearful sensibility in the eighteenth century and after was a many-sided social practice. One key venue was the theater, where tears spread like a contagion through the audience. Another was literature, unfettered by the material constraints of theater. Sensibility disseminated itself most widely through bestselling books: Laurence Sterne's travelogue *A Sentimental Journey through France and Italy* (1768), Henry Mackenzie's moral fable *The Man of Feeling* (1771), Ann Radcliffe's gothic thriller *The*

Mysteries of Udolpho (1794), and above all Johann Wolfgang Goethe's primordial soap opera *The Sorrows of Young Werther* (1772). Werther served for many years as a pan-European guidebook for sensitivity of soul. It stands as a landmark in the history of tears in both Roland Barthes's *A Lover's Discourse* and Tom Lutz's more recent *Crying: The Natural and Cultural History of Tears.*[9]

One scene in particular seems to encapsulate the culture of tearful sensibility at a single stroke. As Barthes describes it:

> The slightest amorous emotion, whether of happiness or disappointment, brings Werther to tears. Werther weeps often, very often, and in floods. . . . By releasing his tears without constraint, he follows the orders of the amorous body, which is a body in liquid expansion, a bathed body: to weep together, to flow together: delicious tears finish off the reading of Klopstock which Werther and Charlotte perform together.[10]

The poem involved—which, incidentally, Werther and Charlotte do not read—is Friedrich Gottlieb Klopstock's rhapsodic "Die Frühlingsfeier" [Festival of Spring], a touchstone of poetic feeling in its day. The scene itself reads like this:

> We stepped to the window. . . . [T]he splendid rain was trickling down upon the land; the most refreshing fragrance rose up to us from the rich abundance of the warm atmosphere. She stood leaning on her elbows, with her gaze searching the countryside; she looked up to heaven and at me; I saw her eyes fill with tears, and she laid her hand on mine, saying, "Klopstock!" I recalled at once the glorious Ode she had in mind, and became immersed in the stream of emotions which she had poured over me by uttering this symbolic name. I could not bear it, I bent down over her hand and kissed it amid tears of the utmost rapture.[11]

Charlotte is moved and her senses aroused by natural forms, but her tears arise at the thought of Klopstock, proving that sincerity and refinement are indistinguishable in her character. Werther's response in kind proves the same of him. The whole episode is figuratively saturated by their tears, which metaphorically shade into the "splendid rain" on the one hand and the "stream of emotions" on the other. This liquid atmosphere, both literal and figurative, also serves as the medium for the eroticism that diffuses itself throughout the scene, released by Charlotte's conjunction of her touch and her tears and reaching a climax in Werther's responsive kiss amid tears of rapture. Finally, the "healthy sentimentality" of the episode declares itself in the pivotal role of Klopstock, whose poem Werther and Charlotte do not need to read because the utterance of his "symbolic name" is enough to unite them. Their tears join them through the mediation of a cultural icon, their joint veneration of which demonstrates their social worth.

The only thing missing here is the nexus of music and sympathy, but that appears elsewhere in the text with a telling narcissistic twist. Charlotte likes to play her favorite tune, "so simple and so full of meaning," at the piano, and in his early acquaintance with her Werther reports that "as soon as she plays the first note of it I find myself cured of all grief, bewilderment, and cares" (53). (The symbolic note acts like Klopstock's symbolic name.) Charlotte's music moves Werther not *to* sympathy but *as* sympathy, which he receives as an offering especially to him. But when Werther hears Charlotte play the same tune after her marriage to another man, the objectified sympathy of the music recoils on him amid the overflow of his tears. The luxury of Barthes's liquid amorous body shrivels up; the tears of sublimation become those of frustration. Werther feels himself suffocating in the "flood" of feelings; "impetuously" he approaches Charlotte and blurts out, "For God's sake, stop!" (119). The moment marks the first serious rupture between the two, and is followed almost immediately by an ominous rupture in the narrative. The fatality in Werther's sensibility, the flaw in the pearl, has now disclosed itself in the same tears by which that sensibility is ratified, and the cause of the disclosure is music.

Our Schubert and Schumann songs recycle the key elements of Werther's musical moments while also making an important expansion in the frame of reference. The songs, too, deal with the mutual mediations of music, sympathy, and tears, but their interest has a double focus. On the one hand they find a continuing validity in the culture of tearful sensibility and therefore seek to continue it, although perhaps with a certain infusion of ironic self-consciousness. On the other hand, they focus on the musical representation of tears as a means of affirming the link between music and individual subjectivity, as opposed to music's aesthetic self-sufficiency or transcendental value. They do so, most likely, not as music but precisely as songs, instances of a genre that prefers to maintain its worldly connections rather than to ride the nineteenth-century cultural wave that offered to free music of its mundane trappings.

The sources of that wave prominently included the aesthetics of instrumental music, which arose in the wake of the perceived "emancipation" of music from language. This line of thought rooted itself in a pair of influential assumptions that would long seem unquestionable: first, that instrumental music was identical with music in its essence; and second, that instrumental music, and therefore music qua music, had no definite content. Although thinkers from Hegel onward tried to establish a coherent relationship between music and subjectivity, these assumptions kept leading them into spheres of pure abstraction. The dilemma can be encapsulated in the work of Theodor Vischer, whose post-Hegelian effort to theorize music as an expression of emotion led to the conclusion that "the individual emotion will find its expression in music ... only as something ... that vanishes into the darkness again as too indistinct the moment anyone wishes to grasp it." Given this conclusion, the only alternatives are to assign the enveloping darkness a quasi-transcendental value or to join formalists like Eduard Hanslick in contemplating the working out of purely musical ideas.[12]

Song seems to offer an obvious stay against music's affective vanishing act: the words of a song link musical expression to particulars. As a genre, the nineteenth-century Lied is ideally suited to use this link on behalf of an aesthetic of particularity. Its texts are lyric poems understood to express personal feeling, and its performance, until late in the era, belongs mainly to the social venues of such feeling, more to the intimacy of the home or conviviality of the salon than to the anonymity of the concert hall. Even more important, perhaps, the genre highlights the individual voice, supporting it discreetly on the piano and leaving it unencumbered by drama, spectacle, or orchestral competition. As Hegel observes, language alone cannot stave off the indeterminacy of musical expression. Although words set up a leaning toward particularity, music often "simply snaps its link with words in order to move at will and unhampered within its own sphere of sounds."[13] But the music of a song cannot simply snap its link with the singing voice. For Hegel, voice endows song with a particularity above and beyond that of words: "In other instruments a vibration is set up in a body indifferent to the soul and its expression. . .but in song the soul rings out from its own body" (K, 922). Not only is song tied to the specific quality of individual voices, but it is also more closely allied with the body, carries fuller traces of the individual body, than any other form of music. It is the form par excellence in which the inner self appears as the manifestation of a unique individual.

Both in their handling of text and the relations they establish between voice and piano, our songs by Schubert and Schumann exemplify the alternative aesthetic based on the particularity of bodies and feelings. More than that, they can be heard as programmatic statements of that aesthetic, specifically on the basis of their treatment of musical tears. By placing their expression of tearful sensibility slightly askew, the songs lightly deface but in no way discredit their own formal design. This technique, which I have elsewhere called "scoring" the subject (with a pun on inscribing and putting to music), develops in the early nineteenth century as a strong sign of subjectivity. The "mark" left on the music—in this case the tear stain—is understood as the self's distinctive handiwork. It combines the idiosyncrasy of the person and the tangible consistency of the body.[14]

Both songs are to texts by Heine: Schubert's from the group of six published posthumously in 1828 in the collection *Schwanengesang* [Swan Song], and Schumann's from *Dichterliebe*. The discussion of each is prefaced by its text.

Schubert, "Ihr Bild" [Her Image]

Ich stand in dunklen Traümen	I stood in dark dreams
Und starrt' ihr Bildnis an,	And stared at her image,
Und das geliebte Antlitz	And the beloved countenance
Heimlich zu leben begann.	Mysteriously came to life.
Um ihre Lippen zog sich	Around her lips there drew
Ein Lächeln wunderbar,	A wondrous smile,
Und wie von Wehmutstränen,	And as from tears of sorrow
Erglänzte ihr Augenpaar.	Glistened both her eyes.
Auch meine Tränen flossen	My tears streamed, too,
Mir von dem Wangen herab—	Down from my cheeks—
Und ach, ich kann es nicht glauben	And ah! I cannot believe
Das ich dich verloren hab'!	I have lost you![15]

The way one reads this poem depends on how much irony one finds in its closure, as is so often the case with Heine. Is the last couplet a mere *façon de parler*, meaning something like "it's unnatural or unjust that I have lost you," in which case the poem ends with the speaker's recognition of his loss? Or does it literally encode a denial of what he knows to be true, in which case the poem ends with the speaker still shrouded in his dark dreams? A reader can choose to have it either way, but the question is impossible to settle. Its contending answers, however, are both consistent with the culture of tearful sensibility. A deluded speaker can be regarded as showing a Werther-like authenticity of feeling, indifferent to mere fact; undeluded, the speaker can be taken to demonstrate the value of "healthy sentimentality" as his tears lead him from self-absorbed reverie to a hard but healing recognition. In both resistance and the glimmer of mournful acceptance, the truth of the speaker's character is embodied by his tears.

It is this process of embodiment rather than the resolution of Heine's ambiguity that most occupies Schubert's song. There is almost a pointed refusal to take a hermeneutic position: the vocal line ends by affirming its disbelief in a supportive B-flat major, but the piano goes on to end the song in a dark-hued B-flat minor. It is impossible to say whether the voice "hears" the piano's contradiction or remains deaf to it. What can be said is that the form of the song is guided by the musical representation of the speaker's tears.

Example 3.1 a–c. From Franz Schubert, "Ihr Bild" (*Schwanengesang*, 1828).

This process begins in the first two measures, which consist entirely of the single note B-flat presented by the piano in a soft and low pair of octaves, divided by a rest (Example 3.1a). Writing in 1928, Heinrich Schenker remarked on the peculiarity of this opening and offered an explanation: "To repeat that note in slow tempo, and to repeat it thus, after a [quarter-note] rest, means: we stare with the note. And as we do so, we are instantly transported . . . to the side of the unfortunate lover."[16] The note transfers to the listener both the temporal character and the compulsiveness of the lover's stare: we can't take our ears away from it. (It even makes the score into a mirror: in the treble clef, the paired notes form a visual emblem of a pair of eyes.) As Christopher Wintle has shown, this staring-eye figure permeates the deeper levels of the song's structure.[17] At the surface level, a version of the figure precedes each of the song's three sections, which correspond to the three stanzas of the poem in an ABA form. The vicissitudes of the figure within this form emerge progressively from the musical contents of the first two sections and steer the third and final section to the point of dramatic crisis.

To characterize the "dark dream" of the poem's first couplet, the song's first section extends the "staring" texture of the opening. The initial octaves, now doubled by the voice, evolve into a somber melody that sounds especially desolate in the absence of harmony. With the second couplet, describing the animation of the image, the missing harmony appears. It seems to bring some comfort, and yet something is palpably wrong with it. As David Schwarz remarks, "The music is in four-part chorale style, as if a phrase from a Bach chorale. There is an incredible discrepancy between the Steven King-esque return of the living dead image in the text and Schubert's conventionally voiced harmonies" (82). The discrepancy masks a secret identity, although this is an open secret, revealed by the pretense of masking: the chorale style here is an archaism, itself a ghostly, reanimated form, and therefore a vehicle for the very uncanny feeling it seems to oppose. The piano postlude to the section also walks the line between the fragility and the persistence of the speaker's illusion. It begins with a pair of stinging exposed dissonances in the deep bass, visceral sounds that cannot quite be appeased by their subsequent passage to resolution.

The second section tries to normalize the atmosphere by bringing the speaker's fantasy under the control of tearful sensibility. The section begins by recalling the "staring" octaves of the opening in both voice and piano, but these soon turn into the top voice of another passage in four-part har-mony, this time a more modern harmony that promises to sustain the speaker's consoling illusion (see Example 3.1b; the entire section is oriented toward the submediant major, a tonal area often associated with imaginary pleasures at this period).[18] The feeling of consolation culminates in the setting of the stanza's second couplet, where the beloved image weeps. The image "mysteriously comes to life" not only in the evocative harmony but also in the song's only vocal ornament, a quivering mordent at the key word "Augen-" [eyes]. The speaker thus seems to receive the tears of the image as an expression of sympathy addressed just to him, and to find com-fort in the associated music, much as Werther does when he first hears Charlotte play.

The third section, however, begins with a recoil of this feeling reminiscent of Werther's reaction when he last hears Charlotte play. The recoil is already implicit at the midpoint of the second section. Between the descriptions of the image's smile and tears, the piano inserts an incongruous little hiccoughing figure (Example 3.1b). The poetic context offers a rationale: the figure can be heard as mimetic, suggesting the sensation of choking up with the access of tears. Nothing is made of this for the moment; the figure simply acts as an irritant within the lyrical texture, perhaps anticipating the tears that the text is about to mention. But the same figure returns to introduce the third section by heralding and then merging with the return of the "staring-eye" figure, which now assumes the form of a pair of heavy, fully harmonized chords, the second of which is the tonic minor (see Example 3.1c). In yet another mysterious reanimation, the staring eyes and the access of tears unite: the eyes weep. Essential to this effect is its synchrony with the formal articulation of the song: the weeping is not an object of representation but the correlative of a felt process. The locus of that process, moreover, is less affective than it is physical: the music embodies the speaker's tearful sensibility precisely by imprinting itself with the sensations of his body.

From here the speaker goes on to mirror the image's tears with his own, as, perhaps, the image has been mirroring his tears all along. The result is a travesty of the kind of sensuous mingling that unites Werther and Charlotte at the symbolic name of Klopstock. The voice and piano mingle without harmonizing. They dislodge the poem's tears from the sphere of consoling illusion by returning to the stark, octave-driven desolation of the opening. But by this point the instability of the speaker's position is irrepressible; as we've seen, he closes his utterance by what is probably a return to illusion. The third section being a reprise of the first, however, this return assumes the "living dead" form of the "Bach chorale" passage and collapses—although not necessarily for the speaker—into the dissonant postlude and a jolting close in the minor. Although the close is harsh enough to suggest a leaning toward tragic or ironic pathos, the final outcome is inscrutable. What remains clear is the speaker's vacillation between Werther's polarized modes of tearful sensibility, each of which has a series of specific musical embodiments. Whatever the truth is, the truth is in the tears, and the tears are in the music.

Schumann, "Ich hab' im Traum geweinet" [I cried in a dream]

Ich hab' im Traum geweinet.	I cried in a dream.
Mir träumte, du lägest im Grab.	I dreamt you lay in your grave.
Ich wachte auf, und die Träne	I woke up, and the tears
Floss noch von der Wange herab.	Still were streaming down my cheeks.
Ich hab' im Traum geweinet.	I cried in a dream.
Mir träumt', du verliessest mich.	I dreamt you left me.
Ich wachte auf, und ich weinte	I woke up and I cried
Nach lange bitterlich.	Still long and bitterly.
Ich hab' im Traum geweinet.	I cried in a dream.
Mir träumte, du wärst mich noch gut.	I dreamt you still cared for me.
Ich wachte auf und noch immer	I woke up, and still ever
Strömt meine Tränenflut.	Streams the flood of my tears.

Like *Werther*, Schumann's *Dichterliebe* is a three-handkerchief work. Seven of the sixteen poems in the cycle involve the shedding of tears, including the "Perlentränentropfchen" I cited earlier. "Ich hab' im Traum geweinet," which occurs late in the cycle (it is number thirteen) and marks its emotional nadir, is the song most preoccupied with the topic.

Like "Ihr Bild," the poem is tricky to interpret because of its in-determinately ironic close. But where "Ihr Bild" is merely ambiguous, "Ich hab' im Traum geweinet" is positively opaque. Its final couplet could equally be, among other things, disconsolate ("But you don't care at all any more"), disillusioned ("Even if you did, you'd just hurt me again"), or jeering ("The real bad dream would be your still caring"). Moreover, the dream of the third stanza may refer ironically to the lovers' whole affair more than to a "real" dream following their breakup. The emotional logic of *Dichterliebe*, however, demands a treatment of tearful sensibility in which irony has no place. Throughout the cycle, tears identify the speaker's obstinate love with fineness of feeling, no matter how humiliating or self-torturing the feeling becomes. The last song claims that this love has finally died, to be buried in a "great coffin" proportionate to the suffering it has caused, although a melancholy piano postlude, quoting music from earlier in the cycle, famously leaves the outcome in doubt. "Ich hab im Traum geweinet" marks the moment at which the speaker's love seems least likely to die, so that it must paradoxically be mourned most bitterly by the very tears that affirm its continuance.

Like Schubert's in "Ihr Bild," Schumann's setting in "Ich hab' im Traum geweinet" depends on a little figure that mimics the weeping body. Schumann's figure is an "organic" element rather than a "painterly" one *ab extra*, but like Schubert's it is articulated so that its vicissitudes coincide with the form of the song. In this case, the form is AAB, one stanza per section, plus a brief postlude. The last section replicates the reversal of direction on which the poem pivots; it rises to a new pitch of intensity by harping on a few key features of the sections that precede it.

Both literally and figuratively, the A sections are broken up. They consist of short, alternating statements by the voice and piano alone, separated by silences. The voice begins with a near-monotonal statement of the title phrase, from which, as in the poem, everything else flows. The piano responds illustratively. Picking up on the monotone, it forms a broken repercussive figure in the bass, lightly sounded but given "body" by a full chordal texture, that can be taken to suggest the sensation of being choked with tears (see Example 3.2). The figure sounds twice, then "breaks up" further into detached chords.

The B section unites the voice and piano as fully as the A sections had divided them. The piano begins by taking over the vocal phrase for "Ich hab'

Example 3.2. From Robert Schumann, "Ich hab' im Traum geweinet" *Dichterliebe*, 1840).

im Traum geweinet"; the melodic difference from its previous monotone figure is just a single neighboring note accentuating the syllable, "-wein" [cry], to which it corresponds. The voice enters shortly afterward by rearticulating the key phrase, but the vocal line soon becomes inarticulate, shunting the voice into a four-bar monotone, as if to reverse roles with the piano. Concurrently, the remainder of the piano part weaves together fragmentary echoes of the key phrase ("-weinet," "in Traum geweinet") in an unbroken chain. The "choking" of the piano's repercussive figure thus becomes continuous sobbing, while the voice's musical enunciation becomes a kind of wail. The earlier silences—of restraint, self-suppression, numbness?—are overrun by a "stream" of sound. Mimetically speaking, the form of the song reenacts the process of breaking into tears, thus anticipating the shift of tenses to the present of perpetual tears in the poem's last line.

The section ends in a state of musical and emotional frustration. The voice wrenches itself to a close on the first scale degree of the tonic, only to find the tonic chord reinterpreted as a dominant (I_5^6/iv); the piano wrenches free from the continuous texture with a short dramatic outburst that compounds the harmonic impasse. A lengthy silence follows. Thereafter the piano returns with a postlude restating and echoing its repercussive figure (once each) amid more oppressive silence. The anticipatory choking-up now becomes a summation, but with an extra dimension of virtual presence: the song that began with the vocal recollection of tears ends with the instrumental embodiment of them. This reversal both completes the articulation of the song's form (by framing it with an "organic" return to the opening) and "scores" it from outside (as a postlude, an extra piece of music neither required nor contained by the AAB sequence.)

Given its key role in this process, the piano's repercussive figure merits some more mulling over. In an earlier discussion of "Ich hab' in Traum geweinet," I suggested that this figure forms a kind of drumbeat.[19] The suggestion still seems tenable; it acknowledges a funereal tone in the music, even the air of an execution, a reference that seems strange until one remembers the program of Berlioz's *Symphonie fantastique* (1830), with its fantasy of sexually motivated murder and the guillotine. (Schumann wrote an extended analysis of the symphony in 1835.[20])

The context of tears, however, may prompt a second suggestion. The song's vocal line uses the semitonal movement but not the characteristic rhythmic gestures of the traditional sob figure. The accompaniment, with its rhythmically marked embodiment of tearful sensibility, seems to make restitution. The bodily dimension of tears has, so to speak, been precipitated out of the vocal line, leaving only an abstracted or etherealized representation behind, but it returns in the choking movement, low register, and thick materiality of the piano's chords. The piano seems to restore the presence of the body from which Hegel's "soul," in song, rings out. The effect is at least double. First, by distributing the musical representation of tears into two parts, the song articulates the dual nature of tears as ideology and as physical substrate: perhaps with special emphasis on the latter, the part that is normally suppressed or sublimated. Second, by specifically severing the material-bodily representation of tears from language, the song intimates a certain model of layered, complex, proto-Freudian subjectivity. The preverbal, unbound, body-oriented energy of tears becomes the hidden truth of the speech act, and, for that matter, of the speaker's dream, which the accompaniment is the first to interpret. At this level my two suggestions come together, the drumbeat-tears at once mourning for the beloved and wishing her dead.

Schubert's "Ihr Bild" also locates its musical tears in the piano, not the voice, as if the relationship of voice and instrument replicated that of voice and body, subjective reflexivity and sensation. Other, closely related songs do the same. Schubert's "Am Meer" [By the Sea], also from the Heine set, embodies the impact of drinking the beloved's tears—one becomes another Werther, obsessed and consumed by desire—in a continuous chain of dissonant tremolos coextensive with a sectional division (see Example 3.3; as written out, the image is also visual, like the eyes in "Ihr Bild"). Schumann's "Wenn ich in deine Augen seh" [When I Look into Your Eyes], also from *Dichterliebe*, is increasingly dominated by the piano's evolution of a "choking up" figure that "scores" the postlude with harmonic ambiguity (see Example 3.4).

In all these songs, the sonorous matter as imprinted by the tear is not permitted to vanish into the abstraction of form, the infinite, the Will, or any other transcendentalizing conception. The scoring of the subject here consists in underscoring, via the bodily mark of tears, the irreducible concreteness of subjectivity. In each case, the musical tear remains incompletely assimilated, a quasi-palpable sign that materializes both the expressivity of

Example 3.3. From Franz Schubert, "Ihr Bild" (*Schwanengesang*, 1828).

Example 3.4. From Robert Schumann, "Wenn ich in deine Augen seh"
(*Dichterliebe*, 1840).

the music and the sensibility of the speaker, terms that thus crisscross in the production of aesthetic pleasure and moral fineness. Barthes's luxuriously bathed amorous body may not appear; indeed, it is violated by this continuation of the tradition that bred it. What does appear is a kind of inventory of the body wrought on and fraught: a catalogue of gasps, shudders, sobs, chokes, and spasms. But this tremulous body is vivid in its pain: vivid enough to hold its own against the formidable power of musical abstraction, vivid enough to mark the music itself with a materiality that is also a mode of feeling.

Schubert's and Schumann's construction of the tremulous body through musical tears has an echo in Hegel's account of the relation of art and feeling, in which tears function like little lenses through which emotion is "fixed . . . fast to one especial content" (H, 189; K, 935):

> it was a good old custom at deaths and funerals to appoint wailing women in order that grief might be brought to intuition in its expression. . . . [To] cry one's eyes out . . . has ever been regarded as a means of . . . relieving the heart. The mitigation of the power of passions . . . has its universal ground in the fact that man is released from his immediate imprisonment in feeling and becomes conscious of it as something external to him, to which he must now relate himself in an ideal way. (K, 49)

This passage identifies crying as the model of art. Tears, like artworks, are external but not foreign to the subject. They depart from the immediacy of feeling while preserving its substance intact. They do not represent or signify the subject's inner life, but form a trace of it that intimates the whole: they simply are that life in external form. The tear is thus literally what artistic production can be only figuratively: a bringing outward, an expressing, of an internal reality, the tangible form of a feeling and the guarantee of the feeling's truth. Musical tears—that is, tears made of music, as in our songs—are precipitates of this process.

Hegel gives the alliance of art and tears an "anthropological" validation by invoking the custom of hired or designated mourners, which alludes to rituals of ancient lineage. But the underlying valuation reflects the same cult of refined sensibility drawn on by Goethe and Heine, Schubert and Schumann, despite Hegel's own sharp critique of the sensibility-laden "beautiful soul" in *The Phenomenology of Spirit*. To relocate feeling in the tear is the quintessential gesture of sensibility. The musical tears of Schubert and Schumann perform this gesture by analogy insofar as they assume the "external" form of a little piece of sound incommensurate with the musical work as a whole. The "piece" is to the work as the tear or the artwork is to the subject. The fragment extracted from subjectivity becomes the guarantee

of that subjectivity, much as a "little piece of the real," according to Slavoj
Žižek, serves to underwrite symbolic fictions.[21] Hegel's account of the "good
old custom" of surrogate wailing takes this point a step further. It suggests
that the relocation of subjectivity in the tear is effectively and perhaps
originally a communal act. Tears turn subjectivity into community property.
Shedding them is a valued social practice that the personal love-laments of
our Schubert and Schumann songs can either aspire to serve or, failing that,
invoke as ideology.

Present-day listeners stand in a peculiar relationship to the tearfulness of
Romantic song, being at once very removed from it and very close to it.
Removed, because the songs themselves can be heard only as historical artifacts. Their social function has long since been taken over by popular ballads,
and their emotional logic depends on a ready susceptibility to tears that is
not currently viable as a social style. Not that we are averse to the spectacle
of tears, quite the contrary; but we tend to want them hard, not easy.
Contemporary tearfulness requires the pretense that the spectator does not
have a quasi-masochistic interest in sharing the lover's tears, which must
therefore dissimulate their own relation to pleasure or bodily validation. The
current model for the spectator's role is that of the caring stranger—the
fiction presupposed by the evening news, another major venue of crying in
public—and not that of the secret sharer or imaginary intimate. Changes
in gender roles have also had an impact. Even though we are no longer
supposed to believe that boys don't cry, the tears of men are still regarded
as more exceptional than those of women, whose world is still defined as
moister than the male norm.

But listeners are still close to these songs, too, because tears remain a
key medium for venting the feelings of love lost and longed for, and music
remains the closest aesthetic equivalent—a good old-fashioned objective
correlative—of that medium. The sheer persistence of this phenomenon
suggests some sort of underlying continuity amid cultural change. I would
like to conclude by speculating on what that might be.

Hegel's notion of external subjectivity offers a clue. It helps explain a
peculiarity attached to tears, or perhaps just enhanced in them, by the culture
of sensibility. Unlike virtually any other bodily secretion, the tear is rarely
an object of disgust once it has been produced. It is sustained in its appeal
because it is never entirely a material object; the tear is always imbued with
subjective value.

What value, then, and for whom? The tear of sensibility is the outcome
and support of a certain mode of subjectivity that, like the tear itself, persists
through the modern era under a host of changing conditions. There is only
one candidate for this office, and its identity is virtually proverbial. The
precious tear is a function of Cartesian subjectivity, the condition of a

consciousness both alienated and rendered autonomous by its unbridgeable distance from its own embodiment. The tear is the golden key that unlocks the prison cell of the post-Cartesian self. It is not an embodiment of the subject's feeling, but the embodiment of the subject as feeling. This construction of the tear helps to explain the close relationship of tearful sensibility to music, which is assigned a slightly more distanced form of the same function in the cultural field. It also helps explain the tendency of music to localize its "own" tears in a particular, unassimilable gesture, a redoubling and reflection of its own never fully assumed powers of "expression." The excess of a dissonance, the skewing of a form, the creation of an oddly iconic image from the abstraction of musical notation, the "underscoring" of the bodily depth of the voice—all work to find in music a dual object-subject that is "precious" in both senses of the word: a little pearl teardrop.

Notes

1. See Anne Vincent-Baffault, *A History of Tears: Sensibility and Sentimentality in France*, trans. Teresa Bridgeman (New York: St. Martin's, 1991); Michael Feher, ed. *Fragments for a History of the Human Body, Parts III–V* (New York: Zone Books, 1989); and Diane Ackerman, *A Natural History of the Senses* (New York: Vintage, 1995).
2. Melodic sobs typically involve several of the following features: semitone motion, melisma, syncopated accent, and short-long phrasing. Examples in Schubert include the settings of "Ei Tränen, meine Tränen" [Ah, my tears, my tears] in "Gefror'ne Tränen" [Frozen Tears], mm. 20–22; "wein'" [cry] in "Letze Hoffnung" [Last Hope], mm. 35–40, both from Winterreise; and "eine Träne wird erweinen" [a tear will be shed] in "An die Türen will ich schleichen" [To the doors I will creep], mm. 38–41, from the sequence *Gesänge des Harfners* [The Harper's Songs] to texts from Goethe's *Wilhelm Meisters Lehrjahr* [Wilhelm Meister's Apprenticeship].
3. From "Allnächtlich im Traume seh' ich dich," set by Robert Schumann as the fourteenth song in *Dichterliebe*.
4. Ann Radcliffe, *The Mysteries of Udolpho* (1794; rpt. Oxford: Oxford University Press, 1966), 534.
5. 1827; text from Robert Schumann, *Dichterliebe*, ed. Arthur Komar (New York: Norton, 1971), 21. All translations of Heine's text are mine.
6. For more on the erotic significance of tears, see Lutz, *Crying: The Natural and Cultural History of Tears* (New York: W. W. Norton, 1999), 38–41, and Peter Rabinowitz, "'With Our Own Dominant Passions': Gottschalk, Gender, and the Power of Listening," *Nineteenth-Century Music* 16 (1993), 242–52. As Rabinowitz notes (citing Xenophon of Ephesus) the association of tears and sexual pleasure is ancient. Its revival in the later eighteenth and the nineteenth centuries may in part derive from the growing need for indirect means for the public expression of sexual feeling, but also clearly depends on the power of tears to "cleanse" sexual feelings of moral and social debasement and to associate them with the "finer" feelings. This cleansing effect forms a bridge to the association of tears with religious ecstasy, a topic that lies outside my scope in this essay but that readily merges with the secular erotics of sensibility, especially in the nineteenth century.
7. Emily Apter, "Splitting Hairs: Female Fetishism and Postpartum Sentimentality in the Fin de Siecle," in Lynn Hunt, ed. *Eroticism and the Body Politic* (Baltimore: Johns

Hopkins University Press, 1991), 167–68; Jan Goldstein, *Console and Classify: The French Psychiatric Profession in the Nineteenth Century* (Cambridge: Cambridge University Press, 1987), 118.

8. The same logic applies to the confessional talk shows that became so popular during the 1990s. It may even apply in inverted form to the more confrontational type where (as in professional wrestling, another version of the same phenomenon recently popular on TV) the ultimate prize is the moan of moral defeat or the penitential tear.

9. Barthes, *A Lover's Discourse*, trans. Richard Howard (New York: Hill and Wang, 1978), 179–82; Lutz, *Crying*, 39, 49–50.

10. *A Lover's Discourse*, 180.

11. Johann Wolfgang von Goethe, *The Sufferings of Young Werther*, trans. Bayard Quincy Morgan (New York: Frederick Ungar, 1957), 38.

12. Vischer is quoted by Carl Dahlhaus, *Esthetics of Music*, trans. William Austin (Cambridge: Cambridge University Press, 1982), 51, translation modified, from the former's *Äesthetik oder Wissenschaft des Schönen* [Aesthetics, or the Science of Beauty, 1840–57]. For general discussion, see Dahlhaus, 46–51, and 52–47 for the formalist initiative centered around Hanslick's *The Beautiful in Music* [*Vom Musikalisch-Schönen*, 1854], trans. Gustav Cohen (New York: Liberal Arts Press, 1957).

13. G. W. F. Hegel, *Aesthetics: Lectures on Fine Art*, trans. T. M. Knox (Oxford, 1975), 960. Subsequent references are given in text with the abbreviation K; references with the abbreviation H refer to my translations from volume 3 of G. W. F. Hegel, *Vorlesungen über die Aesthetik*, ed. D. H. G. Hotho (Berlin: Dunker and Humblot, 1838) in 3 vols.

14. On scoring the subject, see my *Franz Schubert: Sexuality, Subjectivity, Song* (Cambridge: Cambridge University Press, 1998), 27–74.

15. Text as shown in Franz Schubert, *Complete Song Cycles*, ed. Eusebius Mandyczewski (1895; rpt. New York: Dover, 1970), 170–71.

16. Heinrich Schenker, "Ihr Bild (August 1828): Song by Franz Schubert to a Text by Heinrich Heine," trans. Robert Pascall, *Music Analysis* 18 (1999), 263–69.

17. Christopher Wintle, "Franz Schubert, Ihr Bild (1828): A Response to Schenker's Essay in Der Tonwille, Vol. I," *Music Analysis* 18 (1999): 270–88. Wintle offers a subtle reading of the song as a study in incomplete mourning. For another contemporary approach, centered on the Lacanian concept of the Real, see David Schwarz, *Listening Subjects: Music, Psychoanalysis, Culture* (Durham: Duke University Press, 1997), 72–86.

18. See Susan McClary, "Pitches, Expression, Ideology: An Exercise in Mediation," *Enclitic* 7 (1983): 76–86.

19. See my *Music and Poetry: The Nineteenth Century and After* (Berkeley: University of California Press, 1984), 53–56.

20. Robert Schumann, *On Music and Musicians*, trans. Paul Rosenfeld, ed. Konrad Wolff (New York: W. W. Norton, 1969), 164–88.

21. Slavoj Zizek, *Looking Awry: An Introduction to Jacques Lacan through Popular Culture* (Cambridge: MIT Press, 1993), 29–34.

Sensual
Transgressions

4

Untying the Music/Language Knot

Elizabeth Tolbert

Communities of Collaboration

The postmodern attitude of irony and displacement draws our attention to various curious concepts about music implicit in Western discourses, among them its characterization as feminine, and therefore sensual, emotional, and bodily. As many scholars have pointed out, music is elided with the subordinate term in oppositions such as culture/nature, human/animal, mind/body, or reason/emotion.[1] Implicit in music's feminization is its opposition to language, exhibiting qualities such as non-referentiality, syntax without semantics, pure form, the music "itself." For example, Shepherd claims that timbre, music's "tactile core," has a feminizing influence because it lies outside of form.[2] Similarly, Barthes's "grain of the voice" or Kristeva's "geno-text" are the sensual aspects of vocality deemed separate from signification, ripe for assignation as feminine.[3] These ideas about music have found fertile ground in post-Lacanian concepts of music as linked to the infantile, pre-symbolic, pre-Oedipal body, a body undifferentiated from the all-encompassing body and voice of the mother, and one that can exist as such only before entry into the fully Symbolic realm of language and its break with the materiality of sound.[4]

Yet these exalted affirmations of the "sonorous envelope"[5] of the maternal voice and music's attendant femininity cannot completely quell the suspicion that music has become the victim of logocentrism. As Dunn, among others, has pointed out:

> ... the theoretical identifications of music with a "mad" or "feminine"
> discourse, outside the structures of patriarchal signification, themselves

remain firmly within those structures. In blurring the distinction between music and musical metaphor, they essentialize music itself; it becomes the discursive "other" through an act of linguistic appropriation.[6]

In light of this "linguistic appropriation," it becomes clear that music's feminization is not about music at all; it merely reinscribes the binary structures that affirm the dominance of language over music.[7] Paradoxically, this use of music for logocentric aims is exposed by the fact that music cannot be fully contained within its feminization. When music is defined in reference to language, it becomes tinged with masculinity, as evidenced in its syntactical structure and its coziness with the utmost in pure reason, mathematics. This emphasis on syntactic structure in Western music valorizes music that is implicitly language-like and hence free of its feminine, "musical" attributes.[8] Logocentric concepts of music thus uphold the hegemony of language, at least in part, by maintaining the hegemony of musics that disavow their emotional and sensual qualities.

Although much feminist ink has been spilt on critiques of logocentrism and their attendant binaries, and feminist musicologists have long noted the alliance of music and the feminine in both historical and contemporary discourses, perhaps underappreciated is the extent to which music so construed is inimical to these projects. The music/language dichotomy creates a music that is both harder to hear and more complexly imbricated in issues of representation than generally acknowledged. However, there are indications that ideologies of music and language are finally beginning to show signs of wear. Increasingly, scholars are refusing to capitulate to tired music/language dualisms. Abbate, for example, deliberately resuscitates a notion of musical presence despite Derridean critiques, optimistically proclaiming that "the trope of music as a language needs to be resisted. Music may thus escape philosophical critiques of language, perhaps even escape language entirely."[9] Tomlinson, in his intertextual readings of philosophies of subjectivity and their operatic manifestations, takes a different tack, proposing that our theoretical blind spot is the assumption that music is an expression of the Kantian noumenal. In the grip of post-Kantian subjectivity, contemporary Western subjects want music to be both present and beyond presence, both "music-like" and "language-like." In the process, music has been pushed to the point where the illusion of the metaphysics of presence and the illusion of the noumenal are exposed, their interdependence only becoming visible in their threatened collapse.[10]

Abbate and Tomlinson, among others, offer provocative insights; however, it seems unlikely that music will be able to "escape the philosophical critiques of language" without further scrutiny of the "music" that upholds these critiques, or that "presence" will go away as a theoretical issue without acknowledgment of the bodily conditions of representation. In sympathy with these scholars, I suggest that an epistemological critique of contemporary ideas about music and language must begin with an awareness of their intellectual history, specifically, of their roots in Enlightenment discourses about human nature and the origins of human culture. As Europeans began to define themselves in opposition to Nature and non-Western Others, language became the defining characteristic of humanity, leaving music ambiguously positioned between the human and the non-human. Several authors have begun to chart the broad philosophical and historical trajectories that would place this emergent music/language ideology in a rich historical and sociocultural context. George Rousseau, in his interdisciplinary musings on premodern constructions of mind and body grounds contemporary understandings of mind/body dualisms in the Enlightenment, traces of which, by implication, surely inform contemporary understandings of music.[11] Thomas locates more precisely the specifically musical underpinnings of this history in eighteenth-century French writers such as Rousseau, who posited the origins of representation in the origins of music.[12]

Musicologists have also begun to place the feminization of music in specific contexts. Austern traces the emergence of music's vacillating status between nature and culture in early modern England, in light of its feminization, opposition to language, and its place within "Natural Philosophy."[13] Similarly, Tomlinson's readings of Derrida, although not engaging with the feminization of music per se, uncover logocentric assumptions in contemporary accounts of Aztec song, assumptions that have their roots in colonialist responses to Others.[14] Although I cannot unravel these fascinating and complex histories here, there is enough evidence to suggest that contemporary Western discourses on music, language, and the origins of human culture not only have common roots in the intellectual traditions of the Enlightenment, but that they continue their intertextual dialogue across current disciplinary lines, even if only implicitly.

The principal task of this essay is to uncover veiled references to the feminization of music in contemporary humanistic and scientific discourses on representation and human origins. These covert allusions to a feminized music ideology, although seemingly peripheral to the theories of representation that invoke them, are actually a crucial component of these discussions, in that human nature continues to be defined in reference to a universal male subject who has recourse to language. Therefore, implicit in music's feminization is not only its opposition and natural inferiority to language, but its opposition to the fully human. If music, no less than language, is among our few species-specific traits, then the lines imagined both between them and between human and non-human are especially relevant for an understanding of the role of "music" in the broader intellectual concerns of the Academy at large.

Before I go any further, I would like to issue a warning to the faint of heart. In bringing together Western academic discourses on music, language, and human origins, I have had to roam widely for collaborators, from Derrida to evolutionary psychologists, musicologists, linguists, neuroscientists, and feminist philosophers. My community of collaboration thus consists of scholars who in the flesh would cringe at my attempts to bring them together, and who would also probably not approve of my methodology, casting them sometimes as informants and other times as reliable authorities, depending on my purposes. For example, I will imagine the human/non-human divide in terms of the evolutionary body/mind, a body/mind not usually invoked within a humanistic context for fear of essentialist consequences. This bow toward the biological body is due to my conviction, along with a growing cadre of feminists such as Grosz, Wilson, and Kirby, that the elevation of the constructed body merely essentializes the culture half of the nature/culture dichotomy, and leaves us conceptually with a reinscription of the very dichotomy we wish to undo.[15] Therefore, the body invoked here is specifically *not* the textualized body of much current critical theory, but rather one that encompasses the perceptual and cognitive and evolutionary body, a sensate embodiment that extends Merleau-Pontys insight that the body is not an object per se, but rather "our point of view on the world."[16] The constructedness of categories such as "music" and "language" is inextricably tied to our bodily capabilities to construct these categories, and therefore it makes sense to know as much as possible about these human capabilities, how they evolved, and the stories we tell ourselves about our "human nature." This knowledge is not easy to come by, however, because my collaborators do not speak to one another; indeed, they encroach on each other's territory in rather threatening ways, attempting to subsume each other into their own "master" discourses. The only way to weave among them is to show where they already intersect and to go from there.

The Mythological Origin

Derrida, with characteristic wit and obfuscation, points us to the trouble spot between music and language in his by now oft-quoted passages in *Of Grammatology* concerning Rousseau's theories about the origin of language. He identifies this trouble spot as the space between signifier and signified, the non-identity inherent in the sign, which can only lead to the magical belief that there was a time when there was no space between signifier and signified, in other words, when signification did not exist, the era of the "transcendental signified."[17] This, of course, is an evolutionary story.[18]

A cluster of assumptions concerning the nature of language results from this belief in the original and impossible transcendental signified. As Tomlinson points out in his "Ideologies of Aztec Song," the Western model of the relationship between music and language is based on the logocentric and hence ethnocentric privileging of referential meaning, sound as presence, and the privileging of metaphorical, as opposed to metonymic, thinking.[19] However, logocentrism not only colors our musical encounters with the Other, but is also responsible for feminizing and "Othering" the music we claim as Ours. The high value placed on referential meaning denigrates music as an inferior form of communication, devoid of propositional content, and tainted by the "primitive" and emotional prosodic elements of speech. Need I point out that this is also an evolutionary story, placing Music at an earlier stage of evolution than Language?

Similarly, the high value placed on sound as presence, the "absolute proximity of voice and being, of voice and the meaning of being, of voice and the ideality of meaning,"[20] plays into this implicit evolutionary scenario. Derrida proposes that this equation of sound and presence, which he terms "phonocentrism," drove Rousseau to look for the origin of language in an imagined pure vocal presence, something in between animal cries and human language. This vocal presence therefore signals a missing link in human evolution, a link between the "before" and "after" of signification, a link that is "[n]o longer the animal cry before the birth of language; but not yet the articulated language, already shaped and undermined by absence and death."[21] Philosophical fallout from this idea continues to surface in contemporary evolutionary accounts that postulate a musical protolanguage as the missing link between ape and human communication, or in poststructuralist accounts that posit music as the missing link between the undifferentiated infantile cry and true, symbolic language.[22]

Yet there is a problem with this evolutionary story. It depends on the missing link between animal cries and language, and by extension between music and language, a link that could not have existed because it harkens back to a time before signification, and music, of course, has already crossed the "thetic" threshold of signification, to use Kristeva's term, in that it is already a sign system.[23]

To counteract the myth of pure presence, Derrida famously invokes Peirce's indefiniteness of reference, and hence the arbitrariness of the sign, as "the criterion that allows us to recognize that we are indeed dealing with a system of signs," and therefore with the impossibility of a transcendental signified.[24] This consciousness of the indefiniteness of reference is indeed a benchmark of human achievement, one that is not confined to our present moment, and one that itself has an evolutionary history. It is right here where Derrida's evolutionary story and mine part company. His is the dismantling and destabilization of an evolutionary myth. I would like to tell an evolutionary story that keeps this myth in mind, but that attempts to account for the indefiniteness of reference and the arbitrariness of the sign as *bodily* conditions of representation.

Philosopher of anthropology Sheets-Johnstone, in her remarkable book *The Roots of Thinking*, reminds us that "[w]here meanings are represented, animate bodies represent them corporeally."[25] She maintains that the Derridean body lacks corporeality and evolutionary history; Derrida has rewritten the history of the body as the history of the *gramme*, thereby emptying signification of bodily content.[26] In sympathy with Sheets-Johnstone, I contend that confusion over the music/language relationship arises from unexamined assumptions about the origin of symbolic capabilities as grounded in the arbitrariness of the sign, one that necessarily entails a disembodied notion of signification. Therefore, in order to destabilize further this problematic dichotomy, it is necessary to insert the evolutionary body/mind into the narrative.

Another Evolutionary Story

In contrast to the Derridean impulse of subsuming evolution into a theory of signs, evolutionary linguist Steven Pinker seeks to subsume a theory of signs into a scientific discourse on evolution. According to Pinker, the evolution of the human mind is implicitly understood as the evolution of language, because, after all, what other than language is the mark of humanity? However, every theory about language is also a theory about music, and vice versa, a theory that burdens music with a feminized materiality of sound while granting language freedom from the material by virtue of its arbitrariness. As already argued, language has been the primary player in this duality, asserting and maintaining its boundaries at the expense of music. Curiously enough, Pinker's present-day search for the origin of language and mind is following a similar phonocentric path to the one trod earlier by Rousseau, with music in a similar handmaiden position and muddied with a similar ideology of the missing link.[27]

Pinker, who has written a tome modestly entitled *How the Mind Works*, digs around in the phonocentric sandbox to propose that music is an evolutionary by-product, an epiphenomenon of other evolved pre-dispositions. That is, music is "auditory cheesecake, an exquisite confection crafted to tickle the sensitive spots of . . . our mental faculties."[28] To prove this point, he notes the intertwining of music and language, and the intermediate quality of many speech-music forms: hardly news to ethnomusicologists and anthropologists.[29] But for our purposes, the important point is an evolutionary one; these mixed forms show us that language is the "real" adaptation, and music the excess on top of language, the "auditory cheesecake." Ironically, Pinker, in espousing the conventional wisdom of evolutionary psychology, has placed himself squarely within the music-as-feminine-excess ideology espoused by the poststructuralist throng.

Pinker also touches on sound as presence when he posits that harmonic sounds—that is, "harmonic" in the physical sense of having clear overtones—are "good to hear" because they "exaggerate the experience of being in an environment that contains strong, clear, analyzable signals from interesting, potent objects."[30] Tonal melodies are part of this scheme in that they are conceptualized as mere extensions of harmonic sounds; they are essentially "serialized overtones" of "potent objects."[31] Disregarding for a moment the ethnocentric scale system that this scheme implies, what are these potent objects? Animate beings, of course, perhaps socially important members of the group, but in any case, the clear, analyzable signals are reliable indicators of their presence, and knowledge of their presence will ultimately enhance survival. Here we have timbre as presence, melody as serialized presence, and music as an evolutionary by-product of the "grain of the voice," an idea that might be promising, although not in its Pinkerian form, as will be shown below. It is interesting to note that timbre unfolded becomes melody and is in effect masculinized through serialization. Reminiscent of Shepherd's description of timbre as music's feminine "tactile core," this feat of serialization could only be accomplished if timbre were first understood as an index of presence, coded as feminine, yet a presence whose essence could only truly be revealed when masculinized through capture and remade within the stability of a tonal structure.

And what about music as the missing link, something in between animal cries and true language? Pinker has already placed himself in agreement with this position by positing that language is the real adaptation and music the by-product. However, Pinker addresses this issue head-on when he asserts that some melodies are skeletal forms of our species' innate emotion calls, such as crying, moaning, or laughing.[32] Although anthropologists of emotion exhort us to consider emotions as socially constructed, and ethnomusicologists have long considered such things as sigh motives to be based on stylized, rather than natural, crying, Pinker again intersects provocatively and I would contend, not coincidentally, with contemporary poststructuralist conceptions of music by "proving" its emotional, bodily, and animalistic nature, albeit with evolutionary, rather than Lacanian, evidence.[33]

One of Pinker's most interesting ideas for my purposes here—although a rather banal and naive one from the point of view of almost anyone who has thought about such things—is that music has an ineffable quality about it. But Pinker does actually have a specific proposal as to what this ineffability is all about, namely, that it is rooted in neuronal circuits firing together.[34] In other words, this "tickling" of other mental faculties is in and of itself meaningful. Now why does Pinker consider this an evolutionary explanation, or even a useful one? My guess is that we are back into the ideology of sound as presence and the transcendental signified, feminine presence/masculine absence. "Neurons that fire together wire together"[35]; there is no space between signifier and signified. Music need not have crossed the symbolic threshold; triggered by sound, firing neurons engrave pure, unmediated meaning directly onto the brain.[36]

Although Pinker's story pushes the wrong buttons for many of us, it is not wholly wrong, and furthermore, it is tempting to label it wrong for many of the wrong reasons. Pinker and others of this ilk are not wrong because they are reductionist (although they are) or overly simplistic (although they are) or because evolution has nothing to do with music (it almost certainly does), but because Pinker's evolutionary story operates within the confines of phonocentrism and its attendant feminization of music, and hence does little to undo the myth about how signification works, let alone how music works.

However, simply pointing a Derridean finger at the underlying phonocentrism of Pinker's evolutionary psychology is not enough, at least for me. So now I will tell yet another evolutionary story, one that partly confirms Pinker's assertions, yet seeks to temper them with a dose of Peircian semiotics and some more nuanced proposals concerning the evolution of our symbolic capabilities.

"Becoming-Unmotivated"[37]

Quibbling with Saussure's notion of the arbitrariness of the sign, and building on the Peircian insight that so-called arbitrary symbols grow from prior icons and indices, Derrida proposes that arbitrariness is not a *property* of symbols but rather a hierarchical *process* inherent in symbolization.[38] For example, icons are *motivated* by a perceived similarity between the sign and its object. Similarly, indices are motivated by contiguity; to take Peirce's famous example, smoke indexes fire. Furthermore, indexicality is built on prior icons: icons of smoke, icons of fire, and icons of their co-occurrence. Following this logic, for a sign to be perceived as arbitrary and hence unmotivated, there must be an awareness of prior motivation, a prior indexicality that can only be unmasked within the possibility of its lack. Any story about the evolution of language and music must therefore account for this process of the sign becoming arbitrary, in other words, of the sign "becoming-unmotivated."[39]

Deacon, in his writings on language evolution, provides an interesting counterpoint to this question of arbitrariness by arguing persuasively that the unique quality of language is not arbitrary reference, as is commonly believed—because many animals have calls that have arbitrary referents— but rather the capability for indexical reference outside of the specific context in which it arose.[40] For example, vervet alarm calls that arbitrarily refer to specific predators are indices of particular situations, and are not used in the absence of these predators. Animals' emotion calls are also of this type, being involuntary indices of the organism that produced them in response to specific stimuli in the environment.[41]

Therefore, contra Pinker, I propose that when we come to the "grain" of the musical voice or a melodic contour we cannot conflate it with animal calls, because we do not have a simple index, symptomatic of the organism that produced it. Rather, we have a deliberately produced and therefore potentially arbitrary symbol, but one that is simultaneously an index of the possibility of presence, and therefore potentially motivated as well. In other words, a vocal timbre or melodic contour is simultaneously a potential symbol and a potential index, an index of an index of presence. The indexical trace of presence exists in the symbolic voice because the possibility always exists that the arbitrary is a lie, that the "grain" of the voice is after all a "true" symptom of the organism that produced it. Here we have a symbol showing its indexical slip, if you will, a symbol "becoming-unmotivated."[42]

So what is the evolutionary story that accounts for how vocal presence became potentially indexical, an index of an index, and therefore symbolic? Surely not by way of music, as implicitly put forth by both evolutionary psychologists such as Pinker and various poststructuralist theorists such as Barthes and Kristeva. I propose we got there because representation evolved prior to both language and music. The mistaken and pervasive ideology of the missing link obscures this basic point because it seeks something in between language and music, rather than something prior to both. Derrida offers us Writing as the answer to the conundrum; but at this point I will look for my answers among more concrete proposals.[43]

"Writing": Or, Mimesis

Perhaps somewhat counterintuitively, the first step toward tracing the evolution of representation apart from music and language is to question the relationship between representation and vocality itself. This requires us to heed Derrida's warning that the logocentric privileging of the voice renders the conditions of representation invisible; it also requires that we look outside of voice to sense the movements of "arche-writing . . . the pattern uniting form to all substance."[44]

From an evolutionary point of view, there is much evidence to support the idea that representation evolved prior to language, is socially motivated, and is materially grounded in our perceptual and sensory motor systems. Sheets-Johnstone theorizes that representation evolved from species-specific capacities to move, which she terms "tactile-kinesthetic invariants."[45] For example, human corporeal invariants are such things as the experience of a bipedal gait, or the capacities to make sound with our species-specific vocal tract. In Sheets-Johnstone's view, representation first emerged among non-human animals in the context of socially understood movement that was iconic to corporeal invariants, interpreted by others in relation to their own capacities to move. These corporeal invariants "predispose organisms toward iconicity since the most easily formulated, consistently utilizable, and readily understood signals are those that are similar to bodily behaviors and experiences shared by all of the members of the species."[46] This assertion of the fundamentally gestural, embodied, and social nature of representation allows us to consider that sociality itself is based upon intercorporeal meanings borne out of iconic gesture.

Providing a complement to Sheets-Johnstone's proposal, neurobiologist Donald hypothesizes that the first step toward hominid representation was an improved capacity to imitate movement, a "supramodal [in other words, across the sense modalities], motor-modeling capacity called mimesis."[47] The major cognitive difference between human and non-human primates is that humans have greater voluntary access to their memories. Although apes are able to comprehend and analyze events at a high level, they do not have access to memories of these events without environmental cues. Donald suggests that mimesis allowed early humans to use intentional motor modeling as a memory cue, in effect using the body itself as a substitute for context, greatly increasing both access to memory and representational possibilities. Juxtaposing Sheets-Johnstone and Donald, I further suggest that mimetic gesture is iconic to embodied memories of movement, and therefore functions as an intracorporeal index to memory. Mimesis thus exposes the roots of abstract thought in sensory-motor representations because access to memory is an indexical process grounded in iconicity to perceptual and proprioceptive states.

Strong interpretations of embodied iconicity are beginning to gain adherents across disciplinary lines. Studies in neurobiology have long shown that perceptual information is represented iconically in the form of sensory maps;[48] newer studies in psychology suggest that perceptual information retains its iconic structure when incorporated into higher level sensory-motor and cognitive representations, implying that "much conceptual inference is, therefore, sensorimotor inference."[49] "Mirror neurons"— neurons that fire both when observing and performing a motor action— point to a neural mechanism that might partially underlie mimesis and therefore a theory of mind, in that observing actions of others as accommodated to one's capacity for movement allows for the understanding of others as social agents.[50]

The capacity for mimesis may also underlie grammatical structures, placing linguistic representation in a larger-than-language mimetic context.[51] As Deacon notes:

the structure of syntax often only vaguely conceals its pragmatic roots in pointing gestures, manipulation and exchange of physical objects, spatial and temporal relationships, and so on. For example, it is not uncommon for languages to demonstrate number, intensity, importance, possession, etc., by corresponding conventional iconicity of repetition, inflection, adjacency, and so on, in their syntactic forms.[52]

Studies on infant development likewise lend support to the social, mimetic foundations of representation in general and language in particular. At birth, infants are able to imitate facial expressions and respond to vocalizations with vocalizations, revealing a mimetic capacity that kicks in with the first social interactions.[53] Mimetic capacity may also account for infants' earliest preverbal conceptual representations. Infants' earliest representations are thought to be spatial representations derived from visual analysis of moving objects, and it is not unreasonable to suppose that they are understood mimetically, in other words, in reference to bodily experience. Furthermore, these spatial representations must be learnt prior to language, and are in turn reflected in linguistic structure.[54] Needless to say, these positions are not compatible with Lacanian-inspired theories of symbolization that depend upon a pre-symbolic, undifferentiated infant or pre-symbolic, feminized music.[55]

If we are to entertain Donald's proposal, the first transition from ape to human culture was the becoming-unmotivated of the sign through the development of a mimetic motor ability that allowed for the voluntary retrieval of memories outside of the context in which they were created. This prelinguistic, and of course, premusical, change was necessary to bring humans out of the here and now of indexical representation and into an awareness of the arbitrariness of the sign. This was accomplished by using the body representationally, by translating perceptions into action through an "implementable self-image."[56] The so-called arbitrariness of the sign is thus a *bodily* condition of representation, rooted in corporeal iconicity and indexicality. Representation in this general sense is therefore not inherently vocal, and furthermore, is anything but arbitrary.

"Another Sensitive Being Is Present": Vocal Mimesis and the Symbolic Threshold[57]

If representation is not inherently vocal, and is not inherently arbitrary as it is grounded in intercorporeal iconicity, what does this imply? At the very least, it demonstrates that mimesis and the resulting becoming-unmotivated of the sign define a symbolic threshold that cannot uniquely account for either music or language, in that the "arbitrariness of the sign" preceded them both. What, then, have we accomplished by following the mimetic path? What *is* the evolutionary story that accounts for how vocal presence became potentially indexical, an index of an index, and therefore symbolic? In order to understand how vocal presence defines the uniquely human symbolic threshold, it is necessary to interrogate the becoming-unmotivated of the specifically *vocal* sign, a sign grounded specifically in *vocal* mimesis, and one that is modeled on our species-specific, emotion-call system.

As noted previously, the emotion-call system of non-human primates is largely involuntary; it is not possible for chimps to vocalize dispassionately.[58] Therefore, chimps' emotion calls are understood by conspecifics as inherently unfakeable. But once our hominid ancestors were able to model the voice mimetically, new representational possibilities were born. Specifically, new forms of deception became possible. A mimetically modeled emotion call can only be understood as propositionally "true," that is, as an involuntary index rather than a mimetic impostor, and it can only be understood as emotionally "true," that is, as an index of a "true" emotional state, if there is a meta-representation of the possibility of unreliable communication.[59] Therefore, the conceptual separation of emotional "content" and propositional "form" is only possible after the advent of *vocal* mimesis.

The link between indexical, emotional representation and propositional representation is thus specifically vocal, and marks the specifically human symbolic threshold. Indeed, vocal mimesis not only links emotional and propositional representation, but produces the precondition for the arbitrary use of linguistic sound by guaranteeing propositional "truth" with emotional "truth." This linkage only arises in vocal communication, because the propositional truth of non-linguistic gestures is guaranteed by the non-arbitrariness of intercorporeal icons, of movements understood by others in reference to their own capacities for movement. However, in vocal mimesis this guarantee is destabilized by the potential for emotional "lying," for iconically representing the "unfakeable." The intercorporeal understanding of modeled emotion calls is also an intercorporeal understanding that emotion calls can be modeled. We aren't in Kansas anymore, and there's no going back.

"The Privilege of the *Phone* Does Not Depend upon a Choice That Could Have Been Avoided"[60]

This short story, as brief as it is, suggests a few things. The heightened emphasis on vocal mimesis and presence in the musical voice is an insistent reminder of the bodily conditions of representation, of the emotional guarantee that underlies seemingly arbitrary vocal signs. The musical voice is thus in the first instance a meta-commentary on the nature of representation; it not only reminds us that our socially embodied selves are grounded in mimesis, but perhaps more importantly, it reminds us that we are socially and materially enmeshed in representations of emotionally guaranteed "truth."[61]

Therefore, the uniquely human symbolic threshold is defined by an appeal to the becoming-unmotivated of the *vocal* sign. Vocal mimesis unleashes the semiotic power of a dually articulated potential, a potential for arbitrariness married to a potential for indexically guaranteed "truth," preconditions for both music *and* language. But the mimetic voice as the precondition for both music and language is hard to hear over the din of logocentric "music," music that is considered to be simply the emotional excess on top of language. Likewise, arbitrary, free floating "language" could not be arbitrary without audible traces of its prior iconicity and indexicality as guarantors of truth. Indeed, "the privilege of the *phone* does not depend upon a choice that could have been avoided," as it is grounded in the bodily conditions of representation.[62]

The feminization of music is thus deeply implicated in discourses on the evolutionary emergence of human representational abilities, a claim for music that is actually more of a claim for the uniqueness of human language as grounded in the arbitrariness of the sign. This claim is the predetermined end of a long chain of logic that begins with the wrong-headed proposition that the arbitrariness of the sign is coincident with the birth of language. Clearly, then, it does little theoretical good to fall back on post-Lacanian concepts of the feminization of music as a point of departure for explanations of the constructedness of the category "music," in that these kinds of explanation merely uphold the hegemony of language as the arbiter of the truly human, with music as the evolutionary and developmental missing link.

The focus on the arbitrariness of the sign makes it seem as though symbolization came into being all at once, magically, at the moment of awareness of the split between signifier and signified. However, there has been an evolutionary development of the capacity for symbolization; it did not spring full-blown out of the blue. To begin to uncover assumptions inherent in our contemporary music ideologies, to defeminize "music," if you will, we would need to untangle entertwining discourses on "music," "language," and "human nature" in light of evolutionarily plausible proposals concerning the embodied nature of human representational systems. What kind of theories are reasonable to postulate? Although I have hinted at only a few possibilities in this essay, I can say for sure, as does Rousseau, that "as soon as vocal signs strike your ear, they proclaim a being similar to yourself. . . . Birds whistle, man alone sings, and one cannot hear either a song or an instrumental piece without immediately saying to oneself:

another sensitive [in other words, sensible] being is present."[63] To apprehend the voice as "another sensitive being" is to apprehend musical voices as though they literally have subjectivity and bodiliness, that we react to them on the basis of what it feels like to know them as social, emotional, and animate beings, and that this is what motivates their meanings, no matter what the context.

Notes

1. The literature on this topic spans several disciplines, including performance studies, musicology, ethnomusicology, film theory, and literary criticism. For an overview of some of the issues see Susan McClary, *Feminine Endings: Music, Gender, and Sexuality* (Minneapolis: University of Minnesota Press, 1991), 3–34; idem, "Reshaping a Discipline: Musicology and Feminism in the 1990s," *Feminist Studies* 19, no. 2 (1993): 399–423; idem, "Paradigm Dissonances: Music Theory, Cultural Studies, Feminist Criticism," *Perspectives of New Music* 32, no. 1 (1994): 68–85; Ellen Koskoff, ed., "An Introduction to Women, Music, and Culture," in *Women and Music in Cross-Cultural Perspective* (New York: Greenwood Press, 1989 [1987]), 1–23 ; Ruth A. Solie, ed., "Introduction: On 'Difference,'" in *Musicology and Difference: Gender and Sexuality in Music Scholarship*, (Berkeley: University of California Press, 1993), 1–20; Leslie Dunn and Nancy A. Jones, eds., "Introduction," in *Embodied Voices: Representing Female Vocality in Western Cultures* (Cambridge: Cambridge University Press, 1994), 1–13.
2. John Shepherd, *Music as Social Text* (Cambridge: Polity Press, 1991), 90.
3. Roland Barthes, "The Grain of the Voice," in *Image, Music, Text* (New York: Farrar, Straus, and Giroux, 1977), 179–89; Julia Kristeva, *Revolution in Poetic Language*, trans. Margaret Waller (New York: Columbia University Press, 1984), 86–89. Barthes's "grain of the voice" refers to the embodied aspects of vocality that transcend referential meaning. Kristeva similarly posits that the "geno-text" is revealed in those aspects of the text that are "nonsignifying" such as prosody, rhyme, or alliteration (86). Barthes's "geno-song" is a reconfiguration of "geno-text" for musical purposes ("Grain of the Voice," 178). For a critical exploration of Barthes's love affair with music, see Barbara Engh's, "Loving It: Music and Criticism in Roland Barthes," in *Musicology and Difference*, 66–79.
4. For a brief overview of music as pre-symbolic from the perspective of literary theory, see Leslie Dunn and Nancy Jones, "Introduction," in *Embodied Voices*, 1–6; Leslie Dunn, "Ophelia's Songs in *Hamlet*: Music, Madness and the Feminine," idem, 52–55; Nancy Jones, "Music and the Maternal Voice in *Purgatorio* XIX," idem, 35–49. For an overview from a cultural studies perspective, see John Shepherd and Peter Wicke, *Music and Cultural Theory* (Cambridge: Polity Press, 1997), 56–94.
5. The term was coined by Guy Rosalato, in "La Voix: Entre Corps et Langage," *Revue Francaise de Psychoanalyse* 38, no. 1 (1974): 81, trans. in Kaja Silverman, *The Acoustic Mirror: The Female Voice in Psychoanalysis and Cinema* (Bloomington: Indiana University Press, 1988), 84–85. Cited in Jones, "Music and the Maternal Voice," 35.
6. Dunn, "Ophelia's Songs," 55.
7. Terry Threadgold explicitly addresses the limits of logocentric, metaphorical understandings of performance in her "Performativity Voice Corporeality Habitus Becoming Assemblage: Some Reflections on Theory and Performing Metaphors," in *Musics and Feminisms*, eds. Sally Macarthur and Cate Poynton (Sydney: Australian Music Centre, 1999), 63–77. She notes that much poststructuralist theory was formulated as a foil to logocentrism, drawing on reified metaphors of performance. While unsettling to logocentrism, performance metaphors tend to uphold unproblematized concepts of the body, voice, and music, thus promulgating theory that "[forgets] the materiality of which it is born" (64). For further comments see Elizabeth D. Tolbert, "Review of

Musics and Feminisms," Women and Music 4 (2000): 75–81. For additional critique of the invocation of "music" to further the aims of "theory," see Carolyn Abbate's *Unsung Voices: Opera and Musical Narrative in the Nineteenth Century* (Princeton: Princeton University Press, 1991), 10–19; idem, "Opera; or, the Envoicing of Women," in *Musicology and Difference*, 229–234; idem, "Ventriloquism," in *Meaning in the Visual Arts: Views from the Outside*, ed. Irving Lavin (Princeton: Institute for Advanced Study, 1995), 305–11.

8. For an assertion of language-like music as masculine, see John Shepherd, "Difference and Power in Music," in *Musicology and Difference*, 60. McClary states that music from the late eighteenth century onward has been masculinized "by defining music as the most ideal (that is, the least physical) of the arts; by insisting emphatically on its 'rational' dimension; by laying claims to such presumably masculine virtues as objectivity, universality, and transcendence" (*Feminine Endings*, 17). Philip Brett, in his "Musicality, Essentialism, and the Closet," in Philip Brett, Gary Thomas, and Elizabeth Wood, eds., *Queering the Pitch: The New Gay and Lesbian Musicology* (New York: Routledge, 1994), 13–14, similarly suggests that music was masculinized in the nineteenth century by cleansing it of expression and reifying its formal characteristics. For a historical account of the gendering of musical discourse in Western culture, see Leo Treitler, "Gender and Other Dualities of Music History," in *Musicology and Difference*, 23–45.

9. Abbate, *Unsung Voices*, 18.

10. See Gary Tomlinson, *Metaphysical Song: An Essay on Opera* (Princeton: Princeton University Press, 1999). Tomlinson frames the issue in terms of the competing formulations of music as a site of autonomous, transcendent meanings and music as a site of intersubjective, social meanings. Using Britten's singing ghosts in *The Turn of the Screw* as an example, Tomlinson asserts that ghosts represent an intersubjective self reauthored as autonomous; therefore, when ghosts sing, the materiality of their voices and bodies tips the balance too far toward autonomy, drawing attention to the complicity between intersubjective and autonomous selves, and therefore between social and transcendent musical meanings (153–56).

11. George Rousseau, "An Anthropology of Mind and Body in the Enlightenment," *Pre- and Post-modern Discourses*, v. 1 in *Enlightenment Crossings: Pre- and Post-modern Discourses: Anthropological* (Manchester and New York: Manchester University Press, 1991), 210–46.

12. Downing Thomas, *Music and the Origins of Language: Theories from the French Enlightenment* (Cambridge; New York: Cambridge University Press, 1995). Thomas notes that "[m]usic serves as the anthropological 'missing link' in the eighteenth-century attempt to trace semiosis to its origin, to pinpoint the semiotic moment which separates culture from nature, and human beings from animals. Through its natural link to the passions (for as a natural sign, music already represents the passions), music is the triggering mechanism of representation itself" (9–10).

13. Linda Austern, "Nature, Culture, Myth, and the Musician in Early Modern England," *Journal of the American Musicological Society* 51, no. 1 (1998), 1–47.

14. Gary Tomlinson, "Ideologies of Aztec Song," *Journal of the American Musicological Society* 48, no. 3 (1995); 343–79. For a contrasting view, see Abbate, "Ventriloquism," 305–6, 309–10, and idem, *Unsung Voices*, 16–17. Abbate contends that the current feminized musical metaphysics emerged at the beginning of the nineteenth century in the writings of Romantic poets and philosophers, and that Derrida's and De Man's writings on voice and presence betray an ahistorical projection of nineteenth-century thought onto eighteenth-century writers. She states that "[i]deas of music as mere structure resonate less from Rousseau than from the musical aesthetics of nineteenth-century formalists" (*Unsung Voices*, 17).

15. See Elizabeth Grosz, *Volatile Bodies: Toward a Corporeal Feminism* (Bloomington: Indiana University Press, 1994), 8: "The natural sciences tend to treat the body as an organic system of interrelated parts, which are themselves framed by a larger ecosystemic order. The humanities reduce the body to a fundamental continuity with brute, inorganic matter. Despite their apparent dissimilarity, they share a common refusal to acknowledge the distinctive complexities of organic bodies, the fact that bodies con-

struct and in turn are constructed by an interior, a psychical, a signifying viewpoint, a consciousness or perspective." See also the theme issue of *Australian Feminist Studies* on Feminist Science Studies for a more detailed exposition of this idea from a feminist poststructuralist perspective, in particular Elizabeth Grosz, "Darwin and Feminism: Preliminary Investigations for a Possible Alliance," *Australian Feminist Studies* 14, no. 29 (1999): 39–45; Vicki Kirby, "Human Nature," *Australian Feminist Studies* 14, no. 29 (1999): 19–29; Elizabeth Wilson, "Introduction: Feminism, Biology, and Science," *Australian Feminist Studies* 14, no. 29 (1999): 7–18. Grosz, for example, states that "there is a certain absurdity in objecting to the notion of biology itself, if this is (even in part) what and where we are. If we are our biologies, then we need a complex and subtle account of that biology if it is to be able to more adequately explain the rich variability of social and political life. It needs to be an open question: how does biology, the bodily existence of individuals (whether human or non-human) provide the conditions for culture and for history, those terms with which it is traditionally opposed?" (31–32). There have been other recent attempts to bring biological perspectives into the humanities, particularly in literary studies, and from theoretical positions that are highly critical of poststructuralism. See Glen Love, "Ecocriticism and Science: Toward Consilience?" *New Literary History* 30 (1999): 561–76, and volume 30 of *New Literary History* devoted to Ecocriticism (1999).

16. Maurice Merleau-Ponty, *The Primacy of Perception*, ed. James Edie (Evanston, Ill.: Northwestern University Press, 1964), 5.

17. Jacques Derrida, *Of Grammatology*, trans. Gayatri Spivak (Baltimore: Johns Hopkins University Press, 1976), 20.

18. Or more accurately, an originary story. Derrida posits a point of origin in order to deconstruct the assumptions that uphold its originary status. The impossibility of an ultimate origin is revealed by the fact that an origin is always the effect of another origin, *ad infinitum.*

19. Tomlinson, "Ideologies of Aztec Song," 345–55. Other commentators who approach Rousseau and Derrida's reading of Rousseau from the perspective of music ideology include John Neubauer, *The Emancipation of Music from Language* (New Haven: Yale University Press, 1986), 85–102, and Thomas, *Music and the Origins of Language*, especially 82–142. Thomas carefully analyzes eighteenth-century French writings on music and the origins of language to show how they laid the groundwork for later theories of the autonomy of music, a doctrine that is still operative in much current musicological and ethnomusicological work, even among those well-versed in Derridean deconstruction and/or postmodernist cultural theory. The separation of music from language spawns the idea that music is separate from culture and beyond ideology. Although this stance has been vigorously refuted by both ethnomusicologists and the "new" musicologists, some of its more insidious forms remain, most notably in the concept of the arbitrariness of the sign.

20. Derrida, citing Hegel, in *Of Grammatology*, 12.

21. Ibid., 247.

22. Similar to Rousseau's original formulation, contemporary notions of protolanguage are conceptualized as emotional, song-like communication with vague reference. See Nils Wallin, Bjorn Merker, and Steven Brown, eds., *The Origins of Music* (Cambridge: MIT Press, 2000), for a variety of proposals on protolanguage and the evolutionary origins of music, especially Steven Brown, "The 'Musilanguage' Model of Music Evolution," 271–300. Brown proposes a "musilanguage" that is neither music nor language but that communicates both emotion and referential meaning. For a discussion of protolanguage and its relationship to song more generally, see also Merlin Donald, *Origins of the Modern Mind* (Cambridge: Harvard University Press, 1991), especially 37–41, 180–86; idem, "Precis of Origins of the Modern Mind: Three Stages in the Evolution of Culture and Cognition," *Behavioral and Brain Sciences* 16 (1993), 737–91; idem, "Mimesis and the Executive Suite: Missing Links in Language Evolution," in *Approaches to the Evolution of Language: Social and Cognitive Bases*, ed. James R. Hurford, Michael Studdert-Kennedy, and Chris Knight (Cambridge: Cambridge University Press, 1998), 44–671; idem, "Preconditions for the Evolution of Protolanguages,"

in *The Descent of Mind: Psychological Perspectives on Hominid Evolution*, ed. Michael C. Corballis and Stephen E. G. Lea (Oxford: Oxford University Press, 1999), 138–54.
Post-Lacanian concepts of music shift the assumptions of the missing link onto the developmental axis; music is posited as the developmental missing link between pre-symbolic and symbolic, between emotion and reference, or more explicitly, between the emotional, bodily, infantile cry and arbitrary, linguistic sound unmoored from its bodily referents. See Kristeva's writings on the "semiotic" and the "symbolic," for example, in *Revolution in Poetic Language*, 21–106.

23. Kristeva, *Revolution in Poetic Language*, 43–45.

24. Derrida, *Of Grammatology*, 49.

25. Maxine Sheets-Johnstone, *The Roots of Thinking* (Philadelphia: Temple University Press, 1990), 121.

26. Maxine Sheets-Johnstone, *The Roots of Power: Animate Form and Gendered Bodies* (Chicago: Open Court, 1994), 95–116.

27. Steven Pinker, *How the Mind Works* (New York: Norton, 1997), 528–29. Pinker asserts that language is an adaptation, whereas music is "useless," a mere "technology." "Compared with language . . . music could vanish from our species and the rest of our lifestyle would be virtually unchanged" (528).

28. Ibid., 534.

29. See Steven Feld and Aaron Fox, "Music and Language," *Annual Review of Anthropology* 23 (1994), 25–53.

30. Pinker, *How the Mind Works*, 536.

31. Ibid.

32. Ibid., 537.

33. The relationship between the sociocultural expression of emotion and music has been well-studied by anthropologists and ethnomusicologists, particularly in reference to the ritual lament. Laments are found in almost all known cultures, appear in similar forms and contexts throughout the world, and are usually performed by women in a style that mixes weeping, singing, and ritual speech. Pinker's ethologically based conflation of emotion calls and music ignores ethnomusicological and anthropological work that links stylized presentations of emotion to core elements of sociocultural identity. Nevertheless, the presentation of highly stylized musical emotion in the lament has the potential to be an ideal case study, perhaps even a pivotal one, from which to interrogate relationships between the ethology of emotions and expressive culture. For an overview of lament studies in an interdisciplinary context, see Feld and Fox, "Music and Language," 39–43. Anthropological and ethnomusicological case studies of lament that focus on the stylized presentation of emotion include Charles Briggs, "Since I Am a Woman I Will Chastise My Relatives: Gender, Reported Speech, and the (Re)production of Social Relations in Warao Ritual Wailing," *American Ethnologist* 19, no. 2 (1992): 337–61; idem, "Personal Sentiments and Polyphonic Voices in Warao Women's Ritual Wailing: Music and Poetics in a Critical and Collective Discourse," *American Anthropologist* 95, no. 4 (1993): 929–57; Steven Feld, "Wept Thoughts: The Voicing of Kaluli Memories," *Oral Tradition* 5, nos. 2–3 (1990): 241–66; idem, Sound *and Sentiment: Birds, Weeping, Poetics, and Song in Kaluli Expression* (Philadelphia: University of Pennsylvania Press, 1982); Constantina-Nadiia Seremetakis, *The Last Word: Women, Death, and Divination in Inner Mani* (Chicago: University of Chicago Press, 1991); Elizabeth Tolbert, "Women Cry with Words: Symbolization of Affect in the Karelian Lament," *Yearbook for Traditional Music* (1990), 80–105; idem, "Magico-Religious Power and Gender in the Karelian Lament," in *Music, Gender, and Culture*, eds. Marcia Herndon and Susanne Ziegler (Wilhelmshaven: F. Noetzel, 1990), 41–56; idem, "The Voice of Lament," in *Embodied Voices*, 179–94; Greg Urban, "Discourse, Affect, and Social Order: Ritual Wailing in Amerindian Brazil," *American Anthropologist* 90 (1988): 385–400.

34. Pinker, *How the Mind Works*, 538.

35. This maxim is popular in the neuroscience community, and alludes to Hebb's idea that connections between co-active neurons tend to be strengthened. See Donald O. Hebb, *The Organization of Behavior; a Neuropsychological Theory* (New York: Wiley, 1949).

36. Again, Pinker has seized on a pervasive trope in Western culture. The idea of music as less mediated than language hinges on the paradox of the arbitrariness of the sign, which has played out in the musicological arena as the relationship between form and content. The paradox results from the fact that if materiality of musical form is taken to be the immutable ground of free-floating representation, both materiality and representation are essentialized, reducing to yet another version of the mind/body problem. This is most aptly illustrated in canonical, musicological, and ethnomusicological understandings of the relationship between form and content. Musicologists have traditionally located meaning in musical form, thereby essentializing musical structure. Conversely, while most ethnomusicologists reject the idea of immanent meaning in musical structure, the tacitly accepted notion of music as an empty sign to be filled with culturally appropriate content merely reifies content, and likewise devolves into essentialism.

   Ethnomusicological moves toward overcoming the arbitrariness that underlies form/content binaries have generally been framed in terms of Peircian "iconicity," an approach that grounds meaning in similarities between sound structure and social structure, such as that of Feld, in his *Sound and Sentiment*. For a recent reinvigoration of this idea, see Thomas Turino, "Signs of Imagination, Identity, and Experience: A Peircian Semiotic Theory for Music," *Ethnomusicology* 43, no. 2 (1999): 221–55. Drawing on the Peircian insight that signs are structured hierarchically, Turino suggests that music is emotionally meaningful because it relies primarily on iconic and indexical signs, signs that are lower on the semiotic chain, and hence "less-mediated," than conventional linguistic signs (224). Although this line of inquiry is promising, it is at least partially complicit with logocentric music ideology in that it reifies the iconic and indexical aspects of music as emotional, bodily, and immediate.

37. Derrida, *Of Grammatology*, 48.

38. Ibid., 44–49. See also Charles S. Peirce, *The Philosophy of Peirce: Selected Writings*, ed. Justus Buchler (London: Routledge and Kegan Paul, 1956 [1940]), 102–3, for a discussion of the hierarchical nature of the sign.

39. For a discussion of the sign "becoming-unmotivated" see Derrida, *Of Grammatology*, 47–48.

40. For an interpretation of Peirce's hierarchical notion of the sign and its relationship to human and animal representational abilities, see Terrence Deacon, *The Symbolic Species: The Co-evolution of Language and the Brain* (New York: Norton, 1997), 69–101.

41. Ibid., 54–68. Deacon slightly oversimplifies the involuntary nature of animal's emotion calls; according to Chris Knight ("Ritual/Speech Co-evolution: A Solution to the Problem of Deception," in *Approaches to the Evolution of Language)*, chimps are able to suppress their calls for deceptive purposes, even though they are not able to vocalize dispassionately (72–73).

42. A disclaimer: I invoke Pierce within the context of Derrida's concept of "becoming-unmotivated," and do not mean to offer a comprehensive Peircian approach to musical signification. Therefore, many of Peirce's ideas about semiosis, perhaps most significantly, the concept of the interpretant, are omitted from my analysis. However, my placement of the symbolic threshold at the point of "becoming-unmotivated" might be reconfigured in Peircian terms as a meta-threshold between rhematic and dicent indices, one that propels the sign toward the symbolic. For another application of Peirce for evolutionary purposes, one that focuses on sign-object relations, see Deacon, *Symbolic Species*, 92–191. Deacon characterizes the threshold between index and symbol as an unlearning of unique indexical associations and their subsequent recoding as indexical associations between *sets* of indices.

43. See Derrida, *Of Grammatology*, 60, for a discussion of "arche-writing" as the condition of representation, one that is external to language per se. "This arche-writing . . . would constitute not only the pattern uniting form to all substance, . . . but the movement of the sign-function linking a content to an expression. . . . [A]rche-writing . . . cannot, as the condition of all linguistic systems, form a part of the linguistic system itself."

44. Ibid.
45. Sheets-Johnstone, *The Roots of Thinking*, 17.
46. Ibid., 126.
47. Donald, *Precis*, 738–39; idem, *Origins of the Modern Mind*, especially 162–200.
48. See, for example, Vernon B. Mountcastle, "The View from Within: Pathways to the Study of Perception," *Johns Hopkins Medical Journal* 136 (1975): 109–31.
49. George Lakoff and Mark Johnson, *Philosophy in the Flesh: The Embodied Mind and Its Challenge to Western Thought* (New York: Basic Books, 1999), 20. See also George Lakoff, *Women, Fire, and Dangerous Things* (Chicago: University of Chicago Press, 1987). For a discussion of perceptual iconicity in sensory motor and cognitive representations, see Lawrence Barsalou, "Perceptual Symbol Systems," *Behavioral and Brain Sciences* 22: 4 (1999): 577–660.
50. Giacomo Rizzolatti and Michael Arbib, "Language within Our Grasp," *Trends in Neuroscience* 21: no. 5 (1998): 188–94.
51. Ibid., 192.
52. Deacon, *Symbolic Species*, 354.
53. Andrew N. Meltzoff and Shaun Gallagher, "The Earliest Sense of Self and Others: Merleau-Ponty and Recent Developmental Studies," *Philosophical Psychology* 9, no. 2 (1996), 211–33.
54. Jean Mandler, "Preverbal Representation and Language," in *Language and Space*, ed. Paul Bloom, Mary Peterson, Lynn Nadel, and Merrill Garrett (Cambridge: MIT Press, 1996), 365–84.
55. Although they might admit some traffic with Diotima's Symbolic Order of the Mother, a concept introduced to the participants of Feminist Theory V by Suzanne Cusick, in a talk entitled "Music, Subjectivity, and 'The Symbolic Order of the Mother': Challenges from the Feminist Theory of Diotima," Feminist Theory and Music V, London, July 1999. According to Cusick, Luisa Muraro, a member of the feminist collective Diotima, directly challenges the Lacanian idea of the male Symbolic Order and replaces it with a theory of a feminized Symbolic Order based on the child's enculturation by the mother.
56. Donald, *Precis*, 740.
57. Jean-Jacques Rousseau, "Essay on the Origin of Languages," in *Essay on the Origin of Languages and Writings Related to Music*, trans. and ed. John T. Scott (Hanover and London: University Press of New England, 1998), 326. "[A]s soon as vocal signs strike your ear, they proclaim a being similar to yourself; they are, so to speak, the organs of the soul. . . . Birds whistle, man alone sings, and one cannot hear either a song or an instrumental piece without immediately saying to oneself: another sensitive being is present."
58. Knight, "Ritual/Speech Co-evolution," 72. See note 41.
59. See Sheets-Johnstone, *Roots of Thinking*, 144–58. She places propositionality in evolutionary perspective, suggesting that the dichotomy between emotional expression and propositional expression is a false one, based on the assumption that truth and falsity only exist in the linguistic realm.
60. Derrida, *Of Grammatology*, 7.
61. This socially embodied and emotionally guaranteed "truth" is a far cry from the metaphysical, logocentric Truth that so worries Derrida. For Derrida's passages on "The Signifier and the Truth," see *Of Grammatology*, 10–18.
62. Ibid., 7. I ascribe to the evolutionary mind/body what Derrida ascribes to the "historico-metaphysical epoch" of the Western philosophical tradition (6). However, it is possible that my position is compatible with some interpretations of Derrida; if the body is "written," then biology itself could be considered a site of Writing. For a biologically inflected notion of Derridean Writing, see Kirby, "Human Nature," 19–29.
63. J. J. Rousseau, "Essay on the Origin of Languages," in *Essay on the Origin of Languages and Writings Related to Music*, 326. See also note 57.

5

Sensational Sacrifices

Feasting the Senses in the Bolivian Andes

Henry Stobart

Kasiru wiraqa khuyay ulukipa	Married life feels like ulukipa [peppers]
Sultiru wiraqa asukar kanila	Single life is cinnamon sugar
Sunchu t"ikitay, amapulitay,	Sunchu flower, poppy
Amapulitay, suchu t"ikitay	Poppy, sunchu flower
Ñampaq munasqay	I used to love you
Ñampaq reqsisqay	I used to know you
Imanasqallantaq?	What has happened now?[1]

The current interest in the senses in a number of branches of the humanities may largely be traced back to a reaction against the perceived hegemony of visualism in Western scholarship.[2] However, it might also be argued that when we think, write, or talk about music there is a common tendency to present it or conceive of it in terms of "sound," and consequently as primarily monosensorial aural/oral experience.[3] This is not surprising as the auditory dimension can hardly fail to be at the heart of any standard definition of "music." Indeed, the word "music" as a point of reference, for example in a library or scholarly discourse, or as a marketing category, serves to privilege the idea of essentially acoustic phenomena.[4] This perception of music is further encouraged by audio recordings, where other sensory aspects of a particular performance context—whether visual, kinaesthetic, gustatory, or olfactory—are not registered.[5]

Western concert hall performances, in which special efforts are made to eliminate other sensory experiences—through, for example, restrictions on movement, insistence on silence, and typical prohibitions against food and drink—are in many ways exceptional from a worldwide perspective. It would appear that for most forms of music making, the presence of other modes of sensory experience are considered not only desirable but often integral to the event, and may shape the music or be crucial to the meaning of its actual sounds.[6]

A concern with music's interaction with the other senses is by no means new to ethnomusicology. Eric von Hornbostel was pondering this question in the 1920s, and Alan Merriam included a chapter entitled "synaesthesia and intersense modalities" in his 1964 volume *The Anthropology of Music*; yet this was to have little impact on later generations of scholars.[7] Bruno Nettl has suggested that Merriam's failure to devote attention to interactions between music and taste may explain why ethnomusicologists have found his approach of limited utility.[8] The word "taste" is indeed applied to music in many languages, and, as I shall demonstrate, close links also exist between music and the sense of taste in the Southern Andes. But perhaps Merriam's discussion of intersensory analogy (metaphor or iconicity) in almost the same breath as the more specific phenomenon of "development synaesthesia,"[9] such as "colored-hearing,"[10] may help to explain why scholars have avoided this type of approach.[11]

A more helpful and influential perspective has been that of Barbara Tedlock in her work on Zuni aesthetics. She has stressed the need for an approach that "crosses sensory domains."[12] She demonstrated how the contrasted Zuni aesthetic categories *tso'ya* (clear, bright, new, beautiful, multicoloured, chromatic) and *attanni* (muffled, dark, old, fearful, taboo, static) are applied to expressions and qualities from a variety of sensory modalities, including music.[13] Clearly, exclusive focus on any single sensory realm would lead to an impoverished understanding. Consequently, in my discussion of a rural community of the Bolivian Andes in this chapter, I shall focus on how music works alongside and interacts with other sensory modalities, and the ways in which many of the meanings, affects, and ideas about musical process depend, to a considerable degree, on interaction between a variety of sensory domains.

Sensory Landscapes: Daily Life in the Andes

The contrast between the modern conveniences, comforts, and rapid communication systems available to people living in highly industrialized nations and the lives of a community of Andean peasant farmers is stark and in many ways shocking. The residents of the rural community of *ayllu* Macha, in northern Potosí, Bolivia, with whom I have lived for a total of about two years, inhabit a harsh, arid, and treeless environment at an altitude of over 3,000 meters. Their lives revolve around a cycle of daily chores and seasonal activities focused principally on the provision of basic needs, such as food, water, shelter, heat, and clothing.[14]

Typical daily meals include soups, gruels, or dry dishes made primarily from barley, potatoes, chuño (freeze-dried potatoes), maize, or broad beans, sometimes together with rice or pasta. Toasted barley or maize are also common snacks. Green vegetables (with the exception of green onion stems) are simply not an aspect of the diet, and fruit, bread, and sugar are purchased luxuries, which are eaten only rarely. The principal flavorings include salt, chili peppers, garlic, or onions when available. A tiny piece of dried meat *(charki)* or a bone is sometimes added to soups or gruels, otherwise meat is only consumed on very special occasions. The sheep and llama herds serve as people's bank accounts. They are reserved for sacrifice in ceremonial events, and only sold during times of extreme hardship or in order to make very special purchases; it would be unthinkable to slaughter and eat this crucial asset on a day-to-day basis.

As people cross the treeless landscape, going about their essentially solitary daily activities of agricultural work and herding, there is often an intense sense of emptiness. Much of the land consists of rocky or bare earth, and little vegetation grows naturally except clumps of hard, sharp *icchu* grasses, and a few straggling bushes. Especially during the dry winter months, when there is little birdsong, the silence sometimes seems almost tangible, giving the impression that sound is somehow swallowed up by the vast open landscape. Although most men play at least four types of musical instruments, music is rarely heard on a daily basis. Young men are occasionally heard strumming a *charango* or *kitarra* as they walk to town, or sounding a *pinkillu* flute on their journeys to work the fields, but this is a rarity, except on the days leading up to a major feast.

Feasts: Saturating the Senses

It is difficult to convey the extreme contrast between the austerity and largely solitary nature of daily life and the sensory explosion that marks a fiesta. Indeed, sensory saturation would appear to be one of the key aims of a major feast, when large numbers of people congregate together in a particular place, enlivening it with conversation, laughter, shouting, movements, music, dancing, drinking, eating, flirtation, decoration, special aromas, festive clothing—and sometimes fighting. Many individuals explained to me that a sense of *allegría* should be created, a Spanish loan word meaning "gaiety" or "mirth," but perhaps better translated in this context as "liveliness" or "enlivening." This enlivening and sensorial saturation is largely conceived in terms of the release and circulation of animating energies, as a form of sacrifice. Similarly, in her ethnography of Sonqo, Peru, Catherine Allen has described how such animating essences, locally termed *sami,* are said to be present in the foods, coca leaves, and alcohol, and should be shared with the earth and sacred places.[15] It is precisely these fragrances, tastes, sounds, movements, and other sensorial aspects that signal the presence of life, and paradoxically also potentially its destruction, as these potent sensory qualities are circulated and consumed or experienced by others. Accordingly, as in many other South American cultures, festivals seem to serve as "some kind of rupture or interruption of a preexisting temporal condition."[16] For my hosts, the annual cycle of feasts—totaling about thirty days each year— serves to punctuate and shape people's understanding of time.

I shall now explore a few of the principal sensorial expressions that contribute to these ruptures in the daily sensory landscape, focusing in particular on music, drinking, and meat.

From Silence to Sound

Although rarely heard at other times, music is played almost constantly during feasts. It is almost as though the background of silence against which people play out their daily lives is replaced by one of perpetual sound. Indeed, on several occasions, I have heard older people complain bitterly when young musicians, almost too drunk and exhausted to stand, have stopped to take a rest, leaving a period of silence.[17] In these contexts, music was referred to as *kunswilu* (consolation), which the elders insisted must be played in recognition of the sacrifices of the ancestors, saints, and other powers who enable human well-being. Thus, music was explicitly presented as an exchange medium, where human energy is translated into sound and in many senses serves as a form of sacrificial offering.[18] It is not simply the human senses that are seen to be experiencing a feast's burst of sensorial activity: a large pantheon of deities and spirits of the animated landscape, whose desires, sensations, actions, and transformations are presented in much the same way as those of their human dependants, also participate.

At certain moments during a feast, music is foregrounded. For example, when members of a *jula jula* panpipe ensemble arrive at a church, after a many hours or even days walk to a pilgrimage site, the players kneel and perform a special melody called *kupla* (or *kulwa)* in adoration of the sanctuary. This short melody is usually played three times, with considerable solemnity, and the performance framed by silences.[19] More often, music is less clearly framed and serves as an ongoing medium for participation or interaction, and, although a crucial dimension of the proceedings, only dominates the majority of the participants' attention from time to time. Indeed, the repetitive nature of most musical genres does not require the listener to follow musical development but instead to embody semi-consciously the cyclical structure of the melody. Furthermore, instead of the occasion and venue serving the music, the music is used to enliven the place, even if this means playing flutes and dancing in a corral deep with wet and slippery sheep dung (Figure 5.1).

The insistence, in certain genres, on the performance of new tunes each year stresses the idea of melodies as identities, comparable to those of individual living beings. At Carnival or All Saints, for example, a single new *pinkillu* flute melody may sometimes be played almost constantly for three or four days, repeated thousands of times. Yet, as the musicians dance, run, or stagger drunkenly from one homestead to the next—constantly playing— there is no sense that this melody becomes dull or boring. Rather, as the fluidity of the performance increases, and the players find the instruments' full voices and explore the full range of the melodic gestures, the melody seems to develop its personality and potential, in the same way as does a living being. This analogy with a developing being is highly appropriate because these melodies appear to symbolize the soul-substance of the new emerging generation, which during the Carnival season temporarily remains outside the confines of a body, thus is heard as musical sound.[20] With the highly ritualized dispatch of these melodies and of the *pinkillu* flutes at the end of Carnival, this melodic soul-substance is embodied in the new generation of potatoes and other food crops of the year.[21]

A crucially important point about these melodies is their power to generate transformations. This was brought home to me when my host

Figure 5.1. *Pinkillu* flute performance in a very mucky sheep corral for the *k"illpa* ceremony (early January) in which the sheep's ears are cut and decorated (Photograph by Henry Stobart).

described old melodies from previous years as *q'ayma,* meaning "tasteless" or "insipid," a word more usually applied to the flavor of food. There is no point playing these older melodies except for pure nostalgia, he explained, because "they cannot do anything." This particular example emphasizes two of the central points of this chapter: (1) music and the other intense sensory qualities of a feast are expected to contribute to transformation in other spheres of experience, such as atmospheric conditions or plant growth; (2) ideas about music and the sensations with which it is associated interact with, and are often informed by, other sensory modalities.

I shall now consider some of these themes in the context of courtship song.

Sensual Songs

Present at almost any feast are groups of young people who sing and dance in circles, and periodically saunter, jog, or sprint between bars or homesteads. Much of the time these bands consist of extended family members from the same community. From this vantage point of relative safety, young girls develop their song repertoires, and young men their accompanimental skills on the *charango* (during the dry season) or *kitarra* (during the rains). But as confidence grows, fiestas develop and alcohol flows increasingly freely, predatorial young men from other communities eye up *(qhawan)* particular girls and start to move in on the female dominated groups of singers. As soon as an opportunity presents itself, a young man will interpose himself as the *charango* player. It is no coincidence that the sly fox, who features in so many local stories, is often known as *charangero:* "the *charango* player" (Figure 5.2).[22]

Sometimes the predatorial male player is rejected, but at other times his arrival adds renewed vigor and excitement to the performance. As the singing continues, the girls' downcast eyes and flirtatious glances from beneath their low-brimmed hats gradually give way to nervous giggles and witty repartee. Serious amorous interest is often expressed by the stealing of an object of clothing and feigned fighting. At subsequent feasts, these initial encounters may be developed; couples may slip away for lovemaking and arrange other less public meetings, leading potentially to cohabitation in the man's community, the normal preliminary to marriage.[23] The poetic language of songs, expressed from the man's point of view, but created and sung by the women, frequently refers to "stealing" a woman away to live in a man's hamlet. This is reflected in the following song text, which resembles a riddle.[24] When the woman does eventually leave her home hamlet to live with a man, she is accompanied on the journey by a group of predatorial young men playing *charangos.*[25]

Figure 5.2. Young men with *charangos* during a dry season feast in Sacaca, northern Potosí (Photograph by Henry Stobart).

Kaychu chay Macha plazita?	Is this the town square of Macha?
Kaychu chay Macha cholita?	Is this the girl from Macha?
Imanallapitaq suwasqayki?	How shall I steal you away?
Tutallachu yaykumusaq?	Shall I come at night?
P"unchayllachu yaykumusaq?	Shall I come during the day?
Imanallapitaq suwasqayki?	How shall I steal you away?
Wayramanchu tukupusaq?	Shall I turn myself into the wind?
P"isqumanchu tukupusaq?	Shall I make myself into a bird?
Imanallapitaq suwasqayki?	How shall I steal you away?
Phuyumanchu tukupusaq?	Shall I turn myself into a cloud?
Paramanchu tukupusaq?	Shall I make myself into rain?
Imanallapitaq suwasqayki?	How shall I steal you away?
Kunturman avioniyuq	As a condor airplane[26]
Chayamuchun ripunanchispaq	Let it arrive for us to depart
Imanallapitaq suwasqayki?	How shall I steal you away?

For all the feigned modesty, the eroticism of the interaction in courtship songs is sometimes most explicit and, I suggest, largely explains the local prohibition against a woman singing following marriage or cohabitation with a man.[27] This was brought home to me when a young woman, who I had recorded singing on several occasions and who seems to have viewed me with a certain amount of amorous interest, was "stolen away" from my host hamlet to live with a young man from a neighboring community. Some weeks later, she returned to the hamlet to visit her mother and I innocently enquired whether her new status would mean the end of her singing. "Will I never be able to record you singing again?" I asked. She eyed me saucily and simply responded "that depends on you." The erotic implications were blatantly obvious; opening a woman's mouth to a man in song was equivalent to sexual access, and the exclusivity of the relationship that this implies.[28]

A similar association would seem to underlie my hostess's consistent refusal to allow me to record her singing, or to sing for me in any other context, despite her reputation as an excellent singer in her youth.[29] To sing to me would clearly have been seen as immoral, a view supported by my host who was also adamant that it was no longer appropriate for his wife to sing.[30] The sensuality of song is highly explicit and seen as a crucial dimension of almost any feast. But this sexual energy and intense desire expressed in songs is not simply seen as restricted to the young people engaged in courtship but, along with other sensory aspects of the feast, is channeled into the fertility of domestic animals and crops.

As I discovered from my host's instruction, *charango* performance technique is principally aimed at motivating and sustaining women's singing and the dancing, which is integral to almost every musical genre. The fast and virtuosic strumming patterns, which are often featured in urban, pan-Andean styles, would get in the way of the singing, it was explained, thereby shifting the musical focus and destroying the social dynamic of the music. Concepts such as the soloist or virtuoso technique are redundant to the socially interactive nature of most rural Andean music. Instead, music emerges from social interaction and, in turn, serves to stimulate, sustain, and develop further interaction. To reduce these songs to their sonic aspect, as if somehow independent of, for example, the carefully prepared clothing, decoration, body movements, unfolding poetry, and flirtatious glances of courtship performance, would be to miss much of their significance and the piquancy and dynamics of their sensorial effect.

The Biography of a *Charango*

I shall briefly leave the intensity of the fiesta to focus on an actual musical instrument and explore how preparations for musical performance and ideas about how to achieve beautiful and affective music are by no means limited to purely sonic considerations. The story begins with my plan to buy a *charango* to replace one that had been broken. Before setting off to the local town—several hours walk away—to make this purchase, I mentioned my plan to my host. Knowing that I would doubtless lend him the instrument from time to time, he offered me some advice. But, rather than focusing on the sorts of details I would have expected from my guitarist friends in Britain, such as the height of the action or the spacing of the frets, my host simply insisted that the soundboard should be decorated with two parrots and then it would "weep beautifully" *(kachitu waqan)*.

I followed my host's advice, as closely as possible, and returned to the hamlet several days later with a *charango* decorated with a single parrot because none were available with a pair (Figure 5.3). The instrument was considered to sound very good and was greeted with considerable approval. It was a large laminated type, locally known as a *panti charango* due to the black color with which its body is painted.[31] Parrot decoration immediately identifies a *charango* as having been constructed in the hamlets around the village of Pocoata, where many respected makers live and where this form of decoration was quite common. However, because the local market for *charangos* was dominated by instruments made in Pocoata, it would appear that the presence of parrots was not simply a form of quality assurance, linking it to a respected tradition of makers. For my host, at least, it seems that the parrot was itself significant, its image and the sound of the *charango* intrinsically linked.

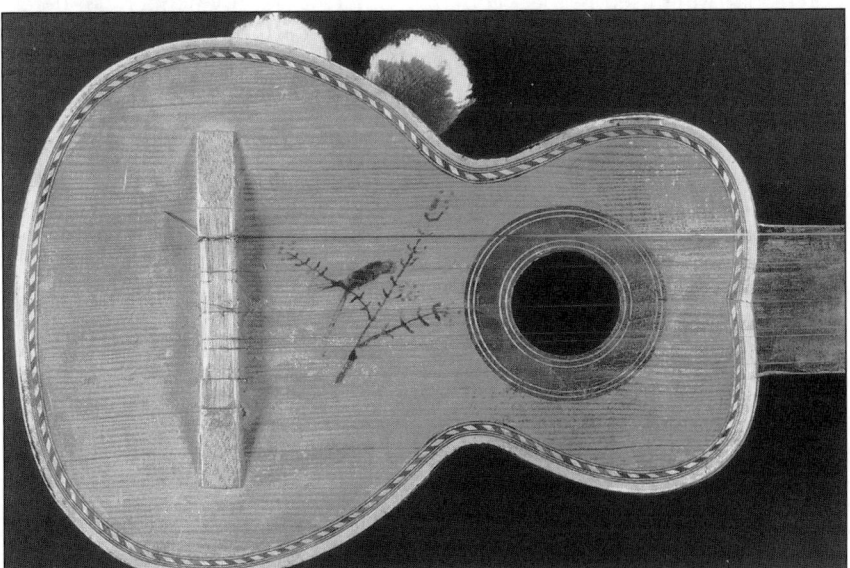

Figure 5.3. The author's *panti charango*, showing the parrot image (Photograph by Henry Stobart).

There are a number of possible interpretations for this insistence upon parrot iconography. First, as in many other cultures, parrots are considered insatiable talkers. A *charango* that speaks continually and effortlessly would be a considerable advantage in its principal role as accompaniment to young women's singing. A player whose instrument falters when accompanying a group of female singers is likely to be quickly replaced by another predatory young man eager to demonstrate his prowess to the young women. Parrots, I was also told, are very difficult to kill. This invincibility is another crucial consideration because *charangos* are extremely fragile and are often inadvertently smashed during feasts. Furthermore, I was told that parrots know everybody's name and thus are seen as somewhat threatening due to their potential power over people, especially because names can be used in sorcery. This would seem to add to the existing association of the *charango* with enchantment, where young women are lured by its sound.[32]

Another vivid intersensory association was made by my host when, just before departing for a nearby festival, he placed a dried hot red chili pepper *(uchu)* inside the body of my new *charango* to give it "voice" *(kus)*,[33] make it "sound well" *(sumaq malqananpaq)*,[34] and "weep really loudly" *(sumaq waqan jatunmanta)*. It must be loud, he explained, so as to dominate and be heard above the other charangos in the noisy bars where alcohol and corn beer are sold. Girls would not sing along with a quiet *charango* that couldn't be heard.[35]

The intersensory imagery here is very powerful. Chilies are the most potent flavoring used in local cooking, and a single tiny pepper can defeat the bravest and strongest man, literally reducing him to tears. As Anne-Marie Hocquenghem has observed, eating chilies may be compared to combat between the pepper and the eater, in which the pepper also serves to stimulate bravery, resistance, and aggression.[36] Spicing my *charango* with a chili apparently invoked a similar sense of aggression and sensory dominance where it was used to vie with other instruments in the battlefield of courtship song.

In summary, some of my host's major considerations concerning the musical quality and effectiveness of this *charango* focused on visual and gustatory aspects, rather than just the sonic ones. To separate artificially these sensory domains by ignoring their creative interaction, as happens in much music scholarship, stifles some of the richness and key meanings operating in many musical performances.

Making Sense of the Year

The punctuation of the year by the periodic sensorial explosions of calendrical feasts is especially important to local understandings of time.[37] People rarely refer to particular dates or months, and instead use feasts as their primary points of reference.[38] Thus, it is common to speak of *Cruz timpu* (the period around the feast of the Holy Cross, May 3), *Todos Santos* ("All Saints"—early November), *San Andrés* ("St Andrew"—late November through early December), *Carnaval* (the period leading up to Carnival and the feast itself), or *Carnaval timpu* (the entire rainy season, culminating with Carnival).[39] These temporal reference points immediately evoke a series of multi-sensorial associations, linked with these particular feasts, seasons, and calendrical activities.[40] In some ways this may be approached in terms of a basic sensorial need. For example, Lawrence Sullivan has suggested that "calendars nourish people with a well rounded diet of temporal experience," acting as a series of "rotating episodes suited to the impulsive human senses of human beings, whose interest soon flags."[41] For my Andean hosts, at least, time appears to be articulated principally in terms of sensory experiences rather than as abstract measurements. [42] (Undoubtedly, this is also, at least partially, true for literate societies who widely use clocks, dates, and months.)

Through the course of the year a calendrically ordered series of musical instruments are played, intended for performance out of doors and sounded using a powerful dynamic style. The sound and other associated qualities of each seasonally alternated instrument, tuning, or musical genre gives a particular quality or flavor to each season, which with few exceptions must be savored singly, rather than mixed together. In certain ways this propriety and ordering can be compared to the sequence of dishes and contrasted flavors in a meal, where it would be unthinkable and possibly repugnant to mix certain types of flavors together in a single dish. To mix *pinkillu* flute music of the rains with *jula jula* panpipe music of the dry winter season would not only be sensorially unthinkable but also seen to threaten the very ordering of the seasons and consequently agricultural production.[43]

Intoxication: Sensuous Senselessness

Alcohol is crucial to any feast and, in my host community at least, is rarely consumed at other times.[44] The two main forms of alcohol are home-brewed corn beer *(aqha)* and purchased (96 percent) cane spirit, which although occasionally consumed undiluted is more often mixed with water. The corn beer is usually made from maize or barley, which is malted (through soaking, sprouting, drying, and milling) several weeks in advance by the family sponsoring the feast, and then brewed communally a week or ten days before the feast is due to begin. This fermentation of alcoholic beverages, where decay is hastened leading to a process of rebirth, may, as Lawrence Sullivan has suggested, be seen to mark "a calendrical node where time cycles can be gathered symbolically."[45] In other words, the festive brewing and consumption of alcohol, like the shifts in musical genres and instruments that occur at feasts, signal major calendrical turning points or transformations.

Music and drinking are particularly identified with one another. This was emphasized to me by a flute maker from another region of Bolivia who had become a member of an Evangelical church that prohibits the consumption of alcohol. As the only surviving maker of this particular type of flute, he held grave ethical doubts about his craft, which involved making instruments that encourage people to get drunk at fiestas.

On several occasions, I was told that drinking alcohol is essential to music-making because it gives the players "courage," increases stamina, and "oils" the performance. Indeed, alcohol temporarily improved my own stamina for playing music and, along with chewing coca leaves, to some degree numbed the sense of pain from, for example, raw and bleeding lips resulting from many hours of panpipe performance. I also discovered that in ensemble performance, alcohol helped me increase my integration with the other players, enabling a sense of technical fluency, melodic fluidity, and increased freedom of expression. Many of these experiences are also undoubtedly shared by my Andean hosts, for whom drinking is not just a sensuous act but also a sacred and social duty that unites people, much of whose lives are spent in relative isolation.[46] As such a salient aspect of the culture, a considerable amount has been written about the ritual and integrative functions of drinking in the Andes, whether as an expression of reciprocity and sharing, a means to question the status quo, or of bringing people into communication with spirit beings.[47]

In most feast contexts, musicians are supplied with corn beer, served from a large earthenware pot *(wich"i* or *lak"ina)* with a half-gourd ladle, and often a bottle of watered-down cane alcohol. These are typically placed in the center of the circle formed by the musicians, and alcohol is circulated during almost any break from playing (Figure 5.4). Thus, for the players, and everyone else attending the feast, the music is almost always filtered through the sensory effects of alcohol. The constant flow of music as sound is matched by that of alcohol, the two interacting with one another in the release and recirculation of sensory energy. The serving of alcohol marks the start of any feast, when music should also begin to flow, and the finishing of the corn beer signals the end of a feast when the music will almost automatically cease.

While evident sensual pleasure is derived from those participating in the musical performance and from drinking alcohol, this consumption is widely treated as a form of offering rather than as self-indulgence. Before drinking takes place, when a person is handed a bottle of alcohol or half-gourd filled with corn beer, a libation to a named power is usually muttered, and a small amount of the liquid is flicked or spilt on the ground.[48] There seems

Figure 5.4. An earthenware pot of corn beer *(aqha)* encircled by a group of *pinkillu* flute players and singers in a llama corral during the feast of Carnival (Photograph by Henry Stobart).

to be no contradiction here in merging human sensory pleasure with offerings to distant powers.[49] Rather, it is crucial that these sacrifices should give sensual pleasure to the human participants and be of the highest quality if they are to be efficacious. Perhaps rather than thinking of offerings as destined to specific unitary powers, the consumption and release of vivid sensorial energies that characterize an Andean feast should be thought of more in terms of recirculation, invoking ideas of both destruction and renewal. This is particularly evident in the case of animal sacrifice, which, in turn, reveals alternative ways for approaching the release and recirculation of musical sounds.

Sensational Sacrifices

The consumption of special foods, usually in large quantities, is a central feature of festivals throughout the world. In certain types of Andean fiestas, it falls upon sponsors, usually a married couple, to provide the food and alcohol, and often to engage and pay musicians.[50] The extreme sacrifices made by individual families are sometimes difficult for outsiders to comprehend. During a fiesta, a large proportion of a family's annual resources can be consumed within a matter of days.[51] Such immense investment in these transitory bursts of sensory energy has been identified by some, especially the members of Evangelical churches, as a root cause for the continued extreme poverty of many rural communities in the Andes. However, despite the immense personal commitment and hardship necessitated by sponsoring a feast, my host was in no doubt that sponsorship would ultimately reap dividends. He, and many others, explained this to me in terms of the future fertility and abundance of the animal herds and crops, resulting from this major sensorial offering to the landscape, ancestors, and community. The sponsoring of a feast also has many other direct practical benefits in terms of boosting a family's integration and status within a community. Indeed, as in many parts of the Southern Andes, leading positions of community authority are typically preceded, or sometimes accompanied, by the completion of feast sponsorship duties.[52]

For my Andean hosts, the central focus of fiesta food is meat, which acquires heightened symbolic and sensory significance due to its rare consumption at other times. The slaughter of the animals *(uywa ñakakun* —"slaughter of the nurtured ones")* for major feasts is usually performed on the eve of the actual feast day. In many respects, it serves to initiate the fiesta proceedings, which may continue for several days. It is also at the *uywa ñakakun* ceremony that alcohol is consumed and music is usually heard for the first time during the feast. The music, I was told, is played to the animal herd as "consolation" *(kunswilu)* and to ensure the future "multiplication" *(mirananpaq)* of the herd (Figure 5.5).

The *uywa ñakakun* ceremony is typically performed in a llama corral near the sponsoring family's homestead, where female and young llamas are kept at night. Following a lengthy series of libations and coca leaf chewing to honor the patronal saints and domestic animals, the sponsoring wife (or sponsor's mother) carries a potsherd or flat stone of burning incense around the inner perimeter of the corral in an anticlockwise direction (to the right). This sensuous act, which draws on Catholic practices, serves as a form of purification and blessing for the corral itself and its power to regenerate new life within its walls. The sponsor's llamas are then herded into the corral, a few animals selected—their legs tied, forcing them to the ground—and the others herded out again. As the animals depart for the mountain pastures, they are sprayed with corn beer, and for the first few dozen yards followed by musicians playing panpipes or flutes. In this way, notions of regeneration are invoked using a powerful sensory language involving alcohol, coca, incense, and music. To suggest that music is some kind of autonomous or "absolute" monosensory aural medium in this context would be ridiculous. Instead we are given the impression that music is somehow scattered or sprayed over the departing animals in the same way as the corn beer and pieces of food offerings, thereby invoking the initiation of new life.

Figure 5.5. *Siku* panpipe players with a *bombo* (bass drum) circling the llamas and sheep selected for slaughter at the *uywa ñakakun* ceremony (Photograph by Henry Stobart).

A few sheep are often brought to be slaughtered with the llamas, and each animal is covered with a beautiful hand-woven carrying cloth. The description of the animals as *uywa* (nurtured ones) and their dressing in cloths, as if representing human children, considerably heightens the sense of sacrifice. Blood from each animal's slit throat is caught in a half-gourd vessel and, to muttered incantations, sprayed in different directions as offerings to the church tower, various saints, and animated features of the landscape. A little blood is also wiped on each person's cheeks and onto the musical instruments as a blessing *(bendición),* and immediately the animals are skinned and the meat carried away to be cooked or stored for later meals during the feast. During certain feasts, the animal skins are carefully laid out on the ground, and in a dance accompanied by panpipe music the sponsoring couple weave between the skins led by the *pusariq* (puller) dance leader. This focus on the empty skins seems to stress the idea of vessels that shortly before had enclosed the flesh and animation of living animals.[53]

The Aesthetics of Giving

Through this rite of sacrifice and the communal consumption of the meat, the stored up sensory potential of the animals, as flavors and the color red (blood), are released from within the skins and circulated. The significance of this sacrifice for understanding music, and many other dynamics within this society, may be better understood when we consider it in the context of the paired aesthetic/ethic concepts *tara* and *q"iwa*. These terms are used to describe two contrasted qualities of musical sound but are also used in a variety of other contexts.[54]

Tara is applied to strong, vibrant sounds, suggesting the full and unrestrained release of energies, and is linked with notions of social harmony and equilibrium.[55] *Q"iwa*, in contrast, is applied to thin clear sounds, which are aesthetically less appreciated, and seen to hold back their potential energies; literally, they "do not give." Similarly, a mean or ungiving person is likely to be described as *q"iwa*, as is a castrated llama that retains its sexual energies and thus, unlike a stud llama, grows fat. White potato plants, without chlorophyll, are also said to be *q"iwa*, presumably for failing to release the sensorially rich green color. This word also conveys notions of social and practical disequilibrium or dissonance, such as a cowardly person, a string instrument that fails to stay in tune, or an awkward-shaped mud brick that will not fit well into a wall.

While *tara* concerns unrestrained sensorial release leading to recirculation and exchange, *q"iwa* conveys ideas of containment and the avoidance of excessive exchange or release of energies. Clearly, both these ideas are crucial to life in this part of the rural Andes. On the one hand, people need to store up provisions and eke these out gradually over the course of the year in order to survive; on the other, harmonious and equitable social relations depend on unrestrained exchanges where no individual is seen to accumulate a disproportionate share of resources or power.[56] In certain ways, the contrasted concepts of *q"iwa* and *tara* might be seen to characterize the unfolding of the year, where extended periods of austerity, during which resources are carefully safeguarded, are punctuated by fiestas, as bursts of relatively unrestrained release and exchange of energies.[57] However, the crucial distinction between *tara* and *q"iwa* concerns the release or failure to release potent inner energies that are expressed as vivid and enlivening sensory qualities, such as tastes, sounds, colors, scents, and kinaesthetic or tactile sensations.

Sensing Life in Flux

Feasts provide an important focus for community energy and are a primary means by which people conceptualize time. They also mark critical moments of symbolic transformation or reversal, such as the start of the rainy growing season (All Saints) and its end (Carnival).[58] This notion of reversal was especially evident to me in the final dances of Carnival when a pair of men and women enacted gender reversal or transvestism by exchanging clothes.[59] At the climax of the ceremony, alongside a radical alternation of musical genres and dance forms, the men and women swiftly replaced their own clothing, as though reversing (and thereby reclaiming) their respective genders. At this climactic turning point, all the other participants also removed their outer garments, turned them inside out, and replaced them.

This focus on external wrappings, where inside and outside are reversed, is reminiscent of animal sacrifice in which, through a rite of reversal, the inner flesh and animation of the animals are exteriorized and circulated as collectively shared sensations. The final rite of Carnival appears to symbolize a converse process in which the abundant external sensory expressions of Carnival are moved inside and literally silenced, to be embodied and transformed into living organisms: the year's new generation of food crops.[60]

As the sensory exuberance of Carnival is removed from human experience and a new period of austerity begins, the vitality of this new life that is about to be revealed as embodied beings would seem to depend directly upon the *allegría* (enlivening) of Carnival itself: its sensory abundance, energy, and interactions.

Although these rites are specific to Carnival, they hint at a more general view that the release or externalization of inner energies and potencies from living bodies, as a form of sacrifice, is intensely associated with regenerative potential. Indeed, these vivid and ephemeral sensory expressions come to signify a moment of release and reconfiguration in the regenerative processes of living things. From this perspective, our experience of, for example, musical sounds, tastes, scents, and bright colors begins to take on a rather different meaning. Instead of the idea that these qualities may somehow exist as abstract and autonomous phenomena, it is our relationship with, and interdependence upon, the (animated) sources of these expressions, as sentiment, that is highlighted.

Conclusion

When you approach a village or hamlet in the rural Andes and your ears are greeted by music, this is a sure sign that a fiesta is underway. Following weeks of musical inactivity and what sometimes seems an almost oppressively silent soundscape, these sounds are remarkable and literally "sensational." But, as you hasten toward the sounds, the music does not simply signal its own presence. Its sounds promise a diversity of other sensual experiences and intense human interactions, as people leave their solitary daily lives and, in a burst of sensory energy, come together to be realized as a form of community.

This convergence of people's lives during feasts, where separate strands come together in a vivid knot of sensorial activity, is crucial to the future directions they will take. For example, many—if not most—couples initially meet during song performance at feasts, the status of a married couple depends on their role as feast sponsors, and feasts are the primary context in which people define their ethnic identity and other social allegiances. I hope to have conveyed the idea that, from a multiplicity of perspectives, feasts serve as pivotal moments of change, and that the culturally proscribed activities and multisensorial saturation that characterize them are crucial catalysts to this transformation.

These transformations or movements from one form, time-space, or phase to another are particularly linked with sensorial effect, such as the succession of sensory configurations found in the seasonal use of music, or the vivid alternation between sensory austerity and saturation. Crucially, sensorial saturation depends on the release and recirculation of the energies or animating essences of "live" beings. The bright colors, flavors, aromas, and vivid sounds that characterize Andean feasts are intimately associated with the expression of the inner energies of bodies: be these humans, animals, food crops, magical rocks, or the animated earth itself. But it would also seem, conversely, that the vitality enclosed in the bodies of future generations—and presumably of the animated earth itself—is seen to depend on the intensity of the multisensorial saturation achieved during these feasts.

Notes

1. Text from a song recorded in Charka province, northern Potosí (November 1, 1986). Married and single life are wittily contrasted according to taste. *(Ulukipa* or *ulupika*—Capsicum conicum—are tiny but particularly potent peppers.) The Sunchu plant referred to in the refrain also symbolizes the distinction between youth and old age. During the rains, the Sunchu has beautiful yellow flowers, but in the dry winter season—its seductive sensory powers spent—its desiccated stalks are used for firewood.

2. This is discussed by, for example, Paul Stoller in *A Taste for Ethnographic Things: The Senses in Anthropology* (Philadelphia: University of Pennsylvania Press, 1989), 7–9; David Howes, "Introduction 'To Summon all the Senses,'" in *The Varieties of Sensory Experience*, ed. D. Howes (Toronto: University of Toronto Press, 1991), 3–21; and Steven Feld, "Waterfalls of Song: An Acoustemology of Place Resounding in Bosavi, Papua New Guinea," in *Senses of Place*, ed. S. Feld and K. Basso (Santa Fe, N.M.: School of American Research Press, 1996), 91–136.

3. Paradoxically, the argument that notated music is a visual format would seem to support, rather than undermine, this argument. With the exception of tablatures, which represent kinaesthetic aspects of music-making, rather than sounds, most notations actually tend to concentrate our focus on sound as "the music," thus reducing the focus on other sensory aspects that might be involved in any given performance.

4. It is significant, in this context, that many languages do not include equivalents for the English words "music" or "sound."

5. The recording is played in a new multisensorial context, but through this process of transmission the idea that intersensory linkages are a critical dimension of the performance appears increasingly tenuous.

6. Ruth Stone's (1982) study on the Kpelle of Liberia was groundbreaking in focusing specifically on the idea of the musical event. However, despite her evocative and revealing title, *Let the Inside Be Sweet* (a comment made by an audience member at the beginning of an event), she does not stress the multisensorial aspect of the event. Ruth

Stone, *Let the Inside Be Sweet: The Interpretation of Music Event among the Kpelle of Liberia* (Bloomington: Indiana University Press, 1982).

7. Eric von Hornbostel, "The Unity of the Senses," *Psyche* 7 (April 1927): 83–89; and Alan Merriam, *The Anthrolopogy of Music* (Evanston: Northwestern University Press, 1964).

8. Bruno Nettl, "Mozart and the Ethnomusicological Study of Western Culture," *Disciplining Music: Musicology and Its Canons,* ed. K. Bergeron and P. Bohlman (Chicago: University of Chicago Press, 1992): Nettl has drawn attention to some amusing, yet thought provoking, intersensory associations between the nature of Mozart's music and the abundance of Viennese sweets or desserts named after him. Both Mozart's music and such sweets "go down easily," as if both are intended to delight the senses. By contrast, there seems to be an absence of sweets, or even stews, named after the composers of less digestible music such as Beethoven or Schoenberg (147–48).

9. John Harrison and Simon Baron-Cohen, "Synaesthesia: An Introduction," in *Synaesthesia* (Oxford: Blackwell, 1997), 11.

10. Lawrence Marks, "On Coloured-Hearing Synaesthesia: Cross-Modal Translations of Sensory Dimensions." *Psychological Bulletin* 82, no. 3 (1975): 303–31.

11. A number of anthopologists have taken to using the word "synaesthesia" to refer to intersensory metaphor or multisensory effect, which contribute to deeply felt recognition or memory of, for example, place. See Bradd Shore, "Twice-Born, Once Conceived: Meaning Construction and Cultural Cognition," *American Anthropologist* 93, no. 1 (1991): 9–27; and Michelle Bigenho, "Sensing Locality in Yura: Rituals of Carnival and of the Bolivian State," *American Ethnologist* 26, no. 4 (2000): 957–80. I am grateful to Michelle Bigenho for our interesting conversations on this theme.

12. Barbara Tedlock, "Crossing the Sensory Domains in Native American Aesthetics." *Explorations in Ethnomusicology: Essays in Honour of David P. McAllester,* ed. C. J. Frisbie (Detroit: Information Coordinators, 1996), 187–98.

13. Ibid., 189.

14. This fieldwork consisted of a stay for one year (1990–91) followed by several shorter visits spread over nearly a decade. I also draw on experiences from a previous year of fieldwork in other parts of rural Bolivia (1986–87).

15. Catherine Allen, *The Hold Life Has: Coca and Cultural Identity in an Andean Community* (Washington, DC: Smithsonian Institution Press, 1988), 148. My hosts did not use the word *sami* in the same context as Allen describes, but the associations of *sami* in Sonqo have many similarities with these for my hosts' concept of *animu*. See Henry Stobart, "Bodies of Sound and Landscapes of Music: A View from the Bolivian Andes," in *Musical Healing in Cultural Context,* ed. P. Gouk (Aldershot: Ashgate, 2000), 26–45.

16. Lawrence Sullivan, *Icanchu's Drum: An Orientation to Meanings in South American Religions* (New York: Macmillan, 1988), 197.

17. While I heard public criticism concerning lack of music, I did not hear complaints about performance quality voiced in public, although this was sometimes encountered in private. See also Thomas Turino, *Moving Away from Silence: Music of the Peruvian Altiplano and the Experience of Urban Migration* (Chicago: University of Chicago Press, 1993), 62.

18. My use of the word "sacrifice" here is intentional as it highlights the idea that such musical performance demands the consumption of human energies, and, as I shall argue later in the chapter, shares many parallels with animal sacrifice. Such "sacrifice" may also clearly be seen to function as what Leach has described as "an expression of the principle of reciprocity" (p. 83), echoing the system of reciprocity described in Mauss's famous theory of "the gift, and the obligation to reciprocate" (p. 18). However, I wish to downplay mechanistic views of exchange (such as the Andean *ayni* system, which has been widely discussed in the literature) in favor of notions of sensory flux and recirculation. See Edmund Leach, *Culture and Communication: The Logic by Which Symbols Are Connected* (Cambridge: Cambridge University Press, 1976); Marcel Mauss, *The Gift: The Form and Reason for Exchange in Archaic Societies* (1950), trans. W. D. Halls (London: Routledge, 1990).

19. This practice is less common in *ayllu* Macha than other parts of northern Potosí.
20. The idea that the soul, when journeying outside the body, may be heard as the sound of a flute is common to a number of South American cultures and is suggested in the tale of the singing bone, which is widely known in the Andes and parts of Europe. See Robert Randall, "Communication with the Other World: The Tale of Isicha Puyto," *Journal of Latin American Lore*, 13 no. 2 (1987): 155–81.
21. Henry Stobart, "Flourishing Horns and Enchanted Tubers: Music and Potatoes in Highland Bolivia," *British Journal of Ethnomusicology* 3 (1994): 45–46.
22. For further details of the *charango* and its strong association with courtship see Thomas Turino, "The Charango and the *Sirena:* Music, Magic and the Power of Love." *Latin American Music Review* 4 (spring/summer 1983): 81–119.
23. Ibid, 91–92.
24. This song was recorded in November 1992 and was accompanied by the *kitarra*, a slightly larger local strummed guitar, usually decorated with bright colors and images of growing plants. For more details of this instrument, see Stobart, "Flourishing Horns and Enchanted Tubers."
25. Today, the young man's parents usually visit those of the girl to formally request cohabitation in the man's community. Evasion of a definite answer, my host explained, was widely understood to signify refusal.
26. In myth, the predatorial condor is often associated with "stealing" women away. See Olivia Harris, "Condor and Bull: The Ambiguities of Masculinity in Northern Potosí" *Sex and Violence: Issues of Representation and Experience*, eds. P. Harvey and P. Gow (London: Routledge, 1994), 40–65.
27. Married women are allowed to sing wedding songs and theoretically may sing during Carnival. In other regions of the Bolivian Andes it is quite common to encounter married women singing, such as in some of the songs discussed by Denise Arnold and Juan de Dios Yapita, *Rio de vellón, rio de canto* (La Paz, Bolivia: ILCA/HISBOL, 1998).
28. The reproductive associations of women's singing in the Andes (especially for animals) has also been noted by other ethnographers, for example, Arnold and Yapita, 118.
29. The only exception to this was an urban song she had learned at school. Only one married woman in the locality was prepared to sing almost any genre for me to record (accompanied by her husband on the *charango*). Exceptionally, this woman had traveled widely, had lived in towns, and her brother is a famous recording artist in the region on whose commercial releases she has appeared.
30. As far as I know, married women do not usually sing to their husbands in private. This is hardly surprising as music making, as I have already noted, is principally confined to the public context of fiestas.
31. The word *panti* is used to refer to a number of highly saturated colors, including dark reds, black, or deep purple.
32. See also Thomas Turino, "The Charango and the *Sirena*" (1983).
33. Presumably from the Spanish *voz*.
34. *Malqa* was related to a full open-throated or a hoarse voice, a sound quality that is much appreciated. My host pointed to his own throat in explaining this idea and related *malqa* to vibrant *tara* timbre. See Henry Stobart, "Tara and Q'iwa: Worlds of Sound and Meaning." In *Cosmología y Música en los Andes*, ed. M.P. Baumann (Frankfurt/Madrid: Vervuert/Iberamericana, 1996), 67–81.
35. A well-known parallel to this custom of "spicing up" an instrument is found in many parts of Northern Potosí where a *cascabel* (rattle from the tail of a rattlesnake) is placed inside a *charango* and glued, pointing downward, at the juncture between the neck and body. On entering a bar, a *charango* with a *cascabel* is claimed to render the player irresistible to women and to cause the strings of any other *charangos* to break. It is specified that the *cascabel* must be taken from a living snake and that the snake must continue to live for at least a year; if the snake were to die, the cascabel would be useless. See also Ernesto Cavour, *El Charango: Su Vida, Costumbres y Desventuras* (La Paz: CIMA, 1987), 173.

36. Anne-Marie Hocquenghem, *Iconografía Mochica* (Lima: Pontifica Universidad Católica del Peru, 1987), 199.

37. The majority of feasts are calendrical, but in certain respects weddings, which although mainly celebrated during the dry winter months, represent a form of non-calendrical fiesta.

38. The principal exception, where the name of the month predominates, is the common observation that the "mouth" of earth is "open" during the month of August, when ritual offering for it should be made. This has also been noted for the case of Peru by Michael Sallnow, *Pilgrims of the Andes: Regional Cults in Cusco* (Washington, D.C.: Smithsonian Institution Press, 1987), 131–32.

39. Although the associations of these feasts are strongly linked with locally specific weather patterns, agricultural activities and seasonal variations in diet, the feast dates themselves are derived from the Catholic church calendar. In many cases these were fused with existing prehispanic festivals. (See, for example, Sallnow, *Pilgrims of the Andes* (1987), 156; Gary Urton, "Calendrical Cycles and Their Projections in Paqariq-tambo, Peru," *Journal of Latin American Lore* 12, no. 1 (1986): 45–64; and R. Tom Zuidema, "The Incaic Feast of the Queen and the Spanish Feast of Cabañuelas," *Journal of Latin American Lore* 20, no. 1 (1997): 143–60.

40. For a Peruvian example, see Gary Urton, *At the Crossroads of Earth and Sky: An Andean Cosmology* (Austin: University of Texas Press, 1981), 32. A case from Papua New Guinea, in which body paint color encodes reference to life cycle, is mentioned by Alfred Gell in *The Anthropology of Time: Cultural Constructions of Temporal Maps and Images* (Oxford: Berg, 1992), 43.

41. Sullivan, *Icanchu's Drum* (1988), 166–67.

42. See also Pierre Bourdieu, *Outline of a Theory of Practice* (Cambridge: Cambridge University Press, 1977), 103.

43. These shifting calendrical sound qualities, as a form of sensorial language, are in many ways comparable with the flavors, aromas, colors, images, and textures, and their various potencies, blends, and arrangements used in ritual offerings. These have been discussed by, for example, Gabriel Martinez, *Una mesa ritual en Sucre: Aproximaciones semióticas al ritual andino* (La Paz: Biblioteca Andina 3, HISBOL/ASUR, 1987); Veronica Cereceda, "Approximaciones a una estetica andina: De la belleza al *tinku*," *Tres reflexiones sobre el pensamiento andino*, T. Bouysse-Cassagen, O. Harris, T. Platt, V. Cereceda (La Paz: Hisbol, 1987); Gwenneth Armstrong, *Symbolic Arrangements and Communication in the Despacho* (Ph.D. thesis, University of St. Andrews, Scotland, 1988); Gerardo Fernández Juárez, *La banquete aymara: Mesas y yatiris* (La Paz: HISBOL, 1995): Gerardo Fernández Juárez, *Entre la repugnancia y la seducción: Ofrendas complejas en los Andes del Sur*, Archivos de historia Andina 24 (Cusco, Peru: CBC—Centro de Estudios Regionales Andinos "Bartolomé de las Casas," 1997). Stressing the sensuality of these offerings, Gerardo Fernández has observed that, above all, a ritual offering *(mesa)* must be seductive or tempting to the specific tastes of the spirit for whom it is destined (1995: 351).

44. Despite alcohol's immense ritual importance, in practice this infrequent drinking is due to lack of availability rather than any explicit value in abstinence; alcohol is made for and purchased for feasts and is rarely a priority at other times. However, on trips to town, men (in particular) will often indulge in drinking bouts and commonly purchase a liter of cane alcohol or *singani*, much of which is likely to be consumed before arriving home. This fuels the false urban stereotype of peasants as lazy and constantly drunk.

45. Sullivan, *Icanchu's Drum* (1999), 196–97.

46. On the theme of drinking as a social duty in the Andes, see Penelope Harvey, "Drunken Speech and the Construction of Meaning: Bilingual Competence in the Southern Peruvian Andes," *Language in Society* 20 (1991): 1–36, esp. 7.

47. See, for example, Catherine Allen, *The Hold Life Has: Coca and Cultural Identity in an Andean Community* (Washington D.C.: Smithsonian Institution Press, 1988), 148-, and Harvey, "Drunken Speech" (1991).

48. In ritual contexts, long and often complex series of libations are made in sequences to named powers (such as the sun = God, moon = Mary, lightning = St. James, mountain peaks, animals, ancestors, etc.). In turn, each person accepts a drink and coca leaves, to chew destined for a particular power. These are usually supplied by the sponsor of the occasion or host and circulated to each adult in turn (moving around the group in a counterclockwise direction).

49. Offerings to non-human powers tended to be presented in terms of the provision of nourishment—as the spiritual essences of food, coca leaves, or alcohol—and it was not rare to hear of such spirits being described as "hungry." Therefore, it seems likely that my host would reject Leach's assertion that, "Gods do not need presents from men; they require signs of submission." Leach, *Culture and Communication* (1976), 83.

50. In certain regions where it is customary to engage semi-professional musicians, such as brass bands, the hire of musicians is sometimes the single greatest expense of a feast. It should also be pointed out that certain feasts are more familial in character and not hosted by recognized public sponsors. Compare, for example, Roger Rasnake, *Domination and Cultural Resistance: Authority and Power among an Andean People* (Durham and London: Duke University Press, 1988), 178.

51. See Rasnake, *Domination and Cultural Resistance* (1988), 69; and William Mitchell, *Peasants on the Edge: Crop, Cult and Crisis in the Andes* (Austin: University of Texas Press, 1991), 157.

52. Rasnake, *Domination and Cultural Resistance* (1988), 67–69.

53. A link between music and the skins is again heightened through the local practice of giving one of the skins of the sacrificed animals to the leader of the panpipe band a few moments before the musicians' final departure from the feast.

54. Henry Stobart, "Tara and Q"iwa: Worlds of Sound and Meaning," *Cosmología y Música en los Andes*, ed. M. P. Baumann (Frankfurt/Madrid: Vervuert/Iberoamericana, 1996), 67–81.

55. The vibrancy or beating effect produced by what European musicologists would describe as acoustic "dissonance" is a crucial aspect of the *tara* sound. In this sacrifice context, this might usefully be compared with a death rattle. Locally this vibrant sound is also equated with the vibrant sound made by llamas during mating. See Henry Stobart, "The Llama's Flute: Musical Misunderstandings in the Andes," *Early Music* (August 1996), 470–83, esp. 478.

56. Accordingly, a few individuals discreetly described the man with the largest family and llama herd in the community as *q"iwa*, whilst the word *tara* was sometimes used to describe two people walking side by side, suggesting some sort of balance or equality between them as equal exchange partners.

57. However, I am hesitant to develop this analogy any further.

58. Olivia Harris, working among the Laymi in northern Potosí, has related seasonal transformation (and other forms of conceptual reversal) to the indigenous concept *pachakuti*, which has sometimes been translated as "world-turning" or "cataclysm." Olivia Harris, "De la fin du monde: Notes depuis le nord-Potosí," *Cahiers des Amériques Latines, No. 6 Bolivie: Fascination du temps et organisation de l'apparence* (Paris: IHEAL Institut des Hautes Études de l'Amérique Latine 1987, 93–118), 96–98.

59. The feast of Carnival is associated with conceptual reversals in many parts of Europe and Latin America. See, for example, Viacheslav Ivanov, "The Semiotic Theory of Carnival as the Inversion of Bipolar Opposites," *Carnival!* ed. T. A. Sebeok (Berlin, Amsterdam, New York: Mouton Publishers, 1984, 11–36), and in the same volume, Umberto Eco, "The Frames of Comic Freedom," 1–10. Ivanov discusses gender reversal and transvestism in some detail, and focuses on the idea of Carnival as the inversion of opposites. It is possible that the roots of the performed transvestism I witnessed are historically drawn from European models.

60. These new tubers and seeds are widely compared to human babies, which must be nurtured and cared for, and which will weep "like infants" if abandoned. Henry Stobart, "Flourishing Horns and Enchanted Tubers."

References

Allen, Catherine. *The Hold Life Has: Coca and Cultural Identity in an Andean Community.* Washington D.C.: Smithsonian Institution Press, 1988.

Armstrong, Gweneth. *Symbolic Arrangement and Communication in the Despacho.* Ph.D. Thesis, University of St. Andrews, 1988.

Arnold, Denise, and Juan de Dios Yapita. *Rio de vellón, río de canto.* La Paz, ILCA/HISBOL, 1998.

Bigenho, Michelle. "Sensing Locality in Yura: Rituals of Carnival and of the Bolivian State." *American Ethnologist* 26:4 (2000): 957–980.

Bourdieu, Pierre. *Outline of a Theory of Practice.* Cambridge: Cambridge University Press, 1977.

Cavour, Ernesto. *El Charango: Su vida, costumbres y desventuras.* La Paz, CIMA, 1988.

Cereceda, Veronica. "Aproximaciones a una estetica andina: De la belleza al *tinku.*" *Tres reflexiones sobre el pensamiento andino* (T. Bouysse-Cassagne, O. Harris, T. Platt, V. Cereceda). La Paz: Hisbol, 1987, 133–231.

Eco, Umberto. "The Frames of Comic 'Freedom.'" *Carnival!* ed. Thomas A. Sebeok. Berlin, New York Amsterdam: Mouton Publishers, 1987, 1–10.

Feld, Steve. "Waterfalls of Sound: An Acoustemology of Place Resounding in Bosavi, Papua New Guinea." *Senses of Place,* ed. S. Feld and K. Basso. Santa Fe, N.M.: School of American Research Press, 1996, 91–136.

Fernández Juáraz, Gerardo. *La Banquete Aymara: Mesas y yatitris.* La Paz: HISBOL (Biblioteca Andina), 1995.

———. *Entre la repugnancia y la sedicción: Ofrendas complejas en los Andes del Sur.* Archivos de historia Andina 24, Cusco (Peru): CBC (Centro de Estudios Regionales Andinos "Bartolomé de las Casas"), 1997.

Gell, Alfred. *The Anthropology of Time: Cultural Constructions of Temporal Maps and Images,* Oxford and Washington, D.C.: Berg, 1992.

Harris, Olivia. "De la fin du monde: Notes depuis le nord-Potosí," *Cahiers des Amériques Latines, No 6 Bolivie: Fascination du temps et organisation de l'apparence,* Paris: IHEAL (Institut des Hautes Études de l'Amérique Latine, 1987): 93–118.

———. "Condor and Bull: The Ambiguities of Masculinity in Northern Potosí." *Sex and Violence: Issues of Representation and Experience,* ed. P. Harvey and P. Gow. London: Routledge, 1994, 40–65.

Harvey, Penelope. "Drunken Speech and the Construction of Meaning: Bilingual Competence in the Southern Peruvian Andes." *Language in Society* 20 (1991): 1–36.

Harrison, John and Simon Baron-Cohen, "Synaesthesia: An Introduction." In *Synaesthesia.* Oxford and Cambridge, Mass.: Blackwell, 1997, 3–16.

Hocquenghem, Anne-Marie. *Iconografía Mochica.* Lima: Pontifica Universidad Católica del Peru, 1987.

Hornbostel, Eric von. "The Unity of the Senses." *Psyche* 7 (April 1927): 83–99.

Howes, David. "Introduction: To Summon All the Senses." *The Varieties of Sensory Experience,* ed. D. Howes. Toronto, Buffalo, London: University of Toronto Press, 1991, 3–21.

Ivanov, Viacheslav. "The Semiotic Theory of Carnival as the Inversion of Bipolar Opposites." *Carnival!* ed. Thomas A. Sebeok. Berlin, New York, Amsterdam: Mouton Publishers, 1984, 11–36.

Marks, Lawrence E. "On Coloured-Hearing Synaesthesia: Cross-Modal Translations of Sensory Dimensions." *Psychological Bulletin* 82 no. 3 (1975): 303–31.

Martinez, Gabriel. *Una mesa ritual en Sucre: Aproximaciones semióticas al ritual andino.* La Paz: Biblioteca Andina 3, HISBOL/ASUR, 1987.

Merriam, Alan. *The Anthropology of Music.* Evanson: Northwestern University Press, 1964.

Mitchell, William. *Peasants on the Edge: Crop, Cult and Crisis in the Andes.* Austin: University of Texas Press, 1991.

Nettl, Bruno. "Mozart and the Ethnomusicological Study of Western Culture." *Disciplining Music: Musicology and Its Canons,* ed. K. Bergeron and P. Bohlman. Chicago and London: Chicago University Press, 1992.

Randall, Robert. "Communication with the Other World: The Tale of Isicha Puyto." *Journal of Latin American Lore* 13/2 (1987): 155–81.

Rasnake, Roger. *Domination and Cultural Resistance: Authority and Power among an Andean People.* Durham and London: Duke University Press, 1988.

Sallnow, Michael. *Pilgrims of the Andes: Regional Cults in Cusco.* Washington, D.C. and London: Smithsonian Institution Press, 1987.

Shore, Bradd. "Twice-Born, Once Conceived: Meaning Construction and Cultural Cognition." *American Anthropologist* 93:1 (1991): 9–27.

Stobart, Henry. "Flourising Horns and Enchanted Tubers: Music and Potatoes in Highland Bolivia." *British Journal of Ethnomusicology* 3 (1994): 35–48.

———. "Tara and Q"iwa: Worlds of Sound and Meaning." *Cosmología y música en los Andes.* ed. M.P. Baumann. Frankfurt/Madrid: Vervuert/Iberoamericana, 1996a, 67–81.

———. "The Llama"s Flute: Musical Misunderstandings in the Andes." *Early Music* (August 1996b): 470–83.

———. "Bodies of Sound and Landscapes of Music: A View from the Bolivian Andes." *Musical Healing in Cultural Contexts,* ed. P. Gouk. Aldershot: Ashgate, 2000, 26–45.

Stoller, Paul. *A Taste of Ethnographic Things: The Senses in Anthropology.* Philadelphia: University of Pennsylvania Press, 1989.

Stone, Ruth. *Let the Inside Be Sweet: The Interpretation of Music Event among the Kpelle of Liberia.* Bloomington: Indiana University Press, 1982.

Sullivan, Lawrence. *Icanchu"s Drum: An Orientation to Meanings in South American Religions.* New York: Macmillan Publishing Company, 1988.

Tedlock, Barbara. "Crossing the Sensory Domains in Native American Aesthetics." *Explorations in Ethnomusicology: Essays in Honour of David P. McAllester,* ed. C. J. Frisbie. Detroit: Information Coordinators, 1996, 187–98.

Turino, Thomas. "The Charango and the *Sirena:* Music, Magic, and the Power of Love." *Latin American Music Review* 4 (spring/summer 1983).

———. *Moving Away from Silence:Music of the Peruvian Altiplano and the Experience of Urban Migration.* Chicago and London: Chicago University Press, 1993.

Urton, Gary. *At the Crossroads of Earth and Sky: An Andean Cosmology.* Austin: University of Texas Press, 1981.

———. "Calendrical Cycles and Their Projections in Paqariqtambo, Peru," *Journal of Latin American Lore* 12 (1986): 45–64.

Zuidema, R. Tom. "The Incaic Feast of the Queen and the Spanish Feast of Cabañuelas." *Journal of Latin American Lore* 20 (1997): 143–60.

6

Siren Sensualities in Physical Theatre

Lloyd Newson's *Strange Fish* (1992)

Janet Adshead-Lansdale

Goddesses, witches, and sirens, all closely linked in Western thinking and dangerous to the male in their capacity to "bewitch" or even to castrate, drive the sensual and imaginative landscape of Lloyd Newson's *Strange Fish*. Dance and music share a history of association with these particular types of women, capable of evoking madness, death, excess, and sensory fragmentation. However, even if desire, eroticism, and sensual pleasure are the lifeblood of both arts, they each construct them in different ways and both shift as genres and times change. The collision of these ideas in the detailed formal constructions of movement and sound in *Strange Fish* offers an intoxicating feast for the "reader." My analysis starts from, and remains with, the dance/act of theatre/performance and its music, rather than pursuing theory, valid as that might be for other purposes. I recognize a "mosaic" of theoretical positions on the notion of the "text" and "intertext" and draw on them where they seem most pertinent. These chosen texts and intertexts, while to some extent shared by the choreographer, film director, and performers as well as other readers, are also peculiarly my own.[1]

Gender and the Construction of Narrative

It has escaped few serious scholars in the arts that music was, for many years, largely free (or ignorant) of the feminist theorizing that has had such an impact in theatre studies, literature, and dance. It seems obvious that the emphasis on structure, in the ideology of abstract formalism, was sufficient excuse not to attend to the position of women (or people of color, or of sexual dispositions other than heterosexual). It was long possible to sidestep, neatly, such inconvenient political questions.

However, since the 1990s there has been much change, initially evident in Susan McClary's work, for example in her use of Bartók's *Bluebeard's Castle* as an analogy for her own relationship with music analysis:

> Just as Bartók's Judith discovers telltale traces of blood on the treasures in the first six chambers ... so I have always detected in music much more than I was given license to mention. To be sure, music's beauty is often overwhelming, its formal order magisterial. But the structures graphed by theorists and the beauty celebrated by aestheticians are often stained with such things as violence, misogyny and racism. And perhaps more disturbing still to those who would present music as autonomous and invulnerable, it also frequently betrays fear—fear of women, fear of the body.[2]

This fear—of the body, of excessive movement and sound, and their powers—becomes a leitmotif of this essay, although with attention to the subtle flow of traces of mediation between notes, movements, and meanings.[3]

It is not just feminism that was for so long ignored, but the political and racist implications of music and dance theory. As Snarrenberg demonstrates, the authority of one of the most recent "gods" of music analysis, Schenker, can only be sustained if his philosophies are seen as irrelevant.[4] Schenker's theories of the organic, biological dimension of music rely on conventional, but now highly controversial, ideas of "nature," as well as according a higher value to the male than the female.

A similar lack of sociopolitical awareness can be seen in dance theory. In the writings on movement and dance of Rudolf Laban, the underlying conceptual framework is just as important as the analytical ideas. A shift can be seen from romantic organicism to the pseudo-scientific "Labananalysis" that his followers developed.[5] For example, Valerie Preston-Dunlop, even in the most recent of her many publications on Laban, has promoted a view of his work that downplays the significance of his mystical beliefs as well as his Nazi involvement.[6]

Analytic concerns in music and dance that are relevant to this essay focus on vocabularies of sound and movement that might represent male and female characters, or more subtly, femininity and masculinity: a semiotics of gender as revealed in a set of conventions. I consider how sensuality and fluid gender identities might be evoked through images, sounds, and the discourses of these arts. Both music and dance have had to fight off charges of effeminacy or risk mockery, with the scientific detachment of abstraction through formalism seen as an attractive way out.[7] This position in its turn has been revised through poststructuralism not only in the arts but also within science revealing the gendered basis of supposedly impartial disciplines. As Spanier notes, gendered ideologies do far more than reflect society; they create and support dominant value systems, privilege, and deprivation.[8] The interface between these ideas and Lloyd Newson's *Strange Fish* is the subject of my analysis.

Possibly one of the most-cited phrases in poststructuralist dogma has been Jean-François Lyotard's "incredulity towards metanarratives," and it bears reiteration in this context in terms of the stories we tell ourselves.[9] Lyotard challenges the narrative construction of science as the only discourse that can legitimate itself. Science refuses to see disciplines that take a narrative form as anything other than "fables, myths, legends, fit only for women and children."[10] The very idea of musical narration—that it can connect with life in some significant way—is both seductive and problematic. Ideas of "true" and "false" are foreign to the discourse, musical meaning remains ambiguous. It can be argued, however, that other narrative domains, into which the arts seem apparently naturally to fall, are equally complex and equally "legitimate." In part this is what I de-objectify here.

Recent strands of dance and music theorizing have moved these disciplines on, albeit in a multitude of sometimes conflicting directions. John Shepherd, for example, argues that "as discursively constituted, music can evoke and refer to, give life to, our corporeal existence," and he makes quite precise links between physiological states and our interpretation of the world:

> Sound, the basis of music . . . reflects and articulates the internal physical properties, the movements, and the surface textures of the bodies that generate it. . . . it is further shaped by the structures, movements and surface textures of the physical objects that reflect it. Sound is shaped and shaping, structured and structuring.[11]

Other writers would focus more strongly on the cultural, rather than physical, construction of narrative. "Narrativity," in both dance and music, has to be understood as a metaphor, given that it is neither possible nor desirable to establish a one-to-one correspondence between movement or musical elements and dramatic events. As Abbate says of opera—and I would add that this is as relevant to dance—these stories are "denatured by fragmentation and nonsensical repetition" and are created to bear such acts.[12] Nonetheless, understanding these metaphors requires methods for tracing the mediation process between the creating of the product and the process of creating cultural meaning.

Lloyd Newson and DV8

Strange Fish, a piece made in 1992 by Lloyd Newson and his collaborators and later filmed for television, seems to invite analysis of a gender-conscious and narrative kind, despite the fact that its subject matter is neither dealt with in separate episodes nor in a single irreversible "story."[13] Events recur, each reiteration irrevocably changed by virtue of what has happened in between. *Strange Fish* hovers in angelic embodiment over the borders of expressionist theatre, heavily politicized by a gay male agenda, and contaminated by a view of women as sirens. Its themes are sometimes contradictory, but together they render the work capable of generating, and allow the reader to construct, a matrix of interlocking interpretations.

Strange Fish draws on massive and constantly recurring themes in Western culture, notably from Greek stories of sirens, Christian rituals and practices, particularly the crucifixion, and representational practices in music, dance, and the visual arts that have grown alongside these narratives (see Figure 6.1).[14] To be productive, approaches to the work have to draw on a vast range of "bodies of knowledge" and disciplines. A discussion of the siren figure illustrates their interlocking character and the intertextual nature of the methods applied in analysis.[15]

Newson's work, commonly referred to as Physical Theatre, sometimes as Visual Theatre, is often thought of as a hybrid of dance and theatre; it

Figure 6.1. *Strange Fish,* scene 1.

is visual, rich in movement, musical, and dramatic. Newson and his company, DV8 (deviate), have been credited with contributing to a revival of both theatre and dance practices in Europe through groundbreaking work.[16] Physical Theatre claims a European heritage that is distinctive from anything current in North America. The Expressionist theatre and modern dance movements of the early part of the twentieth century, matched by shifts in classical theatre and dance toward expressionistic treatments of traditional subject matter, are peculiarly European in character. Their focus on the intensity of emotion and the use of images, words, sound, and movement—separately and together—in dealing with personally and socially relevant issues, invokes politically intense, controversial subject matter.[17] Despite its European base, the issues that the work raises are as relevant to Australians and North Americans as to Europeans because we share much of the same (white, Greek-based, Christian) cultural history.

Lloyd Newson was born in 1957 in Australia and, while studying psychology, danced in an amateur group with release and improvisational interests.[18] Following a Dance Umbrella (London) appearance, Newson started his own group in 1986 as an independent collective with one of its stated aims "to re-invest meaning in dance." He has worked in Europe for some twenty-five years creating powerful sociopolitical pieces.[19] These works are generally created directly with digital technologies in collaboration with composers. Newson's meteoric rise to fame is reflected in the number of awards he has received, including the Prix Italia for the television version of *Strange Fish* with David Hinton, in 1994.[20]

Sensually Responsive Methodologies

How dance and music come to be adopted as metaphors is an interesting question. Dance stands for the play between life and death, between mortality and immortality, in its ability to contrast human frailty, grossness, and ugliness, with a technically exquisite, ethereal, and apparently transcendent bodily spirit. The essentially spiritual nature of Western views of dance is thus exposed, reinforced by its uses in early Christian religious practice to glorify God through metaphors such as the dance of the angels. Paradoxically, dance also represents fear, in the dance of death, and in the power of dance to provoke wickedness in the licentious practices of heretics and women, both drawing on and creating superstitious "pagan" belief.[21]

The disadvantage of such metaphorical speculation is that it denies the physicality, or reality, of dance and music and (dis)places them as "absent." Here I extend Abbate's argument about music directly to dancers' bodies, because it is not just the voice but the whole body that has suffered in these debates. The singing voice, however, is crucial in *Strange Fish*:

> Voice [movement] . . . has suffered some battering . . . through arguments that
> attempt to dislocate or disembody speaking subjects, in order to demonstrate
> how the subject is constituted through language. . . . But [dance and] music's
> voices, unlike the voices assumed to reside in written texts . . . cannot be
> summarily stilled in these terms . . . its own voices are stubborn . . . they
> manifest themselves . . . as different kinds or modes of music that inhabit a
> single work.[22]

Dance and music share this position because both are "live" arts, both
exist in the present as a physical and sensual force, as performance lodged
directly in the human form. In common with other arts theorists, I argue
that dance and music are radically unlike language, even while we might
recognize that language is a useful *analogy*, and even while acknowledging
the inescapably verbal constitution of dance and music discourse in
language systems. In Abbate's writings on music, and my own on dance,
the primacy of linguistic systems is denied; Abbate and I open up a more
complex relationship between these performed arts and social/linguistic
constructionism, in common with some versions of a semiotics of
performance.[23]

The specific methodological issue that has to be confronted here is that
of the appropriateness or validity of linking insights from anthropology,
religious history, and psychology with those from dance or music analysis.
The self-consciousness associated with deconstruction is useful to
contradict the coherence and completion of structuralism.[24] Deconstruction
acts as the "menace from within," an expression that itself rests on a
metaphor of light and dark, the founding metaphor of Western philosophy.[25] In *Strange Fish,* the menace is Wendy Houstoun, and she both
destroys and deconstructs the intentions of others, presenting the dark side
of human imagination.

Critical analysis tends to rest on common binaries such as tension/release
and attraction/repulsion, even toward the end of the twentieth century, and
these binaries are deeply dependent on a male/female dichotomy. The male,
as in myth, is always the active, creative force, and the female the opposite.
While this is often blindingly obvious at the level of the subject matter of
opera and ballet, it can be seen to operate widely, and also insidiously, within
the formal conventions of both dance and music.[26] As more and more
theories are constructed within a pluralist postmodern world, the choice
of methods becomes more, not less, problematic because justifications have
to be made for the use of particular approaches.

The once-fashionable practice of studying small groups of works under
"genre" labels fell foul to the poststructuralist pitfalls of elevating single
works to some kind of monolithic status. Defiantly, despite the difficulties

of installing too close a relationship between notes, movements, and meanings, I return to this idea to draw out the necessity of close reading. Walser, a theorist of heavy metal music writing on his own education recalls:

[A]s a musician, I cannot help but think that individual texts, and the social experiences they represent, are important. . . . I had to acquire the ability to recognize, distinguish, and deploy the musical possibilities organized in styles or genres by various communities. . . . [B]ecoming a musician . . . is a process of learning to understand and manipulate the differences intrinsic to a style, which are manifested differently in each text and performance.[27]

There are parallels in dance analysis in the early 1980s.[28] Ideas that have to be stated through any language, whether explicitly or by analogy, dancerly or musical, cannot escape. These dance and musical languages have technically specific vocabularies and physical counterparts that need to be subjected to meta-analysis.

A methodological parallel to my own study of *Strange Fish* can be found in a fascinating analysis of Philip Glass's *Akhnaten* by John Richardson.[29] Ranging from larger abstract issues to a close reading of the opera, from musicological detail to specific periods in history, in both archaeological and musical terms, he makes each directly relevant to, and reflective of, the other, never losing sight of the vivid experience of the music theatre it evokes.

A Parody of Gendered Excess

For the purposes of this essay, I concentrate on a brief extract from the 55-minute work *Strange Fish*. The fourth scene starts approximately 11 minutes into the video-recording of the work and lasts for 4.38 minutes. It follows the scene of religious observance with which the piece starts, and two scenes of a conversational kind between the actors/dancers conducted in movement and music. In Scenes 2 and 3, the performers jostle for position and make and break alliances, often along gendered lines.

Jocelyn Pook's music for Scene 4, created in collaboration with the performer Melanie Pappenheim, provides a striking contrast to earlier plainsong-based musical themes found in Scenes 1–3. Scene 4 presents the ecstatic and wild end of dance and music that speaks both "with and across the text" in layered narrations.[30] I give this scene the descriptive title "Sexual play, two against one (female-male)," but interpret it as "The blonde terrorists' duet."

Jordi Molina enters the empty bar where, with lighted candles placed one on each shoulder, he performs slow, curving, and sinking movements, arms held outstretched, reminiscent of a very elegant Spanish bull fighter or a Balinese dancer in a complex mixture of male sensuality and skill (see Figure 6.2). A whining cry, almost like a cat, and a "pssst" call the dreamy viewer to attention. The cry announces footsteps that, through rapid movement, enhance the rhythm of voices, as if feet and bodies could "chatter."

Surreptitiously, Wendy Houstoun and Lauren Potter slink around the door and enter the bar. They wear blonde wigs—shoulder length and fluffy for Lauren, straighter and shorter for Wendy—very short, shiny, silvery dresses, black tights, and shoes. They adjust their clothes, play with their hair, and admire each other before targeting Jordi Molina, circling him, and drawing him into their game (see Figure 6.3). It is a teasing game in which the women's repetition of unison movement and their canon-like phrases are much enhanced by the close-up camera action that conveys extremes of distraction and motion as the women swirl around him, beckon, insinuate, and seduce. Lauren and Wendy circle Jordi like animals moving in for the kill, drawing nearer and nearer to him. They are predatory, siren figures, and he cannot escape. This is the stuff of nightmares or satanic ritual practice (see Figure 6.4).

The women (in fact, Melanie Pappenheim's voice on pre-recorded tape) emit small high-pitched shrieks, almost as squeaks, starting quietly at first

Figure 6.2. Jordi Molina.

Figure 6.3. Wendy Houstoun seduces Jordi Molina.

Figure 6.4. Wendy Houstoun, Lauren Potter, and Jordi Molina.

and interspersed with sighs and silences. These pauses between events are themselves interrupted by an abrupt, repeated keyboard chord. The sirens mimic this vocal madness, creating their own version of "shrieks" in subtle and small shifts of parts of the body, often moving a small part out of alignment with the rest, as though commenting on the sound, and reflecting the paradoxical countertensions heard within it.

This virtuosic "blond terrorists" duet combines extremes of voices, movement, and film. It is based on the repetition of highly skilled, complex, fast movements, often arrested by pauses at unlikely moments that in turn stop the whirl and create vertigo for the observer.[31] Their threatening movement observes no known dance techniques or styles. The dancers move at high speed, rapidly changing level and direction, leaping high and rolling to the ground, splitting the body into parts. The directorial filming choices combine to fragment any phrase of movement just as the voices are fragmented by silence and intermittent, unrelated shrieks.

The singing voices, which initially mock each other with brief and varied phrases based on vocalizing "ooh" and "aah," develop into a series of repeated nasal chants in repetitions of "na." Cells are added and subtracted from rhythmic patterns across a huge vocal range and not "placed" in a particular pitch. These fragments of rhythm are given force by a syncopated pulsating beat. Changes in the density and complexity of the polyrhythmic fabric, from a thin texture of a single call to a multitude of voices and sounds in overlapping cycles, are echoed in the bodies; a single gesture becomes a whirl of complex movement rippling through a single body, then across two, and finally all three bodies.

These rhythmic cells alternate between patterns of three's and two's, giving an emphasis as though in triple time, then in duple time using the repeated exclamation: "**na** na na/ **na** na na/ **na** na/ **na** na// **na** na na/ **na** na na/ **naaaaaa**," overlaid with whoops and shrieks and footsteps. This changes to an "ooh ahh" construction, equally wordless but inviting surprise and excitement, as distinct from the more aggressive, nasally produced "na na" sounds: "ooee . . . ooee . . . ooee . . . **a** . . ./ ooee . . . ooee . . . **a** . . . **a**. . . ." The volume fades and increases in unpredictable fashion—creating further tension—layering dynamic textures onto this shifting ground. A bemused Jordi follows the women responding to them in turn as though they were animals in heat, until Wendy spitefully pulls Lauren's wig off. Silence and stillness, heavy with menace, reign (see Figure 6.5).

Lauren and Jordi, however, have made a different kind of contact, and she follows him down the corridor. Wendy brings up the rear, petulantly, no longer the prime mover. Finally the sound fades away into single voices, unpicks its own density, reveals its bare structures, and ends on a sighing "oohing" thread and occasional light keyboard chords.

Figure 6.5. Jordi Molina and Lauren Potter.

Sapphonic Cries

The overload and repetition of frantic calls, apparently arbitrary but with a strong enough structure in the vocal line to create a vibrant and threatening rhythmic pattern, compel the listener into the drama. For the Blonde Terrorists, this madness is not the excessive ecstasy of the diva in lyric opera. The staccato nature of the sound and the movement emphasizes discontinuities and reinscribes the action. The association is now with animal instinct, bare emotion, and hence demonic pleasures. Poizat's comment that language disappears and is "superseded by the cry" is directly relevant to this scene.[32] There are no real words here. The cry should instead be understood as a fully intentional progression from speech, to speech sung as language, to the detachment of the sound from language as it reaches the highest notes and culminates in the extreme upper ranges—it is at its most ecstatic when it is least intelligible.

As Poizat argues, voices can signify the transgression that is found in the "cry," where the voice expresses "a paroxysmal vocal emission beyond the range of music and out of the reach of the word."[33] Cries are not notated, neither are they exclamations of a particular word. Thus this scene of gender parody in *Strange Fish* is in every sense a potent and dangerous "cry." It follows scenes of pure and lyrical singing and adopts traces of it; but, like heavy metal, it also says that we have the freedom to respect "no love, no law, no responsibility," all the things our puritan ancestors fought against.[34] In Physical Theatre, as in opera, "the masquerade of gender, and aural delusion come together in an intricate web . . . challenged by perceptions of multiple voices, a dispersal of authority . . . [that lies] at the heart of transvestism."[35] Basing the argument in psychoanalytic theory, it might be said that Melanie's singing with herself is both schizophrenic and erotic, and thus can be constructed as a complex and multiply layered form of madness.

On one level, this "excess" is simply a reflection of the women's attempt to take control. To the extent that they succeed, they raise the fear referred to at the start of this essay. But the terrorists' intentions are subverted by the very evident contribution of David Hinton, the director, and by implication, Lloyd Newson himself. Distortion is critical to the filming. As Houstoun and Potter tease Molina, darting around him with light, playful movements, the camera, by close focus techniques, directs the reader's attention very specifically to faces and body parts to whirling hair and complicit smiles. The singing voices contain faint echoes of an earlier musical theme which I call the Siren song, perhaps in ironic commentary, before high-pitched female chattering, giggling, and laughter take over.

The viewer's sense of location in space, like Molina's in the middle of the action, is utterly lost as the dancers whirl across the screen unpredictably, sometimes appearing from behind the camera as well as from the sides. Molina's evident confusion about what is real and what is illusion poignantly reinforces the message of the movement text. The apparently harmless, teasing message is made menacing by being filmed so close up, and the perpetrators seem completely mad. The camera forces the reader to see these events through particular eyes, both by its perspective and by bringing faces and movement in and out of focus. Dislocation, rather than rootedness, is a direct consequence of these video techniques.[36] The wildness of women is evoked rather than serious questioning of gender roles through the music/sound and the movement/dance, which draw attention to the body that produces them. Where the body lacks the physical attributes associated with the particular sound or movement, the discrepancy opens up questions of maleness and femaleness.[37] The voices in *Strange Fish* are the subversive voices of women.

At the climax of this scene, the excessively high soprano voices (which may also transgress to resemble deeper contralto sounds) challenge the way the dominant gender order is normally manifest in musical melody. Ellizabeth Wood's theory of the voice is based on the constructs of sexual preference. She points to the disturbing effects of big, strong female voices of unusual range such as a chest sound or baritone quality that speaks of masculinity, a falsetto voice in a male, and the high "uncannily queer lost sound of a castrato or male falsetto . . . [or] a sexless boy chorister" where the voice seems to be outside the body.[38]

Within these cultural traces can be found others that echo conflicting attitudes toward the female body. On the one hand, the eroticism and sexual power of the female is evident, tracing a particular kind of stereotype directly juxtaposed with another, that of female vulnerability, naiveté, and purity: whore and virgin, the ever-present tension for women. The sexual identity crisis that *Strange Fish* recalls is one where male, female, and transsexual biological identities are compounded by choices in terms of gender identity. In this way, I position the singing in Scene 4 a long way from the highly controlled declamation and enunciation of traditional theatre. It is also a long way from the sacred plainsong-based sections in *Strange Fish,* but still makes reference to them through fragments of the same angelic melodies, just as fragments of the women's movement appear again.

Example 6.1. Melodic fragments in Strange Fish.[39]

There is a fully recognized eroticism created in the singing, particularly where Melanie Pappenheim sings with herself on pre-recorded tracks, whether in the angelic phrases of the earlier scenes or in Scene 4 referred to here. This use of counterpoint creates a crossing of borders that Wood calls "sapphonic," offering "a space of a lesbian possibility, for a range of erotic and emotional relationships among women who sing and women who listen. . . . It is characteristically powerful and problematic, defiant and defective."[40]

For Wood, this "integration of sameness and difference in one solo and undivided voice" is hugely seductive.[41] Melanie Pappenheim accomplishes this by singing both the melodic lines, while the two soprano voices heard together deny the culturally dominant male/female pairing found in representations of love, ecstasy, and conflict. Whether realized by two castrati voices, or two women, in a situation where two *equal* voices work together but at the extremes, such pairings evoke the terror of gay/lesbian difference, and thus are doubly subversive. These voices work with and against Melanie Pappenheim's actions. By analogy, the vertical chords of harmonies accompanying these narrative melodic lines provoke an excess of fugal intoxication.

Conclusion

If it is possible to parody gender, then gender itself can be constructed as a kind of performance under the witting control of the participant. It is a style with particular gestures, positions, and modes of speaking in which known codes are traded against new contexts where they would not normally appear. From the point of view of gender politics, what Lloyd Newson's setting and David Hinton's filming tells the reader is that the events of *Strange Fish* are disastrous, not something to be celebrated. Women are still not seen in a positive light or able to take control of their own lives, neither does it open up existing constructs to greater flexibility since the outcome that the work depicts, ultimately, is Christ's death and Wendy's utter isolation. On this basis, it is possible to question whether Newson dismantles the homo-hetero sexual hierarchy or simply retrenches, as Diana Fuss's work might suggest. The "imaginative enactment of sexual redefinitions" is sadly lacking.[42] If Lloyd Newson's political aims are reasonable, then support might be found in Sue-Ellen Case's point that retaining referents to the outside world, and refusing the poststructuralist dissolution of identity, is vital.[43]

Lloyd Newson's choice of mythic material is highly significant and an unavoidable clue to interpretation. The fit between his material and his treatment of it makes the theme of misogyny inescapable. As Morris argues, it may be that powerful theatrical and musical forms are attractive because they offer the chance to identify with so-called illegitimate meanings without in fact disrupting heterosexual male values.[44] This is not peculiar to *Strange Fish;* opera and some forms of contemporary dance—as well as Physical Theatre—frequently become the crucial locus for these issues. *Strange Fish* is a striking example of both this conflation of ideas and of the power of theatre, music, and dance.

Notes

1. The theoretical perspective that I adopt is drawn from readings of Roland Barthes *Image, Music, Text* (London: Fontana, 1977); Umberto Eco *The Role of the Reader* (Bloomington: Indiana University Press, 1979, 1984); Marco de Marinis *The Semiotics of Performance* (Bloomington: Indiana University Press, 1993); and, most particularly Michael Worton and Judith Still, eds. *Intertextuality: Theories and Practices* (Manchester: Manchester University Press, 1990). A more detailed account of an intertextual methodology applied to dance studies can be found in the first chapter of Janet Adshead-Lansdale, ed. *Dancing Texts: Intertextuality in Interpretation* (London: Dance Books, 1999).
2. Susan McClary, *Feminine Endings: Music, Gender and Sexuality* (Minneapolis: University of Minnesota Press, 1991), 4.
3. McClary, in opening up a greater range of possibilities of meaning that music may

evoke, has been criticized, as poststructuralist music analysis has evolved further, but at the time her work was a vital spur to reworking ideas of meaning.

4. Robert Snarrenberg traces the American abandonment of Schenker's organicism where attempts to take his theoretical constructions independent of their conceptual basis are exposed, in Craig Ayrey and Mark Everist, eds. *Analytical Strategies and Musical Interpretation: Essays on Nineteenth and Twentieth Century Music* (Cambridge: Cambridge University Press), 1996.

5. See for example Irmgard Bartenieff, et al. "The Potential of Movement Analysis as a Research Tool: A Preliminary Analysis," *Dance Research Journal* 16, no. 11 (1984): 3–26.

6. Valerie Preston Dunlop, *An Extraordinary Life* (London: Dance Books, 1999); and Lilian Karina and Marion Kant *Tanz Unterm Hakenkreuz* 1996; 1999; and Carol-Lynne Moore, "The Choreutic Theory of Rudolf Laban," (Ph.D. thesis, University of Surrey, 1999).

7. However, the position of dance scholarship is very different from that of music. Ignored and deprecated as an art for women or queers, its largely female exponents and theorists have been grateful to be noticed, only to be taken over and appropriated often for male, often queer, purposes.

8. Bonnie Spanier points to "actual males and females . . . whose actions contradict predominant stereotypes" in *Impartial Science: Gender Ideology in Molecular Biology* (Bloomington: Indiana University Press, 1995), preface.

9. Jean-Francois Lyotard, *The Postmodern Condition: A Report on Knowledge* (Manchester: Manchester University Press, 1979; trans. 1984), xxiv.

10. Lyotard, *The Postmodern Condition*, 27.

11. Quoted in Ruth Solie, *Musicology and Difference: Gender and Sexuality in Music Scholarship* (Berkeley: University of California Press, 1993), 51–52.

12. Carolyn Abbate, *Unsung Voices* (Princeton: Princeton University Press, 1991), 68.

13. Lloyd Newson and David Hinton, *Strange Fish* (BBC/RM Arts), 1994.

14. Photographic images are taken from the video of *Strange Fish* and used by permission of BBC/RM Associates.

15. This essay is a version of part of a book-length discussion of interpretative strategies focused around an analysis of *Strange Fish*, in preparation 2000.

16. Along with a small group of companies, including Theatre de Complicité.

17. As in the work of de Valois for the ballet in England.

18. Newson came to the UK in 1980, studied briefly at the London School of Contemporary Dance and joined Extemporary Dance Theatre in 1981. There he produced a company piece alongside another newly emerging, and equally controversial, choreographer, Michael Clark. See Jan Parry, "Outside Dance," *Dance Theatre Journal* 8, no. 3 (1990): 43.

19. Writings on Newson's works are not plentiful and are mainly found in newspapers and journals. A small number are referred to here, see Nadine Meisner "Strange Fish" *Dance and Dancers* (July 1992): 10–13; Lloyd Newson on "Strange Fish," *Dance and Dancers* (July 1992): 10–13; and DV8 Packs 1 and 2 (Arts Admin, Toynbee Studios, 28 Commercial Street, London, E1 6LS); and Jan Parry, "Strange Fish," *Dance Now* 1, no. 3 (1992): 22–27.

20. Lloyd Newson and DV8 have received more than ten awards since 1987, including the Evening Standard Ballet Award in 1989 and the Frankfurt Dance Screen award in 1990, both for Dead Dreams of Monochrome Men, and the Digital Dance Production Award for Dance in 1991. A brief introduction to their work can be found in Alan Robertson and Donald Hutera, *The Dance Handbook* (London: Longman 1988), 236–37, and in the Choreographer Fact Card: Lloyd Newson (1956-) (National Resource Centre for Dance, University of Surrey, Guildford, Surrey, GU2 5XH).

21. The literature on this theme is not extensive, from the dance point of view, but a useful survey can be found in E. L. Backman, *Religious Dances in the Christian Church and in Popular Medicine* (London: Allen and Unwin, 1952).

22. Abbate, *Unsung Voices*, 12.

23. See de Marinis, *The Semiotics of Performance*.

24. See Adshead, ed. *Dance Analysis: Theory and Practice* (London: Dance Books, 1988) and *Dancing Texts*. Anthony Pople, on the same problem in music, reflects on the development of "analysis itself as a kind of theory through which a range of possible meanings can be described, prescribed or circumscribed. At the same time, and perhaps ironically, the interpenetration of analysis and theory—so evident in the explicitly scientistic wave—has revealed theory, too, as a construction." *Theory, Analysis, and Meaning in Music* (Cambridge: Cambridge University Press, 1993), x.

25. Naomi Cumming in Ayrey and Everist, *Analytic Strategies*, 26.

26. Susan McClary's exposition in *Feminine Endings* of the same narrative paradigms operating in absolute or abstract music in terms of the trajectory of keys and other formal features challenged accepted views and has in its turn been critiqued as essentialist.

27. Robert Walser *Running with the Devil: Power, Gender, and Madness in Heavy Metal Music* (Hanover and London: Wesleyan University Press, 1993), xii.

28. See Adshead, *Dance Analysis*.

29. John Richardson, *Singing Archaeology: Phillip Glass's Akhnaten* (Hanover and London: Wesleyan University Press, 1999).

30. Abbate, *Unsung Voices*, xiv.

31. My references here are solely to the video version. Since image and sound are so closely intertwined, it would make no sense to refer to the stage recording.

32. Michel Poizat, *The Angel's Cry: Beyond the Pleasure Principle in Opera*, trans. Arthur Denner (Ithaca, N.Y.: Cornell University Press, 1992), 37.

33. Poizat, *The Angel's Cry*, 76.

34. Robert Walser, *Running with the Devil*, 52.

35. Abbate, qtd. in Solie, ed. *Musicology and Difference*, 229.

36. A discussion of the changes which arise from filming dance and a description of DV8's work for video can be found in Sarah Rubidge's, "DV8 Physical Theatre on Television," in Stephanie Jordan and David Allen, *Parallel Lines* (Arts Council of Great Britain, 1993), 204–7.

37. Abbate, in *Musicology and Difference*, intriguingly uses analysis of the modern film *Mascara* (1978) to reveal entangled motifs, from vocal characteristics to political purposes, to show how together they can question received positions. In her example, the archetypal female Salome is revealed as male, a nice inversion of Christ in *Strange Fish*.

38. Ellizabeth Wood in Phillip Brett, et al., *Queering the Pitch: The New Gay and Lesbian Musicology* (New York: Routledge, 1994), 31. McClary identifies Schubert's homosexuality with musical techniques that challenge prevailing narratives of a conventional kind, thus deflecting and exploring other ideas freely instead of driving to a conclusion—creating ambiguity, yielding to pleasure—notably feminine attributes as conventionally constructed. Drifting and oblique modulations between keys seem to open up alternative narratives.

39. Musical illustration created for this purpose by Dr. S. Goss and used with his permission. I am grateful also for his advice on musical matters.

40. Wood, in *Queering the Pitch*, 27–28.

41. Wood, in *Queering the Pitch*, 36–37.

42. Diana Fuss, *Inside/Out: Lesbian Theories, Gay Theories* (New York: Routledge, 1991).

43. Sue-Ellen Case, *The Domain-Matrix: Performing Lesbian at the End of Print Culture* (Bloomington: Indiana University Press, 1996).

44. Morris, in *Musicology and Difference*, 192.

7

Heroism Undone

The Erotic Manuscript Parodies
of Jean-Baptiste Lully's *Tragédies en Musique*

Catherine Gordon-Seifert

In late-seventeenth-century France, political erotica emerged as a means of dislodging myths of heroism promoted by Louis XIV.[1] Found in a number of manuscript sources and in a few published works, political erotica attacked the King and anyone associated with the royal body, including courtiers, the King's doctors, military leaders, and favored artists of all kinds. By using subjects related to sex, these works challenged and undermined the language of heroism advocated by Louis XIV.[2] Two specific genres of political erotica were literary and musical parodies, hereafter referred to as erotic parodies. Government-sanctioned works of art were were often erotic parodic objects because they served as the very tools of propaganda that promoted images of the King as hero. It is not surprising that after 1673, authors found Jean-Baptiste Lully's *tragédies en musique* as suitable works to parody. The operas not only reflected the King's vision of heroism as an extension of his own person, they were also extremely popular and well-known to audiences whose social worlds never intersected directly with that of King and court.[3]

The erotic parodies of Lully's *tragédies en musique* are not to be confused with the better-known collections published at the end of the seventeenth century and performed at the Ancien Théâtre Italien.[4] Erotic parodies differ from these and other types in their use of sexually explicit language and subjects. Many are found in a manuscript collection entitled *Chansonnier Maurepas*, named after an aristocrat who, during the eighteenth century, paid to have opera parodies (among other works) copied into beautifully bound, neatly written volumes, now housed at the Bibliothèque Nationale in Paris.[5] Fifty parodies of Lully's *tragédies lyriques*, authors unidentified, are included in five volumes of the Maurepas manuscripts, dating from 1673 to 1696; of these, thirteen are erotic.[6]

The erotic parodies of Lully's works found in the Maurepas manuscripts include a variety of songs, dances, and scenes from *Alceste, Atys, Bellérophon, Roland, Amadis,* and *Acis et Galatée.* I have chosen to analyze one of the most extended parodies: the parody of Act 2, scenes 6 and 7, of *Bellérophon,* which targets a courtier named Marie de Bautru, the widow of the Marquis Charles de Rambure.[7] This is not only the longest, most detailed parody found in the collection, it is also the most sexually explicit and the only one that directly focuses on women.

The parodied scenes from *Bellérophon* are among the most memorable in the opera. Seventeenth-century audiences, who knew them well, perhaps even by heart, would have fully understood the meaning and humor of the parody in relation to the original.[8] My analysis focuses on the multitextual synthesis of original scenes, parody texts, dramatic function, and musical expression as multiples of parodic objectives. This particular example demonstrates better than any other how the original meaning of Lully's music, composed to represent a specific text—in this case, magicians conjuring monsters from the underworld—could be reinterpreted to convey new meaning. Here, the original context is transformed into representations relating to sexual acts.

Whether or not Lully composed his music with any direct references to sexuality, it clearly inspired just such an interpretation, the parody text readily making explicit the sexual implications of Lully's musical setting in these scenes. So doing, the parody underscores the notion that Lully's music could be dangerously provocative. Critics of Lully's operas warned that the sounds of his music could kindle the "flames of love" in women, leading to infidelity, deviant sexual behavior, and even madness.[9] This particular parody also demonstrates how humorous references to sex, in text and music, were used to attack nobles at court, targeting their private parts, their passions, and their obsession with heroic images, attacks ultimately directed at the hypocrisy and immorality that many associated with Louis XIV's reign.

Many scholars have studied the attempt by Louis XIV and his ministers, particularly Jean-Baptiste Colbert, to elevate the King's person and to present a vision of the monarch as omniscient and invincible.[10] This glorified and heroic image of the King was projected in a variety of media: in literary sources, paintings, monuments, sculptures, theater productions, ballets, and operas.[11] The King was particularly compared to and associated with mythological gods and heroes. In these allegories, Louis was given the valor of Mars, the wisdom of Minerva, and the strength of Hercules. Artists also likened him to Jupiter, Neptune, or Apollo. His image was often described or shown with a phallic-shaped scepter, sword, or baton in hand as symbols of authority and virility.

The connection between power, masculinity, and sexual prowess provided the primary mode of attack for authors of erotic parodies. Although many sources of political erotica assaulted the King himself, the erotic opera parodies targeted those closest to him. Every parody included in the Maurepas manuscript collection is accompanied by commentary that identifies and explains the people and events to which the texts refer. Most erotic parodies targeted male courtiers, and most used venereal disease, impotence, and sodomy to attack violations of proper heroic and masculine conduct.[12] During the seventeenth century, a man's sexual function was viewed as both a private and a social matter.[13] Within marriage, sex existed for procreation to benefit family and state. Behavior identified as sexual excess, whether with prostitutes or homosexuals, was thought to lead eventually to sexual inadequacy, either physically, from contracting syphilis, which caused impotence, or psychologically, from a disinterest in women.[14] Deviant sexual behavior compromised fundamental moral and social laws that affected the health and well-being of family and state. Erotic parodies that accused courtiers of sexual malfunction underscored the hypocrisy of nobles who sought to personify an heroic image.

Like all such parodies, that of *Bellérophon* attacks courtiers, but unlike most examples, it targets women at court, specifically a widow and her entourage. The parody has two important features in common with Lully's opera: the main character is a widow and she is represented in an un-complimentary manner. Both parody and opera reflect misogynous attitudes toward widows, yet the opera clearly differentiates between the widowed, morally corrupt protagonist, Stenobée, and the high-minded, righteous hero, Bellérophon. By contrast, the parody directly attacks a widow and her entourage of women and only indirectly, men at court, presenting no honorable male character. Even while underscoring female sexual appetite, it reflects, nonetheless, on masculine sexual inadequacy, specifically the brutality, impotence, or disinterest associated with the King's men in many prose and poetic sources of political erotica. Several from the Maurepas manuscripts, including two opera parodies, refer directly to this phenomenon: men at court were interested in every other form of sexual relations except those with their female counterparts.

In the original opera by Lully and librettist Thomas Corneille, Stenobée, a widow of the deceased King of Argos, is infatuated with the young hero, Bellérophon. He, however, is in love with Philonoe, the daughter of the present King, and she returns his affection. After a celebration of the young couple's engagement, Stenobée, the widow, reveals her passion to Bellérophon, but he is repulsed by her advances. In her anger, she summons a magician who loves her, Amisodar, to help her seek vengeance. Amisodar summons up a terrifying monster from the underworld to destroy both Bellérophon and the land of Argos. Ever the hero, Bellérophon volunteers to destroy the monster even though he is sure he will die. What he does not know is that he is the son of Neptune and object of an oracle that claims he will defeat the monster and marry the Princess. With the aid of Pallas, Bellérophon obliterates the monster and marries Philonoe at the end of the opera.

The parody reworks Act 2, scenes 6 and 7, of the opera, wherein Amisodar summons his fellow magicians to conjure up the monster. In the parody, a sex-starved widow summons "prostitutes," the daughters and wives of important nobles, to help her conjure up a monstrous penis from hell. The parody, then, substitutes the male magician with a female widow, a group of male magicians with servants of a brothel, and a monster with a gigantic penis.

The widow in the parody does not replace just any ordinary man, but rather she supplants a male magician who executes magical spells and incantations. Widows were often portrayed in literary works as witches or women with special, bewitching powers that could turn an orderly world, ruled by men, into chaos.[15] In the opera, the monster conjured up by the magician at the command of a widow turns Argos into a horrific land of desolation, destroying almost all of its citizens and the countryside. In the parody, the monster is a giant penis, conjured up and controlled by a widow. Such a situation, too, could turn a world upside down.

The connection between widows, specifically, and females, generally, with magicians in both opera and parody likens these women to witches.[16] Indeed, females, and especially widows, were thought of as the weaker sex and more likely than men to exhibit unrestrained passions and desire, and thus prone to reject Christian faith and become witches.[17] Although images of the sorceress throughout Europe varied according to region and country, certain traits were commonly attributed to most. Witchcraft, or the capacity to bewitch, demonstrated perverse power over legitimate authority, and many convicted witches were widows who were accused of engaging in antisocial behavior that threatened the establishment.[18] Witchcraft often took the form of vengeful acts, such as the destruction of property and crops or causing illnesses and death.[19] Witches were frequently accused of engaging in sexually perverse activities, such as seducing other women's husbands or having sex with the devil and animals.

All of these common manifestations of the sorceress are evident in opera and parody. Although Stenobée is never accused of being a witch in the opera, she behaves like one. She attempts to take control of Bellerophon, but when he refuses her, she becomes vengeful and turns to magic (the magician) to help her retaliate by devastating the countryside in an attempt to kill the hero.[20] Yet unlike the implied connection between Stenobée and witchcraft in the opera, La Rambure, in the parody, becomes a witch; she replaces the magician and engages in perverted sexual activity. The gathering of La Rambure and her entourage of young women is not unlike a witches' sabbath with frenetic dancing and copulation with the devil himself. The parody scenes and the following description of a sabbath from 1613 present similar narratives: "to dance indecently, to banquet filthily, to couple diabolically, to sodomize execrably, to blaspheme scandalously, to pursue brutally every horrible, dirty and unnatural desire...."[21] The monstrous penis in the parody could be construed as that of the devil as it ascends from the underworld. The night, darkness, black (the color of the devil's bodily organs), and the creation of a diabolical "antiworld" in the parody are all images readily associated with witches and their defiance of cosmic order.[22]

In addition to the portrayal of widow as witch, the representation of La Rambure as a male character, particularly one who is sexually frustrated, underscores an anxiety directed at widows in general. Widows posed a specific and real threat to men in early modern Europe. Still second-class citizens, widows were, nonetheless, the closest women could get to enjoying many of the privileges reserved for men. By law, widows had rights that no other women had, namely, the right to manage property, make contracts, and remarry without parental intervention.[23] During the reign of Louis XIV, the number of widows grew as military activity intensified, and the more widows there were, the greater the threat to the patriarchal system promoted and enforced by the monarch.

Young widows were especially problematic. Many young girls, even as young as twelve, were married off to older men. Thus it was conceivable that a woman, still in the prime of her life, could be left a widow. Young widows potentially were not only powerful, but lustful. They had had, after all, a taste of the forbidden fruit. During the reign of Louis XIV, however, widows found it more and more difficult to exercise their legal rights. If a husband died before her twenty-fifth birthday, the young wife could not exercise any freedom but remained under the rule of her father, losing all her husband's assets. Strict codes of conduct for mourning widows also curtailed a widow's autonomy. She had to wear black, was expected to be pious, and had to wait at least a year before remarrying. Widows were urged to become nuns since the next best thing to virginity was a celibate life pledged to God.[24]

Women of any age were thought of as having voracious sexual appetites. From antiquity to the late eighteenth century, females were seen as the sexual aggressors, and men the more level-headed participant in sexual acts.[25] Since widows were acquainted with sex, they were considered all the more dangerous. Older widows (usually those over forty years old) were not likely to remarry, and yet, libidos aroused, were thought most likely to exhibit an ungoverned lust.[26] Add to that the potential for greater legal rights and freedoms afforded older (and richer) widows, those usually reserved for men, and widows seemed all the more likely to disrupt social order.

The apparent potential of widows (the witches) to cause societal disorder is featured in both opera and parody. The following comparison of the original scenes of the opera with the parody reveals the close links between the two.[27]

Maurepas Ms. Fr. 12620, Vol. 5, # 223

1682. Parodie de la VIe et VIIe Scene du IIe Acte de l'Opera Bellérophon, *où l'auteur introduit Marie de Bautru veuve de Charles de Rambures accompagnée d'un choeur des Maquerelles de la butte St. Roch, et des servantes de Bordel, et invoquant des Putains pour evoquer des Enfers un vit monstreux pour son usage. Le Dialogue est entre Elle, et le choeur des Servantes.*

1682. Parody of the 6th and 7th scene of Act 2 of the opera Bellérophon, *where the author introduces Marie de Bautru, widow of Charles de Rambures, accompanied by a choir of "madames" of la butte St. Roch, and the servants of the brothel, and invoking prostitutes to evoke from the underworld a monstrous cock for her use. The dialogue is between her and the choir of servants.*

Scene 6

Amisodar (Opera)

La Rambure (Parody)

1. Que ce jardin ce change en un desert affreux.
   Let this garden change into a hideous desert

1. Que ce Palais se change en un bordel affreux
   Let this palace change into a hideous brothel

2. Noirs habitans du sejour tenebreux,
   Dark inhabitants of the shadowy resting place,

2. Vieilles Putains de ce quartier fameux,
   Old whores of this infamous district,

3. Pour m'écouter dans vos demeures sombres
   In order to hear me in your somber residences

3. Pour écouter mes impudiques Farces,
   In order to hear my obscene farces

4. Redoublez, s'il se peut le silence des sombres;
   Increase, if you can, the silence of the shadows

4. Arestés s'il se peut le cultis de vos garces,
   Stop, if you can, the movement of your prostitutes' asses,

5. Et vous à me servir employez tant de fois,
   And you, employed in my service so many times,

5. Et vous, à me servir employées tant de fois,
   And you, employed in my service so many times,

6. Ministres de mon art accourez à ma voix.
   Ministers of my art, hurry, come when I call you.

6. Servantes de bordel, accourez à ma voix.
   Servants of the brothel, hurry, come when I call you.

SCENE 7

Magiciens	*Choeur de Servantes*
7. Parle, nous voila prests, tout nous sera possible. Speak, we are ready now, all will be possible for us.	7. Parle, nous voila prests, tout nous sera possible. Speak, we are ready now, all will be possible for us.

Amisodar	*La Rambure*
8. Faisons sortir un Monstre horrible, Let us make a horrible monster appear,	8. Faisons sortir un vit terrible Let us make a terrible cock appear
9. Pour l'évoquer employez l'Acheron, In order to evoke it, call upon Acheron	9. Pour l'evoquer employés la Teron, In order to evoke it, call upon La Teron[28]
10. Le Cocyte, Le Phlegeton, Cocytus, Phlegethon	10. La Royan, La Rane, La Broon, La Royan, La Rane, La Broon[29]
11. Faites que vostre voix dans tout l'Enfer raisonne, Make your voice resound throughout all of Hell	11. Faites que votre voix chez les Fertés raisonne, Make your voice resound at the home of the Fertés[30]
12. C'est moy qui vous l'ordonne. It is I who orders it of you.	12. Rambure vous l'ordonne. Rambure orders it of you.

Magiciens	*Choeur de Servantes*
13. Par ce pressant commandement, By this pressing command,	13. Pour ce C[ons] si large et si grand, For this c[unt] so wide and big,
14. Par ce pressant commandement, By this pressing command,	14. Par ce pressant commandement, By this pressing command,
15. Promptement promptement; Quickly, quickly,	15. Promptement promptement; Quickly, quickly,
16. Que le Tenare s'ouvre, Let Tenare open up,	16. Que les plus longs s'empressent, Hurry, longest ones,
17. Que l'Enfer se décourvre, Let Hell expose itself,	17. Que les plus gros parroissent; Appear biggest ones;
18. Que le Tenare s'ouvre, que l'Enfer se découvre, Let Tenare open up, let Hell expose itself,	18. La Royan, La Teron, il nous faut du secours, La Royan, La Teron, you must help us,
19. Cocyte, Phlegeton, il nous faut du secours, Cocytus, Phlegethon, you must help us,	19. La Royan, La Teron, il nous faut du secours, La Royan, Le Teron, you must help us,
20. Pour nous entendre arrestez vostre cours. In order to hear us, stop running.	20. Pour nous entendre, arrestés de vos culs le trop rapide cours. In order to hear us, stop the excessive pace of your asses.

Amisodar

21. Pousuivez, Que pour moy vostre
pouvoir éclate,
Continue, let your power shine,

22. Par Cerbere et la triple Hecate,
By Cerberus and the triple
Hecate,

23. Parlez, pressez, appellez à grand bruit
Speak, hurry, call loudly,

24. Et la mort et la nuit.
Both death and night

Magiciens

26. Nuit, mort, Cerbere, Hecate, Erebe,
Averne,
Night, death, Cerberus, Hecate,
Erebus, Avernus,

27. Noires filles du Stix que la fureur
gouverne,
Black girls of Styx who are governed
by Fury

28. Entendez nos cris, servez-nous,
Hear our cries, help us,

29. Nous travaillons pour vous.
We work for you.

Amisodar

30. Le charme est fait, les monstres vont
paroistre,
The spell is cast, the monsters are
going to appear,

31. La terre s'ouvre et me le fait
connoistre;
The earth opens up and makes it
known to me;

32. Rendons auz sombres Deïtez,
Let us surrender to the gods of the
shadows,

33. Les honneurs que de nous elles ont
meritiez,
The honors they deserve from us,

Magiciens

34. La terre nous ouvre
The earth opens up for us

35. Ses goufres profonds,
Its deep chasms,

La Rambure

21. Poursuivés, qu'a mes voeux tout votre
soin s'aplique
Continue, take care to follow my wishes

22. Par La Baume, et son front lubrique;
By La Baume and her lecherous front
side;

23. Pressés, parlés, appellés a grand bruit
Hurry, speak, call loudly

24. La Chaulieu et d'Alluy.
La Chaulieu and d'Alluy[31]

Choeur de Servantes

26. Comtesse de Grammont, Thiange,
Lenclos, d'Olonne,
Countess of Grammont, Thiange,
Lenclos, d'Olonne[32]

27. Vielle et noire Bregny, et vous [?]
Lionne[33]
Old and dark Bregny, and you
Lionne[34]

28. Entendés nos pleurs et nos cris,
Hear our tears and our screams,

29. Nous demandons des lis.
We demand beds.

La Rambure

30. Le charme est fait, le vit montre sa
teste,
The spell is cast, the cock shows its
head,

31. Mon front qui souvre a l'engloutir sa
preste,
My front side which opens up prepares
to swallow it,

32. Rendons a ce vit souhaite,
Let us surrender to this desired
cock

33. Les honneurs qui sont deus à son
imancité.
The honors that are owed its enormity.

Choeur de Servantes

34. Que la Rambure ouvre,
Let La Rambure open (up)

35. Son gouffre profond
Her deep chasm

36. L'Enfer se découvre:
   The Underworld reveals itself:

37. Chantons, triomphons,
   Let us sing, let us triumph

38. On void l'onde noire
   One sees the black wave

39. Pour nous s'arrester.
   Stop for us.

40. Victoire, Nous avons la gloire
   Victory, we have the glory

41. De tout surmonter,
   Of surmounting everything,

42. Triomphe, Victoire,
   Triumph, victory,

43. Nous avons la gloire
   We have the glory,

44. De tout surmonter,
   Of surmounting everything,

45. Non, rien ne peut nous resister.
   No, nothing can resist us.

36. Le vit se découvre.
   The cock reveals itself.

37. Grands Dieux qu'il est long.
   Great gods, how long it is

38. Que sa couille est noire,
   How black its testicle is

39. Qu'il est souhaité,
   How desired it is,

40. Victoire, elle aura la gloire,
   Victory, she will have the glory

41. De le surmonter,
   Of surmounting it;

42. Triomphe Victoire,
   Triumph, victory,

43. Elle aura la gloire
   She will have the glory

44. De le surmonter,
   Of surmounting it,

45. Jamais vit n'a pu lui resister.
   No cock has ever been able to resist her.

Amisodar

46. Un Monstre seul causeroit plus
   d'effroy,
   One monster alone would cause more
   terror

47. Il faut unir ces trois Monstres
   ensemble.
   The three monsters must be united
   together.

48. Par un charme plus fort & plus digne
   de moy,
   By a charm stronger and more worthy
   than I,

49. Faisons qu'un seul corps les assemble,
   Let us make them into a single body,

50. Pour en venir à bout descendons aux
   Enfers,
   In order to make it happen let us
   descend into the ends of Hell.

51. Les gouffres nous en sont ouverts.
   The chasms are open to us.

La Rambure

46. Un vit tout seul seroit trop peu pour
   moy,
   One cock alone would be too small for
   me

47. Il n'en est point d'une trempe si
   dure,
   There are none so hard,

48. A l'aspect de mon front qui ne
   tremble d'affroy,
   That they don't tremble in fear at the
   sight of my front side

49. Il en faut trois pour ma nature,
   Three are necessary for my inclination

50. Je vais les assembler pour en faire un
   parfais,
   I am going to assemble them (all three)
   to make a perfect one,

51. Qui tienne beaucoup du Mulet.
   Which very much resembles a
   mule's.

Throughout the parody, women's spaces are likened to the dark and evil underworld. In line 1 of the opera/parody text, for example, a garden turned into a desert by a magician in the opera is replaced, in the parody, by a palace turned into a brothel by the frustrated widow. Like Eve in the Garden of Eden, a woman, either by taking control of a man, as in the opera, or by using her own bewitching forces, as in the parody, destroys innocence and changes beautiful, protected places into hostile and evil habitats; the desert, in the opera, an environmental wasteland, is linked with the moral wasteland of the brothel, in the parody. In line 2, the shadowy resting place, in the opera, is connected to the infamous districts of prostitution, and in line 11, the parody equates the home of the Fertés, a prominent and wealthy noble family closely connected to Louis XIV, with the underworld.

Throughout the parody, women and prostitutes are likened to magicians, evil beings, or witches, along with specific areas in the underworld. In many lines, there is an intriguing juxtaposition between seventeenth-century perceptions of magic (witches), pornography, brothels, prostitutes, and ancient mythological images. In line 6, ministers of the art of magic, in the opera, correlate with servants of the brothel, in the parody. In line 2, dark inhabitants, in the opera, are linked to old whores, in the parody. In lines 9 and 10, the parody likens specific noble women to mythological rivers of the underworld, from the opera. In line 22, the noble woman, La Baume, is linked with Cerberus, the dog with three heads and a serpent's tail who guards the underworld, and her "lecherous front side" with Hecate, the triple-headed goddess associated with witchcraft, ghosts, and magic of the underworld. In line 24, two noble women, La Chaulieu and d'Alluy, are connected with death and night, respectively, and in line 26, other noble women are linked with Erebus, a section of the underworld through which the souls of the dead must pass, and Avernus, the entrance to the infernal regions. Finally, in line 27, black girls of the Styx are linked specifically to the old and dark Bregny, the wife of a marquis, and Lionne, whose husband was secretary and minister of state.

The head magician, Amisodar, is directly connected to the widow herself, La Rambure, throughout the parody, and the horrible monster that he conjures up in the opera becomes a hideous penis that she conjures up in the parody. Beginning in line 34, La Rambure is identified as the vessel through which evil flows. Her "front side," or genital region, is likened to a chasm in the earth that leads to the underworld. We learn at the end of the parody that La Rambure's genitals are so cavernous that even a gigantic penis cannot satisfy her.[35] Just as three monsters must be joined in strength to attempt to destroy Bellérophon in the opera, so three penises must unite to form one suitable to quench La Rambure's insatiable desire.[36]

Lully's musical setting fits both opera and parody texts. In scene 6, the music is commanding, composed of dotted rhythms in duple meter (in the style of Lully's overtures), repetitions, and movement in the bass by intervals of fourths and fifths (see Example 7.1, measures 1–14).[37] One would expect a commanding affect in the mouths of evil magicians conjuring up monsters, but when put into the mouth of the widow, the musical tones demonstrate her strength, masculine demeanor, and power, an unfitting and uncomplimentary representation of a woman during this period. That she speaks in a bass voice only adds to her hideousness. Like a witch possessed by the devil, she speaks in his voice.[38]

This scene exemplifies a specific type of air, dubbed by Manfred Bukofzer as the "double continuo air," wherein the bass voice fulfills two functions, both the bass line of the basso continuo and the melody.[39] Lully frequently used this type of air for supernatural beings, grotesque characters, or exotic foreigners who share one common trait: they are all disappointed lovers.[40] Thus a voice type (the bass) and a certain style of air (the double continuo air) are associated with a particular dramatic situation (the rejected lover). In *Bellérophon* and its parody, the double continuo air is sung by deleterious characters who are discarded paramours. When melody and bass line are one and the same in the mouths of such personages, the functional bass line, with its leaps and insistence on tonics, dominants, and subdominants, achieves an effect opposite to that of conventional tender expressions that one would normally associate with those who are in love. The effect is instead crude and suitable to more hideous characters.

In *Bellérophon*, Amisodor, who loves Stenobée, is the rejected lover. He conjures up a monster from the underworld at her command in order to please her. Yet Stenobée has no intention of rewarding Amisodor for his efforts by returning his love. Amisodor's predicament also reflects on the widow, Stenobée, because she, too, is a rejected lover, spurned by Bellérophon. As such, Amisodor's actions are an extension of her rage and jealousy. The dramatic function of the double continuo air in this scene, then, represents rejection times two. Like the double continuo air sung by Amisodor, this style of air is well-suited to the widow in the parody. It is applicable to her as a grotesque character—La Rambure speaks in a male voice and has magical powers—and to the dramatic situation—she is a frustrated lover. Even after succeeding in conjuring up the colossal penis, her desire goes unfulfilled because three united are not big enough for her.

In scene 6, the increasing urgency of the summons in the opera and sexual desire in the parody are first suggested by the use of bass-line chromaticism (see Example 7.2, measures 46–49). In the opera, the chromatic passage accompanies the words "ministers of my art," but in the parody, chromaticism appears on the words "servants of the brothel." Particularly in French airs from this period, and to some extent in other examples from Lully's operas, ascending chromaticism in the melody represented sexual desire associated with "the burning fires of love" to

O: Amisodar Que ce jar - din   ce   chan - ge_en un de - sert af - freux.
P: La Rambure Que ce Pa - lais   se   chan - ge_en un bor - del af - freux.

Opera: How this garden changes into a hideous desert.

Parody: How this Palace changes into a hideous brothel.

Example 7.1. *Bellérophon*, Scene 6, measures 1–14.

portray rising sexual tension.[41] Here the music seems especially suited to accompany the mention of prostitutes (implied witches) who were associated with unrestrained sexual desire.

Excitement—evil fervor in the opera and sexual stimulation in the parody—is also demonstrated rhythmically and metrically in both scenes 6

Opera: Ministers of my art, hurry, come when I call you.

Parody: Servants of the brothel, hurry, come when I call you.

Example 7.2. *Bellérophon*, Scene 6, measures 46–51.

and 7. At the end of scene 6, beginning in measure 51 (see Example 7.3), the meter changes from a slow and quasi-noble 2/2 to a lively 3/8. The effect is one of excitement and anticipation on the part of Amisodor, as he calls on his fellow magicians to respond to his command. In the parody, the effect becomes one of sexual excitement, particularly when we consider that references to love in vocal music of the period were often accompanied by musical devices associated with the number three: triple meter (though usually 3/2 or 3/4), melodies that move by thirds, and harmonies in first inversion.[42] In this passage, however, any musical reference to tender love is distorted by the driving movement associated with 3/8, more akin to the provocative and frenetic dance of a witches' sabbath.[43]

Opera and Parody: Hurry, come when I call.

Example 7.3. *Bellérophon*, Scene 6, measures 51–57.

The first chorus that begins scene 7 continues the frenzied pace established at the end of the double continuo air and the following dance, through melodic and rhythmic repetitions and major harmonies in root position (Example 7.4). In response to the chorus, Amisodar and La Rambure use a commanding tone as they order their servants to conjure up a monster and gigantic penis, in the opera and parody respectively (Example 7.5). The first mention of the monster and penis (Example 7.5, measures 74–75) is accompanied by a serpentine melody. The serpent, of course, is a symbol of evil, of sexual temptation, and the devil (the witches' master), an appropriate musical representation of both monster and penis, the former in the hands of an evil magician under the widow's control, and the latter in the hands of the widow herself.

In the second chorus, the magicians/servants respond to the command by restoring the frenetic pace and excitement established earlier in the scene through melodic repetitions, the unrelenting eighth-note movement, and strong root-position harmonies that frequently formulate dominant-tonic relationships, a fitting setting in both opera and parody on the words "pressing command" and "quickly, quickly" (Example 7.6).[44] Contributing to the frenzy is the change in meter from simple duple to compound time (Example 7.6, at measure 83). This agitated affect generated by the chorus

Opera and Parody: Speak, we are ready now, all will be possible for us.

Example 7.4. *Bellérophon*, Scene 7, measures 68–71.

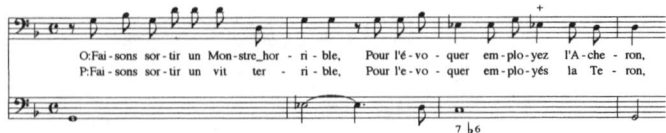

Opera: Let us make a horrible monster appear, In order to evoke it, call upon Acheron

Parody: Let us make a terrible penis appear, In order to evoke it, call upon la Teron

Example 7.5. *Bellérophon*, Scene 7, measures 74–77.

Opera: By this pressing command, Quickly, Let Tenare open up, Let Hell expose itself

Parody: (For this cunt so big and wide,)
By this pressing command, Quickly, Hurry, open up, Appear biggest ones

Example 7.6. *Bellérophon*, Scene 7, measures 81–88.

in the opera is certainly appropriate for the evil zeal needed to conjure up
a monster from the underworld, yet it also suits the sexual excitement in the
parody as La Rambure's entourage proceeds to conjure up the monstrous
member.

At this point in the opera, the magicians ask the rivers of the underworld
to stop their rapid flow and open up (see Example 7.7). The fast pace of the
music in 3/8 expresses not only the urgency of their command, but also
represents the rapidity of the rivers' movements. In the parody, as La
Rambure becomes lustier by the moment, the music depicts the excessive
pace of the prostitutes' "asses," and marks their incessant participation in the
sex act (Example 7.7, measures 97–100). As Amisodar in the opera and La
Rambure in the parody intensify the urgency of the situation with the words
"hurry, speak, call loudly" (see Example 7.8, measures 119–123 and 130).

Opera: you must help us, In order to hear us, stop, stop, stop running.

Parody: you must help us, In order to hear us, stop, the excessive pace of your asses.

Example 7.7. *Bellérophon*, Scene 7, measures 91–100.

Opera: Continue, let your power shine, By Cerberus and the triple Hecate, Speak, hurry, call loudly, Both death and the night

Parody: Continue, take care to follow my wishes, By La Baume and her lecherous front side, Hurry, speak, call loudly, La Chaulieu and d'Alluy

Example 7.8. *Bellérophon*, Scene 7, measures 113–133.

The choral response to Amisodor and La Rambure becomes breathless, as their words are punctuated by frequent rests. In the opera the rests occur between the words "nuit," "mort," and so forth, but in the parody they occur in between the syllables of the names of La Rambure's helpers, the daughters and wives of famous ministers and aristocrats, "Com-tes-se de Gram-mont" and "Thian-ge" to imitate panting lovers (see Example 7.9, measures 134–137). The parody connects these names with night, the hours for love, death, a common metaphor for sexual climax, and characters and regions of the cavernous underworld. Where the magicians of the opera conclude with cries, the servants utter tears and screams in the parody as the excitement builds (Example 7.10). The cries of the opera are an appeal to the black daughters of Styx, and in the parody, pleas for beds, indicating readiness to complete the sex act (Example 7.10, measures 146–148).

The scene draws to an end as the monster appears and as the giant penis rears its head, in opera and parody, respectively. The anticipation and exhilaration as the monsters penis are about to be revealed are accompanied by an ascending melody, representative of the monsters' ascent to earth and an erect penis (Example 7.11, measure 149). Just as the earth opens up in the

Opera: Night, Death, Cerberus, Hecate, Erebus, Avernus,

Parody: Countess of Grammont, Thiange, Lenclos, d'Olonne,

Example 7.9. *Bellérophon*, Scene 7, measures 134–139.

Opera: Hear our cries, help us, We work for you.

Parody: Hear our tears and our screams, We demand beds.

Example 7.10. *Bellérophon*, Scene 7, measures 144–48.

opera to free the monsters, La Rambure opens up in the parody (see Example 7.11, measures 150–152, and Example 7.12, measures 156–160). In both works, the choruses proclaim victory (Example 7.12, beginning in measure 168), because nothing can resist the magicians' power nor La Rambure's lust. This final chorus is again in triple meter, but here a dance-like 3/4 is used instead of a frenetic 3/8. Even though the use of 3/4 may suggest a slower tempo, it nonetheless takes on a driving and relentless

Opera: The spell is cast, the monsters are going to appear, The earth opens up and makes it known to me:

Parody: The spell is cast, the penis shows its head, My front side, which opens up prepares to swallow it,

Example 7.11. *Bellérophon*, Scene 7, measures 148–152.

motion, indicative of the sex act, as the repetition of the same melodic and rhythmic pattern in the bass line and voices occurs every four measures until victory is proclaimed. Here the monsters and demonic penis are in the process of fulfilling their duty.

The scene ends as Amisodor and La Rambure announce that neither separate monsters nor one massive penis are enough. It will take three joined together to ensure success. Here again the reference to the monsters and penises is accompanied in the music by a serpentine melody (Example 7.13, measures 190–191). The snake-like melody of the final recitative, along with the triadic gestures, represent the unification of three monsters and penises of opera and parody, respectively.

In sum, La Rambure in the parody cannot be satisfied by mortal men; she needs three phalluses that come close to resembling a mule's.[45] While the parody was most certainly a misogynous attack on the widow, it was also a thinly veiled commentary on the men who surrounded her at court. In many other sources of political erotica, women told tales of impotence, homosexuality, and brutish behavior in connection with the King's men.[46] The parody reveals a scenario that was especially dangerous to a patriarchal society. It tells of women taking sexual matters into their own hands and dismissing the need for man and his penis. A woman could conjure up her own phallus, whether animal or mechanical.

Indeed, the monstrous penis from hell is, if not that of the devil, an enormous dildo, often the subject of erotic poetry and novels during this period. In the pornographic novel *L'Académie des dames* (Latin edition, 1660; French edition, 1680), Tullie, the sexually experienced woman, tells Octavie, the innocent one, that a dildo can be used for pleasure if a husband is unavailable.[47] An illustration of a store that sells dildos appeared as the frontispiece to later French editions of this seventeenth-century erotic novel.

Opera: The earth opens up for us, Its deep chasm, The Underworld reveals itself: Let us sing, let us triumph, One sees the black wave stop for us, Victory, we have the glory of surmonting everything.

Parody: Let La Rambure open (up) Her deep chasm, The penis reveals itself. Great Gods, how long it is How black its testicle How desired it is, Victory, she will have the glory of surmounting it.

Example 7.12. *Bellérophon*, Scene 7, measures 156–175.

The illustration shows a store selling dildos in all shapes, sizes, and even national types (Italian, Turkish, German, etc.) stacked on tables and shelves.[48] Noble women are crowded into the small shop; a long line extends from the sale's counter, where clerks are showing their wares, to the door and beyond.

As several conversations from *L'Académie des dames* make explicit, women could also pull together to satisfy each other. In the fifth conversation, Tullie prepares Octavie for her wedding night by engaging in sexual relations with her.[49] After the fateful night, Tullie asks Octavie to describe what transpired in bed, and in the course of the conversation, they become so sexually excited that Tullie asks Octavie "to play the role of the husband," which she does.[50] Indeed, both lesbianism and masturbation were perceived as viable alternatives for a woman who wanted to be sexually fulfilled whenever she felt the desire.[51] Like syphilis, a disease linked with sexual excess which caused eventual impotence, and like sodomy, sex between men, lesbianism and the use of a dildo were sexual activities that challenged the very essence of the heroic ideal: fertility, virility, and one's duty to procreate for the health and well-being of the State.

Opera: One monster alone would cause more terror The three monsters must be united together
    By a charm stronger and more worthy than I, Let us make them into a single body,
    In order to make it happen, let us descend into the ends of Hell, The chasms are open to us.

Parody: One penis alone would be too small for me There are none so hard,
    That they don't tremble in fear at the sight of my front side Three are necessary for my inclination
    I am going to assemble them to make a perfect one, Which very much resembles a mule's.

Example 7.13. *Bellérophon*, Scene 7, measures 190–198.

This parody and other forms of political erotica from this period show the King's men, and by association, the King himself, as essentially impotent, both in sexual activities and as rulers. Katherine Hoffman, in her book *The Society of Pleasures*, describes the King's phallus/sword, particularly toward the end of his reign, as being "broken and useless, dangling imprudently about in the bushes of Versailles for all to see."[52] As a literary corpus, political erotica exposed the private passions (and private parts) of the King and anyone in his favor, fed the public's desire for details of royal intimacy, and yet also expressed an anxiety toward powerful women, weakened men, and an immoral State. The erotic parodies of Lully's operas not only enabled the public to visualize in their minds perverse sexual activity at court, but also permitted them to experience, through the music, a powerful sexual energy that ran counter to images of the hero and heroine in control of their passions. Ultimately, the erotic parodies of opera, as part of the larger corpus of political erotica, played a role in the destruction of king, hero, heroine, and noble ideals: exposing moral hypocrisy and perverting the very principles that structured and vivified the royal community.

Notes

1. For more information about political erotica as a literary genre, see Kathryn Hoffman, *Society of Pleasures: Interdisciplinary Readings in Pleasure and Power during the Reign of Louis XIV* (New York: St. Martin's Press, 1997). For a history of pornography, see Lynn Hunt, *The Invention of Pornography: Obscenity and the Origins of Modernity, 1500–1800* (New York: Zone Books, 1992). In early modern Europe (1500–1800), pornography was used as a vehicle for criticizing religious and political authorities. As Hunt explains: "pornography . . . emerged as a distinct category in the centuries between the Renaissance and the French Revolution thanks, in part, to the spread of print culture itself. Pornography developed out of the messy, two-way, push and pull between the intention of authors, artists and engravers to test the boundaries of the 'decent' and the aim of the ecclesiastical and secular police to regulate it" (p. 10). During the sixteenth century, pornography was limited to an educated elite (many works originally appeared in Latin), and these examples became prototypes for the seventeenth- and eighteenth-century political pornography. Though largely written and published for an aristocratic audience, its appeal to a broader audience grew between 1600 and 1800. It was during the middle of the seventeenth century that pornography seemed to reach its height of maturity. Sex became intellectualized, and the use and availability of sex aids increased. The center for pornography also moved from Italy to France during this period (pp. 26–30).
2. For a complete account of the King's use of Lully's operas as sanctioned propaganda, see Robert M. Isherwood, *Music in the Service of the King: France in the Seventeenth Century* (Ithaca: Cornell University Press, 1973), and Manuel Couvreux, *Jean-Baptiste Lully: Musique et Dramaturgie au Service du Prince* (Paris: Marc Vokar Editeur, 1992).
3. The popularity of Lully's operas has been well-documented. Opera's popularity is noted (and even complained about) by such writers as Jean de La Fontaine, Marie de Rabutin-Chantal de Sévigné, Charles Denis de Saint-Évremond, Lean Laurent Lecerf de la Viéville, Jean de La Bruyère, and Charles Perrault. See Donald Grout, "Seventeenth-Century Parodies of French Opera," *The Musical Quarterly* 27, no. 2 (1941): 211–19 and 27, no. 4 (1941): 514–26.

4. The parodies performed at the Ancien Théâtre Italien were quite different from those that appear as manuscript parodies. First and foremost, the parodies performed at the Théâtre were not erotic and were most often of airs that were usually incorporated into a newly composed work. Sometimes the text alone was parodied; sometimes the original version of an air, both text and music, would appear in a burlesque setting; sometimes a portion of the text using Lully's music would be used in a new context; and sometimes the original text would be used with a new musical setting. A few comedies parodied a central idea and plot of an entire opera by Lully and his librettists, Philippe Quinault or Thomas Corneille. Several parodies were first published as *Le théâtre italien de Gherardi* in 1685 in Brüssels by Henri Frick. Most of these seventeenth-century parodies were presented on the stage of the Ancien Théâtre Italien in the old Hôtel de Bourgogne on the Rue Mauconseil. The Italian troupes were permanently established in Paris in 1662 and originally improvised comedies in the style of the *commedia dell'arte*. In 1697, the Italian troupe was expelled from Paris, but the theater eventually reopened in 1716 (known as the Nouveau Théâtre Italien). See Cecilia Campa, "Il Teatre-Italien: La parodia e le querelles del primo Settecento," *Nuova rivista musicale italiana* 23 (1989): 342–77; Grout, "Seventeenth-Century Parodies of French Opera," 27, no. 2 (1941): 211–19 and 27, no. 4 (1941): 514–26; Renzo Guardenti, *Gli Italiani a Parigi: La Comedie Italienne, 1660–1697* (Rome: Bulzoni, 1990); Pierre Larderet, "Humour, ironie, satire, parodie dans la musique française des XVIIe et XVIIIe siècles," *Aspects de la musique baroque et classique à Lyon et en France* (Lyon: Université de Lyon, 1989); François Moureau, "Lully en visite chez Arlequin: Parodies italiennes avant 1697," in *Jean-Baptiste Lully* (Laaber, Germany: Laaber Verlag, 1990), 65–76; Herbert Schneider, *Die Rezeption der Opern Lullys* (Tutzing, Germany: Hans Schneider, 1982); and Marcello Spaziani, *Il Théâtre Italien de Gherardi* (Rome: Edizioni dell'Ateneo, 1966).

5. For a detailed description and account of the manuscript parodies of Lully's operas, see Schneider, *Die Rezeption der Opern Lullys*, 37–49 and 157–244. The Comte de Maurepas (1701–1781) played an important role in State affairs under Louis XV as *ministre de la marine* and was well-known for his scandalous verses. The works from the seventeenth century that appear in the Maurepas manuscripts were copied directly from the *Chansonnier de Clairambault*. Pierre Clairambault (1651–1740) was the genealogist to King Louis XIV who made it his business to know about everyone and anyone associated with the King and aristocracy. For more information on the Clairambault-Maurepas manuscript collections, see Paul d'Estrée, "Les origines du chansonnier de Maurepas," *Revue d'histoire littéraire de la France* (1896): 332–45; Claude Grasland, "Timbres, chansons, politique à Paris sous l'Ancien Régime" (Travail de maîtrise, Université Paris I, 1984–85); Claude Grasland, "Chansons et vie politique à Paris sous la Régence," *Revue d'histoire moderne et contemporaine* 37 (1990): 537–70; Claude Grasland and Annette Keilhauer, "'La Rage de Collection': Conditions, enjeux et significations de la formation des grands chansonniers et historiques à Paris au début de XVIIIe siècle (1710–1750)," *Revue d'histoire moderne et contemporaine* 47, no. 3 (2000): 458–86; Annette Keilhauer, *Das französische Chanson im spaten Ancien Regime: Strukturen, Verbrettungswege und gesellschaftlicke Praxis einer popularen Literaturform* (New York: Georg Olms Verlag, 1998); and Émile Raunié, *Chansonnier historique du XVIIIe siècle (Receuil Clairambault-Maurepas)* (Paris: A. Quantin, 1879).

6. Besides the compiler of the manuscripts, it is not known who might have had access to the parodies, as very little information is known about the composition of texts and reception of the collection. Some of the general texts were written by Louis XIV's courtiers (for example, the princess de Conti and the duchess de Bourbon, the King's illegitimate daughters) and circulated at court, but some others were penned by the famed Pont-Neuf storytellers/singers known as the Savoyard and the Cocher de Monsieur de Verthamont. There is even evidence that some of the parodies were composed and sung in cabarets located in the *quartier du Temple* by the literary greats Boileau, La Fontaine, and Racine (d'Estrée, "Les Origines du Chansonnier de Maurepas," 334, and Keilhauer, *Das französische Chanson*, 162).

7. The widow of Charles de Rambure, Marie de Bautru, was the object of a number of parodies and was even mentioned by Mme. de Sévigné in her *Correspondance* (III, S. 654 and 674) for her follies and inconceivable lust (*les folies et les fureurs inconcevables*). Madame de Rambure was notorious for having many lovers and for her insatiable sexual desire. One parody from the Maurepas manuscripts (1676) on a verse from *Alceste* states that if a man is able to satisfy La Rambure, his penis (implied) would have to be as "big as the mast [of a sailboat]" (Schneider, *Die Rezeption der Opern Lullys*, 198).

8. Fans of Lully's operas would have known by heart not only airs from his various works, but also entire scenes. In his article "Seventeenth-Century Parodies of French Operas," Grout even claims that "many Parisians would have sung all of Lully's operas from beginning to end, and certain favorite scenes were so familiar that Addison in 1699 was able to observe: 'I have sometimes known the performer on the stage do no more in a celebrated song, than the clerk of a parish church, who only serves to raise the psalm, and is afterwards drowned in the music of the congregation'" (Grout, "Seventeenth-Century Parodies of French Opera," 213–14).

9. Critics of Lully opera, such as Charles Denis de Saint-Évremond or Nicolas Boileau-Despréaux, warned that opera corrupts women. In his *Contre les femmes*, Boileau cautioned husbands that by allowing a wife to attend the Opera, she will lose all virtue. Women, who are by nature unfaithful and lascivious, are aroused by the luxurious voices of singing and are inspired to seduce unsuspecting men. For an account of the antifeminist rhetoric used to criticize Lully opera and the relationship between women, opera, and sexually deviant behavior, see Georgia Cowart, "Of Women, Sex and Folly: Opera under the Old Regime," *Cambridge Opera Journal* 6, no. 3 (1994): 205–20.

10. For a thorough account of projected images of Louis XIV, see Peter Burke, *The Fabrication of Louis XIV* (New Haven: Yale University Press, 1992).

11. In two books, Claude-François Menestrier (1631–1705) explores emblematic devices used as symbolic imagery. His *La Philosophie des Images* (in two volumes, 1682) is a study of the "science" of iconography; his *L'Art des Emblèmes* (first edition, 1662; second, 1684) is a study of the art of pictorial symbolism (see Burke, *The Fabrication of Louis XIV*, 115–19).

12. Perhaps the best example of a parody that attacks proper heroic or masculine conduct with reference to venereal disease, sodomy, and prostitution is the parody of Act I, Scene 5 of *Alceste* (Maurepas Ms. Fr. 12619, Vol. IV, #165, 1674). For a discussion of representations of sodomy in the *Chansonnier Maurepas*, see Lewis Seifert, "Masculinity and Satires of 'Sodomites' in France, 1660–1715," *Homosexuality in French History and Culture*, ed. Jeffrey Merrick and Michael Sibalis (Binghamton, N.Y.: Haworth Press, forthcoming).

13. Jeffrey Merrick, "Impotence in and at Court," *Studies in Eighteenth-Century Culture* 25 (1996): 199–215.

14. Venereal disease was directly associated with having sexual relations with prostitutes. For more information on a history of venereal disease, see Jon Arrizabalaga, John Henderson, and Roger French, *The Great Pox: The French Disease in Renaissance Europe* (New Haven: Yale University Press, 1997), and Laurence Brockliss and Colin Jones, *The Medical World of Early Modern France* (Oxford: Clarendon Press, 1997), 45–46, 97, 131, 147, 161, 219, 319, 437–38, 408–9, 446, 573–74, 624–26, 633–36, 668, 698, 770, 773–76, 785, 795.

15. See Deborah Hahn, "The School for Widows: Gender, (Re) Marriage, and Comedy on the Absolutist Stage (Seventeenth-Century French Theater)" (Ph.D. diss., Brown University, 1999).

16. See Robin Briggs, *Witches and Neighbors: The Social and Cultural Context of European Witchcraft* (New York: Viking Penguin, 1996) for a history of witchcraft in seventeenth-century France. Anxiety about witchcraft existed at least to some extent during the reign of Louis XIV, as exemplified by accusations of sorcery that seriously maligned the court during the late 1670s. Known as the *affaire des poisons*, the scandal

involved "love magic, black masses, poisonings, and child murder . . . involving the king's mistress and other leading figures" (Briggs, *Witches and Neighbors*, 251). See Simone Bertière, *Les Femmes du Roi-Soleil* (Paris: Éditions de Fallois, 1998), 245–72, and Robert Mandrou, *Magistrats et Sorciers en France au XVIIe Siècle* (Paris: Librairie Plon, 1968), 467–72.

17. Nancy Tuana, *The Less Noble Sex* (Bloomington: Indiana University Press, 1993), 59–60 and 96. It was also believed that women after menopause were especially prone to believe in witchcraft and succumb to the devil's seduction.

18. Briggs, *Witches and Neighbors*, 42. See also Andrew Sanders, *A Deed without a Name: The Witch in Society and History* (Oxford: Berg Publishers Limited, 1995), 1–9 and 30. Robin Briggs explains that in France, accused witches were men, women, peasants, aristocrats, young women, old women, married people, and widows and widowers; whereas in other countries and regions (particularly in the German lands), the majority of witches were women, and many were old and unmarried. Two important primary sources on witchcraft in France are Jean Bodin, *De la démonmanie des sorciers* (Paris, 1580) and Pierre de Lancre, *Tableau de l'inconstance des mauvais anges et demons, ou il es amplement traicté des sorciers et de la sorcellerie* (Paris: J. Berjon, 1612). Secondary sources include Sigrid Brauner, *Fearless Wives and Frightened Shrews: The Construction of the Witch in Early Modern Germany* (Amherst: University of Massachusetts Press, 1995); Robin Briggs, *Communities of Belief: Cultural and Social Tensions in Early Modern France* (Oxford: Clarendon Press, 1989); Carlo Ginzburg, *Ecstasies: Deciphering the Witches' Sabbath*, ed. Gregory Elliot, trans. Raymond Rosenthal (London: Hutchinson Radius, 1990); Mandrou, *Magistrats et Sorciers en France;* Jonathan L. Pearl, *The Crime of Crimes: Demonology and Politics in France, 1560–1620* (Ontario: Wilfred Laurier University Press, 1999); Diane Purkiss, *The Witch in History: Early Modern and Twentieth-Century Representations* (London: Routledge, 1996); Lyndal Roper, *Oedipus and the Devil: Witchcraft, Sexuality and Religion in Early Modern Europe* (New York: Routledge, 1994); Gerhild Scholz Williams, *Defining Dominion: The Discourse of Magic and Witchcraft in Early Modern France and Germany* (Ann Arbor: University of Michigan Press, 1995).

19. Briggs, *Witches and Neighbors*, 137. See also Sanders, *A Deed without a Name*, 11.

20. Unlike in other countries, such as Germany, where accused witches were overwhelmingly women, in France, male witches were just as common as female (Briggs, *Witches and Neighbors*, 21).

21. de Lancre, *Le Tableau de L'Inconstance*, sig û i (translated and quoted in Briggs, *Witches and Neighbors*, 32).

22. Briggs, *Witches and Neighbors*, 26–28, 45, 99, 101–2.

23. The exact nature of a widow's condition varied according to region and socioeconomic status. In most areas of France, the bulk of the husband's assets would return to his family, but she was entitled to her dowry and use of her husband's property after his death (some husbands, however, used up the dowry, leaving their wives penniless). If she had children, she might stand to gain a greater monetary settlement. See Maïté Albistur and Daniel Armogathe, "Le féminisme à l'age classique," *Histoire du féminisme français du moyen age à nos jours* (Paris: des femmes, 1977); Roger Duchêne, "La Veuve au XVIIe siècle," *Onze études sur l'image de la femme dans la littérature française du dix-septième siècle*, ed. Wolfgang Leiner (Tübingen: Gunter Narr Verlag, 1978), 221–42; Sarah Hanley, "Engendering the State: Family Formation and State Building in Early Modern France," *French Historical Studies* 16, no. 1 (1989): 4–27; Julie Hardwick, "Widowhood and Patriarchy in Seventeenth-Century France," *Journal of Social History* 26, no. 1 (1992): 133–49; Merry E. Weisner, *Women and Gender in Early Modern Europe* (Cambridge: Cambridge University Press, 1993), 73–78. Primary sources that discuss marriage and widows include Claude Decret, *Le Vraye Veuve, ou l'idée de perfection en l'estat de viduité* (Paris, 1650); François de Grenaille, *L'Honneste veuve* (Paris, 1640); Claude Maillard, *Le bon mariage ou le moyen d'estre heureux avec un Traité des veuves* (Paris, 1643); François de Sales, *Introduction à la vie dévote* (1609); and Girard de Villethierry, *La Vie des veuves ou les devoirs et les obligation des veuves chretiennes* (1697).

24. Hahn, "The School for Widows," 20–21.
25. Hahn, "The School for Widows," 20–21. For a comprehensive account of female sexuality in early modern Europe, see Merry E. Wiesner, *Women and Gender in Early Modern Europe*, 41–81. Wiesner points out that women were considered as being sexually insatiable due to their ability to have multiple orgasms (Wiesner, *Women and Gender in Early Modern Europe*, 46).
26. Olwen Hufton writes: "Theologians and moralists dealt with the widow as if she was part of a homogeneous group. The aim of much prescriptive writing was to contain a woman who had experienced sex and hence had had her libido aroused. Now her husband was not there to control her, her ungoverned lust was seen as a threat. . . . The implications of medical writing on the widow are also that, having had her sexual appetite whetted, she was an aroused and lusty force and hence predatory, needing a male replacement" (Olwen Hufton, *The Prospects Before Her: A History of Women in Western Europe [1500–1800]*, vol. 1 [New York: Alfred A. Knopf, 1996], 226).
27. In the following example, spelling and punctuation marks are those of the original texts; translations are my own.
28. La Teron was the daughter of Colbert who separated from her first husband and took the name of Mlle. du Teron. She then married Prince de Carpegna of Rome.
29. La Royan was the wife of the Marquis de Royan; La Rune was a sister of La Rambure and widow of the Marquis de Rane (who died in Germany in 1678). She remarried Jean-Baptiste-Arman de Rohan. La Broon was the wife of the Marquis de Broon.
30. This refers to the home of Madeleine d'Angennes, widow of Henry de Sennecterre, Duc de la Ferté, and her daughter-in-law Maire de Sennecterre.
31. La Chaulieu was the wife of Sr. de Chaulieu; d'Alluy was the wife of the Marquis d'Alluy.
32. The countesse of Grammont was the wife of Philber, Count de Grammont; Thiange was the wife of the Marquis de Thiange; Lenclos was Anne de Lenclos, commonly referred to as Ninon, "the famous Courtisan"; d'Olonne was wife of the Count d'Olonne and sister of Mlle. de la Ferté.
33. The adjective preceeding Lionne in the parody text was illegible.
34. Bregny was the wife of the Marquis de Bregny; Lionne was the wife of Hugues de Lionne, secretary and minister of the state.
35. "A cunt so wide and deep" is a phrase often used in seventeenth- and eighteenth-century erotic literature to malign women, especially older females. A wide vagina could not satisfy any "normal" man; and likewise, no "standard-sized" man could fulfill a woman whose vagina was too large. Such a woman was of no use to men because she could not please them. A woman with a "wide and deep" vagina was someone who had had so many lovers that she was stretched out and deformed, an indication that she was perverted and immoral.
36. As indicated in n. 5, the size of La Rambure's genital region is referred to in other parodies as well: a man's phallus would have to be as big as the mast of the sailboat in order to please her (*Chansonnier Maurepas*, Ms. Fr. 12619, S. 305, 1676).
37. Please note that musical examples taken from scenes 6 and 7 include both the opera and parody texts and translations, labelled "O" and "P," respectively. These examples are taken from the printed edition of *Bellérophon*: Jean-Baptiste Lully and Thomas Corneille, *Bellérophon* (Paris: Ballard, 1679). Measure numbers do not reflect the dances that occur in the scenes (which are not part of the parody), as such, the measure numbers begin in measure one of scene 6 and continue directly on to scene 7.
38. La Rambure's "inconceivable lust" is referred to by Sévigné in her letters (Sévigné, *Correspondance*, III, 654 and 674). Sévigné's choice of words and her association of sex with violence are revealing (*les folies*, madness, and *les fureurs*, lust, rage, or fury). Sex and violence are linked in many seventeenth-century sources: the phallus is referred to as a weapon; death, a metaphor for organism; and love making, regarded as amorous combat (Hoffman, *Society of Pleasures*, 155). See Linda Austern, "'For, Love's a Good Musician': Performance, Audition, and Erotic Disorders in Early Modern Europe," *The Musical Quarterly* 3, no. 4 (1998): 614–53. Austern notes that Neoplatonic writers

on love during the late sixteenth and early seventeenth centuries believed that (certain) music could actually cure lustful feelings (Austern, "'For, Love's a Good Musician,'" 620–23). This stands in stark contrast with opinions expressed later in the century by French critics of opera, who warned that Lully's music *caused* irrationality, madness, and lustful feelings, particularly in women.

39. Manfred Bukofzer, *Music in the Baroque Era* (New York: Norton, 1947), 158.

40. In "Lully and the Ironic Convention," *Cambridge Opera Journal* (1989): 139–53, Patricia Howard states incorrectly that the double continuo air was used exclusively by Lully for supernatural beings, grotesque characters, or exotic foreigners. Even though Howard's contention is applicable to this particular scene (a magician with supernatural powers), I would like to thank Rebecca Harris-Warrick for pointing out to me that the double continuo air was indeed used by Lully for many other types of characters as well and not exclusively for disappointed lovers who are exotic or grotesque.

41. For a more detailed discussion of chromaticism in French airs, see Catherine Gordon-Seifert, "The Language of Music in France: Rhetoric as a Basis for Expression in Michel Lambert's *Les Airs de Monsieur Lambert* (1669) and Bénigne de Bacilly's *Les Trois livres d'airs* (1668)" (Ph.D. diss., The University of Michigan, 1994), 150–56.

42. The association of the number three with Venus and love is discussed in Gordon-Seifert, "The Language of Music in France," 147. I first became aware of the association of love, Venus, and the number three in a paper delivered by Mary Rasmussen, "Viols, Violists and Venus in Grunewald's Isenheim Altar," given at the AMS New England Chapter Meeting at Harvard University on February 13, 1992.

43. The association of witches and their ability through music to arouse a man's sexual desire was regularly represented on the English stage. See Linda Austern, "'Art to Enchant': Musical Magic and Its Practitioners in English Renaissance Drama," *Journal of the Royal Musical Association* 115 (1990), 191–206.

44. This is the only place in the parody where an extra line of text has been added without a matching line in the opera (*Pour ce Con si large et si grand*—For this cunt so big and wide). The added text fits into the first musical phrase without a problem; however, this phrase of music must be repeated to accommodate the second line of the parody text, measures 81 and 82 of Musical Example 7.6.

45. References to having sex with animals were also a common accusation used to malign suspected witches (Sanders, *A Deed without a Name*, 30).

46. Hoffman, *The Society of Pleasures*, 151–55.

47. *L'Académie des dames*, ed. Jean-Pierre Dubost (Arles: Picquier, 1999). *L'Académie des dame* was first published in Latin as *Aloisiae Sigaeae Toletanae Satyra Sotadica de arcanis Amoris et Veneris* in 1659 or 1660. An edition in French was published in 1680. For more information on this seventeenth-century pornographic "classic," see Hunt, *The Invention of Pornography*, 15, 18–20, 27, 28, 29, 30–31, 167, 169, 170–72, 181, 207, 251, and 286. Hunt also points out that during the middle of the seventeenth century, there was an increase in the availability (and use) of sex aids, particularly the dildo. In the 1660s, imported Italian dildos and condoms became readily available in London.

48. Hunt, *The Invention of Pornography*, 169.

49. The fifth conversation begins on page 95.

50. *L'Académie des dames*, 102.

51. Hoffman, *The Society of Pleasures*, 158.

52. Hoffman, *The Society of Pleasures*, 156.

Transcendence

Chant: "et non me paenitentem, timor mortis conturbat me."

8

Processions for the Dead, the Senses, and Ritual Identity in Colonial Mexico[1]

Grayson Wagstaff

If the ear of the musician is like the eye of the painter, that is a great thing
. . . in art one cannot put things into words, because in truth the best of such
art (if not all arts) cannot be put into words

—El Greco, unpublished glosses
on Daniel Barbaro's commentary on Vitruvius

During a lecture that I attended with some trepidation, Camille Paglia made one of her many provocative asides. While discussing approaches in various scholarly fields that encourage what she described as "deconstruction" of history to the point of denying the existence of events and objects themselves, Paglia stated that all scholars should have had the same experiences that she did as a young woman in the Egyptian art exhibit at the Metropolitan Museum. Before the new air conditioning system was installed, she knew that history was real because, in her words, "I smelled it."[2] Her senses made Egypt, at least some impression of it, "real" to her. However, Paglia's aside underscores our difficulty understanding how the senses are manipulated. Her nose and all of the neurosensory apparatus attached to it were interpreting ancient Egypt because of the way she had been taught to do so, not least of all because of the way it was presented in that exhibit.

In November 1559, one of the century's most momentous events for European music took place, not in Europe, but in Mexico City. There, a multiday commemoration (called *exequies*) was celebrated to honor the Holy Roman Emperor, Charles V, who had died the previous year.[3] Because of his Habsburg ancestry and his father's marriage into the royal family of Spain, Charles had ruled much of Europe and Spain's New World colonies. The *exequies* were important not only because of the amount of music performed but more importantly because music composed in Mexico was sung alongside works imported from Spain.[4] During these services, participants heard music by the great Spanish composer Cristóbal de Morales and works composed specifically for the event by the chapel master of Mexico City. But the music was only one element in the complex ceremonial of these events. In fact, *exequies* were a coordinated spectacle of sight, sound, smell, and choreography, much like an opera in terms of the interconnections of these media. Although they were similar to other ceremonies in early modern life, these *exequies* in colonial Mexico were also meant to communicate to non-Europeans. This added complexity of communicating across cultural and linguistic barriers makes these rituals some of the most interesting in sixteenth-century life.[5]

The procession winds its way through the streets of Mexico City. One line is lead by the archbishop, who is followed in order of their importance by other members of the ecclesiastical hierarchy and members of various orders; in a second rank, the viceroy heads the civil authorities of the colony and members of the nobility. In yet another file, there are native leaders from many regions of Mexico. Each of these groups of dignitaries stops at preplanned locations, where the choir of the cathedral sings a responsory. Each member of the procession—by his location in line—represents the chain of connections that run throughout Spanish society from the king, God's representative on earth, down to the poorest native of the colony. As the dignitaries enter the church, they see the hundreds of candles that cover the funeral catafalque. The light of so many candles and torches shocks them upon entering the typically dark building. The few who can read Latin understand the tributes on the catafalque. The majority of people see the visual magnificence of the catafalque, almost as tall as the ceiling of the church, and know that it symbolizes Charles's power and piety. They smell the incense and the smoke from all the candles. Each one is taught about the emperor and the new society of Mexico. Like Paglia's reaction to Egypt, each participant in Mexico in 1559 hears, sees, smells, and feels what the colony of New Spain is.

The incorporation of native peoples, "los naturales," added a new element to the organization of these events. Francisco Cervantes de Sálazar, a professor of rhetoric at the university, wrote an account of these ceremonies in which he makes clear that the Spaniards watched the Native people with great interest:

> Saint Andrew's day having come, the Viceroy was in the royal palace when he was joined by all the attendants and the Knights and nobility of the city, who had joined together there. There were ordered so that each would be placed in his position. . . . The complete procession had four parts; in the first were the natives, who entered the street of San Francisco with noble behavior and having such great sentiment beyond sadness that the rest of us were provoked by them to tears.

In the mid-sixteenth century, the assumption that one was represented after death by Catholic rituals was transplanted to colonial Mexico. It seems that this tradition of endowing rituals that involved the community in corporate mourning was adopted by many native Mexicans.[6] These death rituals in Latin America served a pedagogical purpose because they provided a moment when the new "journey" of Christianity could be solidified in the new converts' minds. The interconnection of visual, auditory, and other sensory experience in these events was similar to the way that native people had been taught Christian tenets through visual representations.[7] Charles's model rites manifested his good death and his reward. Those who accepted the new way were given the all-important ceremonial sendoff, the soul was "ferried" to its paradise accompanied by the sacred song. Of course, those receiving the most elaborate funeral rites were the wealthy Spaniards and ecclesiastical officials; their deaths were to be models to all,[8] and the greatest in terms of sensory stimulation.

This repertory did not originate in Mexico: the earliest identified works in the Hispanic repertory for the Mass and Office for the Dead were written in late-fifteenth-century Spain, although the concept of improvised music for these rituals may go back earlier.[9] It is likely that composers were encouraged by ecclesiastical authorities to create music for burials and commemorations that more closely reflected the Christian belief in calm acceptance of death than did the laments, wails, and other emotional displays decried in church documents.[10] This would mean that Spaniards had been taught by these works and rituals (and continued to be taught by them) in a similar way as the native peoples of Mexico were instructed in the 1550s. In Spain, the fact that the new polyphonic works were sung by choirs of clerics and boys was also considered a positive aspect, because it removed women from the spotlight at this crucial time. The etiquette of the rituals is directly related to the senses and their use as part of the religious experience intended by Church leaders. The music, choreography, and visual elements of these rites were altered to control what ecclesiastical officials viewed as dangerous behavior.

Although related to the Requiem tradition in France, the Low Countries, and later in Italy, the repertory in Spain and colonial Mexico is unique in that it emphasizes music for the processions and other ceremonies, not just the Mass for the Dead. All the Spanish and "Mexican" composers wrote settings for Matins and for the processions. This emphasis on what I term the more ritually *active* portions of the liturgy is a distinguishing characteristic of the liturgical style of these *exequies*. The most important element of these ceremonies in terms of this public interaction was the procession.

Processions, particularly those of the standard Catholic liturgy, have received relatively little attention from scholars in ritual studies and anthropology, especially when compared with a similar journey through "sacred" space, the pilgrimage.[11] The use of processions extends back to the early Church and seems to have included various elements borrowed from Imperial Roman practice.[12] Processions create various relationships among those participating in them through the power symbolized in the sacred element being presented, how close one is to it, and the ceremonial actions completed en route. The use of public ceremony, including such ritualized movements as processions, seems to have resonated quite strongly with Pre-Columbian religious life.[13] Indeed, public rituals in sixteenth-century Mexico assumed a grandeur that impressed visitors from elsewhere as well as the native inhabitants.[14] In general, the theatrical nature of much Spanish devotional activity—sacred dramas of various kinds, mock battles of good versus evil, processions with costumed participants, and the use of such basic theatrical elements as scenery, music, and acting—was warmly accepted by Native inhabitants of New Spain.[15] The processions were indeed theatrical; the dramatic elements included the assumption that participants were to display the proper demeanor of mourning. As noted, the native participants evinced, or "acted" with, such noble bearing in their sadness that Spanish-born observers were moved to tears. This is ironic in that the appropriate response, judged by the theological tenets of the time, would have been more stoic. As we shall see, the emotions that the senses were supposed to produce were carefully planned aspects in these rituals.

During this time, Spaniards understood sacred rituals as forums to display emotions, which emotion being determined in part by the theological underpinnings of the event being marked. As William Christian demonstrated in his study of provoked weeping, emotions, especially during Holy Week, were intensified by various stimuli that each participant sought out.[16] In essence, one went to a certain ritual, especially during Holy Week, in order to cry. Art historian Susan Verdi Webster has connected the outpouring of grief and tears to specific characteristics of statues used in Holy Week processions.[17] Tears flowed because artists sought ways to promote this venting of emotions.[18] The sensation, created by these physical stimuli, fostered a physical manifestation of the theological interpretation of Holy Week: it was a time to honor the suffering of Jesus, a week that would mark a contrast to the celebration of his resurrection on Easter. However, tears were appropriate only in certain rituals. In one of the ironic contrasts of early modern rituals, burial and commemoration processions—unlike those for Holy Week—were governed by the belief that the death of a Christian was to be marked by calm acceptance.

This concern with the orthodox representation became the focus of tracts on how to prepare for death. *Ars Moriendi* treatises in Spain emphasized the sanctity of death rituals as opposed to the themes of personal piety found in Erasmus's writings on death. [19] In Spanish and later Spanish colonial thought, one was to die "well," but perhaps more importantly, one was to be processed, buried, and commemorated with orthodox ritual. The senses were to be used to create the correct impression, that the deceased had died a calm death assured of his/her reward. Each participant was to manifest this successful death. Burial music, visual representations, and choreography were to channel the proper emotions just as Holy Week statues provoked tears. This is perhaps the most striking aspect of the account by Cervantes de Sálazar: he admits that the natives were such successful actors that they triggered an inappropriate demonstration of tears.

Like the theatrical elements, the hierarchical nature of the processions seems to have been accepted by native participants. The placement of participants according to rank in these processions could be seen reflected in various other aspects of the visual representation of the emperor's power. Spaniards had extended this hierarchy even into the planning of cemeteries, perhaps the most concrete symbol of how the power structure of society extended into death.[20] Specific people, such as the archbishop and the leaders of each order, were given places of honor in the procession. They in essence became the "sacred" element because the king's body was not present. The music included similar delineation according to prestige, specifically the role of the cantors.

The traditional format of the burial processions included the chanting of psalms while the body was carried from the home, where it had been washed and prepared, to the church in which the Mass for the dead or Requiem and other services would be celebrated. The other services included Vespers and Matins. At some point, probably in the fifteenth century, it became customary in Spain to use the responsory chants from Matins in processions with the body. Improvised part music was sung originally by the cantors, but later this practice was replaced by written, polyphonic music. This practice seems to have been widespread by the mid-sixteenth century. Carlos M. N. Eire has examined dozens of wills that request *responsos* to be sung during these processions; he described the obvious metaphoric interpretation that this ceremony represented a "ferrying of the soul" to a new place.[21] Each one of these rites was designed to draw in observers through various physical stimuli. Like the later *exequies*, each procession was a theatrical presentation in which sight, sound, touch, and smell intertwined.

The importance of these musical traditions in colonial Mexico can be seen in one of the earliest publications with music, *Manuale Sacramentorum secundum usum ecclesiae Mexicanae* (Mexico, 1560), which gives a fairly comprehensive presentation of how the chant melodies were to be incorporated in the burial processions. The lengthy responsory melody for each pause in the procession follows a series of prayers:

Procession for the dead: Responsory chants,
Manuale Sacramentorum (Mexico, 1560)
Station 1: *Memento mei*
Station 2: *Kyrie*
Station 3: *Qui Lazarum*
Station 4: *Peccantem me*
Station 5: *Requiem aeternam*
(not the same melody as the "Requiem" Mass)
Upon entering the church: *Subvenite Sancti Dei*

The written polyphonic works usually incorporate the traditional chant as the highest voice of the new work, making it the most obvious element.[22] Would the native listeners have recognized the chant melodies in these works? Perhaps a few would have, but the more important issue is that they would recognize the manner in which these polyphonic works were sung as being similar in many ways to the chants they had heard missionaries and priests sing. The polyphonic works would be a more elaborate version of the chant performance. In this context, these works would be a symbol of the emperor's power as well as his Christian, orthodox beliefs. One knew that Charles was headed for paradise in part because of the appropriate serenity of the music that marked his transition. What each participant heard, saw, smelled, and felt was creating the correct physical manifestation, the behavior that represented this calm death.

There was an ancient tradition in Christian theology concerning music's power and how the senses created religious experience.[23] St. Augustine wrote eloquently on his struggles with the senses and their power:

I used to be much more fascinated by the pleasures of sound than the pleasures of smell. I was enthralled by them, but you broke my bonds and set me free. I admit that I still find some enjoyment in the music of hymns, which are alive with your praises, when I hear them sung by well-trained, melodious voices, but I do not enjoy it so much that I cannot tear myself away. . . . For sometimes, I feel that I treat it with more honor than it deserves. I realize than when they are sung these sacred words stir my mind to greater religious fervor and kindle in me a more ardent flame of piety than they would if they were not sung. . . . But I ought not to allow my mind to be paralyzed by the gratification of my senses, which often leads it astray. For the senses are not content to take second place.[24]

In late medieval and early modern Spain, the understanding of music and its powers became intertwined with attempts to cleanse the Church of inappropriate behavior.[25] Various diocesan constitutions from the late fifteenth and sixteenth centuries advise priests to replace such "foreign" practices as excessive laments with more appropriate sacred music for funerals and commemorations.[26] The "appropriate" music was presumably the polyphonic works that began to be written in ever larger numbers during this time. As was already discussed, behavior at rituals was governed at least in part by theological concepts of what the event symbolized.

The participants in the rituals in Mexico in 1559 saw a large number of visual symbols: the giant catafalque or monument, text phrases, emblems, the shape of the procession, and even such details as how the members of the choir arrayed themselves to sing the responsories. [27] Music mixed with these various visual stimuli. There were obviously different "levels" of signification that function simultaneously in the visual and auditory elements, but different levels of education would have affected what each participant understood. Likewise, aspects of the music's structure function on different levels. Each person who heard the responsories knew that these texts and the priests who sang them were somehow important, and that the portion of each sung in part music was made more solemn than the rest of the text. Just as did the visual monuments, these polyphonic responsories encode the hierarchical organization of the new power structure in Mexico.

It is now commonly accepted that European courts and governments in the fifteenth through eighteenth centuries used ceremony as propaganda.[28] In terms of understanding the "projective" nature of these rituals, music scholars owe much to art historians.[29] Since the publication of Roy Strong's *Art and Power: Renaissance Festivals, 1450–1650*, many art historians have studied how power, politics, and theological precepts were encoded in visual elements of many different kinds of ceremonies, such as royal entries, court entertainments, weddings, and funerals.[30] Likewise, in the study of colonial Mexico, many scholars have examined both the pedagogical and propagandistic elements of visual features.[31] As did the art and architecture of these events, the rituals and music all communicated, but determining what their method of communication is remains difficult.[32] The music had texts, but because its Latin language was opaque to any but a tiny segment of the listeners, the power of the music in the ceremonies had to have exceeded its textual limitations. Ethnomusicologist Thomas Turino has applied Peircian semiotics—based on the theories of American philosopher Charles Sanders Peirce (1839–1914)—to understand music in "imagination, identity, and experience." [33]

Two aspects of Peircian theory are relevant here: that symbols are not automatically tied to linguistic meanings, although they may connect in some way to linguistically mediated ideas; and that what are termed "chaining processes" often connect symbols through time. For instance, a performance of *Peccantem me quotidie*, one of the processional responsories involves this process. Taken at face value, this text/chant/polyphonic work requests, "have mercy on me oh God, and save me." Even if the Native inhabitants did not know what the words meant, they had some understanding of requesting grace for the departed. Many native Mexicans adopted Spanish rituals, as witnessed by the number of natives who requested memorials in their wills. Peircian analysis allows us to posit that this request for grace became entwined with the symbols of the emperor's power. A Native man from the region of Puebla asks the living emperor (perhaps the living archbishop and viceroy as well) for grace at the same time that he asks God for help for the dead monarch. This was not stated, but, by trying to satisfy the wishes of the organizers of this memorial, processing with proper body position, displaying the correct "nobility," and listening with proper reverence, the man is granted a role, what Grimes called a "ritual office."[34] He is given more respect and credibility as a participant in the ritual of the colony. The participant is told whether or not he has successfully participated. The account implies that there was punishment for inappropriate behavior.

A key element in Charles's identity was his role as defender of the true Catholic faith, a soldier fighting against Lutheranism and other heresy. His death had to be a model; his music, ceremony, and liturgy had to project the orthodox beliefs of the Church with its sanctioned music, chant, being the basis for the repertory. The newly written polyphonic works were composed in a very conservative, perhaps intentionally archaic style that presents the preexistent chant melodies as the most important aspect of each piece. Example 8.1 is a typical setting of *Peccantem me quotidie*. The top voice is almost identical to the chant melody.

These polyphonic responsories present a musical analogy for the hierarchical nature of the surrounding ceremony. Items such as *Peccantem me quotidie* preserve the distinctions of the older practices with their respect for the role of the cantors, who were always allowed to sing specific portions of some chants. Its text shows how the portions reserved for the cantors would be set off from the rest of the text, sung by the whole choir, which was left to be sung in chant: *Peccantem me quotidie* shown as set by a composer in Mexico City Cathedral MS 3 (text set polyphonically in all caps):

PECCANTEM ME QUOTIDIE, et non me paenitentem, timor mortis
    conturbat me:
        QUIA IN INFERNO nulla est redemptio, miserere mei, Deus, et
        salva me.
    V. DEUS, IN NOMINE TUO SALVUM ME FAC, et in virtute tua libera
    me.

QUIA. . .

The fear of death troubles me, as I sin daily and do not repent.

> Since in hell there is no redemption, have mercy on me, O God, and save me.

V. O God, by Your name save me, and by Your might deliver me.

> Since. . .[35]

The native participant was probably struck by the fact that this music was more elaborate than other Spanish funeral music. The difference in status determined who would have just the chant melodies sung over their graves versus those who would have had polyphonic music sung. The polyphonic music necessitated the presence of trained musicians, priests, and choirboys who would be paid for their services. This would make all music heard in the processions—at least in theory—Church sanctioned, cleansed of all inappropriate music and behavior. In this way, only those appropriate sensations, those connected to the proper interpretation of death and reward, would be created. Tears or any other "display" could counteract the model that the emperor's death had set.

Those who participated in the *exequies* for Charles were changed by their involvement. Through this sensory spectacle, these people emerged sharing some view of their world. Their senses helped them relate to an unimaginably far off leader who now controlled many aspects of their lives. This identity, shaped by sensual means, would continue to be manipulated by public events throughout the colonial period. Theologian Michael Aune has examined this process of identity evolution in ritual:

> The problem of the "subject" is basic to any humanistic or social scientific inquiry that seeks to better understand the dynamic nature of culture (and ritual is certainly a cultural matter!). . . . A *subject* is not a source and master of meaning or signification but emerges through the discourses and practices of a culture—"the 'I' is not something given but comes to exist. . .as that which is addressed by and relates to others. . . . Instead of approaching this activity [ritual] as a relatively enclosed dramatic frame having to do primarily with a group or a community, *the focus is now on how to understand what is said, seen, and done as formative of a distinctive experience of personhood or self-definition.*[36] [Emphasis mine]

As each of the native people watched or marched toward the memorial service to honor the dead emperor, they learned something about their role in the new power structure of the colony. Each would have heard the new order in the music. Each person learned how to process with the proper bearing of the body. Each learned his place in the order. Each was assaulted by a sensory experience of sight, smell, and sound, and felt the choreographic

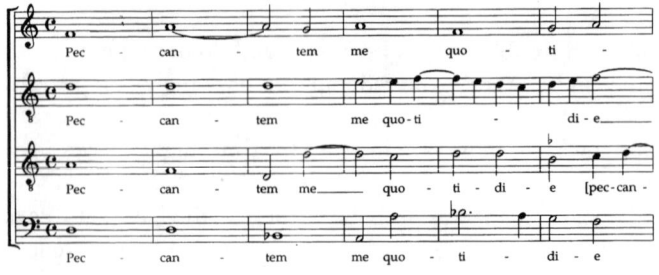

Chant: "et non me paenitentem, timor mortis conturbat me:"

Example 8.1. Anon., *Peccantem me.* Responsory for Matins for the Dead. Mexico City Cathedral Manuscript 3.

use of the body as a stage device. These events had a veneer of sacred ceremony, theologically based ritual, but they were in fact much more about political power and maintaining the civic status quo than they were concerned with any sacred elements. *Exequies* were media events, staged to represent the stability of the Habsburg line.[37] Those who heard the music in 1559 were being taught about the decorum of colonial life, the calm acceptance of the Christian way and colonial rule, just as fifteenth-century Spaniards were taught about the theology of death when these polyphonic works replaced the older laments specifically labeled "foreign" by the Church. Identity had been projected through ritual in this manner since the early days of conquest: Hernando Cortés's going out on his knees to greet

Chant: "nulla est redemptio, miserere mei, Deus, et salva me."

Example 8.1. (continued)

the first missionaries is just the most obvious of the uses of religious symbolism and ritual to control the development of the new society.[38]

On this day in 1559, each participant—Spanish, Mexican, Creole, or Mestiza—was an actor in political ritual. These *exequies* included thousands of native Mexican participants, leaders from many different cultures who had been summoned to Mexico City, then the viceregal capital, to create a web of connections to all regions of the colony. This network of power was emphasized by the organization of the procession, based on the ancient hierarchical practices of the Catholic Church. The music that they heard was crafted to be a direct link to the chant melodies and practices surrounding death. Since its inception in Spain, this polyphonic repertory for burial processions seems to have been employed to foster proper calmness in death rituals.

A "distinctive experience of personhood" might be one way of describing Paglia's perception that Ancient Egypt was real. She knew something about the concept of Egypt from the way the museum's curators and designers had shaped her experience of it. They had provided a sensory introduction to it, including an unintentional one from the poor air circulation, but one that created a perception through the senses. Ecclesiastical and civic leaders of Mexico City in 1559 created an induction into Spanish society for the native participants. Each one who processed that day underwent a transformation, passing through the liminal state of the ritual, and became a member of Spanish colonial society.

Notes

1. An earlier version of this essay was presented in an interdisciplinary symposium *Religious Transformations: Colonial and Post-colonial Encounters*, Oct. 1996, at the Center for Historical Analysis, Rutgers, State University of New Jersey. I would like to thank anthropologist Michael Murphy and musicologists Denise Gallo and Amy Graziano for their suggestions. Financial assistance for this project was provided by the Research Advisory Council of the University of Alabama and the Committee for Cultural Cooperation between Spain and U.S. Universities.
2. Camille Paglia, "The Religion of Art," lecture, University of Richmond, February 1996.
3. Francisco Cervantes de Sálazar, *Túmulo Imperial de la gran ciudad de Méxcio* (Mexico City: Antonio de Espinosa, 1560). On this account, see Lota Spell, "Music at the Cathedral of Mexico in the Sixteenth Century," *Hispanic American Historical Review* 26 (August 1946), 305–6; Robert M. Stevenson, *Music in Mexico* (New York: Crowell, 1952), 89–90, and *Music in Aztec and Inca Territory* (Berkeley and Los Angeles: University of California Press, 1968), 200–2. My re-creation of the procession is based on Cervantes de Sálazar's account and various discussions of these events.
4. On the growth of musical repertory during this period in one Latin American center, see Robert J. Snow, *A New World Collection of Polyphony for Holy Week and the Salve Service: Guatemala City, Cathedral Archive, Music MS 4* (Chicago: University of Chicago Press, 1996), 1–26.
5. Gary Tomlinson, *Music in Renaissance Magic: Toward a Historiography of Others* (Chicago: University of Chicago Press, 1993), 1–43, has examined the complexity of discussing European music from the standpoint of the "other."
6. James Lockhart, *The Nauhaus after the Conquest: A Social and Cultural History of the Indians of Central Mexico, Sixteenth through Eighteenth Centuries* (Stanford: Stanford University Press, 1992), 172–74.
7. On the Catechism or "doctrina" see Robert Ricard, *The Spiritual Conquest of Mexico*, trans. by Lesley Byrd Simpson (Berkeley: University of California Press, 1966), 96–108. He discusses several missionaries who carried pictures representing hell and purgatory to clarify these concepts for the Indians. Jean Pierre Dedieu, "'Christianization' in New Castile: Catechism, Communion, Mass, and Confirmation in the Toledo Archbishopric, 1540–1650," trans. Susan Isabel Stein in *Culture and Control in Counter-Reformation Spain*, ed. by Anne J. Cruz and Mary Elizabeth Perry (Minneapolis: University of Minnesota Press, 1992), 4–10.
8. Carlos M. N. Eire, *From Madrid to Purgatory: The Art and Craft of Dying in Sixteenth-*

Century Spain (Cambridge: Cambridge University Press, 1995), 300–22 and 401–24, examines how the deaths of Philip II and Teresa of Ávila were used as pedagogical models.

9. Wagstaff, "Music for the Dead and the Control of Ritual Behavior in Spain, 1450–1550," *Musical Quarterly* 82 no. 3/4 (fall/winter 1998): 551–63. This obsession with orthodoxy in funeral ceremonies may have been connected to attempts to cleanse the region of Moslem and Jewish practices.

10. Ibid.

11. Mircea Eliade, et al., eds, *The Encyclopedia of Religion* (New York: Macmillan, 1987), vol. 12, 1–3, S. V. "Procession" by Ronald Grimes, makes the connection to the pilgrimage in terms of shared symbolism in making the journey itself one of spiritual discovery. Terence Bailey, *The Processions of Sarum and the Western Church*, Studies and Texts no. 21 (Toronto: Pontifical Institute of Mediaeval Studies, 1971), 112–19, on the traditional order of processions.

12. Stanley Sadie, ed., *The New Grove Dictionary of Music and Musicians* (London: Macmillan, 1980), vol. 15, 278–81, S. V. "Processional" by Michel Huglo, states that one of the ancient processions, the Major Litany or St. Mark's Procession, "represented the christianizing of an old pagan procession held on the same day, the *robigalia*, which had persisted until the Late Empire."

13. On pilgrimages in Latin America, see Robert Shadow and María Rodríguez Shadow, "La peregrinación religiosa en América Latina: Enfoques y perspectivas," in *Las peregrinaciones religiosas: Una aproximación*, ed. by Carlos Garma Navarro and Robert Shadow (Iztapalapa: Universidad Autónoma Metropolitana, 1994), 15–38.

14. Luis Weckmann, *The Medieval Heritage of Mexico*, trans. Frances M. López-Morillas (New York: Fordham University Press, 1992), 296–301.

15. Giovanna Recchia, *Espacio teatral en la Ciudad de México: Siglos XVI-XVIII* (Mexico City: Centro Nacional de Investigación Teatral Rodolfo Usigli, 1993).

16. William A. Christian, Jr., "Provoked Religious Weeping in Early Modern Spain," in *Religious Organization and Religious Experiences*, ed. J. Davis (New York: Academic Press, 1882), 97–114.

17. Susan Verdi Webster, "The Processional Sculpture of Penitential Confraternities in Early Modern Seville" (Ph.D. dissertation, University of Texas at Austin, 1992), 263–75. See also her *Art and Ritual in Golden-Age Spain: Sevillian Confraternities and the Processional Sculpture of Holy Week* (Princeton, N.J.: Princeton University Press, 1998).

18. David Summers, *The Judgement of Sense: Renaissance Naturalism and the Rise of Aesthetics* (Cambridge: Cambridge University Press, 1987), 125–50, examines fifteenth- and sixteenth-century discussions of viewers' reactions to art.

19. Eire, 24–34.

20. Manuel José de Lara Ródenas and David González Cruz, "Piedad y vanidades en la ciudaded de moguer: Un modelo de mentalidad religiosa y ritual funerrario en el barroco del 1700," in *Huelva en su Historia 2.*, ed. Javier Pérez-Embid and Encarnación Rivero Galán (Huelva: Colegio Universitario de la Rabida, 1988), 491–552. Huelva is west of Sevilla, in the region of Andalucia in Spain.

21. Eire, *From Madrid to Purgatory*, 114–67.

22. G. Grayson Wagstaff, "Music for the Dead: Settings of the *Officium* and *Missa pro defunctis* by Spanish and Latin American Composers before 1630" (Ph.D. dissertation, University of Texas at Austin, 1995), 75–150.

23. Piero Weiss and Richard Taruskin, eds., *Music in the Western World: A History in Documents* (New York: Schirmer Books, 1984), 25–32. In addition to Augustin, James McKinnon, *Music in Early Christian Literature* (Cambridge: Cambridge University Press, 1987), 29 and 101, quotes Clement of Alexandria.

24. Weiss and Taruskin, 31–32. McKinnon, 154–55.

25. On fifteenth- through seventeenth-century discussions of music's powers, see Don Harrán, "The Musical Encomium: Its Origins, Components, and Implications," *Actas*

del XV Congreso de la Sociedad Internacional de Musicolgía vol. 4 [*Revista de Musicolgía*, 15, no. 4 (1993)]: 2187–97.

26. Wagstaff, *Musical Quarterly*.

27. Andrew Stephen Arbury, "Spanish Catafalques of the Sixteenth and Seventeenth Centuries" (Ph.D. dissertation, Rutgers, State University of New Jersey, 1992).

28. Concerning rituals and their political purposes, see David I. Kertzer, *Ritual, Politics, and Power* (New Haven: Yale University Press, 1988).

29. Robert I. Levy, "The Quest for the Mind in Different Times and Places" in *Social History and Issues, Religious and Social Ritual: Interdisciplinary Explorations*, ed. Michael B. Aune and Valerie DeMarinis (Albany: State University of New York Press, 1996), 18. "Another of the ways that one is tempted to go from public forms to private mind is via the symbolic forms of community life. . . . Such forms, and not say, economic and subsistence activities, were taken in conjunction with the idea of *projective culture*, as being—as dreams were for individuals—royal roads to ethnic unconsciousness."

30. Roy Strong, *Art and Power: Renaissance Festivals, 1450–1650* (Suffolk, U.K.: Boydell Press, 1984; first edition 1973). See also Richard Trexler, *Public Life in Renaissance Florence* (Ithaca, N.Y.: Cornell University Press, 1980) and Edward Muir, *Civic Ritual in Renaissance Venice* (Princeton, N.J.: Princeton University Press, 1981).

31. See the special issue of *The Americas: A Quarterly Review of Inter-American Cultural History* 52, no. 3 (January 1996), particularly Linda A. Curcio-Nagy, "Introduction: Spectacle in Colonial Mexico," 275–82; Nancy H. Fee, "*La Entrada Angelopolitana*: Ritual and Myth in the Viceregal Entry in Puebla de Los Angeles," 283–320; and Steven Flinchpaugh, "Economic Aspects of the Viceregal Entrance in Mexico City," 345–66. Also Clara Garcia Aylaurdo, "A World of Images: Cult, Ritual, and Society in Colonial Mexico City," in *Rituals of Rule, Rituals of Resistance: Public Celebrations and Popular Culture in Mexico* ed. William H. Beezley, et al. (Wilmington, Del.: Scholarly Resources, 1994), 95–114.

32. Tess Knighton and Carmen Morte, "Ferdinand of Aragon's Entry into Valladolid in 1513: The Triumph of a Christian King," *Early Music History*, 18 (1999): 119–63, examine musical and visual elements employed in royal entries.

33. Thomas Turino, "Signs of Imagination, Identity, and Experience: A Peircian Semiotic Theory for Music," *Ethnomusicology* 43, no. 2 (spring/summer 1999): 221–56.

34. Ronald L. Grimes, *Beginnings in Ritual Studies* rev. ed. (Columbia: University of South Carolina Press, 1995), 34–36. Grimes poses the question, "Which roles extend beyond the ritual arena and which are confined to it?"

35. Translation after *The Hours of the Divine Office in English and Latin* (Collegeville, Minn.: The Liturgical Press, 1963), vol. 1, 1010.

36. Michael B. Aune, "The Subject of Ritual: Ideology and Experience in Action," in *Religious and Social Ritual: Interdisciplinary Explorations*, 157.

37. Sophie Menache, *The Vox Dei: Communication in the Middle Ages* (Oxford: Oxford University Press, 1990), 175–90, discusses the use of rituals as propaganda. For different examples of a projected construction of reality in the late twentieth century, see Marjorie Gerber, et al., *Media Spectacles* (New York: Routledge, 1993).

38. Pauline Moffitt Watts, "Languages of Gesture in Sixteenth-Century Mexico: Some Antecedents and Transmutations," in *Reframing the Renaissance: Visual Culture in Europe and Latin America 1450–1650*, ed. Claire Farago (New Haven: Yale University Press, 1995), 140–51.

9

Between Life and Death

The Funeral and Mourning Rituals
of the Southeastern Hungarian Vlach Roma

Irén Kertész Wilkinson

When an exotic custom fascinates us in spite of (or on account of) its singularity, it is generally because it presents us with a distorted reflection of a familiar image, which we confusedly recognize as such without yet managing to identify it.

—Claude Levi-Strauss, *The Mind of the Savage*

In the spring of 1999, Hungarian Television showed a short scene from a Roma funeral with the coffin surrounded by the grieving family of the deceased singing Gypsy songs and drinking. Hungarians I talked to were shocked and confused at the same time: "Why were they behaving as if *mulatnának* (revelling)"? In the village where I did my research, Hungarians who witnessed Vlach Roma singing in the local cemetery regarded their songs as "religious hymns of their own," or "prayers," something the Roma themselves found amusing.

The Roma in General

The Hungarian Vlach Roma, like any other Roma/Gypsy or Traveller group, have been living for centuries, if not always, in the social space of others and in economic and social interdependency with the dominant society. This relationship involves an enormous power imbalance, in which the Roma have been marginalized and stigmatized in the extreme. Under perpetual pressure to assimilate, locked into the worst conditions and bombarded daily by negative stereotypes, the Roma, in order to survive, have resorted to being adaptive and flexible on one hand, yet without relinquishing essential aspects of their own values on the other.

At the center of Vlach Roma resistance is their creation of a moral superiority to the *gaje* (non-Roma) who, according to the Roma, do not live in an ethical way, have no sense of shame, and do not know how to show respect.[1] This moral hierarchy is replicated within Vlach Roma society, where men—socially equal amongst themselves—occupy a higher social status than women. Their construction of a moral discourse, as in any other society, is based on the bodily experienced schemes. For the Hungarian Vlach Roma, this results in a physical, functional, and ideological division between upper/lower and inner/outer parts, with embodied meanings of pure and polluting that generate containment and force.[2] Accordingly, women who menstruate and give birth are seen as potentially soiled and thus incorporating in their engendered body the ambiguous social "other." Everyday and ritual performances amongst the Roma thus emphasize bodily based divisions in more or less elaborate ways of dressing, cooking, washing, spatial design of dwellings, etc. Most significantly, the bodily based moral discourse also governs the proper interactions between gendered Roma persons in their musical practices.

The death of an individual challenges the lifelong effort of the social group to maintain boundaries and to keep Roma members within the group. In this essay, I will discuss how the southeastern Hungarian Vlach Roma deal with the problems of death, with special attention to the role of music.

The Vlach Roma of Southeastern Hungary

The Vlach Roma communities I studied are in Békés County, a territory sandwiched between the Transylvanian mountains of Romania and the Hungarian Great Plain and also within easy reach of the Serbian border. Its population is an ethnic mixture of various Gypsy groups (Vlach, Romungro,[3] Beash[4]), Slovaks, Romanians, and Serbs interspersed among the Hungarian majority. The dominant religion is Calvinist Protestant, although there are also Roman Catholic villages as well as Greek Catholics in Romanian and Eastern Orthodox enclaves, along with a longstanding tradition of Evangelist Pentecostals in some areas. The Vlach Roma I researched are largely Roman Catholic by denomination, joined by a few Calvinists who also prefer to call on the services of the Catholic priests (as they say: "there is only one God") at birth and death.

The warm climate and fertile soil of Békés favors agriculture, which was one factor that, by the 1980s, allowed Vlach Roma men to revert to their traditionally favored occupation of full-time horse dealing after several decades of being obliged to take "proper" waged jobs (e.g., manual work in brewing, forestry, road construction, or cart-driving for the cooperative farm), in contrast to most Hungarian Vlach Roma elsewhere, whose dealings in horses remained a side occupation.[5] At the time my research began in the late 1980s, a declining light industry provided work for some of the Vlach Roma women alongside occasional jobs for Hungarians such as domestic cleaning, white-washing walls, plucking poultry, and gathering onions, etc. For these jobs, they received payment in kind or in money. Seasonal work carried out by a family team (collecting herbs, edible snails for export, picking blueberries, cutting sorghum, etc.) is still a popular way of supplementing their generally meager incomes.

Most Vlach Roma families live in houses abandoned by Hungarians. In the past, they were generally concentrated in a few streets on the outskirts of the village. Since the late 1980s, however, they have increasingly tended to invade Hungarian space and move toward the center of the villages. Younger married couples have set up separate households following the birth of their first child and obtained places either to have more convenient access to the main roads or to distance themselves from internal rivalry. With this drift, previously obvious differences between Roma and non-Roma houses are becoming less visible: the gates are not open to the yards nor is washing hung out on the fence.

"Don't Look Back!"

The Vlach Roma, the second largest group, comprise 20 percent of the total Roma population. They are relatively recent migrants having arrived in Hungary from Romania, as their name indicates, from the mid-nineteenth century onward. They are bilingual in Romany and Hungarian, and remained itinerant, at least seasonally, up until World War II. The use of the Romany language is regarded by the Vlach Roma themselves as a key element in their identity construction. It differentiates them not only from the dominant society but also from other Roma groups, making them "true Rom," as opposed to the Romungro, who now speak only Hungarian and are considered by the Vlach Roma to belong somewhere between themselves and the Hungarian population: "not [real] Rom anymore but not yet gajo[6] either."[7] Although I worked with groups who were among the last wave of those who left Romania,[8] by the time I encountered them any recollection of that sojourn had already sunk into oblivion, along with any attachment they may have had to a nomadic existence; they now consider the latter to be a pointless hardship compared to a fixed domicile.[9] The ultimately Indian origin of their ethnic group, although a significant factor in Roma politics, holds little interest.[10] It would be misleading to conclude, however, that they are as settled as Hungarians. Even the younger generation extend their feelings beyond the dominant society's conventional concept of a Magyar/Hungarian "homeland": "We would not say 'my country' but 'world' (luma)."[11]

Their interest in the present, which typically for Roma/Gypsy and Traveller groups comprises the three living generations,[12] is also apparent in their songs. Song texts are mostly in the first person and present tense, often in the form of a dialogue. Hardships suffered at the hands of the outside world are not specified in songs but indicated by references to *gajo* (non-Roma) protagonists and institutions (such as prison or hospital), nor are horrific events discussed in everyday life. The ritual injunction "Don't look back" that I was given by one family on the way to church to baptize their baby does indeed embody a "whole cosmology, an ethic, a metaphysic, a political philosophy."[13]

Purity and Pollution: Rites of Passage and Musical Practices

Birth and Baptism

The moral implication embodied in purity concepts is that only those who act according to the laws will be lucky, healthy, wealthy, and the object of the respect and honor of other Roma. Misfortune suggests infringement of the laws, so that shame may even be attached to some forms of illness.[14] The sexual act, which is clean within marriage provided it is kept private (that is, provided that no other Roma knows about it) becomes public knowledge with pregnancy and birth. Because babies at birth leave the "clean" inner wombs through the mother's polluted external sexual organs they themselves become polluted, which is a strong reason for having childbirth assisted by *gajo* doctors and midwives. The first child also marks a major transition for the mother in her new role as an initiator of life, albeit in polluting circumstances. Furthermore, because mother and child share the pollution of childbirth, this produces the strongest, most abiding emotional tie for a Rom, making it of the most positive relationship featured in song lyrics[15]: stronger than father, "brothers," or "sisters."[16]

Babies must be "cleansed" through the ritual of baptism, significantly carried out by a non-Rom priest.[17] Following the six-week period of pollution after birth, there is a considerable pressure to mount baptism if "the baby cries a lot" due to fear that an unbaptized child "would not go to heaven if it died suddenly" or "could get exchanged" during its sleep, when the soul leaves the body temporarily. Until they are baptized, babies are protected by providing them with an amulet, such as a red ribbon tied around the wrist. Through baptism, the child is officially adopted into Rom society; that, I was told, is when "their face turns rosy" and the process of becoming a Rom starts. Baptism may be celebrated after the ceremony by a larger gathering of cognates and affines or just by the immediate family. It comprises performances of both slow songs and dance songs, with the latter eventually dominating. No professional Romungro band is invited.

As babies, children of both genders are adored. One of the most remarkable expressions of Gypsies' love for their babies is that kissing and cuddling can encompass the whole body, including the genitals, areas that in later life become highly suspect for pollution and, accordingly, a central concern of the culturally constructed sense of shame. What this practice creates, however, is a deeply felt unity between love and sensuality, generating close social interaction amongst the members of family and community, while its expression is soon channeled into the socially ascribed ways. Gypsy music-making, singing, and dance both perform and engender this culturally sensualized, feeling body in highly expressive but controlled ways.

Weddings

At puberty, a girl must learn how to control her body so that she may marry as a virgin with honor (*patjiv*). Her family's reputation and her own are celebrated by a large gathering of kinfolk and affines including community members at her wedding. What is ritually sanctioned here is the girl's passage from girlhood to womanhood, to the socially "intermediate" position of wife—reflected in the typical use of music provided by the ethnically "intermediate" Romungro band to mark the occasion—rather than, say, the bribe's transition from one family unit to another, because newlywed couples do not always reside with the groom's family. Both husband and wife keep their descent lines open and alive and can return to these as and when necessary: the essential thing is that their movements remain within Roma society.[18]

Although the wedding music is a mixture of Roma and Hungarian dance songs, the latter are at least partially "Vlachified" through Vlach Roma dance steps and movements. Various levels of kinship are performed in dance: grandmother dancing with grandchildren, fathers with daughters, and mothers with sons, etc. Weddings are also occasions for playful competition and challenges to ascribed social roles through dance (the Romany word *khelel* [dance] relates to the verb *khelel pe* [play]): men provoke the bridegroom; unmarried girls dare men, and so flout their own ascribed social position by "cheating" to get behind their partners' back;[19] and married couples perform sexually explicit movements (like the husband dancing closely behind his wife).

The gender hierarchy is embodied in the performance structure of dance songs. In these, a melody is accompanied by "mouth bass" elaborations (in imitation of instruments), and hand clapping, foot stamping, or leg slapping, both on and off main beats, to create a dense texture of rhythmic and tonal polyphony, filling up every space. Is it not, perhaps, a soundscape version of Vlach Roma households filled with relatives and children? This contrasts with the monophonic performance structure of the slow songs, a musical metaphor of men's equality amongst each other. These are delivered with a subtle heterophony between the exchangeable roles of "leader" and "helpers" enacting both the mutual dependency of Rom individuals as well as negotiating subtle discrepancies in social roles. The performance of slow songs requires singers to make long pauses, or silences, between their main musical lines, which can be interpreted as musical markers of the social boundary and distance between Vlach Roma society (sung lines) and *gaje*.

Singing and Cleansing; Pollution and Creation

Song, or "true speech,"[20] holds great social and moral value for the Vlach Roma collectively as well as psychological significance for the individual Rom. Voice production is located in the upper, inner (i.e., clean) part of the body. One of the Romany words for singing, indeed, is *phurdel* (to blow), which also denotes a cleansing and curative technique among the Rom.[21] It allows feelings about shame, death, love, and other aspects of life to be "told," that is implicated and shared (confessed)[22] with others through the ambiguous symbols of the song texts. Furthermore, through song, shame can be transferred to someone else. In the case of a male singer that transference will be to his wife, who, being an affine, is in a socially ambivalent position, both loved and distrusted, whereas a woman singer would choose a non-kin female as a subject of her projections.

In practice, Roma morality is more complex than a simple choice between right and wrong. Any breach of law is judged according to its particular context, the extent to which family prestige is involved, and, most significantly, whether it threatens social unity, and increases or decreases the social cohesion of the group. At the time of my research, for example, elopement—a socially accepted and institutionalized alternative to marriage amongst the Roma—still entailed the woman being excluded for a period of time by her immediate family as a punishment.[23] Nowadays, it is not uncommon for a number of girls in their twenties (a mature age for a Vlach Roma girl) to have children without getting married and still stay at home with their own parents without any retribution. Whatever the initial embarrassment to the woman and her parents, her children, including offspring of *gajo* fathers (or even, in one case known to me, born to a *gaji* mother), are incorporated into the community as they are strengthening the social group. A parallel may be seen here in the way that Vlach Roma divide their own Romany songs from adapted Hungarian songs even though the "otherness" of the latter is largely obliterated in performance trans-formations. What is important is, that musical distinctions are made through a process of selective inclusion that simultaneously enriches Roma musical practice, or in the same way, a good non-Roma-born singer may be accepted because of the contribution that singer makes to Roma heritage. Leach's notion that "clean/dirty" corresponds to the dichotomy "impotence/potency," with its implication that social power ultimately is located in "dirt,"[24] is useful here in underlining attributes that operate flexibly in the maintenance of Vlach Roma morality and identity.

Death Rituals and Music

Types of Death and Their Relation to the Mulo

Death is an irreversible loss and an extremely traumatic event for the Roma because it affirms their fragile social position as a threatened minority. Consequently, they, like Travellers,[25] never regard death as something good or to be wished for, even when old or ill, the way that some societies do.[26] Nevertheless, the southeast Vlach Roma of Hungary also differentiate between an individually or socially bad death, and the most despicable kind of death, suicide. This classification guides their efforts to assess and guard against the malevolent response of the *mulo*, the spirit of the dead, toward the living.

The *mulo* stands at the center of the Vlach Roma belief system as other Roma and Gypsy/Travellers.[27] As Okely noted,[28] the *mulo* is a personification of the *gajo*, projected as an alter ego of the living Roma: unpredictable, wild, and likely to be provoked into returning by anything unfinished.[29]

In case of death by violence, a *mulo* would be unable to rest unless living relatives provided retribution. Nowadays, however, the vendetta that was once sanctioned by Romany *kris* (law) is so closely associated with pollution that retribution is left for the *gajo* authority, the police.

A child who dies young, besides the natural grief this occasions the immediate family, leaves non-kindred essentially unaffected because its spirit is not considered dangerous. Furthermore, the one wake for a child in the village where I stayed was reported by the men who attended as being "boring because there was hardly any singing since the child did not have his favorite songs yet." (The Vlach Roma have no separate children's songs: children learn to perform adult songs as part of the process of becoming a Rom.) Suicide is very rare among them. The communities where I worked knew of only one Rom suicide, and when references were made to him the speaker would spit on the ground to demonstrate a physical need felt to cleanse oneself of such a polluting thought: "No one went to his funeral. He died like a dog."

It is different with those who are old and whose death is expected. In the summer of 1999, my friend in the village where I did my research whispered to me that her uncle's cancer, despite initially successful treatment, had returned. He was at home and although unaware of his illness, was receiving a steady stream of visitors who were coming "to pay up their debts" as the song lyrics state. My friend was worried that this would arouse his suspicion because, in 1987 when his mother had been close to death of old age, members, both close and distant, had visited her constantly for two weeks prior to her death. They had congregated around her bed, joking when she was awake, and reckoned "they had her back to life three times by making her sing" before it failed to work the fourth time.

Death as a Process

Hungarian Vlach Roma death rituals start with a three-night wake preceding the funeral. It is then followed by two commemoration services, *pomana*, held at six months and a year after death, when the deceased person's soul finally separates from the body and the family mourners are reincorporated into the society of living. When clinical death sets in, a small glass is placed before the nose and mouth of the deceased, used to make sure she or he really has breathed his or her last. The body is then washed and dressed, either by a female or male relative who is not of the immediate family, before transferring it to the mortuary. For some Roma, being left unburied and alone in the cemetery for three nights is feared more than death itself, since their earlier practice of keeping the corpse in the house for the three-night wake[30] has been outlawed by *gajo* health regulations. Nevertheless, at one recent wake I attended the deceased was permitted to remain with the mourners, largely because the bitter cold weather presented less risk of bodily decomposition, but also because the family passed a handsome bribe to the health officials to turn a blind eye. Whether the body is in the house or not, the soul is still nearby because the body is still intact; it needs to be respected and cared for in order to pacify any malevolent feelings it may have for the living relatives.

Death rituals amongst the Vlach Roma, as in other societies, focus on the processes of separation between flesh and bone, body and soul, and the dead and living.[31] For the Hungarian Vlach Roma, the decomposition process enacts the breakdown of social divisions that the deceased faced when alive: Roma versus non-Roma; man versus woman. The dead spirit becomes a *gajo* and thus the previously pure Rom is now polluting. Life processes of "entering," "becoming," "being part of," and "proliferating" are reversed and performed as separation-transition-aggregation[32] in order to reconstitute normal life.

Wake

Like the English Travellers,[33] the Vlach Roma I worked with consider wakes and funerals the biggest events in their lives: "It is bigger than weddings." The only instruction I had from my hostess was that both customary greetings and smiling were forbidden during the wake. I was surprised to see the lack of remorse shown by many community members who were not from the direct family of the dead person; indeed, it is quite usual for joking and merrymaking to proceed alongside the mourning of the relatives.[34] Unmarried men and girls play practical jokes on adults, try to get them drunk, or create other mischief, and parents may look for a wife for unmarried sons. Parents of unmarried girls keep a particularly close eye on them at these events because bride-stealing reputedly may still occur at such gatherings. In this heightened atmosphere of fear and excitement, of almost palpable liminality, all women tend to stick together, especially when venturing outside.

The seating arrangements in the room in which the wake is held follows age and gender, with older male and female participants taking up central positions and the younger members of the community on the periphery. Children are present but, unlike at other social events, they do not participate in singing. Women tend to group together with each other, or with men to whom they are related. If space allows, a room is set aside for women who come unaccompanied, and this is respected by the menfolk, which reverses the everyday practice of women having to respect an exclusive male-attended *mulatsago*.[35] Close relations demonstrate their participation in the pollution of death by wearing black clothing;[36] less immediate kin and friends of the deceased will avoid brightly colored garments, especially reds, greens, or blues. Great care is taken to cover mirrors and windows lest the dead spirit get a chance to see its difference from the living (uncovering of either arouses near panic). If the body is in the next room, people visit it from time to time. Over the course of the three-night wake, hundreds of Roma come to pay their respects; significantly, these are also occasions for reconciliation of grievances and exercising forgiveness.[37]

Music, Death, and Burial

The songs performed at a Rom wake are mostly of the slow variety and embody various levels of the social structure. Performances involve participation by all or most of those present through subgroups of older and younger male or female singers, community and family groups, down to specific individuals who are invited to sing on account of their acknowledged aesthetic skill or social standing. Even during long "suites" of songs, the lead is not allowed to alternate between different genders. Lyrics emphasize departure and are regularly sung in the form of dialogue between the deceased and an offspring ("I must go away, my son, I must leave you" answered by "Don't sleep the whole night, mother").

As each evening progresses, any joviality of mood subsides into growing solemnity. If the body is laid out in the house, the mourners will sing until before midnight. After that, people keep checking the time and huddle together until early morning, when the mood starts to lift again, generally prompted by performances from the menfolk of highest status, who are often also the most exceptional performers. As these men turn, each picking up and completing the current song before starting a new song of their own choice, the participants are lifted from gloom and anguish to *voja* (a heightened state of mind) that transcends sorrow. Hopefulness emerges: "It is getting dark, but the dawn will come."

Toward dawn, the deceased gradually becomes distanced through the musical performance. Song lyrics such as "Who had the idea of having to go to a cemetery, with no window or door to let my mother out" comes to dominate. It is also customary to perform the favorite song of the deceased, which at both wakes I attended happened to be a Hungarian slow dance song, but which is performed without the polyphonic vocal parts typical for deliveries in other social contexts. The non-Vlach performance of a Hungarian dance song, accompanied by a Romungro band (if already invited for the wake), embodies the liminal position of the soul being in between Vlach Roma and *gajo* society, and symbolically marries the deceased to the *gajo* world.

Funeral

The burial is invariably arranged to take place the morning after the third night of the wake. All mourners start at the house where the wake was held, and are joined by a hired Romungro Gypsy band, if one has not already been playing at the wake itself. There is much crying and sobbing from relatives, male or female, with demonstrative gestures of sorrow (ripping of shirts by men) or near-catatonic shock. The mourners insist that the coffin be turned so that the deceased's feet will be first out of the house (so the body cannot return). The coffin is first laid outside on a table with continued singing as bottles of hard liquor are passed around (spirits are the obligatory drinks at wakes and funerals). The arrival of the priest leads into the service, which opens with a prayer. Then the priest speaks a farewell on behalf on the deceased in acceptance with a list prepared by the immediate family to include members of all Roma families present and away, lest they become the possible targets for revenge by *mulo*. The relatives will then cut small pieces from the shroud of the deceased for both their own protection and as one of the few direct mementos that they allow themselves to keep. [38]

Once the coffin has been closed and placed on a horse-driven Gypsy cart, an extremely slow procession starts toward the cemetery. Close relatives stop the cart at every few yards in a show of pulling it back to postpone the departure of the deceased. When the cart reaches the main road, the traffic is stopped, a point of pride for the Roma. The grander the funeral, the longer the obstruction; this is one of the few occasions when the Roma publicly demonstrate their strength in number amongst the *gaje*. When the graveside is eventually reached, often taking several hours, candles are lit at the head with the family singing. The coffin is slowly lowered into the grave, which is the last moment of great anxiety in case the coffin is accidentally dropped. The grave is lined with tiles and red carpet—like "Brezhnev had at his funeral"[39]—and favorite objects of the deceased are placed in it. Drink is poured into the grave, and also a cigarette, by extended family members.

In the distance, Roma are chatting and joking as people start moving slowly home before dark sets in.

The Cemetery

Hungarian cemeteries typically lie well outside of the village. Traditionally, the Roma were forced to bury their dead in a far corner of the cemetery. According to their customs, wooden crosses displayed only the *gajo* name of the deceased as Travellers of England.[40] By the time I started my work, however, that tradition was starting to transform. Roma graves were being located in previously *gajo*-only burial areas—roughly parallel to, though preceding, the Roma penetration of *gaje* living spaces already referred to. Furthermore, the Roma have adapted the *gajo* customs of marking the grave with a headstone, though typically they decorate this with photographs of the deceased and horse figurines to differentiate them from the *gaje* graves. I know of one case when the family erected a little plastic roof over his tomb to prevent "snow and rain falling on him." The following summer, this grave had a fence around it, with a gate opening onto a "garden," and a bench to sit on to make it look "like a little house."

Pomana

The first six weeks after a funeral—the transition period between being alive and "fully" dead—are when the deceased is the most polluting because the corpse is still near to life, as evidenced by the observation that "the hair and the nails are growing." All members of the extended family observe a compulsory six weeks' mourning period, while for close cognates, along with husbands and wives, the period may continue for one year. During mourning, men do not shave (a symbol of the still growing hair of the deceased), married women wear black dresses and a head scarf, while unmarried girls tie a black ribbon into their hair. This requirement to enact[41] pollution is often expressed in physical terms: "I hate this black scarf; it drags me down and gives me a headache." As hands are possible vehicles of pollution, mourning women are forbidden to make cakes or noodles in order to avoid passing any contagion to their families. Families with babies may leave dim lights on during the night during these six weeks. Mourning is also marked by a conspicuous avoidance of singing; although a Rom may hum a slow song quietly to him- or herself, dancing is categorically prohibited. A young man told me how ill he became when he once broke that prohibition during the mourning for his grandmother. He and other male relatives had paid a visit to his dying uncle, the son of his grandmother, who on seeing them unshaved became suspicious that something had happened to his mother. Disbelieving their claim that only a local (non-related) Rom man had died, he asked his nephew to dance in order to prove that they were telling the truth, so he had felt obliged to do so to spare his uncle's feelings.

The ritual *pomana* commemoration for a deceased person is held at around the end of the six-week mourning period—when "the face will turn black" and decay starts—and repeated again one year after death. It takes the form of a meal in which the deceased's favorite dishes are offered, usually having been "asked for" in a dream that a close relative will claim to have had. Given the high risk of pollution associated with food handling, most guests take great care over what they eat. In both communities where I worked, these meals were prepared separately for the Rom and the invited older Hungarian guests. Cooking for the Roma was done by an older Hungarian woman and for invited Hungarians by a mourning female relative of the dead person with the help of men; this would ensure that any evil or malicious feelings associated with the dead would only be transmitted to non-Rom.

At the six-weeks *pomana*, Hungarians were served meat with bone (chicken),[42] which changed to stuffed pepper with minced meat by the last, one-year *pomana*. The fear of contamination prompts many Vlach Roma to arrive deliberately late for the lunch to avoid ingesting the "wrong type of food," warning me personally about the danger of "eating the soul of the dead." The few men who are willing to eat under these arrangements will often claim to feel ill the next morning, despite taking food from a supposedly "pure" source.

Men who are permitted to "break the mourning" come already shaved; women bring colorful clothes that they will change into. They first join performances of slow songs with those who will carry on before moving to a different room to start dancing. At some point during the dancing, each person pours red wine over a black piece of clothing they have worn during the mourning period, which then they trample on with dance steps and never wear again. Although close relatives will resist the end of mourning even at the one year *pomana*, convention obliges them to do so and to mark a return to full life by dance; refusal to do so is taken as an invitation for death to claim further victims. The soul is now separated from the body and the transition is finished for both dead and living.

Return to Life

Hungarian Vlach Roma, like other Roma/Gypsy groups,[43] make a point of avoiding any mention of the dead by name in order to avoid seeming to invite a return of the deceased's *mulo*, though I have noticed there is less reluctance about this more recently. The traditional approved manner of invoking a dead person's memory is to perform songs that she or he was associated with, which, by being sung words, concurrently purify the performers' soul.[44] The room in which someone has died is repainted and rearranged to associate all possible material association with the dead. In an extreme case, this may even mean selling the home, as happened with the unmarried son and daughter of one already widowed woman, who preferred to sell the mudbrick house that the three had been sharing up until the mother's death. The Hungarian who bought it paid only a nominal price and dismantled it to use the mudbricks. The unmarried son and daughter who had lived with the deceased woman moved to the home of their brother and his family. Two married sons of the deceased who had lived next to one another for decades also separated. One moved to a house near to his children (which was only a few hundred yards away from his previous house). The death of elders of an extended family has gradually given rise to the formation of a number of subgroups marking the beginning of future extended families.

After the one-year *pomana*, deaths are marked only within the family on intimate family occasions, such as New Year's and, more especially, All Saint's Day, when they take the form of wake-*pomana* rituals compressed into a few hours. The Roma go in groups to the cemetery with flowers and bottles of alcoholic drinks to visit the graves of kinfolk and common ancestors, and offer the dead a drink and a cigarette. At dusk everyone hurries away from the cemetery, cheering themselves by singing dance songs as they progress. The menfolk and their older sisters tend to continue with singing and dancing at a local bar that antagonizes Hungarians who are present because they often misinterpret it as a sign of disrespect for the dead.[45]

Conclusion

The death rituals of the Roma, like those in other societies, are intended not only to cope with individual loss but also with revitalizing the remaining social group. For the Roma, lacking land of their own to live on or even to cultivate, the focus is on maintaining their separateness as an ethnic group from the dominant society on which they depend economically and to which they must therefore, to some extent, adapt. A deep-seated Roma fear of being engulfed becomes all too real when they face the physical disintegration of an individual Rom body, on which their sense of superior morality is premised. To renew and reinforce their morality, the Roma identify with the processes of disintegration, immerse themselves in its pollution by enacting processes from a selection of their ritual and everyday practices, accentuating some while reversing others.

To renew the boundaries of their separation from the *gaje* and other Roma groups, the Vlach Roma engage "specialists" from these groups onto whom they can transfer the pollution of death and thus regain their cleanliness. By officiating over the funeral, as at baptisms, the priest personifies the polluted body and soul through spoken words that are opposed to the Roma's "true speech" of singing. The enlistment of a Romungro Gypsy band, as at weddings, marks the intermediate position of the deceased in transition from Roma society to the non-Roma world of the dead. The band's "wordless" instrumental music embodies both the materialistic *gajo* world (for whom the Romungro usually perform) and the pure, non-materialistic concerns of the Vlach Roma.

Complex transformations and reversals are observed in relation to Roma and *gaje* women, too. A selected *gaji*, who in an everyday context would represent the antithesis to the "clean" Roma women, becomes the one clean person permitted to prepare safe meals for the Roma, while the cooking of the "dirty" mourning Roma woman transfers her pollution to invited, older non-Roma guests. Symbolically this also hastens separation of the flesh from the bone, which the Roma themselves must demonstratively postpone. Furthermore, the potential pollutedness of flesh that is normally associated with women in an everyday context is also extended to men during mortuary rites. To re-create male purity, the usual Roma division between the genders is overlaid by a division according to generations. The flesh is now associated with the younger generation, whose social task is to proliferate Roma society through the body, while the renewal of Roma spiritual life is the task of the older, mostly, but not exclusively, male generation.

The musical performances during mortuary rites emphasize the various stages of passage. The longest and musically most dense performances are those that take place during the wake, when body and soul are still together and the corpse is nearby. Each night enacts a transition from life to death and back to life, with performances of the older generation providing the spiritual continuity of Roma life. The funeral, at which hundreds of Roma walk (as opposed to dance) and sing their way to the cemetery, is a major public demonstration of Roma unity. After the funeral, the long silences of the slow song performances transform into "dead silences" of the mourning period that sharply marks the living and the deceased, while re-creating the boundaries between Rom and non-Roma, men and women. Separation is complete when the flesh has parted from the bone, and the soul has gone to its proper resting place. Then the return to normal life is celebrated by dance and dance songs. Vlach Roma life is fully restored with all the hierarchies of engendered and sensualized joy of existence performed in the dance-song performances.

The funeral rites also display less-fixed aspects of evolutionary significance. While distancing and "*gajofying*" the dead remain, at least during the wake, for all the elements of evident continuity of the southeastern Hungarian Vlach, yet in the death rituals the seeds of change are already apparent. The large funeral processions have always been performances of local "politics"—as demonstrations of Roma unity, their spiritual and moral integrity[46]– but they have by now turned into a proper political dialogue between Roma politicians and the dominant society. Slow but appreciable economic advancement has allowed at least some Roma to commission professional video recordings of funerals that are kept as treasured mementos along with other possessions associated with the deceased. More usually, the communities are keen to obtain through researchers the recorded voice and images of dead while they were alive. Roma are now preparing their resting places, which only a few years ago would have been a very un-Roma request. Are we witnessing new strategies emerging in response to a change in their lives: a sense of "We are here to stay, ready to mark and take our dead back, and with them our memory and past"? Are the local Vlach Roma death rituals performing their demand for a new history that they regard as worth remembering?

Notes

1. See also Judith Okely, *The Traveller Gypsies* (Cambridge: Cambridge University Press, 1984); Michael Stewart, *The Time of the Gypsies* (Boulder, Colo.: Westview Press, 1997); and Paloma Guy y Blasco, *Gypsies in Madrid. Sex, Gender and the Performance of Identity* (Oxford: Berg, 1996).
2. The generation of bodily experiences in the creation of image schemata in language is discussed by Mark Johnson in his book *Body in the Mind* (Chicago: University of Chicago Press, 1987).
3. The Romungro were the earliest migrants to Hungary, first entering the country in the sixteenth century. They are also the largest group, totaling about 350,000, or 70 percent of Hungary's Roma population. (Hungary has a total population of ten million). Many Romungros are professional musicians.
4. Beash, or the Boyash, are Romanian- and Hungarian-speaking Gypsies famous for their woodcraft and making various household utensils.
5. See Stewart, *The Time of the Gypsies*, 97–109.
6. The word *gajo* itself among Hungarian Rom primarily designates a "peasant," one who digs the "impure" earth. However, they make a further distinction within non-Gypsies between *gaje* (peasants) and non-Gypsy gentility (*raj manuš* [R] or *úri ember* [H]), who are higher and cleaner than the former through occupational and social rank.
7. Péter Szuhay, *A magyarországi cigányok kultúrája, ethnikus kultúra vagy a szegénység kultúrája?* [The culture of Hungarian Gypsies: Ethnic culture or the culture of poverty?] (Budapest: Panorama, 1999), 32.
8. *Erdœs Kamill Cigánytanulmányai* [Gypsy studies by Erdös Kamill], ed. J. Vekerdi, (Gyula: Erkel Ferenc Múzeum, 1989), 66.
9. One young man remembered his grandmother talking once of relatives in Romania, while a woman told me about her parents who were still nomadic during the summers before World War II.
10. Questions like "Is it true that we come from India?" for the older generations, it has little more significance than being reassured that Roma are everywhere, while the younger generation is increasingly interested in other Roma, especially in their music.
11. Irén Kertész Wilkinson, "Differences among One's Own and Similarities with the Other: Dual Role of Adopted Songs and Texts among the Hungarian Vlach Gypsies

in *Echo der Vielfalt* [Echoes of Diversity] ed. U. Hemetek (Vienna: Böhlau-Verlag, 1996), 229.

12. Guy y Blasco, *Gypsies in Madrid. Sex, Gender and the Performance of Identity*, 4.

13. Pierre Bourdieu, *Outline of a Theory of Practice* (Cambridge: Cambridge University Press, 1972), 94.

14. One woman almost died after a miscarriage because shame of disclosure made her keep it secret for days while her husband's brothers were staying with them; she did not allow her children, who were daily visitors to other households, to leave home during this period. The problem was only resolved by my telling the husband, where-upon the brothers left immediately in order to avoid further pollution. Another woman in the community, commenting on this incident, blamed the woman herself for the miscarriage because of her earlier carelessness in stepping over a rope on the road: because it was snake-shaped, it was seen as an evil force. When the same woman had a stye in her eye, she projected the blame onto a nursing mother's curse so as to avoid any suspicion that she herself might have breached the purity laws.

15. Kertész Wilkinson, "Genuine and Adopted Songs in the Vlach Gypsy Repertoire: A Controversy Re-examined," in *British Journal of Ethnomusicology* 1, ed. J. Baily, D. Hughes, C. Pegg and R. Widdes (ICTM UK Chapter, 1992), 118.

16. A Rom who assured me of his brotherly love was honoring me when he said, "I treat you as if we came out of the same cunt." It follows that brothers and sisters cannot transmit pollution to each other. One woman used to go to her brother's yard for water in the period after childbirth, saying this was all right because they were related.

17. Priests are also called on to "sanctify" new or redecorated houses before a Rom moves in. Economically well-off Roma make a big celebration of this, entirely comparable to a large baptism.

18. Although the Hungarian Vlach Roma, being sedentary, show differences from nomadic Gypsy groups like the English Travellers, their use of kinship system is still very similar. Both have a "cognatic system whereby an individual can claim member-ship of both his or her father's and mother's kindred. . . . After marriage each spouse retains their original kin connections, so the couple can choose to associate with mem-bers of either the husband's or wife's kindred, often alternating between the two. . . . Residence is neither virilocal nor uxorilocal" (Okely, *The Traveller Gypsies*, 172).

19. Kertész Wilkinson, "Musical Performance: A Model for Social Interaction between Vlach Gypsies in South-Eastern Hungary," in *Gypsy Culture and Gypsy Identity*, eds. T. Acton and G. Mundy (Hatfield: University of Hertfordshire Press, 1997), 111.

20. Stewart, *The Time of the Gypsies*, 198–202.

21. See also Anne Sutherland, "Health and Illness among the Rom of California," in *Journal of the Gypsy Lore Society*, Fifth Series, No. 1/2, ed. Sheila Salo, (Cheverly, Md.: Gypsy Lore Society, 1992), 25.

22. Kertész Wilkinson, "Therapeutic Aspect of Vlach Gypsy Singing," in *Voice and Ritual*, ed. K. Dorothova (Moscow: Institute of State Art, 1995), 107–23.

23. Kertész Wilkinson, "Genuine and Adopted Songs in the Vlach Gypsy Repertoire: A Controversy Re-examined," *British Journal of Ethnomusicology* , 111–36.

24. Edmund Leach *Culture and Communication: The Logic by Which Symbols Are Connected* (Cambridge: Cambridge University Press, 1976), 62.

25. Okely, *The Traveller Gypsies*, 230.

26. For example the English; see Nigel Barley, *Dancing on the Grave. Encounters with Death* (Cambridge: Cambridge University Press, 1995), 110–11.

27. See also Erdœs, *Erdœs Kamill Cigánytanulmányai* [Gypsy studies by Erdös Kamill], 40–41; and Patrick Williams, *Nous, ou n'en parles pas. Les vivant at les morts chez les Manouches* (Paris: Éditions de la Maison des Sciences de l'Homme, 1993), 5–53.

28. Okely, *The Traveller Gypsies*, 228.

29. I was told by a Rom woman how a dead person had visited a friend of hers during the night to ask for the return of a skirt she had lent previously; after the woman returned the garment to the family, the visits by the *mulo* stopped. A Rom man was generally so afraid of his dead father's spirit that he never walked alone after dark and had to be

accompanied if he left the house. Nighttime sightings of *mulo* on the road or near to a cemetery are common among the Vlach Gypsies.

30. According to some Roma, in the past the deceased used to be made to sit with the mourning relatives, fed and given drink as if he or she had not died.

31. R. Herz, "Contribution á une étude sur la représentation collective de la mort," *Année sociologique* (1907), 48–137.

32. Arnold van Gennep, *The Rites of Passage* (London: Routledge and Kegan Paul, 1960 [first ed. 1908, Paris]).

33. Okely, *The Traveller Gypsies*, 192.

34. Merrymaking at funerals or transformation of mood from sad to happy, at least at some of the event, is not unique to the Roma. It is a widespread practice around the world from Latin America, through Western and Eastern Europe to Africa, just to mention a few. See Maurice Bloch and Jonathan Parry, eds. *Death and the Regeneration of Life* (Cambridge: Cambridge University Press, 1982); Peter Metcalf and Richard Huntington, *Celebrations of Death: The Anthropology of Mortuary Ritual* (Cambridge: Cambridge University Press, 1991); and Barley, *Dancing on the Grave.*

35. Stewart, *The Time of the Gypsies*, 187.

36. See also Okely, *The Traveller Gypsies*, 218.

37. Ibid., *The Traveller Gypsies*, 192.

38. Other items, such as the deceased's bed and clothes, are given away to the *gajos*.

39. See also Magda Szapu, *Halotti szokások és hiedelmek a kaposszentjakabi oláh cigányoknál* [Death customs and beliefs among the Vlach gypsies of Kaposszentjakab] (Budapest: Hungarian Academy of Sciences Research Group, 1984).

40. Okely, *The Traveller Gypsies*, 226.

41. Reenactment can be a way of dealing with shame and pollution. For example, the husband of a woman who miscarried was put in a shameful position by his wife having to show the lower part of her body to the visiting doctor in their own home. He overcame this by later dressing himself up as the doctor and thereby enacting the dual role of doctor-husband.

42. The Roma frequently use sayings like "I eat your lung" or "Let me lick your heart," some which are similar to Hungarian sayings, to express special affection. A Roma woman once said jokingly to her ill husband "I eat your flesh," and she was widely frowned on by other Roma because it implied her desire to have him dead.

43. Okely, *The Traveller Gypsies*, 225.

44. When I returned to the Roma in, 1994 after my mother's death, one woman, instead of talking about it, sang me a song with the lyrics "My brother died just as your mother," drawing a parallel between our fates.

45. Kertész Wilkinson, *The Fair Is Ahead of Me. Individual Creativity and Social Contexts in the Performances of a South-East Hungarian Vlach Gypsy Slow Song* (Budapest: Hungarian Academy of Sciences, 1997), 138; Szuhay, *A magyarországi cigányok kultúrája, ethnikus kultúra vagy a szegénység kultúrája?* (The culture of Hungarian gypsies: Ethnic culture or the culture of poverty?), 148.

46. Okely, *The Traveller Gypsies*, 193.

The Call of the Human Voice in Poulenc's *La Voix Humaine*[1]

Michal Grover-Friedlander

New Operatic Voices, New Operatic Sights

Opera in the twentieth century has largely been characterized by a preoccupation with rethinking the quality, and redefining the limits, of the operatic: what can be considered as opera, what determines it as such, and how does opera relate to other twentieth-century multimedia works?[2] One of the main areas of experimentation has concerned the possibilities provided by the medium for admitting and containing voices that have not traditionally been considered "operatic": voices that challenge opera's vocal artificiality and stylization, its exaggerated range, its strained production, its bordering on the inhuman in an impossible quest for the divine.[3]

Redrawing the boundaries renegotiates the balance between the senses in opera, between what is heard and what is seen. Dependant on the tensions between the visual and the acoustic, the operatic medium both regards and disregards the visual; new voices shake the already fragile status of sight in comparison with the stake in the operatic voice, the extraordinary belief in the aural sense.

Despite such innovative conceptualizations, the majority of operas produced, performed, and heard in recent decades have been traditional, mostly drawn from the nineteenth-century repertoire. Operas composed by Monk, Birtwistle, Glass, or Hindemith are heard within the context of earlier operas. A fundamental feature shared by the operatic canon is the presentation of a journey depicting the death of the voice of opera, the culmination of which is played out solely on the acoustic level. These traditional works portray the vicissitudes of voice, striving toward a goal which is only achieved when voice is extended to its extreme: the operatic voice is driven, as it were, to express its own death. An expansion of range, intensification of the degree of difficulty (or intensification of lyric expression), or overembellishment (or oversimplification) are signs of this extreme condition of the stylized voice of opera.[4] The medium of opera is immersed in a ritualization of voices raised to the occasion of expressing death.[5] The actuality, physicality, or ocular testimony of a dead "body" is insignificant within this matrix. In opera, death is the expectation not for an unbelievable sight but for an unimaginable sound.

Contemporary opera has reacted to this tradition by reinterpreting the role played by the senses in delivering death. An important example from the beginning of the twentieth century is Debussy's *Pelléas et Mélisande* (1902), that undermines any correspondence between what is heard and what is seen. As the opera is based on Maeterlinck's symbolist play, what is referred to in words, voices, music, gestures, or staging is not realized— but is to be imagined; the constituents of the opera collaborate, as it were, to enforce a novel balance between realistic and fantasized sights. *Pelléas et Mélisande*'s renegotiation of the senses culminates in the opera's take on the deadening of voice. Not only is Mélisande's death vocally indistinguishable from the rest of the opera, but it is the disappearance of voice from the visible frame—Mélisande's stepping out of the field of vision—that is the sign of her death. The work redefines the inheritance of the ritual-of-vocality-as-ritual-of-death through a final magical gesture in which we no longer count on either of our senses for the interpretation of her death.

An extreme example from the end of the twentieth century is Meredith Monk's opera *Atlas* (1991), which allows the voice to transgress to prelingustic or inhuman modes of communication. The work's expressive powers lie in its expansion of vocal techniques and inclusion of novel sounds produced by dancers professionally trained in unique kinds of vocalization: animal imitation, ululation, syllabic chanting, and shrieks, as well as body movements as extensions of vocality. There is very little verbal text; the vocalized lines are predominantly wordless melodies, a vocal equivalent of dance mime.[6] These new voices redefine the plot, which is cyclic rather than linear, ending not in death but in a return to the conditions of the beginning of the opera: metaphysical rebirth replaces death. The work does not call for complementarity of the senses: the dancers-singers may look human, and tell a tale of humans, but they do not sound human. Although *Atlas* portrays a range of unconventional voices diametrically opposed to the stylized, artificial voices usually associated with the world of opera, it too is attracted to inhuman capacities of the human voice, exhibiting a foundational belief in the fantasies of the sense of hearing, a distrust of the sense of vision.

Opera on the Phone

Taking as my starting point the idea of new operas' attraction to downplay the power of the eye to inform the ear, of sight to explicate voice, with what I would call its fascination with voices of the invisible, I shall discuss an opera centering on the technological mediation of the human senses. Poulenc's one-act opera *La Voix Humaine* (*The Human Voice*) from 1958 has drawn little interpretive attention.[7] The work is based on a play of the same title by Cocteau, which also served as inspiration for a film, by Rossellini. The opera is situated halfway between Debussy's opera of the first decade of the twentieth century and Monk's avant-garde works of the 1990s. *La Voix Humaine* provides a unique conceptual relationship between the voice of opera, its dimension of invisibility, and the death of that voice.

The entire opera consists of one side of a phone conversation.[8] We see and hear a woman whose lover has left her. As he cannot see her, she uses her voice to inform and deceive him. We, the audience, neither see nor hear him; the woman's voice and the musical accompaniment stand for what we do not hear (the lover's voice), whom we don't see (the lover), and for what the lover himself does not see. All that is said and not said on the other side of the line is inferred from her voice, for we are exposed to that voice alone. The conversation is constantly interrupted, cut short, or jammed by the French telephone company. A final farewell is broken up into short "phases" and fragments of conversation stretched over forty tortured minutes.[9] The opera ends with the phone cord around the woman's neck: the woman's anxiety over being disconnected by and from the machine is realized, and cruelly reversed, when the "voice" of her lover—through the wire of the phone—chokes her, leaving her attached to the machine in a death that epitomizes the end of voice. The phone acquires a truly monstrous, unheard of dimension in its power to bring about death by an invisible, unheard voice. The issue I would like to raise with regard to this composition touches upon the very wish to imagine the voice-of-opera-on-the-phone, the ways in which the telephone is employed to renegotiate the relation between the senses—between the eyes and the ears of opera—and the implications it might have on the delivery of death.

Poulenc's choice of the telephone is not intended to distort the singing voice, at least not directly.[10] We do not hear the heroine's voice mechanically reproduced or filtered through the phone, yet the presence of the telephone alters her singing. This technology affects the meanings assigned to the voice as it attributes to it a powerful sense of "hearing" while her voice interprets what is acoustically inaccessible to the audience. It is the telephone's division of hearing and the silencing of one end of the line that summons the voice to its death: what delivers the voicelessness of the other delivers death.

There is no action, no plot, and no voice on the other end of the line. The opera's meaning lies in the extreme power lent to her "vocality." The entire vocal space is the one "created"—heard, performed, voiced, visualized, invented—by the prima donna. She embodies her partner and internalizes the machine as part of her vocal persona. Are we totally trapped within a prima donna's voice? Do we decipher other voices within her voice? And if there are, how are we to differentiate between them and the prima donna's voice, since we hear only her performance? What does it mean for the interpretation of the work that the entire external world we expect to hear and see is swallowed up, devoured by her voice?

I would suggest that indeed we "hear" voices other than the woman's voiced utterances: "musicalized-voices" that are delivered by the voiceless music.[11] There are two such categories in Poulenc's opera. First, there is music that takes the place of the (unheard) voice at the other end of the line, and which the woman's responses "literalize" into a specific text. In this category, music as such (not a specific motive, nor an identifiable tonality) "speaks" the (otherwise) unheard voice of the lover.[12] We are made to "hear" what he is saying. Here, orchestral music shows the capacity to signify a texted voice, that is, to stand for an operatic character's speech (or thought).

The second category of musicalized-voices are those produced, as it were, by the inanimate machine on stage. A distinct instrumental motive renders the diegetic noise of the telephone, in contrast to the music, *any* music, which may stand for the meaning of words and the voice of the lover. Poulenc paints a distinct musical portrait for the ringing of the phone: a single pitch repeated in sixteenth-notes on a metallic xylophone, a timbre which is reserved solely for sounding the ringing of the phone. The pitch and duration of the ringing changes, but the timbre remains constant and imitates the "voice" of the phone.

The distinct musicalized ringing of the phone is first heard after the opera's brief, 18-measure orchestral prelude, and develops into the woman's voice as she answers the phone repeatedly. The orchestral prelude foreshadows the technique employed in the opera as a whole. The opera begins on a trill in the bass, which serves as a semitone-motion drone for the initial few measures of the prelude; for the final measures of the prelude, the notes of the trill ascend a third. The motivic cell of the opera is presented together with these two trill phrases. The cell is comprised of a sharp dotted rhythm, a melodic combination of semitones juxtaposed with large angular leaps, implying a tonality constantly in flux, all of which is repeated, varied but without development, throughout. Together, the drone trill and the varied cell above it draw on the entire chromatic scale. In other words, semitones are employed not for the purpose of emphasizing or clarifying a tonal center, but to constantly reinterpret structural tones and their relation to passing dissonant tones. Poulenc can thus allude to tonality without providing for a tonal center, and perhaps even hint at the possibility of a twelve-note ghost-framework by using equally important semitones, but with "too many" repetitions of them. This does not undermine the sense of tonality as a continual point of departure, but nor does it pin it down to a specific tonal center. In fact, the music is motivically, not tonally, driven, yet the motivic material itself is dominated by tonal colorings—half steps or leading notes, sevenths, or appoggiaturas—which raise expectations for tonal functioning and tonal resolutions. Poulenc's motivic, cell-like aesthetics does not undermine a sense of tonality, but treats it as constantly deferred, or in motion.

The technique of eschewing any grounding of tonal centers is typical of Poulenc's style, as is an accumulative, rather than developmental, technique, which also emphasizes the sense of unanchored tonal centers.[13] However, in *La Voix Humaine*, this technique is drawn into the representation of the phone itself. The phone's music—the slow tremolo played by the xylophone—is a contraction of the overwhelming semitone motion across the opera into a unison tremolo motion. The sound of the phone decontextualizes even further the recurring strategy of the semitone motion and the sense of instability in the piece.

Poulenc restricts his musical means for the sake of expressing the inhuman machine and the repetitive ritualistic dimension of speaking on the phone. Yet this has a crucial impact on the quality of the woman's voice, which is condemned to fragmented, recitative-like, and frequent silences. In other words, the woman's voice—the voice of opera—is balanced by the sound of the telephone, and the machine's orchestral voice approximates that of the woman.

The prima donna's responses, the ritual of picking up the phone, become textual motives in their own right, independent of the music that carries them: *"Allo! Allo!,"* *"On avait coupé,"* and so forth, are the woman's words that are specific to this particular machine. The text is constant, the music flexible. The combination of the woman's and the phone's pitches increases, rather than clarifies, the sense of drifting. Only at the end of the opera is there an arrival on a clear cadence in *a* minor; yet the tonal implications throughout the opera do not prepare for this ultimate closure on *a*. The relationship between the voice of the woman and the voice of the telephone, then, creates the style of the work.

The fragmented impression of the opera is due not only to its tonality but also to another characteristic derived from the phone. The one-act opera is divided into phases that are emotively distinguished from one another: the woman remembers their first days of love, which began with her phone call; lies about her present situation and what she is wearing; describes the reaction of her lover's dog to his departure, and so forth. These phases give a false improvisatory impression, as if the music is taken by surprise by each turn of emotion and is bound to the unexpectedness of her reactions, doomed. The impression of fragmentation is created by the solitary, isolated, and coherent sense of each phase. They could be reordered. Yet separating the phases would cancel the accumulative effect in the construction of the piece as a whole. Time is piled up, causing an illusion of presentness or simultaneity, an illusion of a continuous present.

This continuous musical present conveys the dissonance of several interrupted phases within one continuous phone conversation, the last farewell. The mechanism of the phone—connection and disconnection of one or several call(s)—and the mechanism of the distortion of musical time as linear, in a constant tonal flux, are combined to enhance the phone's overall domination of the opera. Poulenc has achieved the task of including technology as an operatic constituent: the phone's voice determines the musical vocabulary, the span between the phone's ringing and its disconnections determine the opera's structure; telephonic words and the ringing of the telephone are motivic; the prima donna's voice approximates the operatic rendering of the voice of ringing.[14]

Film on the Phone

Poulenc's use of the telephone in his opera is far more radical than Rosellini's in his film *Una Voce Umane*. The film was released in 1948, ten years before Poulenc's opera, and is based, as I mentioned earlier, on the same play by Cocteau. In the preface to the play, Cocteau describes the location—the phone call—as the scene of the crime. At the end, writes Cocteau, the woman is bleeding like a wounded animal, and the room is flooded with blood. Cocteau's violent description does not, cannot, correspond to death by a phone. For opera, however, a plot's context *is* an unavoidable end in death. Opera's telephone, then, must differ from cinema's in the understanding of the death of a human voice, Poulenc's from Rossellini's. In the film, in fact, we *hear* humming sounds from the other end of the line (this is an addition to Cocteau's text). The man's words on the phone are undecipherable, a noise, a mere trace of speech in the materiality of his voice—yet there is, as it were, a presence of another. Rossellini does not adhere to the woman's vocal-sonic omnipresence and allows us, our ears as it were, a degree of independence from her "ear" on the phone. The film fashions this other as an "acousmêtre." Acousmatique is a term borrowed from a Pythagorean sect that forbade seeing the Master, and whose worship followed the Master's voice. Michel Chion coined the term acousmêtre to denote a voice not issuing from a body within the frame of vision.[15] The acousmêtre plays on the difference film creates between the visual and the acoustic "off-screen" (whereas in fact, there is no sense in an *acoustic* off-screen: off-screen always refers to the origin in an image, not in a voice). The acousmêtre relies on the anxiety arising from an encounter with an invisible voice.

The difference in the treatment of Cocteau's voice on the phone in the two media—film and opera—is illuminating.[16] An acousmêtre usually "causes" film to follow a trajectory trying to expose the hidden source issuing the voice, to search for missing bodies to match them to voices. Perhaps because the human voice was lacking in cinema's initial stages, its introduction has since acquired an illusory status of realism or depth for the effigies on screen, as if anchoring a sound would pacify film's yearn to unify images with the sounds emitted.

Opera, on the other hand, has found its kinship in the telephone: opera is attracted to the very properties of the telephone, a land of disembodiment where cancellation of the visual and the bodily is successfully imagined. The medium can conjure a derided acousmêtre: one lacking even its very voice.[17]

Though based on the same text, in Rossellini's treatment it is the "other" who is the cause of death. In the composer's work, death does not necessitate the intervention of another's voice. Death's otherness is internal to the operatic voice, and there exists only the voice of the one to die. Death in opera—according to this opera—resided *within the operatic voice as such*.[18]

The Invention of the Voice on the Telephone

To appreciate Poulenc's transformation of the machine into an operatic constituent, the deadly power assigned to the invisible soundless voice of the other, the operatic phone's power to "hear the unheard," let us turn for a moment to the origins of the machine itself. An article that appeared in 1887 in *The Scientific American* described the anxiety created by the invention of the telephone, arising from:

> ... the mysteriousness, the sense of material non-existence, of that part of the machine and its belongings that lies beyond one's own instrument.... I can imagine my friend at the other end of the line. But between us two there is an airy nowhere, inhabited by voices and nothing else— Helloland, I should call it. The vocal inhabitants of this strange region have an amazing vanishing quality.... The consciousness of such an experience produces in sensitive men, I am sure, a sensation of nervous shock, somewhat akin to seasickness. And sometimes... you hear the confused murmur of a hundred voices. You catch more expressions from private conversations than your nerves can transmit to the central office of your brain; and if you are imaginative, you may undergo, as I have, a feeling as if you had a hundred astral bodies that were guiltily listening at as many keyholes.... The telephone seems to you to have no visible agency.... Your applications and complaints go over the wire to that one impersonal, impalpable voice.[19]

In the invention of the telephone, even before Edison, human and animal organs were employed for the purpose of recording and transmitting auditory signals. In 1829, a talking machine was invented in order to transform frequencies into tones: the machine employed an elastic tongue modeled on a human one. In 1857, in an invention predating the gramophone needle, harsh short hoghair was employed. In 1874, Bell invented the first model of a phone receiver with an ear membrane taken from a human corpse's ear. The first telephone receiver is, in fact, a human ear, a machine that transmits a living human voice by way of a dead human's ear.

The invention of the telephone arouses anxiety in its association with absence and death. The power of the machine lies in its ability to bring forth absent voices. The discrepancy between what is seen and what is heard allows for the possibility of hearing both more and less than what is seen. In her work *The Telephone Book,* Avital Ronell describes the telephone as a machine that connects the voices of disconnected beings—in its power to reseparate voices, the telephone only temporarily connects voices.[20] The unexpected suddenness of the ring of the telephone is associated with the blind cruelty of Fate, with the ultimate message of Death. The bodiless voice over the phone exercises its power over us because its source is unknown. Picking up the receiver summons one to an unknown encounter, according to an advance agreement. As such, the phone is not under our control, not determined by our will. The telephone has the technical ability to transport the human voice (it does not reproduce the voice but transmits the "original" voice), yet it is not in itself human, lying somewhere between an object, a machine, and a piece of art (at least at the beginning). The telephone both transmits life and represents its absence, showing the unclear demarcation between the living and the nonliving, continues Ronell. The telephone is where the outside world, the voice of the other, intrudes; the connection of voices erases geographical, spatial distances between self and other, undermining the relation self-other, subject-thing.

Conceived in terms of Lacanian psychoanalysis, the initial stages of the development of the self are located in an impossible relation with the other. The relation to the other is understood as prior to selfhood. The path to the self is necessarily a detour through the other; "I" is a deposit with the other. This other, which is constitutive of the self, emerges in psychoanalytic treatment, which is based solely on the voice: The analysand does not see the analyst, but only hears a voice, as the voice of the master, as the voice of God.[21]

The anxieties and fantasies underlying the history of the invention of the telephone might remind one of those underlying the myth and the history of the invention of opera, as manifested, for example, in the myth of Orpheus with its elaboration of the relation of voice to the presence of what is absent, to the death of Euridice.[22] The scientific-technological wish to transmit a disembodied voice, to mechanize ghostly non-present presence parallels the highest stake opera places on the presentation of the illusionary faculties of voice. In *La Voix Humaine*, the power of the operatic voice meets its shadow in the uncanny telephone machine.

Calling Death

What is "human" in an operatic call of death? Why a *human* voice? How is Poulenc's "human voice" mediumatically unique?

Only in the opera is the telephone used for showing what is inherent to the aesthetics of its voice: the notion that death is a result of the encounter with an invisible voicelessness—interpreted through the technology of the phone—as resulting from the *prima donna's* own operatic voice. Only in the opera does the voice act out its termination from within itself, expressing death as an outcome of singing as such. Only in opera is the risk taken by voice so high, that inventing new voices for opera—the operatic phone call, the single voice signifying two, the invisible, the voiceless—still results in death.

Poulenc's work radically rethinks the ways in which we hear an operatic voice, without allowing the voice to reign and become a fully "operatic" one: to signify through the power of beauty. The refusal to escape into beautifying and stylizing the voice in this opera is an acknowledgment of the human— within the operatic—voice. Exposing this voice as human, however, reveals the vicissitudes of voice: its longing for response, the always absent desired response, and the cruelty in the unvoiced voice on the other end of the line. In monitoring our senses, the phonic-opera places us, the witnesses, in a position of embodying cruelty, as the voiceless, invisible presence the *prima donna* addresses herself to, the other end of the line. It is we whom she desperately wishes to retrieve. *La Voix Humaine*, the Human Voice of Opera, is the expectation for the other call, that which will never sound.

Notes

1. An earlier version of this paper was read at the *Opera Analysis* conference at Trinity College, Cambridge, 10–11 April, 2000.
2. In relation to the impact of new productions see Tom Sutcliffe, *Believing in Opera* (Princeton: Princeton University Press, 1996). In relation to the media see Jeremy Tambling, *Opera, Ideology, and Film* (New York: St. Martin's Press, 1987); Jeremy Tambling, ed. *A Night In at the Opera: Media Representations of Opera* (London: John Libbey, 1994); Nicholas Cook, *Analysing Musical Multimedia* (Oxford: Clarendon Press, 1998) especially chapter 6 "Reading Film and Rereading Opera: From *Armide* to 'Aria,'" 215–60; and Gary Tomlinson, *Metaphysical Song: An Essay on Opera* (Princeton: Princeton University Press, 1999) especially chapter VI "Ghosts in the Machine," 127–46.

3. On the operatic voice and the aesthetics of the "quest," see Michel Poizat's books: *L'Opéra ou le Cri de L'ange: Essai sur la jouissance de l'amateur d'Opéra* (Paris: Editions A. M. Métailié, 1986), trans. Arthur Denner as *The Angel's Cry: Beyond the Pleasure Principle in Opera* (Ithaca, N.Y.: Cornell University Press, 1992); *La Voix du Diable: La jouissance lyrique sacrée* (Paris: Editions A. M. Métailié, 1991); and *Variations sur la Voix* (Paris: Ed. Economica-Anthropos, 1998).

4. On extreme styles of singing in Italian opera see for instance, John Rosselli, *Singers of Italian Opera: The History of a Profession* (Cambridge: Cambridge University Press, 1992). For Wagner and styles of Bel Canto singing see for instance, Jens Malte Fischer, "*Sprechgesang* or Bel Canto: Toward a History of Singing Wagner" in *Wagner Handbook*, eds. Ulrich Müller and Peter Wapnewski (Cambridge: Harvard University Press, 1992), 524–46.

5. For various interpretations of canonic opera's expressions of death see: Michel Poizat, *The Angel's Cry;* Catherine Clément, *Opera, or the Undoing of Women*, trans. Betsy Wing (Minneapolis: University of Minnesota Press, 1979/1988); Stanley Cavell, "Opera and the Lease of Voice," in *A Pitch of Philosophy: Autobiographical Exercises* (Cambridge: Harvard University Press, 1994), 129–69; Ralph Locke, "What Are These Women Doing in Opera?" in *En Travesti: Women, Gender, Subversion, Opera*, eds. Corinne Blackmer and Patricia Smith (New York: Columbia University Press, 1995), 59–98; Carolyn Abbate, "Immortal Voices, Mortal Forms" in *Analytical Strategies and Musical Interpretation: Essays on Nineteenth-and Twentieth-Century Music*, eds. Craig Ayrey and Mark Everist (Cambridge: Cambridge University Press, 1996), 288–300; Linda Hutcheon and Michael Hutcheon, *Opera: Desire, Disease, Death* (Lincoln: University of Nebraska Press, 1996); Michal Grover Friedlander, "Voicing Death in Opera" *Common Knowledge*, 5 (1996): 136–44; 'Voicing Death in Verdi's Operas', Ph.D.diss., Brandeis University (1997); and her "Verdi's Shakespearean Operas: Voice and Body in *Otello* and *Falstaff*," paper presented at the *Shakespeare on Screen* conference, Malaga, Spain, September 1999; Peter Kivy "Happy Endings" in *Osmin's Rage: Philosophical Reflactions on Opera, Drama, and Text* (Ithaca, N.Y.: Cornell University Press, 1999), 283–96.

6. For discussions of the opera see Max Loppert, "An Introduction to *Atlas*" and Meredith Monk, "Process Notes" in *Atlas* (ECM Records, 1993); and Deborah Jowitt, ed. *Meredith Monk* (Baltimore: Johns Hopkins University Press, 1997).

7. Poulenc composed three operas, all of which, I would claim, reinterpret death's complex dependence on the aural and the visual. *Les Mamelles de Tirésias* (1947), a comic opera based on a text by Apollinaire, toys with a "metamorphosis" of death into a male reproduction of invisible bass-voice babies. *Les Dialogues des Carmélites* (1958) multiplies operatic death: It portrays an "ugly" and "sacrilegious" death and a metaphysical sacrificial, "beautiful" death in the same opera.

8. There is, to my knowledge, one opera besides *La Voix Humaine* that consists entirely of a phone conversation: Menotti's *The Telelphone* (1947). Few recent operas contain a scene or several scenes on the phone: *Jackie O.* (1997) by Michael Daugherty and Wayne Koestenbaum; *Don Giovanni Revisited* by Mozart and Amnon Wolman (1997).

9. "Phase" is Poulenc's term. See Letter to Bernac reproduced in *Poulenc Dialogues des Carmélites La Voix Humaine* L'Avant Scène Opéra, Mai 1983, n. 52, 136.

10. Poulenc shows, through the aesthetics of simplicity and everydayness, a fascination with the human voice in its more popular and mundane forms, perhaps like the voice within cinema—a fascination shared by Les Six and Cocteau. (For Poulenc's attraction to simplicity in relation to the aesthetic of Satie and Cocteau, see Jann Pasler, "New Music as Confrontation: The Musical Sources of Jean Cocteau's Identity," *The Musical Quarterly* [fall 1991]: 255–78). In this context it is interesting to note Poulenc's objection to casting Maria Callas in the role of the woman. Poulenc preferred his collaborator in his two previous operas, Denise Duval, creating for *La Voix Humaine* an operatic role for a non-conventional operatic singer (see Henri Hell, *Francis Poulenc: Musicien Français* (Fayard, 1978), 277.

11. A related term "unsung voices" was coined by Carolyn Abbate. As discussed bellow, "musicalized-voices" has different properties. See Carolyn Abbate, *Unsung Voices: Opera and Musical Narrative in the Nineteenth Century* (Princeton: Princeton University Press, 1991); her "Opera; or the Envoicing of Women," in *Musicology and Difference: Gender and Sexuality in Music Scholarship*, ed. Ruth A. Solie (Berkeley: University of California Press, 1993), 225–58; and her "Debussy's Phantom Sounds," *Cambridge Opera Journal*, 10/1 1998, 67–96.

12. Poulenc's opera-on-the-phone shows the complications in maintaining distinctions between "unheard," "silenced," and "mute" operatic voices. For related issues in cinema see Michel Chion, *La Toile Trouée: La Parole au Cinéma* (Paris: Editions de l'Etoile, 1988); his *The Voice in Cinema*, trans. Claudia Gorbman (New York: Columbia University Press, 1993/1999); and his *La Voix sourde: La société face à la surdité* (Paris: Editions A.M. Métailié, 1996). For implications for the voices of opera see Tambling, "Towards a Psychopathology of Opera," *Cambridge Opera Journal*, 9/3 1997, 263–79; and Carolyn Abbate, "Debussy's Phantom Sounds."

13. See Hell, *Francis Poulenc*; Keith Daniel, *Francis Poulenc: His Artistic Development and Musical Style* (Ann Arbor: UMI Research Press, 1982); *Poulenc Dialogues des Carmélites La Voix Humaine*; Wilfrid Mellers, *Francis Poulenc* (Oxford: Oxford University Press, 1993); Renaud Machart, *Poulenc* (Paris: Seuil, 1995).

14. *La Voix Humaine*'s use of the telephone also preserves the framework, form, and thematics of the traditional operatic death song. We can consider Poulenc's opera as an extreme depiction of what canonic opera traditionally reserves for the very end: character isolation, an apotheosis of song expressing knowledge of death. In Poulenc's opera there is nothing but the death song, but a presence unto death. *La Voix Humaine* is thus an opera-length death song. More specifically, as the musico-dramatic phases rewrite the canonic death song's strophic form, it is the telephone that serves to connect and disconnect the musical-phonic phases; the length of the call is the length of the phrase. Moreover, interruptions typify an operatic death song. In *La Voix Humaine*, interruptions derive from (problems with) the technology of the telephone. Musicalized noise as diegetic sound is also thematic in the death song. These noises emphasize the character's self-absorption and isolation (in canonic death song, there would be a knock, a sigh, the sound of the wind in place of the ringing of the telephone). Eavesdropping is essential to the death song. In Poulenc's opera, eavesdropping is built into the very mechanism of the phone conversation. Yet overhearing an intimate phone conversation has an almost opposite function to canonic opera's convention of overhearing a character's inner thoughts, as the telephone encourages "inauthentic" rather than "authentic" speech. These themes, combined with a declamatory, nearly undifferentiated vocal style, draw us into an extreme condition of an opera-length death song. (For a discussion of the canonic death song see Grover-Friedlander, "Voicing Death in Opera," and *Voicing Death in Verdi's Operas*.)

15. Michel Chion, *The Voice in Cinema*; and his *Audio-Vision: Sound on Screen*, trans. Claudia Gorbman (New York: Columbia University Press, 1990/1994).

16. For an interpretation of Rossellini's film as "operatic" see Michal Grover-Friedlander *Vocal Apparitions: Cinema's Attraction to Opera* (forthcoming).

17. Here it is interesting to note Almodovar's film *Women on the Verge of a Nervous Breakdown*, which takes its inspiration from Cocteau's play *La Voix Humaine*. In Almodovar's film, the function of the voice on the telephone is further tranformed into that of a recording of an absent voice on an answering machine.

18. For the idea of death as the outcome of singing as such see Cavell, "Opera and the Lease of Voice"; Clément, *Opera, or the Undoing of Women*, specifically her interpretation of *Tales of Hoffmann*, 31–33; and Grover-Friedlander, "Voicing Death in Opera."

19. Quoted in Barbara Engh, "Adorno and the Sirens: Tele-phono-graphic Bodies" in *Embodied Voices: Representing Female Vocality in Western Culture*, eds. Leslie Dunn and Nancy Jones (Cambridge: Cambridge University Press, 1994), 122. A classic discussion of technology in relation to the work of art is Walter Benjamin's "The Work of Art in the Age of Mechanical Reproduction," in *Illuminations*, trans. Harry Zohn, ed.

Hannah Arendt (New York: Harcourt, Brace and World, 1968). For anxiety over the invention of the telephone and related technological inventions, which absent the body of a heard-voice, see for instance Theodor Adorno, "The Curve of the Needle" trans. Thomas Levin, *October* 55 (1928, trans. 1990), 48–55; Friedrich Kittler, *Gramophone, Film, Typewriter*, trans. Geoffrey Winthrop-Young and Michael Wutz (Stanford: Stanford University Press, 1986/1999) where he discusses Cocteau and his attraction to new technologies and machines (191–92). See also Kittler's "Opera in the Light of Technology," in *Languages of Visuality: Crossing between Science, Art, Politics, and Literature*, ed. Beate Allert (Detroit: Wayne State University Press, 1996), 73–85; Lana Rakow, "Women and the Telephone: The Gendering of a Communications Technology," in *Technology and Women's Voices: Keeping in Touch*, ed. Cheris Kramarae (New York: Routledge, 1988), 207–28; Avital Ronell, *The Telephone Book: Technology, Schizophrenia, Electric Speech* (Lincoln: University of Nebraska Press, 1989); and her "Finitude's Score" in *Thinking Bodies*, eds. Juliet Flower MacCannell and Laura Zakarin (Stanford: Stanford University Press, 1994), 87–108, where she specifically discusses Poulenc's opera; Felicia Miller Frank, *The Mechanical Song: Women, Voice, and the Artificial in Nineteenth-Century French Narrative* (Stanford: Stanford University Press, 1995), especially Chapter 6 "Edison's Recorded Angel," 143–71, in which she also discusses Paris and the invention of the teleopera in the twenties; Thomas Levin, "Before the Beep: A Short History of Voice-Mail," in *Essays in Sound 2*, ed. Annemarie Jonson (Darlinghurst, Australia, 1995), 59–67; Tambling, "Towards a Psychopathology of Opera"; and Abbate, "Debussy's Phantom Sounds."

20. See also Ronell, "Finitude Score."

21. Freud sees in the long-distance phone call a model for the indirect path and inferral access to the unconscious. See Ronell, *The Telephone Book*, 423–24. For Lacanian psychoanalytical interpretations of voice see for instance Mladen Dolar, "The Object Voice," in *Gaze and Voice as Love Objects*, eds. Renata Salecl and Slavoj Zizek (Durham: Duke University Press, 1996), 7–31. For Lacanian psychoanalytical interpretations of the voice of *opera* see for instance Poizat, *The Angel's Cry*; Tambling, "Towards a Psychopathology of Opera"; and Michal Grover-Friedlander, "The Phantom of the Opera: The Lost Voice of Opera in Silent Film," in *Cambridge Opera Journal*, 11/2, 179–92.

22. I would claim that the myth of Orpheus, at the core of the operatic medium, shows opera's very questioning of human capacities. The medium's original interpretation of the power of voice revolved around its battle with the deadly power of the gaze. Since its invention, opera has attempted to define the Orphic powers of voice and vision anew. For a "technological" interpretation of the myth of Orpheus see Klaus Theweleit, "Monteverdi's *L'Orfeo*: The Technology of Reconstruction" in *Opera through Other Eyes*, ed. David Levin (Stanford: Stanford University Press, 1993), 147–76.

Video
(I See)

II

The Performance of Vision in Peter Sellars's Television Production of *Così fan tutte*

Marcia J. Citron

Mozart's collaboration with librettist Lorenzo Da Ponte created three of the most magnificent works in the operatic repertoire: *Le nozze di Figaro* (1786); *Don Giovanni* (1787); and *Così fan tutte* (1790). Although each has a distinctive tone and none is free of dramatic problems, whether of meaning, structure, or pacing, audiences and critics found *Così fan tutte* especially difficult to comprehend almost as soon as it was premiered. Several themes have dogged the work. One is the idea of a huge gulf between the beautiful music Mozart composed and the "silly" libretto he set. Another is the purported immorality of the story. And yet a third issue, closely related, concerns the ambiguity of the ending and what we are to think of it. A common thread in the critical reception of *Così* is that Mozart wasted his talents on the opera, and we as operagoers should not waste our time on it either.[1]

Così's plot, drawn from lofty literary themes that go back as far as Ovid, is simple.[2] Two pairs of lovers in eighteenth-century Naples appear to be secure in their relationships. Don Alfonso, described as a "vecchio filosofo," is skeptical, and he persuades the men, Ferrando and Guglielmo, to place a bet on the constancy of their lovers, Fiordiligi and Dorabella. They agree to subject the women to a test. The two men are sent on a bogus war campaign and reappear in disguise as new suitors. Despina, the sisters' servant, assists Alfonso in the ruse. Although the women resist at first, they eventually succumb to the advances of the men, in switched pairing from the start of the opera. A double marriage ceremony is arranged but interrupted when the original men return; confusion ensues. Although music and libretto imply a return to the original pairings at the end, this is not entirely clear, and many productions emphasize the ambiguity or leave us with the new couplings.

Compared with the busy plots of *Figaro* and *Don Giovanni*, little happens in *Così*. External events yield to inner feeling, and the narrative is relatively static. Da Ponte's text, which delights in learned references and esoteric phraseology, is partly responsible, because it removes the figures from daily concerns and positions them in an elevated realm. Mozart's music defines that realm as one of feeling and offers many pleasures to the listener. These are produced by certain musical devices, which include lush streams of parallel thirds (especially when the couples exist in their original pairings), warm writing for wind instruments, a reverential quality in slow numbers, and a pervasive Rococo *tinta* that accords with the story's setting by the sea.

The early twentieth century was slow to warm to *Così*, but by the end of the century the opera was viewed more favorably.[3] Many postmodern tendencies, including interdeterminacy, cynicism, and contradiction, can be found in the work.[4] They find expression in the most fundamental matters in the opera, such as the ending and the opera's message and moral. What are we supposed to think of the wager and the events that devolve from it? What does the opera say about gender relations, erotic attraction, and sexual responsibility?[5] And how do we relate to the characters and their behavior? In addition to its postmodern features, *Così* may please millennial audiences because its near eventless plot is less beholden to a specific time or place. This means that the work lends itself to transposition to other settings or time periods more easily than many operas.

American director Peter Sellars performs this kind of transposition on *Così*. Staged at the Pepsico Summerfare Festival in 1986, *Così* became part of the Mozart-Da Ponte trilogy that Sellars prepared for Austrian Television (ORF) in 1991 to celebrate the Mozart bicentennial.[6] Sellars's version of *Così* takes place in contemporary America and emphasizes a land of the hip and the free. Rejecting the charge that he deploys updating as a gambit,[7] Sellars nonetheless unfetters the work from its old European context—it is now set in a Westchester diner in the late 1980s—and exploits pop culture to the hilt. The transposition is not pure, however. Sellars shows his historical leanings by retaining the original Italian text and including every number in the opera.[8] We end up with a temporal multiplicity that rubs the eighteenth century against the 1980s; twenty years later, our perspective adds a third vantage point. The contrast between the literary Italian text uttered by the singers and the slangy, sometimes crude English "translation" in the subtitles also creates friction.[9] These juxtapositions show how Sellars likes to explore "secret worlds" that inhabit the nodes of contradiction and the gaps of meaning in his productions.[10] These gaps are meant to distance the audience from the work and, in a Brechtian way, lead to productive reflection on the meanings of art, culture, history, and modernized versions of old works. In this respect, Sellars reveals his debt to progressive figures of the theater such as Vsevolod Meyerhold and Giorgio Strehler, both of whom he greatly admires.

Così's minimal plot makes the work ripe for reinterpretation through television or film because it allows a camera (and its director) to fill in meaning beyond the original musical and verbal texts. This visual potential ties in nicely with the centrality of vision in the story. The test the women undergo hinges on their ability to recognize their lovers. While any one of several senses might serve to identify the men, vision fails to provide the key to recognition. Thus looking, in the sense of recognizing or not recognizing someone according to how you see the person, is fundamental to the progress of the story. The inability to recognize through sight leads to the complexities of feeling in the story. In Sellars's telecast, these intense feelings take us to an interior realm that suggests that vision is unreliable. As we shall see, Sellars marks this place through a simple but brilliant visual device: the wearing of dark glasses. By controlling their use, the director weaves a pattern that shows us what he thinks of the characters and their passions.

The telecast offers an exterior counterpart to the interior visual realm. On several occasions the narrative breaks the fiction of the story with visual effects that narrow the distance between viewer and story. Through a combination of direct address, a characteristic televisual mode of communication, and visual send-ups of popular culture, Sellars frames the movement into interior realms with an emphasis on the exterior, a place that extends to the viewers. Perhaps he does not wish us to immerse ourselves too deeply in the world of feeling that he intensifies through other tropes of vision. The result is a dualistic, almost schizophrenic exploration of vision and its role in narrative, representation, and drama. The two realms, the interior and the exterior, form the basis of our inquiry into the place of the visual senses in Sellars's telecast production of *Così fan tutte*.

Looking: Inside the Fiction

Sellars's camera emphasizes looking. He uses close-ups frequently, and we often see characters looking at each other, especially when someone is singing to someone else, or when a shot-reverse shot pattern shows successive speakers in a conversation. Sellars enlivens this basic vocabulary with techniques from sit-coms and soap opera. For example, sometimes the camera isolates the gaze of a peripheral onlooker when he or she reacts to the main event; Don Alfonso is often captured this way. The device recalls sit-coms such as *Designing Women*, which like to show the reaction of a peripheral figure, although in Sellars's work these shots are not ornamental and haphazard, but structural and deliberate. From soap opera Sellars has the camera stare long and hard at a character at the end of a dramatic unit as he or she registers deep emotion. These inserted pauses, which mimic the sense of a timeless continuum found in soap opera, contribute to the mannered pacing of the production.[11]

Looking is affirmed through its connection with other senses. Sometimes we see characters listening intently to music, as in the wind serenade "Secondate aurette amiche" (No. 21). Sometimes we see them turning to tactile feeling, as in the moving prayer for safe speed, "Soave sia il vento" (No. 10), where Fiordiligi and Dorabella touch themselves sexually. This number, in dimmed lighting that lessens characters' looking but heightens viewers' looking, also presents subtle hand gestures that are choreographed to the music. Mozart himself pictorialized waves and breezes mentioned in the text through a gentle turning figure in muted violins. "Soave" gives us an example of how Sellars physicalizes music in his productions, drawing on gestural traditions as diverse as sign-language for the deaf and Japanese *Noh* theater. My point in the present context is not the variety of sensual experience in Sellars's *Così*, although it is certainly striking. It is rather that we as television viewers *see* these experiences happening before us and that the other sensory modes that Sellars puts in play are working with, and in many ways dependent on, the faculty of vision. Another way to characterize the situation is to say that there are times when the downplaying of sight in the fiction allows for greater emphasis on other senses.

Sellars's interest in vision builds on references to seeing in the libretto. At their first appearance in the opera, in the duet "Ah guarda, sorella" (Ah look, sister) (No. 4), the women admire their lovers' pictures in a locket. Later on, when passions intensify in the new pairings, references to seeing take on new meaning. In the seduction duet "Il core vi dono" (No. 23), Guglielmo tells Dorabella not to look ("Non guardar"), and Sellars has Guglielmo cover her dark glasses with his hand. After she responds to his advances, Guglielmo twice asks her to look. Seeing is a prominent part of the next series of numbers, which involve the other couple. In the accompanied recitative, Ferrando tries to counter Fiordiligi's description of him as a monstrous creature, and he asks her to look at him ("Non ti chiedo che un guardo"). This introduces "Ah! lo veggio" (Ah, I see) (No. 24), Ferrando's aria on what he sees in Fiordiligi's spirit.

Sellars's production inflects the trope of vision in provocative ways. Instead of having the sisters gaze at a locket, they look at pictures of men in a magazine; this recurs at the start of Act II. Their obsession with manufactured images shows their emotional immaturity. Similarly, Don Alfonso is seen at the start of the opera with his head buried in a newspaper. When Ferrando and Guglielmo enter, Alfonso pointedly avoids looking at them as he continues to read. The lack of visual contact reveals his cynicism toward human interaction. Thus in "Soave, sia il vento," where deep emotions are awakened, Alfonso covers his eyes on the loaded word "desir" (desires, or wishes), a place marked by an exquisitely dissonant chord that extends musical tension. Alfonso cannot face desire and hence his reflexive action to ward it off. The defensive visual gesture appears all the more striking in contrast to the women's overt expression of physical desire in the same number. As the opera progresses, Alfonso's growing consternation at the levels of passion experienced by others adds an ironic *frisson* to Sellars's interpretation.

When Alfonso covers his eyes in "Soave," he performs an act of concealment that hints at a more developed trope of concealment in the production: the wearing of dark glasses. This occurs in a substantial portion of the telecast and is intimately tied with the structuring of passion over the work. It occupies our attention in the next section.

Dark Glasses

Looking, not looking; seeing, not seeing; blindness, avoidance, awareness, and acceptance: these are the terms of engagement that Sellars conjures through the donning and shedding of dark glasses. Often worn in a dark setting, dark glasses invoke the conceit of the masquerade and create an altered or fluctuating identity. In much the same way that Judith Butler conceives of the formation of gender as a process of performative acts,[12] so the use of dark glasses becomes a performance of altered identities that shapes erotic relationships among the characters. The camera is critical in organizing these visual representations.

The function of dark glasses changes over the telecast. At first they serve as a comic device, one element in the men's funky disguises. They provide a shield against recognition and stimulate wacky behavior. In Act II, they become a means of transition to real feeling as they allow the power of Mozart's sensual music to take hold and penetrate the lovers as their literal ability to see is diminished. After the submission to feeling is complete, the dark glasses are removed. Along the way they may be removed temporarily, usually away from direct confrontation. Variations in lighting and the interplay of interior and exterior locations also inflect the device.

The trope of not-looking and avoidance that appears in the text is aptly conveyed by the dark glasses. The characters encountered at the beginning are afraid to face themselves. The glasses allow them to embark on a journey toward self-awareness and self-knowledge, a goal signified by the recognition of passions that have been repressed. But it is a frightening prospect to face oneself at this level. By severing them from their original world and its codes, the dark glasses ease them into an interior realm that represents who they really are or would like to be. They retreat to a place of pure sensuality and sensation, one consisting of erotic touching and rapturous music. The lovers become pure body, inured to the rational world known through the faculty of sight. Thus they enter a feminine world that all four characters, including the women, are afraid of; conventional socialization, after all, mandates that rationality keep people on track. Sellars's trope of visual concealment reminds me of one of the pillars of symbolism in *Tristan und Isolde*, Wagner's paean to ecstatic love. Although Sellars's version does not exalt Night in Wagner's Schopenhauerian way, it too suggests that the ideal path to true passion and self-knowledge is through darkness, here expressed as diminished capacity to see. Thus Sellars's hip telecast inscribes some Romantic elements, an appropriate inflection for an opera whose music touches on the sublime. This quality, by the way, becomes another feminine element of *Così* that Sellars's characters have to deal with.[13]

All four lovers participate in the donning and shedding of dark glasses. Occasionally Don Alfonso also wears them, and this signals his involvement in the progress of passion. In traditional productions, Alfonso is relatively impassive, but here he gets sucked into the emotional vortex in ways he did not foresee. Furthermore, the dispirited Vietnam vet in Sellars's conception is shown to have chinks in his armor as well as failed romances in his past, especially with Despina. His vulnerability becomes a striking feature of the telecast and produces a more complex staging of passion than one usually sees in *Così*.

The first time we see dark glasses in the production is at No. 13, "Alla bella Despinetta," when Ferrando and Guglielmo enter in disguise. The new personalities style themselves as "wild and crazy guys" (a phrase associated with comedian Steve Martin) and sport streaks of paint on face and arms. They do the bogus-trendy movements developed by Martin and Dan Ackroyd in their famous sketch from *Saturday Night Live* of the two Czechoslovakian brothers, and, just as Martin and Ackroyd did, alienate the women. The mood is light, and dark glasses add to the campy feel of the new personas. The glasses stay on in the next few numbers. Ferrando's affective aria, "Un' aura amorosa" (No. 17), marks a change, and Ferrando sings the number without glasses. As Bruce Alan Brown notes, Mozart's aria, a paean to the spiritual delights of love, "reveals a hitherto unsuspected depth of feeling in Ferrando."[14] Slow, lyrical, and formally similar to the old *da capo* aria, the number arrests dramatic time and plumbs personal feeling. In Sellars's production, the dimmed lighting discloses Ferrando's depth. The removal of dark glasses suggests that Ferrando is facing his emotional core in a new way, and that it could lead to complications. The journey inward finds visible expression in a myriad of smooth hand gestures. Meanwhile, we watch Alfonso as he stares in amazement and envy. As we shall see many times, Sellars links rapturous music and expressive body gestures as the visual sense in the fiction is downplayed. At these points, our own visual senses are heightened through the many things we experience with our eyes.

After this aria, Ferrando and Guglielmo wear dark glasses for the rest of the act, while Fiordiligi and Dorabella take up the conceit in Act II. The second number is a duet for the sisters, "Prenderò quel brunettino" (No. 20), where they decide which man each will pair up with. They mock the men's campy gestures and at the end put on dark glasses: Dorabella's with hot pink frames, like Guglielmo's; Fiordiligi's plain black. Seated in a booth, the sisters continue mocking the men, and we see that they view the gambit as a lark. Thus they do what the men did when they first donned glasses: another kind of *Così fan tutti*, or thus do males and females alike (not merely females, as in the opera's title).

Soon the situation changes. Alfonso enters the brightly lit diner wearing dark glasses and in the following recitative invites the women to a party in the parking lot. We see darkness through the doorway. When Dorabella asks "What's going on?," Alfonso responds "You'll see." Then comes the pivotal moment. As the women sit in the booth, beautiful instrumental music wafts in from outside. They hear the seductive strains of a wind serenade (No. 21), the velvety tones of the clarinets on the melody. Unlike the succession of most numbers in Mozart's operas, the tonality of this piece (E-flat) marks a big break with the preceding number (ending in G major). The lights dim inside and approach the darkness outside. The women are stunned by what they hear and sit still, transfixed. The dark glasses on their faces make them look like blind people whose aural senses are heightened as the visual is diminished, and close-ups show their reaching out with their ears to take in the sounds. It is here that the glasses seem to shield against frivolities that can penetrate through vision. Instead, the glasses channel feelings inward as the characters heed the truth of the music. Just as early Romantics such as E. T. A. Hoffmann, Schopenhauer, and Hegel believed in the power of music to access the deepest level of existence, so Fiordiligi and Dorabella appear to sense that music provides the means to discover deep truths about themselves and their feelings. The impact on the viewer, as on the women, is stunning. Meanwhile, the camera intercuts views of Don Alfonso staring out the window into the darkness.

At the recapitulation (we've gone through an A and B section), a pastoral text, "Secondate, aurette amiche" ("Friendly breeze, give my desires a lift" in the subtitles), joins the instruments. It is sung by Ferrando and Guglielmo, outdoors, without dark glasses. At this point they are positioned outside the emotional entanglement and don't need a visual barrier. Their being outdoors and by themselves suggests they are still in a real world, possibly as their original selves. Yet although they are not acted upon in the same way as the women, they too remain still and find themselves caught up in the reverential tone of the music. The camera moves from face to face, in close-up. When Ferrando and Guglielmo enter the diner later in the number, they don dark glasses for the resumption of Alfonso's game. The lights return to normal as the number ends.

We should emphasize that this number, which draws on the pastoral qualities of the wind serenade and the devotional aspects of the hymn, recalls earlier reverential numbers in the opera: "Di scrivermi" (No. 9), "Soave sia il vento" (No. 10), and the Andante section in B-flat in the Finale to Act I ("Dove son"). Sellars uses them as key moments in the structuring of passion. "Secondate, aurette amiche," however, articulates the real point of departure for the lovers. For the women especially, the change occurs because they are literally hearing and heeding Mozart's music.[15] Henceforth deep passions will heat up quickly, and the four will face and, at some level, accept the truth of their feelings.

In the recitative after No. 22, the lovers go out into the night, two at a time. The next number, the duet "Il core vi dono," consummates the erotic attraction of Guglielmo and Dorabella. Against a coy musical style—lots of start-and-stop phrases, with indefinite rests in between—Sellars shows us smoldering passion. We can barely see the two figures against the black background, and the dark glasses block their eyes from us as well as each other (see Figure 11.1). They have entered a private world of night. This sets up a nice interplay with the text, much of it concerned with looking and not-looking. In the developmental part of the aria, Guglielmo removes Dorabella's locket, a token of her original relationship. He tells her not to look as he covers her glasses with his hand. She expresses her sexual excitement in telling him that "Vesuvius is erupting." As the recapitulation begins he removes his hand from her glasses, places a big sticky heart on her chest, and asks her to open her eyes. This is a metaphorical invitation to vision, of course: she is to see and realize this as true passion, while the dark glasses remain and block much of her literal vision. After continued erotic touching and a round on the floor, the two walk off.

Next come Ferrando and Fiordiligi, also in dark glasses. In an accompanied recitative, they avoid looking at each other; even when Ferrando asks her to look at him, and she does, he turns away. This dance of visual resistance continues in Ferrando's aria, "Ah lo veggio" (No. 24), whose title ironically proclaims his ability to see her beautiful spirit. They continue to avoid the gaze of the other. In the faster section, Fiordiligi leaves. At the end of the aria, Guglielmo rushes into the diner, without his glasses. Unhappy with what he has seen, he spends the next number nursing a bottle of whiskey in the diner. Next we see Fiordiligi outside in the dark, alone, and without glasses. In the accompanied recitative and aria, "Per pietà" (No. 25), she speaks of betrayal while wracked with emotional turmoil—so much so that by the recapitulation, after she has entered the diner, she is rolling on the floor. Meanwhile, she sees Ferrando on the outside

Figure 11.1. Doabella (Janice Felty) and Guglielmo (James Maddalena) in the duet, "Il core vi dono" (No. 23), in Peter Sellars's *Così fan tutte*. Photo by ORF. Courtesy Forum Media, Dr. Eberhard Scheele.

gazing at her, still in his dark glasses. Soon he rushes into the diner and she feels pulled between the two men. Sellars gives us a complex visual triangulation: this for an aria that is usually performed when Fiordiligi is alone on stage. She strips down to her bra, symbolically shedding a slew of pressures that have been layered onto her subjectivity.[16] She runs out.

For Fiordiligi, the removal of clothes follows, and in some ways replaces, the dark glasses. The wearing of glasses acted as a transitional device from denial to acceptance; the wearing of inner clothes on the outside signals an openness to erotic experience and to the internalization of deep feelings. Acceptance is imminent. As for Dorabella, she literally throws off her dark glasses in a recitative before No. 28 when she declares, "But he's a little demon." In her aria "Vado, ma dovè" (No. 28), sung in dim lighting, Dorabella falls under the spell of Mozart's sensuous music in the second part of the number. In a slow tempo with prominent clarinets, this section seduces Dorabella and us in much the same way as the other reverential numbers in the opera. Sellars's use of this replacement aria is critical in having us believe in the seriousness of her feelings;[17] Dorabella's conversion is complete.

The duet "Fra gli amplessi," No. 29, completes the conversion of Fiordiligi and Ferrando and marks the climax of the opera. While the two avoid looking at each other at first, by the end they face each other squarely and openly express their joy. The moment they stop singing they embrace furiously and passionately, grabbing at each other. This continues well past the instrumental postlude for some twenty seconds longer—a silent space in which the camera fixates on other characters' incredulous stares. Occurring in dim lighting, theirs is a gaze that is trustworthy because it sees a new truth. Sellars suggests that this is the real truth—they see it, we see it—and for the first time what is seen accords fully with what is known through other senses. Vision, passion, and eroticism are explicit and in sync with each other; dark glasses for sensual suppression are no longer needed.

Looking: Outside the Fiction

The performance of the course of passion is not without interruption, however. Sellars inserts breaks in the fiction, often extravagant ones, and they have important consequences. They alter the viewer's relationship with the spectacle and affect the role of vision in the construction of subjectivity. In this way, they reconfigure the subject-object relationship in looking and diffuse a controlling subject position, which tends within media of mass reproduction to be situated in the viewer.[18] The breaks also have an impact on the construction of meaning. They reinscribe the didactic element that is embodied in the opera's subtitle, "la scuola degli amanti" ("the school for lovers," actually the libretto's official title), and affirm Sellars's updated setting through their emphasis on postmodern strategies of perception. These have the effect of blurring boundaries between perception and production, perception and representation; they even affect the distinction between viewer and character. When we consider that this is an opera about confused identity and problematic distinctions between reason and feeling, then such strategies seem entirely appropriate.

Scattered throughout the opera, the breaks have the feel of an "A" section in a rondo, a dramatic refrain whose intervening episodes in this instance trace the linear progression of passion. Don Alfonso performs the disruptions more than anyone, but the two men and Despina also participate in the conceit. Fiordiligi and Dorabella are noticeably missing. A likely reason is that they are acted upon more than they initiate in the drama, a stance reflective of Western ideological associations of female gender with passivity, especially for upper-class females. Another explanation may be that the sisters fall deeply under the spell of true passion, giving themselves over to societal expectations of feminine emotionalism. Considered from this perspective, it would be odd to have them step outside the fiction and observe what is going on. This would inject a sense of masculine rationality into their personas, something Sellars's production and most treatments of *Così* seem to avoid.[19] Beyond gendered associations, however, lies the practical matter of dramatic structure: Sellars needs some characters to remain inside the fiction so that the departures have something to work against.

Most of the breaks entail the televisual device of direct address, a mode of communication in which an onscreen figure faces the camera squarely, looks straight into the lens, and speaks directly to the audience. According to television theorist John Ellis, direct address in its purest form occurs in news reporting, where the technique is excellent at promoting a sense of liveness, currency, and co-presence.[20] The directness of direct address, especially on television's small screen, creates intimacy between speaker and viewer, so that the viewer feels close to what's presented. Despite the bond, however, the viewer remains at an emotional remove from the screenplay, especially in comparison to the seductive potential of cinema for drawing the spectator into the narrative. We also tend to look at the two media differently. Television does not encourage a controlling gaze in the spectator, whereas cinema does; Ellis dubs the distinction television's "glance" versus cinema's "gaze."[21] Thus the television viewer, especially when confronted with direct address, can remain distant from the narrative at the same time that he or she feels co-equal and familiar with the figure onscreen.

Direct address performs interesting transformations in this particular telecast. In one of Sellars's most brilliant strokes, it becomes a way of generalizing the message of *Così* so that viewers become participants as well as spectators. This comes about when text that is intended for specific characters is aimed directly at us. We become complicit in the moral universe that Sellars criticizes and hence cannot let ourselves adopt a superior gaze toward the complex display of feelings in the story. Don Alfonso is the main agent in these situations. On several occasions he points a finger aggressively at the camera and tells us things "straight," without flinching. Like a TV evangelist or old-fashioned school teacher, he accuses and lectures; and like a "vecchio filosofo" in an updated "scuola degli amanti," he teaches all lovers, not only those on stage, what life is about. Alfonso's strong gaze in such places attempts to overwhelm the viewer—to objectify and dominate the viewer—and disrupt the relatively equal relationship between viewer and spectacle that is characteristic of television.

The first instance occurs early, in the recitative after No. 2. Alfonso has just been discussing the tendencies of women to be unfaithful, and Ferrando and Guglielmo call it "poetic crap." Then Alfonso looks directly at the camera, points vigorously, and exclaims: "Exactly what proof do you have that your lovers are true? Why are you so sure?" We viewers are the targets of this pointed message, not the characters. It not only disarms our comfortable position as distant observers, but forces us to take on, albeit temporarily, the personas of the characters and install ourselves in the moral universe that is the story. Our subject positioning is disturbed, and in doing so illustrates Vivian Sobchack's theory of filmic signification that viewer and film interact intersubjectively and flexibily, not hierarchically in a fixed relationship.[22] At this point in *Così*, does our function approach that of a (silent) Greek chorus, invited to respond? Whatever our reaction, the moment passes quickly, for in an instant Don Alfonso returns to the story and allows us to resume our traditional role as observers. For a brief moment all of us—males and females alike, a further expansion of the title's "tutte"— are involved in the narrative.

Three similar places occur later. In the recitative after "Secondate, aurette amiche," Alfonso turns to the audience, points forcefully, and says: "Wipe that old-fashioned look off your face." The equivalent text in the libretto is "Oh, to the devil with you. Leave off these old-fashioned affectations," lines addressed to Ferrando and Guglielmo because of their awkward attempts at courtship. Sellars's device is meant to deflate our voyeuristic tendencies as judgmental viewing subjects, especially as this is the decisive moment when passions will heat up intensely. The device also deflates the emotional tone created by the exquisite music the characters have just heard. Alfonso may enact this crude gesture in order to fight the personal effects of his dark glasses, which he wears here. He fears his own vulnerability to passion.

In the recitative after Ferrando's aria "Tradito, schernito" (No. 27), Alfonso tells the men that he will change things back if they wish. Suddenly he claps his hands in a dramatic punctuation and points directly at the camera: "Listen! Fiordiligi stayed true to Guglielmo. But Dorabella betrayed you." On the last two words he begins to walk out, effecting a transition to the story proper, and we realize that the words "betrayed you" are meant for viewers and for Ferrando. Alfonso has addressed us as if addressing an objective moral force—another reference to the Greek chorus?—in the first statement. In the second statement, he loses his fighting spirit and returns quickly to the formal narrative frame.

The last instance with Alfonso occurs in his moralistic number, "Tutti accusan le donne" (Everyone accuses women; No. 30). It ends with two statements of the words "Così fan tutte," this after the romantic capitulation of both women is complete. But something unexpected happens. Although direct address and pointing occur on the opening line, by the time we get to the key text, Alfonso's gaze is diffuse and he avoids the camera completely. No assured look affirms the critical didactic line, and the physical organization of the group fragments rather than solidifies. Alfonso's inability to fix a commanding gaze at the viewer tells us that the test-wager has been a moral failure. The lack of direct address indicts him and his project.

Despina also speaks directly to the audience. In a recitative after "Soave, sia il vento," she looks straight at the camera with a cup of hot-chocolate in her hand and says, "Kind sir, dear lady, you get to drink it, I don't." Her directness continues for a long time. After she drinks, her last line is "Good to the last drop," a reference to the famous slogan in Maxwell House coffee ads. In fact, the pose and facial expression of the whole episode resemble a commercial. Thus Sellars displays his schizophrenic tendencies in having a sublime moment ("Soave") near a crass moment: deep emotion juxtaposed with cultural satire. The contrast acts to prevent the viewer from becoming overly invested emotionally in the story and from assuming the standpoint of the characters. We can observe and make judgments at a conceptual remove, and be less susceptible to idealizing the characters or drowning in their emotional excesses. In these respects, Sellars's dramaturgy is highly un-Wagnerian, in contrast to the workings of the trope of darkness discussed earlier.

Other places in the Sellars version offer send-ups of pop culture. One grabs our attention early in the telecast. In No. 3, "Una bella serenata," a trio that closes off the opening tableau between Alfonso and the men, Ferrando and Guglielmo use the music-making topic in the text as a pretext for becoming rock stars. After Ferrando puts coins in the jukebox, he grabs a hand mike and starts the trio with funky movements. Guglielmo continues the gambit at his musical entrance. As they ape pop stars, they enact a performance within a performance—itself an added layer in the narrative—and bring elements of star-power to their personas.[23] When the text toasts the god of love, the three simultaneously pop flip-tops of Miller Lite as though in a beer commercial. Continuing to look directly at the camera, they line up like a 1950s rock group and pitch their line in a self-conscious way. The conceit is a wink at the audience: as if to say that all of us are in on the joke and Alfonso's wager-test isn't to be taken seriously.

The most striking break involving direct address and popular culture occurs in Guglielmo's aria in Act II, "Donne mie la fate" (No. 26). In preceding numbers, Ferrando and Guglielmo have hit the depths of despair over the women's capitulation. After No. 25, Ferrando asks Guglielmo what's to be done to relieve his torment. Unable to provide an answer, Guglielmo throws up his hands and smiles, and a spotlight signals another break in the narrative. Guglielmo performs a huge disruption as he trots into the studio audience to perform his aria. The main visual apparatus, the camera, is thrown off as it effects a blurry and unfocused pan as if losing its way at the drastic change from stage to audience. Next we see Guglielmo shaking hands with the cameramen; the keepers of the visual are now performers in the spectacle. As he sings about the fickle qualities of women in this buffa aria, he plays talk-show host with mike à la David Letterman or Phil Donahue and has women in the audience stand as he pretends to interview them. In the B section, he points at and addresses the camera directly as he says, "Many times I've taken up the sword to save your honor." We women viewers are pulled into the narrative. After taking a phone call and commenting further on women's qualities, Guglielmo begins to lose his cool. Rage intensifies as he walks closer and closer to the camera, his face increasingly distorted (another Letterman trick). Repeatedly he says in direct address, "If your lovers scream, they have a good reason." As he signals for the camera to "cut," we observe the camera that was looking at him. Finally the camera does a quick zoom to the stage and we're back in the regular story.

The temperamental personality on display in this number suggests that Guglielmo is different from other characters. This quality is foregrounded at the arranged wedding ceremony. At one point a toast is made for the couples' happiness. Mozart sets the number as a musical canon: one person starts, another replicates the line after a short distance, and so on.[24] All goes according to plan for the entrances of Fiordiligi, Ferrando, and Dorabella. But when Guglielmo is slated to sing, he spoils the symmetry by singing words of complaint to a collection of angular musical motives that puncture the prevailing texture. A spoil sport, he refuses to play the game. While this seems to mark him as a crazy person—he was shown earlier to be quite vain and superficial, after all—it may also make him the only character who is "in touch with his feelings" and who understands reality beyond the frame of the artifice.

Only when Guglielmo is seen moving into the audience does the television audience become aware of a studio audience, a new narrative element. In fact, we are introduced to other narrative elements earlier. For example, after the pivotal wind serenade ("Secondate"), we see a medium shot of Don Alfonso from the side as he stoops at the edge of the stage to speak to musicians in the orchestra pit. And in a later instance, the camera shows us another camera. As these places rearrange basic aspects of the looking process—who is subject and who is object, and what warrants a gaze and what does not—they leave us with more complex notions of what it means to see and be seen, and how that can affect the meaning of a work.

In the final analysis, what Sellars offers in this *Così* is an intriguing display of the possibilities for visual engagement in telecast opera. Television viewers form new connections with the narrative as they become players as well as observers, while figures in the story reveal depths usually not seen in the opera. And the power of Mozart's music to eroticize is, perhaps ironically, given added strength through the emphasis on vision. The result is a memorable excursion into a disturbing opera that in Sellars's hands finds new ways to play out postmodern tendencies of *Così* and of our age. Just as the characters are unsure of who and what they love, so we may feel the same way toward the work and what we have witnessed. What Sellars does is refocus that ambivalence around our contemporary obsession with seeing and with dismantling boundaries between categories, in this case those concerned with the role of character and viewer, the location of interiority and exteriority, and the senses of hearing and touching as well as seeing. This *Così* opens our eyes to the richness of the opera: its journey into deep passion and its magical sonorities that chart passion, unlock its mysteries, and channel our desires and those of the characters. In its visually guided journey, Sellars's *Così* pays the ultimate tribute to Mozart's exquisite music and the power of sounds to move us. It is a stunning performance. It leaves us with an expanded sensory experience of this very sensual opera and heightens expectations and desires for performances yet to come.

Notes

1. Scott Burnham theorizes connections between the disparity and the biblical fall from grace in "Mozart's *felix culpa: Così fan tutte* and the Irony of Beauty," *Musical Quarterly* 78/1 (spring 1994): 77–98. See also Mary Hunter, *The Culture of Opera Buffa in Mozart's Vienna* (Princeton: Princeton University Press, 1999), 285–96; and Stefan Kunze, *Mozarts Opern* (Stuttgart: Reclam, 1984), 432–36.
2. For the provenance of the plot, see Bruce Alan Brown, "The Sources of an 'Original' Libretto," Chapter 4 of *W. A. Mozart: Così fan tutte* (Cambridge: Cambridge University Press, 1995), 57–81; and Andrew Steptoe, "*Così fan tutte* and Contemporary Morality," *The Mozart-Da Ponte Operas: The Cultural and Musical Background to* Le nozze di Figaro, Don Giovanni, *and* Così fan tutte (Oxford: Clarendon Press, 1988), 121–39.
3. Landmarks in the turnaround include early performances at the Glyndebourne Festival and serious attention in an important book, Edward J. Dent's *Mozart's Operas: A Critical Study* (London: Oxford University Press, 1913; second edition, 1947; revised edition, 1991). An excellent survey of the opera's reception appears in Brown, *Così fan tutte*, 157–82.
4. One of the first to discuss ambiguity in *Così* is philosopher Bernard Williams, in two essays: "Passion and Cynicism: Remarks on *Così fan tutte*," *The Musical Times* 114 (April 1973): 361–64; and "Mozart's Comedies and the Sense of an Ending," *The Musical Times* 122 (July 1981): 451–54.

5. An exploration that links eighteenth-century notions of gender and reason is Angela
   M. Marroy, "Reason and Desire, Education and Regression: Aspects of Rousseauist
   Gender Roles in *Così fan tutte*" (MM thesis [Musicology], Rice University, 1999).

6. For a general study of Sellars and his four television-video productions to date, see
   Marcia J. Citron, "A Matter of Time and Place: Peter Sellars and Media Culture,"
   Chapter 6 of *Opera on Screen* (New Haven: Yale University Press, 2000), 205–48.

7. As quoted in David Littlejohn, "What Peter Sellars Did to Mozart," *The Ultimate Art:
   Essays around and about Opera* (Berkeley: University of California Press, 1992), 142.

8. Sellars is more than complete in this production; he *adds* a musical piece, the opening
   of Mozart's Piano Concerto in G Major, K. 453, to fill in stage time as characters
   move outdoors in the recitative after No. 22. Another new piece enters the score when
   Sellars replaces Dorabella's aria in Act II, "*E Amore un ladroncello*" (No. 28), with a
   weightier independent aria, "*Vado, ma dovè,*" K. 583. Aside from dramatic reasons for
   the change (see discussion below), the substitution is apt on historical grounds: the aria
   was composed for Louise Villeneuve, the first Dorabella, as a substitute aria (in Martín
   y Soler's *Il burbero di buon core*, libretto by Da Ponte); it was written while Mozart was
   working on *Così*; and its text is probably by Da Ponte. Sellars's replacement also makes
   sense in light of the belief of Alan Tyson that Dorabella's "*E Amore un ladroncello*" is
   itself a replacement for an earlier, now unknown aria for Dorabella; see Tyson, *Mozart:
   Studies of the Autograph Scores* (Cambridge, Mass.: Harvard University Press, 1987),
   195. Dorothea Link takes the thesis further, suggesting that the newer "*E Amore,*"
   which has traits of the pastoral, a popular generic topic in the late eighteenth century,
   was composed by Mozart as a "compliment" to Villeneuve, who had gained popularity
   as the character Amore in another opera by Martín y Soler, *L' arbore di Diana*—a very
   popular work that Link sees as a model for *Così*. See Link's essays, "*Così fan tutte*:
   Dorabella and Amore," *Mozart-Jahrbuch* (1991): 888–94; and "*L' arbore di Diana*: A
   Model for *Così fan tutte*," in *Wolfgang Amade Mozart: Essays on His Life and His Music*,
   ed. Stanley Sadie (Oxford: Oxford University Press, 1996), 326–73.

9. For an elaboration see Citron, *Opera on Screen*, 217–18.

10. Sellars's own words appear in Del Ray Cross, "Peter Sellars's Stagings of *Don
    Giovanni*: Directorial Intent and Critical Response" (MA Thesis, Bowling Green
    State University, 1992), 34.

11. Soap opera in Sellars's four television productions is discussed in Citron, *Opera on
    Screen*, 222–29. Time is much more schizophrenic in his productions of *Figaro* and
    Don Giovanni, where there are many more events to manipulate in terms of speed.

12. See Butler's *Gender Trouble: Feminism and the Subversion of Identity* (New York: Rout-
    ledge, 1990).

13. For the feminine tone in the opera see Marroy, "Reason and Desire," especially
    Chapter 4. Citron discusses the gendered ideology of Romantic music in *Gender and
    the Musical Canon* (Cambridge: Cambridge University Press, 1993; reprint Urbana:
    University of Illinois Press, 2000), especially in Chapters 1 and 4. Christine Battersby
    makes astute connections between the sublime and the feminine in *Gender and Genius:
    Towards a Feminist Aesthetics* (Bloomington: Indiana University Press, 1989); pertinent
    discussions appear throughout the book.

14. Brown, *Così fan tutte*, 38.

15. Carolyn Abbate has written extensively on operatic characters' hearing the music,
    although it is usually a reflexive relationship with music they are singing. See especially
    Abbate's "Elektra's Voice: Music and Language in Strauss's Opera," in *Richard Strauss:
    Elektra*, ed. Derrick Puffett (Cambridge: Cambridge University Press, 1989), 107–27.
    For similar relationships in screen versions of opera see Citron, *Opera on Screen*,
    Chapter 4 (for Powell and Pressburger *Tales of Hoffmann*) and Chapter 5 (for Rosi's
    Bizet's Carmen); and Citron, "The Elusive Voice: Absence and Presence in Jean-Pierre
    Ponnelle's Film *Le nozze di Figaro*," in *Between Opera and Cinema*, ed. Jeongwon Joe
    and Rose Theresa (New York: Routledge, 2001), 135–55.

16. Another notable place in Sellars's telecasts of shedding clothes occurs in *Don Giovanni*,
    when Giovanni strips down to his jockey shorts as he intones "*Viva la libertà.*" Here

the device affirms the libertarian sentiments of the text as it pictorializes the individual's right to ultimate personal freedom.

17. See note 8.
18. For a summary of major theories of film spectatorship, see Linda Williams, "Introduction" to her edited volume, *Viewing Positions: Ways of Seeing Film* (New Brunswick: Rutgers University Press, 1995), 1–20. In the same collection, Vivian Sobchack posits a flexible relationship between viewer and film in "Phenomenology and the Film Experience," 36–58.
19. Many of the binary oppositions associated with gender in Western society, especially those involved in musical creation, representation, and reception, are discussed in Citron, *Gender and the Musical Canon*, especially Chapters 2, 4, and 5.
20. The theoretical basis of this discussion comes from Ellis's valuable essay, "Broadcast TV as Sound and Image," excerpted from his book *Visible Fictions* (1982), in *Film Theory and Criticism*, 5th ed., eds. Leo Braudy and Marshall Cohen (New York: Oxford University Press, 1999), 385–94.
21. Ellis, "Broadcast TV as Sound and Image," 386.
22. Sobchack, "Phenomenology and the Film Experience," 36–58; a fuller account appears in Sobchack, *The Address of the Eye: A Phenomenology of Film Experience* (Princeton: Princeton University Press, 1992). Although, to be precise, Sobchack's theories refer to cinema rather than television, I cite her work here because the general point is apt in the present context. Furthermore, some media theorists do not believe there are major differences in spectatorship between television and cinema.
23. Star-power, a prominent feature of MTV, is explored at length by Andrew Goodwin, *Dancing in the Distraction Factory: Music Television and Popular Culture* (Minneapolis: University of Minnesota Press, 1992), 98–130.
24. Dorothea Link explores this piece against the larger musical tradition, in "The Viennese Operatic Canon and Mozart's 'Così fan tutte,'" *Mitteilungen der Internationalen Stiftung Mozarteum* 38 (1990): 111–21.

12

Sensational, Performing, and Promotional Bodies

Sherril Dodds

Music Video and Video Dance

New music-making technologies demonstrated to musicians, critics and audiences more forcefully than ever before that pop performance is a visual experience.[1]

Dance made specifically for the camera . . . should surely appeal to our trendy youth fed on pop videos and instant images.[2]

This chapter examines the relationship between sound and image in music video and video dance, and the implications this has for the position of the auditor-spectator and for the performing body. The term "music video" refers to the promotional clips that accompany popular music singles; and "video dance" is art dance that is specifically conceived and choreographed for the camera. A number of commentators have drawn comparison between the two and, significantly, both developed during the 1980s.[3] Claudia Rosiny states that video dance "paralleled the MTV boom from the middle to the end of the eighties" with "the video-specific possibilities of electronic image modification, fast cutting, and effects," while Michael Bayston notes that "many of the technical tricks [of video dance] are used in commercials and pop promotional videos."[4]

The commonalities between music video and video dance become most evident through an examination of the relationship of sound and image. Within music video and video dance there are close links between sound, image, and physicality; yet the way in which the two forms deal with the interrelationship of these sensations is not always comparable. For this reason, the first section of this essay focuses on ways in which music can act on the senses, particularly in these media. The second section also takes music as its starting point, but considers how sound can participate in constructing a representational or performing body and the implications of this for the auditor-spectator. In conclusion, the chapter considers to what extent music video and video dance diverge and overlap.

The Physicality of Sound and Image

How does the triadic relationship between sound, image, and physicality operate sensorily within both music video and video dance? Dancing bodies frequently operate as a major component of music videos. The dance element may be performed by audience members, professional dancers, or the singers and musicians of the band, and can range from loose, improvised movement through to tightly choreographed routines.[5] Several scholars comment on the interaction of sound, image, and movement and the palpability of this relationship. Simon Frith argues that music video aims to create the impact of live performance on the small screen.[6] He suggests that "movement" becomes a metaphor for sound, through such devices as fast cutting, swirling bodies, and visual excess. He states, "we are overwhelmed with images to compensate for the essential feebleness of TV sound."[7] The way in which the televisual apparatus is employed is paramount to the sense of motion. Theresa Buckland asserts that the energy of the camera is intended to parallel the dynamic of the performers.[8] Similarly, Brigitte Heilmann identifies how filming and editing can provide a choreographic sensibility irrespective of whether the singers and musicians are moving.[9]

Two case studies particularly demonstrate some of these ideas. The first is the promotional video for *Let Me Entertain You* (1997) by Robbie Williams.[10] The video is shot in black and white. Williams is dressed in a style that makes reference to Queen frontman Freddie Mercury and the band members of Kiss: he wears a black skintight jumpsuit, covered in metal studs with a scooped neckline down to his waist, clumpy biker boots, and white pan stick make-up with blackened lips and eyes. The look is an homage to rock theatricality that is echoed in the music, the events of the video, and its style of camera work and editing. In the establishing shot, the camera zooms in to a close-up of Williams hunched down, clutching a white dove. An electronic hum amplifies as Williams slowly opens his mouth as if to bite off the bird's head, but instead he kisses it before launching it into flight. As the dove is liberated, the piano introduction commences that will eventually lead into the full rock soundtrack.

During this introduction, a succession of shots ensues that includes close-ups of Williams, in which he twitches like a madman, rolls his eyes, and sticks out his tongue. The length of these shots allows the spectator sufficient time to take in the image, and their stark composition is reflected by the simple piano riff. Although later there will be a surge of blaring instrumentation and lightning-fast images, at present the spectator can only anticipate the potential eruption. Williams rises as he sings the first two lines of the verse while the camera zooms in. On the final word "scream," he menacingly flashes his tongue and wiggles his fingers around his face. The shot cuts to a tight close-up as Williams sings the next line and lazily rolls his eyes. The rapidity of the edit increases as this time he only sings half a line; when he points to the camera on the word "you," it zooms in so that his body instantly expands as it looms toward the spectator. An unnerving sense of contact is employed in his direct address, underscored by diabolic images of flashing eyes and flicking tongues.

Although the speed of the cuts has gained pace, it is in the next few shots that the song and image truly let rip. In the fleeting break that precedes the chorus, four bullet-quick images fly past: a drum stick strikes the kit, Williams slides down a ramp, hair flies in the air, and the guitarist spins round. With the introduction of drums, guitars, and the anthemic rock chorus, the auditor-spectator is flooded with a giddying onslaught of bodily excess: Williams flamboyantly nods, claps and thrusts his pelvis, while the guitarists strut, pose, and strike their instruments. The explicit borrowing of music industry clichés invites the viewer to participate in the sound and visuals through the pastiche of predictable riffs and heavy rock imagery.

The camera work focuses solely on Williams as he sings the next verse and the pace of the edit temporarily calms. With the return of the chorus, however, a rapid succession of images are revealed through diverse and manic shots: the band members thrash their instruments; sexy backing singers give it their all; and Williams salaciously postures and licks his finger. This mode of delivery continues throughout the video. The spectator is presented with a playful torrent of rock quotations: Williams flies wildly though the air on a wire, runs half-naked down a hotel corridor with a young woman, signs autographs, and ostentatiously smudges his make-up. The images jump from different contexts, shot sizes, and angles.

Toward the end of the song, the visual and aural deluge escalates even further. This prevents the auditor-spectator from becoming too comfortable or familiar with the sensory experience. The chorus is repeated over and over again and is matched by repetitive split-second shots of Williams waving his hands as flashing lights emanate from his body, almost like a stroboscope in quality. The instrumentation is intensified as a new piano part, extra guitars, and back-up vocals are added to the track. A series of rapid zoom-ins cause Williams and the band members to appear to fly toward the screen so that the spectator is almost enveloped by their image. The fleeting succession of images is heightened by flashing lights, explosions, and sparks on stage; as a brass section is introduced on the track, the image of women sliding down poles is added to the mix. The sensory overload of heavy electronic rock and vertiginous somatic images creates a palpable physicality.

Unlike *Let Me Entertain You*, the next video does not rely on a swiftly edited, image-overload aesthetic. *It's Like That* (1998) by Run DMC vs Jason Nevins is a reworked version of the 1980s track of the same name by seminal hip-hop band Run DMC.[11] References to the historical lineage of rap and hip-hop and the classic status of this track contribute to the video. It is based on a "dance out" between two rival gangs; the dancers wear a mix of "old school" styles and 1990s street wear; and the video is occasionally intercut with black-and-white images from the original video. The establishing shot is of a man carrying a large ghetto blaster while walking into a deserted parking lot; the cassette player beats out a drum-machine riff that will form the backbone of the whole soundtrack.

A sharp cut shifts from a close-up of the man to a long shot of a group of youths standing at the far end of the lot. It could be said that the spectator is inserted or positioned into the video by seeing this image from the man's "point of view." Within film theory, it is suggested that this device "sutures" the spectator into the text. The term "suture" refers, first, to the way in which the shots in a film or program are "stitched" together to give an illusion of "seamlessness," and second, to the way in which the spectator is stitched into the narrative through such devices as point-of-view shot structures.[12] These notions of positionality and shifting perspectives suggest a kinetic encounter for the spectator, although this is obviously perceptual rather than actual. This continues as the shots cut back and forth between the man and the gang. On each shot of the gang, the frame is tighter so that the physical presence of the members increases. The cutting to and fro also builds an element of suspense as the man and the gang remain static but ready for action. Eventually, the man crouches by his ghetto blaster and nods, followed by a shot of the opposing gang situated at the other end of the lot. At this point a voice comes onto the track which raps, "Here it goes a little something like this." It is with this introduction that the physical action and the vocal and instrumental layers kick in.

The ensuing images cut in and out of the two gangs as they walk toward each other: the man with the ghetto blaster who beats out the riff with his hand, and shots of the original video of Run DMC walking into a recording studio. The rhythm of the action is set in time to the music, so that the beat is echoed both through sound and image. Eventually the two gangs run toward each other to take up their positions for the dance out. From now on, the video consists of members of the two groups alternately demonstrating a variety of virtuosic street-dance moves as they try to outdance each other. The camera cuts between the dancers themselves and the gang members jeering and goading the other gang. Certain components of the music are foregrounded through the events of the video. For example, a sampled "brass stab" recurs during the track, and this is drawn attention to through a number of devices. On one occasion a woman knocks a man off balance just as the sound occurs. His temporary loss of control and bewilderment is echoed by a rapid high-pitched synthesized note. The brass stab occurs again as a woman motions an insulting yawning action and, later, when a dancer dives over his opponent into a forward roll in an impressive display of showmanship. This key sound always coincides with a significant physical moment. The impact of it thus becomes inscribed in the listening/viewing experience.

One of the features of rap and hip-hop is a distinctive layering of sounds and rhythms, and therefore the movement, camera work, and editing privilege specific components at different times. For instance, at one point, the image cuts back to the original video of two pairs of trainers marching on the spot in time to the drum beat, which momentarily diverts attention to that particular sound. At another, the rapid synthesized notes flitter across the track as a woman performs a body-popping motif. The fleeting, but isolated, articulation of her limbs complements the density of the music sequence.

Similar devices also occur during key vocal moments. The refrain "It's like that" punctuates the track and is always highlighted in some way. On one occasion, all of the dancers suddenly execute some rapid "scissor steps" in unison, in striking contrast to their previous dancing individually or in pairs. Likewise on the "huh" sound, a pair of dancers shunt their bodies downward as if to reflect the low bass sound of the vocals. At the end of the track, the man picks up his ghetto blaster to signify that the "dance-out" is over, and the final shot is of Run DMC in a gallery watching a video monitor on a plinth. Unlike *Let Me Entertain You*, *It's Like That* does not employ an overwhelming excess of visual and aural signification. Yet there is a distinctive physicality: the cutting back and forth and the shift between the new and old video imply a mobile experience for the spectator in terms of the changing contexts. The use of eye-catching movements to foreground key musical components imbues the viewing/listening space with a clearly defined rhythm and dynamic.[13]

With the exception of Annie Bozzini who comments that "a film's novelty value increases in direct relation to its soundtrack," few scholars have addressed the relationship between sound and image in video dance.[14] Yet several writers have commented on the links between the image and the kinetic experience. Fiona Burnside suggests that the spectator is mobilized through shifting camera perspectives, while Sue Merrett conceptualizes the camera as an additional performer due to its physical participation in the dance.[15] Michael Bayston sees a symbiotic relationship between video dance and the camera, and Judith Mackrell and Claudia Rosiny argue that camera work and editing are intrinsic to the movement dynamic.[16]

As with the two music videos already discussed, the next examples consider how music can act on the senses in video dance. The first work, *Bruce McLean* (1994), is choreographed and performed by Bruce McLean and directed by Jane Thorburn.[17] The action takes place in a plain white room with a door against the far wall. Although the shot sizes change, the camera is always positioned face-on to the door. McLean is a stocky, middle-aged man who wears a white suit, a turquoise shirt, and a red tie. The only other flashes of color are bright household objects integrated into the action, and the background behind the door, which is a striking royal blue. The soundtrack consists of fragments of guitar strumming and snatches of a male voice, largely comprised of odd syllables with occasional words and recognizable phrases.

The piece begins with a few guitar strums in the empty space, although a large shadow of McLean, impatiently shifting from foot to foot, is reflected against the wall. The door opens slightly and, through the crack, a second shadow of McLean edgily stepping back and forth is reflected onto the wall, adding to the twitchy effect created by the first shadow. A series of rapidly edited shots draw focus to the left side of McLean's body. In the first frame, his body can be seen from shoulder to knee as he swings his arm to the side. The camera cuts to a close-up as he stretches and folds his arm, then returns to a wider shot as he turns and bends over while gesticulating excitedly. The image then shifts to a close-up of his torso in which he juts, taps, and waves his elbow. His agitated movement and the hiccupping soundtrack of reassembled syllables are made all the more chaotic by the fleeting cuts and dislocated perspectives. Indeed, this type of spasmodic cutting challenges the conventions of "invisible editing" as identified by James Monaco and creates an unsettling viewing experience.[18]

The manic execution of sound and image continues throughout the video. For example, the camera focuses on a close-up head shot, but McLean bobs up and down and side to side, randomly slipping in and out of the frame. While more conventional modes of television-making privilege the human face by keeping it in a tight frame, in this case, an overwrought dynamic is created as the head flies in and out of the still shot.[19] There is also a series of shots based on McLean hurriedly entering and exiting the space. On each occasion, there is a split-second uncertainty as to whether he will emerge or disappear through the door or from the side of the frame. The camera remains still, enhancing the sense of commotion as he races across the screen. Because his absence creates momentary pockets of stillness and calm, his presence is always magnified through the frenetic action. This bedlam is also ameliorated by the primary-colored watering cans, washing-up bowls, and plastic buckets that fly around in the background each time he opens the door.

The organization of the soundtrack is far from arbitrary. To the contrary, there are recognizable patterns of sound that are closely tied to visual ideas. On two occasions, McLean opens the door and the guitar sound is distorted as if a needle is being scratched on vinyl; and during verbal sections of the soundtrack, close-up shots focus on McLean gabbling words at the same frantic pace. The close partnership between sound and image is similar to the music and events seen in the music videos. The piece ends in the same abrupt way that it began. McLean walks in and out of the door and on his third exit does not return; precisely at this moment the soundtrack comes to a sudden standstill. *Bruce McLean* is a formal exploration of time and space in relation to the moving body. The rapid fragmentation of sound and image creates a kinetic rush. Through musical devices and televisual techniques, the performer's body becomes unpredictable and playful, and the sense of movement produced through camera work and editing is potent.

The next example, however, deals with the relationship between sight and sound in a far less obvious way. The piece is called *Monologue* (1994) and is choreographed by Anna Teresa de Keersmaeker and directed by Walter Verdin.[20] Unlike *Bruce McLean*, *Monologue* consists of a single unedited close-up; yet the way in which sound, image, filming, and physicality interrelate is equally significant. The work is shot in black and white and consists of a big close-up of the dancer Fumyo Ikeda's face. Her eyes are closed and the piece begins in silence. This stands in stark contrast to the explosive physicality of the other three examples. The quiet and stillness create a calm not usually associated with the television screen. Slowly she opens her eyes but her focus remains cast downward. She fleetingly glances from side to side and this refusal to make a direct address to the camera suggests an unease for both the performer and the spectator. Although direct address is less common in classic narrative cinema, with television, presenters, commentators, and interviewees regularly address the audience.[21] Ikeda blinks, glances out, but then looks down again. Whereas an uninterrupted gaze suggests surveillance, control, and power, her blinking highlights vulnerability and awkwardness. Because the auditor-spectator is not presented with a flurry of visual and aural signification, a space is created to dwell upon her painfully shy expression. She moves as if to utter some words, but they fail to emerge. Eventually she mutters a phrase in French, but the hesitant quality of her voice renders it almost inaudible. The spectator is made very aware of the persistent claustrophobia of the unedited close-up shot. The apparent emotional difficulty she has in formulating her words can be seen in acute detail. The severity of her face, the choked language, and her uneasy gaze seem to penetrate beyond the television screen.

Ikeda begins to utter a few more words with an increasingly confident tone. It is still difficult to make out what she is saying, although the precise content would seem to be unimportant because the actual sentiments are so clearly articulated in her facial expression. The crevice in her brow and wrinkles around her eyes are concentrated through the close-up. She continues her monologue in a strong, regional French dialect with her eyes now permanently focused out to the camera. After the initial discomfort of her awkward gaze, her piercing stare makes equally uncomfortable viewing. Her language grows in speed and confidence and, at the end of one sentence, she looks stubbornly satisfied. As the language cascades forth, a musical excerpt from Scene 8 of Monteverdi's *L'incoronazione di Poppea* (1643) commences, making it progressively more difficult to translate any of Ikeda's words. The music is a romantic duet between Poppea and Nerone and the lyrics speak of their eternal love and devotion. The clarity of their voices makes a stark contrast to the broken snatches of Ikeda's furious diatribe. As the singing voices become stronger, her anger also intensifies. No longer is she awkward and vulnerable but fired up and irate. She spits out her words with venom. The disjunctive relationship between the calm execution of the classical duet, with its tender words of love, and her bitter verbal attack creates an unsettling, and decentered, viewing experience. While she shouts, the clarity of her language is completely lost and the image begins to be played back in slow motion. This dislocation of sound and image has a striking effect. While her words are spewed out in a wretched tone, they are magnified by the detail of the slow-motion close-up: the contorted mouth; the flecks of spittle that fly out from her lips; her screwed-up eyes; and her complete loss of reserve and control. The verbal and visual signification are made all the more peculiar by the serene, harmonious duet.

Eventually Ikeda reaches the end of her verbal monologue with guttural screech, but her facial monologue continues along with the music. The contrast between the controlled duet and her distraught face is perturbing. What was clearly her final screaming word on the soundtrack is recalled in the image: her face is locked in an agonized shriek; her mouth is wide open like a gaping wound. She then clenches her teeth together and her pained expression settles into a deep, introspective frown. This pose is held until the end of the duet and the stillness of the unedited shot makes for uneasy viewing. As the piece of music comes to an end, she glances out to the camera accusingly and walks out of the frame.

In this video dance, the voice goes out of synch with, and the music is set in radical contrast to, the image. Yet this juxtaposition adds a striking, and at times disturbing, physicality to the work. This is reinforced by the absence of any cuts and the still, close-up frame of the camera. In this instance, sound and image work against each other to produce a disconcerting aural and visual experience. Whereas in the previous examples, the images clearly mirror the pace, rhythm, and energy of the soundtrack, here sound and image operate tangentially. Hence, by comparison, the relationship between sound and image is more open-ended and unpredictable.

The Performing Body:
Promotional Discourses versus Textual Radicality

Whereas the previous section considers how music acts sensorily on the auditor-spectator, this section sets out to investigate the role of the representational or constructed body in music video and video dance. The focus is on the relationship between sound and image as mediated through the performing body and the implications of this for the auditor-spectator. It is apparent from the previous section that the link between sound and image is a vital way to read music video and video dance. In his work on music video, Andrew Goodwin notes that although music television has received much scholarly attention, there has tended to be a marginalization of the aural element in favor of the visual.[22] In order to address the relationship between sound and image, Goodwin proposes a "musicology of the image." To inform this theory, he uses the concept of "synaesthesia," the process by which a sensory impression is transferred from one sense to another. This notion is pertinent to music video, in which images are constructed through the visual associations of a soundtrack. Although this methodology derives from Goodwin's study of music video, for the purposes of this chapter, I use it here to analyze links between sound and image in video dance.[23] In order to address the performing bodies of music video and video dance, two works by French choreographer-director Philippe Decouflé form the focus of investigation: the first is the music video *She Drives Me Crazy* (1988) by the pop band Fine Young Cannibals; the second is the video dance piece *Le P'tit bal perdu* (1994).[24]

She Drives Me Crazy intercuts shots of the band, comprised of a lead singer and two guitarists, with images of the dancers. In a number of ways, the video is coded with familiar pop iconography. During the vocal sections there are recurrent close-ups of lead singer Roland Gift. He is positioned face on to the camera against a number of brightly colored backdrops, highlighting his good looks and "pin up" status. There are also shots of the two guitarists as they strum their instruments. The dancers, however, are very much situated in an art dance context through the costumes, movement, and style of filming. During the drum beat introduction, the camera is placed in an overhead shot as two dancers (respectively dressed in yellow and black shirts, jackets and trousers rolled up to the knees, braces, and goggles) jump forward in time to the rhythm. In a momentary pause before the guitar introduction, the camera disjointedly zooms in and out toward Gift in a rapid series of cuts so that he appears to whiz toward and away from the screen.

Many of the images of the dancers are framed in striking and unconventional ways. In one instance, a man in a black-and-white striped suit is positioned against a purple backdrop in a tight full shot, with his knees bent outward and his head creased sideways. He swings his arms from side to side while his knees twist in and out, and the overall impression is that he is too tall to fit into the tight frame. In another, the man in the yellow suit stands on his hands over a perspex floor. The camera is placed directly beneath the perspex, thus the spectator views his body from an unexpected and eye-catching perspective. Additionally, the dancers engage in strange and unpredictable behavior. One dancer's body is padded with red satin cushions and springs onto its stomach and back, each time rebounding off the floor. The bouncy vitality of the dancer's actions is enhanced by the filming style, which cuts in and out through different shot sizes and angles.

Although the spectator is presented with these seemingly incoherent signifiers, there is an element of logic to the video. The images may appear absurd, but many of them tie in with musical components of the song or general pop music conventions. Just as a backing singer comes in on the soundtrack, two painted faces pop out of brightly striped cylinders to mimic the vocals and, during an instrumental section, the men in the black and yellow suits dance against a split screen backdrop. Although they perform a type of wacky street dance, which includes frog jumps, isolations, and wild gesticulation, the strategy of using dance sequences during instrumental sections is a standard pop music device. Significantly, the lyrics relate how the 'singer' fails to comprehend the actions of 'a woman' and the irrational images could be said to reflect his confusion. The arresting visuals of *She Drives Me Crazy* are perhaps intended to encourage repeated viewings, with the performing body treated in an experimental or innovative way. Yet any aesthetic radicality is counteracted by the close links between the visual components and pop music conventions. Whether by associating the cutting edge imagery with music practices, such as pin-up singers, backing dancers, and formal components of the song, or by giving the band a zany or artsy image, the video serves a promotional function. In a number of ways the performing bodies either advertise the single or the band.

Decouflé's work in video dance offers a significant comparison. *Le P'tit bal perdu* features a man and woman who sit behind a table in the middle of a field of long green grass. Occasionally there are cutaway shots of some black and white cows, and of a stout elderly woman who sits playing an accordion in a field surrounded by a string of white lights. The action is set to a French folk song, "Le P'tit bal perdu," [the little lost ballroom (or dance)] and the lyrics describe a ballroom, the name of which the singer cannot remember. The use of pun is a central device throughout the work. *Le P'tit bal perdu* ideally illustrates Goodwin's "musicology of the image" in that both the form and the content of the movement closely follow the structure and lyrics of the song.[25]

The choreographic content is made up of a complex gestural motif, and the choreographic form mirrors the musical structure. The actual movement closely corresponds with the lyrics to the song and, in some instances, this is through mimetic representation. On the word *guerre* (war), for example, the performers point their fingers like a gun and on *deux* they hold up two fingers. At other times, the gesture is more abstract; yet, it is still possible to read the links between word and image. For instance, with the word *importante* the performers stand up with their hands on their hips as if to demonstrate authority, and on *piste* they mark out a winding trail with their hands as if to represent a *track*. A number of incongruous props featured in the piece also tie in with the punning device. The words, *qui s'appelait*, meaning 'whose name was,' are repeated several times throughout the song, and each time a pun is brought into play around the "... *pele*" or "... *ler*" sound. A telephone appears on the table as a reference to *appeler* (which can mean "to call"), along with several bottles of "milk," which are a play on the *lait* sound. This occurs again with *pelle* as a variety of "shovels" appears, and with *laid*, at which the man pulls an "ugly" face. Through such unstable relationships between language, movement, props, and meaning, the work plays on the problem of semantics. Although the choreographic content closely follows the structure of the song, it is highly unlikely that the auditor-spectator would be able to translate the movement back to the lyrics.

This piece displays several similarities with Decouflé's work in music video. The striking visual design, the gestural vocabulary, the use of humor, the absurd behavior, and the incongruous images are all recognizable hallmarks of Decouflé's style. Indeed, it is perhaps not surprising that there are formal similarities between music video and video dance. Ann Kaplan describes how music video borrows visual conventions from advertising and Stephanie O'Donohoe draws attention to advertising's appropriation of ideas and techniques from other art forms.[26] These ideas are further supported by Goodwin who states that the emergence of music video coincided with the convergence of various media sites in the 1980s, both textually and institutionally.[27] O'Donohoe conceptualizes this intertextuality in terms of "leaky boundaries" to describe the way in which popular texts merge and overlap. This metaphor lends itself well to the dancing body, which can be conceived as fluid and mobile rather than fixed and stable. The manner in which it slips between music video and video dance, with their shared aesthetics, calls attention to this leakiness. Yet the extent of this fluidity is questionable.[28]

There is a fundamental difference between music video and video dance. With *Le P'tit bal perdu*, although the image closely follows the music, there is no promotional strategy connected to the song. The viewer is told that the music is a traditional French folk song, but it is not credited to a songwriter or performer. In *She Drives Me Crazy*, the images both visualize the song and promote various messages and associations in relation to the band. Whereas *Le P'tit bal perdu* is simply a postmodern play of signifiers; eclectic and fragmented images, sounds and actions are placed side by side so that meaning remains deferred and open-ended.[29] Yet there is a danger of polarizing the intentions in each too simplistically by equating commercialism with music video and aestheticism with video dance. Although the body in video dance is not tied to a discernible commodity, with a given "exchange-value," it could nevertheless still be conceptualized as a "promotional body." After all, video dance undoubtedly exposes and promotes the work of individual directors and choreographers. Andrew Wernick proposes that the intertext of promotion has gone radically beyond the advertising media, into all aspects of cultural life.[30] He states that promotion is a signifying system applicable to commercial and non-commercial phenomena and as areas of social life have become increasingly commodified, promotion is now a "cultural dominant." If this is the case, then it appears that the video dance body is unavoidably inscribed in promotional discourses. Innovation is one of the motivating factors behind artistic practice and, at times, this has a commercial aim. Not only are practitioners concerned to a greater or lesser extent with stimulating audience interest through new artistic ideas, but many artists also have a commercial aim in mind; with increasingly limited subsidies available, many practitioners modify their work to suit funding body policy, which seeks to maximize audience targets.

Equally, the contexts for production and consumption of music video are not solely financial. Music video employs artistic strategies as a way to make itself distinctive and innovation is adopted as a means to differentiate one recording artist from another. This is reflected in various industry awards that celebrate and privilege aesthetic achievement in music video. In reference to advertising, Mica Nava posits that young readers consume television commercials as they would other cultural forms, such as pop singles and magazine articles, and O'Donohoe argues that many young people readily divorce the selling message from the aesthetic components.[31] The same practices of resistance and subversion may be employed with music video: readers may admire, comment on, and engage with certain music video texts, yet not necessarily like the music, or wish to buy the single. This again indicates an element of overlap between music video and video dance. Music video can be produced and consumed with its aesthetic properties in mind, and video dance can fulfill a promotional role.

It appears that there is a blurring of boundaries between music video and video dance, in that both genres trade in aural-visual signification, in which bodies are positioned, framed, moved, and filmed in stylized and innovative ways, and both are subject to economic and artistic exigencies. Yet the way in which they are "framed" is somewhat discrete. The economic potential of video dance is questionable due to the marginalization of dance on television, and its limited commercial viability is reflected in the continual struggle to raise funding for new projects.[32] Hence the promotional potential of video dance is relatively limited in comparison to that of music videos, which occupy the commercial territory of dedicated music channels. Although music video can be consumed purely for its aesthetic sensibility, as a genre it is geared toward consumerism.

In all of the music video examples, there is a close/d relationship between sound and image that seeks to create a sensory experience that reflects the character of the singer/band and construct performing bodies inscribed by promotion. Since music video has a commercial agenda, it aims to create a consumerist auditor-spectator who buys into the sound and image of the commodified singer/band. Video dance, on the other hand, lacks this explicitly economic function and the play between sound and image remains far more ambiguous and open-ended. In *Bruce McLean*, the music and movement work closely together to create a manic physicality, but the rationale behind a middle-aged man executing fragments of gesture to a jumpy and disordered soundtrack has no external logic; in *Monologue* the music and image are diametrically opposed to produce an unsettling and decentered viewing experience; and in *Le P'tit bal perdu*, although the choreography mirrors the structure of the song, the stability of meaning in movement and language is disrupted through the bizarre selection of puns. With video dance the unstable relationship between sound and image opens up a discursive space for the auditor-spectator in which textual radicality can be an end in itself.

Notes

1. Andrew Goodwin, *Dancing in the Distraction Factory: Music Television and Popular Culture* (London: Routledge, 1993), 33.
2. Nadine Meisner, "A Particular Affinity," *Dance and Dancers* (October 1991), 17.
3. Vera Maletic, "Videodance—Technology—Attitude Shift," *Dance Research Journal* 19, no. 2 (winter 1987–88) 3–7; Stephanie Jordan, "Dance Screen 1992," *Dancing Times*, LXXXII, 984 (September 1992), 1154–55.
4. Claudia Rosiny, "Dance Films and Video Dance," *Ballet International* (August/September 1994), 82; Michael Bayston, "Dancers on Television," *Dancing Times*, LXXVII, 921 (June 1987), 707.
5. Theresa Buckland, "Dance & Music Video" in *Parallel Lines: Media Representations of Dance*, ed. Stephanie Jordan and Dave Allen (London: Libbey, 1993), 51–79.
6. Simon Frith, *Music for Pleasure: Essays in the Sociology of Pop* (Cambridge: Polity, 1988).
7. Frith, *Music for Pleasure*, 216.
8. Buckland, "Dance & Music Video" in *Parallel Lines*, 51–79.
9. Brigitte Heilmann, "MTV Dances," *Ballet International* 6 (June 1999), 40–42.
10. Robbie Williams, "Let Me Entertain You," *Life Thru a Lens* (London: Chrysalis Records Ltd., 1997).
11. Run DMC vs Jason Nevins, "It's Like That," *The Best Hip Hop Anthemz . . . Ever!* (Circa Records Ltd, 1998).
12. John Fiske, *Television Culture* (London: Routledge, 1989); Robert Stam et al., *New*

Vocabularies in Film Semiotics: Structuralism, Post-structuralism and Beyond (London: Routledge, 1992).

13. I would like to thank Dr. Tim Brookes for his generous advice on technical music terminology.

14. Annie Bozzini, "They Film as They Dance," *Ballet International* 14, no. 1 (January 1991), 40.

15. Fiona Burnside, "Moving Pictures on a Black Marble Frame," *Dance Theatre Journal* 11, 3 (Autumn 1994), 14–17; Sue Merrett, "Video Dance: IMZ Dance Screen in Frankfurt," *Dancing Times* LXXXI, 963 (December 1990), 256–57.

16. Michael Bayston, "Dancers on Television," *Dancing Times* LXXXII, 982 (July 1992), 950; Judith Mackrell, "Making Television Dance," *Dance Theatre Journal* 1, 4 (Autumn 1993), 28–29; Rosiny, "Dance Films and Video Dance," *Ballet International*, 82–83.

17. Anne Beresford, "Bruce McLean," *Tights, Camera, Action!* (Channel Four Television, MJW Productions, 1994).

18. James Monaco, *How to Read a Film* (Oxford: OUP, 1981). Monaco states that according to Hollywood conventions, any editing must remain "invisible" and as unobtrusive as possible. In Bruce McLean, the style of editing is immensely distracting due to its jerky rhythm and sudden changes of perspective.

19. Fiske, *Television Culture*.

20. Anne Beresford, "Monologue," *Tights, Camera, Action!* (Channel Four Television, MJW Productions, 1994).

21. Fiske, *Television Culture*.

22. Goodwin, *Dancing in the Distraction Factory*. See also Will Straw, "Popular Music and Postmodernism in the 1980s" in *Sound and Vision: The Music Video Reader,* ed. Simon Frith et al. (London: Routledge, 1993). The reason for this visual bias may be because much of the analysis has derived from the fields of psychoanalytic, feminist, film and postmodern theory, which are primarily concerned with the image, and thus neglect the popular music context out of which music video has emerged.

23. Goodwin, *Dancing in the Distraction Factory*.

24. Fine Young Cannibals, "She Drives Me Crazy," *The Raw and the Cooked* (London: FFRR Records, 1988); Anne Beresford, "Le P'tit bal perdu," *Tights, Camera, Action!*, (Channel Four Television, MJW Productions, 1994).

25. Goodwin, *Dancing in the Distraction Factory*.

26. E. Ann Kaplan, *Rocking around the Clock: Music Television, Postmodernism and Consumer Culture* (London: Routledge, 1988); Stephanie O'Donohoe, "Leaky Boundaries: Intertextuality and Young Adult Experiences of Advertising" in *Buy This Book: Studies in Advertising and Consumption*, ed. Mica Nava et al. (London: Routledge, 1997).

27. Goodwin, *Dancing in the Distraction Factory*. Instances of the crossover of media texts are seen in pop music used in advertising and star names used to endorse products, or cross-media marketing deals that might incorporate the rights to a film along with a soundtrack and related merchandise.

28. O'Donohoe, "Leaky Boundaries: Intertextuality and Young Adult Experiences of Advertising" in *Buy This Book*.

29. See Lisa Appignanesi, ed., *Postmodernism: ICA Documents 4* (London: ICA, 1986); E. Ann Kaplan ed., *Postmodernism and Its Discontents* (London: Verso, 1988); Madan Sarup, *Post-structuralism and Postmodernism* (Hemel Hempstead: Harvester Wheatsheaf, 1988).

30. Andrew Wernick, *Promotional Culture: Advertising, Ideology and Symbolic Expression* (London: Sage, 1991).

31. Mica, Nava, "Framing Advertising: Cultural Analysis and the Incrimination of Visual Texts," in *Buy This Book*; O'Donohoe, "Leaky Boundaries: Intertextuality and Young Adult Experiences of Advertising," in *Buy This Book*.

32. Dave Allen, "Screening Dance" in *Parallel Lines: Media Representations of Dance* ed. Stephanie Jordan and Dave Allen (London: Libbey, 1993); Meisner, "A Particular Affinity," *Dance and Dancers*, 16–18.

13

Musical Instruments, Glass Cases, and Headsets

Sound and Sensation in France's Museum of Music[1]

Carla Zecher

For critic Alain Lompech of *Le Monde*, the new Museum of Music in Paris is "a CD-ROM incarnated."[2] This museum, which opened in January 1997, houses the French national collection of musical instruments. It combines conventional displays in glass cases with additional, contemporary methods of interpretation, including a dynamic postmodern architectural setting, a sophisticated audio system, interactive video technology, and spaces for live performance.[3] In the Museum of Music, the visually arresting features of the artifacts—with their rich woods, bright metals, inlaid gems and ivories, and varied shapes and sizes—are supplemented by innovative interpretive tools designed to appeal to the other senses as well. Visitors are provided, free of charge, with infrared headsets that allow them to hear musical excerpts and brief spoken commentary as they circulate among the display cases. The interactive video stations installed here and there in the galleries provide further information about musical styles and genres; they are activated by pressing links on their screens, and their recordings are also transmitted by the headsets. A tightly constructed museological program, integrated into an inventive architectural environment, takes visitors on a "journey through the history of music and instruments."[4] Along the way they may find themselves witnesses to live musical production as they pass by one of the museum's small performance spaces. The overall effect of a visit to the Museum of Music is indeed somewhat like stepping into an immense, captivating CD-ROM.

But Lompech's CD-ROM analogy is not entirely complimentary. He finds the notion of progress so omnipresent in this museum to be irritating, rather than illuminating. In some respects, the Museum of Music is as much about late-twentieth-century museology as about the artifacts it houses. Here musical instruments are packaged for visual and aural consumption in a multisensory environment that seeks to bring them to life, to help them "speak" to a public for whom musical experience has become to a considerable extent a media experience. But this method of presentation has a disadvantage in that the objects displayed risk being overshadowed by the wonders of the technology that interprets them. As Michael Ames has noted, this is a common problem with current museology: "When we 'museumify' other cultures and our own past, we exercise a conceptual control over them; and when this 'museumification' involves high technology . . . we are demonstrating and exhibiting the superiority of our technology."[5] In the Museum of Music the delicate balance between object and interpretation sometimes tilts in favor of the latter. When it does, the museum, rather than directly addressing the senses, slips into sensationalism.

Music à la carte

The Museum of Music (*musée de la Musique*) forms part of the City of Music (*cité de la Musique*), an architectural complex situated at the northeastern edge of Paris that serves as a port of entry to the vast park at La Villette.[6] Along with the Museum of Music, its archives, and its boutique, the City of Music houses the Paris National Conservatory of Music and Dance, the management offices of Pierre Boulez's *Ensemble Intercontemporain*, a large concert hall, a small amphitheater, an information center for music and dance, a mediatheque, a gamelan studio, and a café. According to Brigitte Marger, the City of Music's director, the music complex—like the entire park at La Villette—is intended to bridge the frontier between diverse worlds: city and suburbs; outdoor and indoor spaces; traditional culture and new urban arts; historical research and amateur expression.[7] As with the *Théâtre National Populaire* of Jean Vilar in the 1950s, the City of Music has been installed on the urban margin with the general intent of bringing the patrimony to a constituency that comprises all social classes, and the particular hope of reaching the economically and culturally impoverished. "The National Popular Theater," Vilar stated in his manifesto, "is a public service, just like gas, water, and electricity."[8] Similarly, the City of Music's web site presents the music complex as being "at your service."[9] Marger describes it as "a house permanently open to all publics, where music is seen, heard, and played."[10]

Within the City, the Museum of Music aims to make the national collection of musical instruments more widely accessible than it had been in its previous home in the old Paris Conservatory. Established in the early nineteenth century, the collection first consisted of instruments that had been confiscated from the elites during the Revolution.[11] Initially, the museum's mission was to preserve the most beautiful musical instruments extant as models for builders. But during the course of the nineteenth century, this simple function of conservation expanded to include such goals as the education of the public and the elaboration of a national cultural memory.

The Museum of Music endeavors to realize these goals more fully by enabling greater parity of access. Public museums, born in the age of imperialism, have often been criticized for functioning as tools of the ruling classes and corporate powers.[12] In response to this critique, the Museum of Music, like many other new museums, adopts the ideology of consumerism, marketing itself as an attraction, a source of entertaining education, of "infotainment."[13] Specifically, it aims to bring France's art-music tradition into the country's heritage industry. Marger stresses the intention to offer a musical program varied enough to attract a broad spectrum of the public:

At a time when museums are wondering how to reconcile patrimonial and scientific policies with the creation of events likely to draw, and draw back again, an expanded public, it is an unusual opportunity for a museum dedicated to music to be situated at the heart of a city animated with the rhythm of a diversified program which seeks to interest all categories of the public in music.[14]

Although the museum has been removed from its former home in the old Conservatory in the heart of Paris, it has been relocated to the heart of another "city," the City of Music, where it becomes one among many musical wares to be sampled.

The City of Music's democratizing mission is communicated to consumers in terms that evoke the notion of a visit to a restaurant or cafeteria. Its pocket-sized promotional brochure offers a musical menu "à la carte":

The cité de la musique was created to meet the needs of a new public who, over and above the traditional concert format, seeks to experience music as a living art. This explains the decision to bring together the musée de la musique, concerts and shows, and various services related to music and dance in one place. Henceforth, you choose your activities "à la carte," for this cité is first and foremost yours . . .[15]

This equation between music and eating, this invitation to musical consumption, has particular implications for the Museum of Music, within the larger context of the City. It brings to mind the conception, elaborated by Ames in his study of the anthropology of museums, that museums are a form of cannibalism made safe for polite society. In these institutions we stand in front of glass cases, gazing at objects, as if we could thereby absorb into ourselves some of the energy that once flowed through them.[16] Museums, like eating, serve as a safe form of travel. Just as today's sophisticated diners seek out the "exotic" in ethnic restaurants located comfortably close to home, museumgoers carefully ingest the "other" (be it the otherness of the past or of another contemporary culture) from behind glass and metal partitions. What Ron Scapp and Brian Seitz have noted about eating is also true of museumgoing; both activities are "largely about creation and self-creation, and about the production and reproduction of human life."[17] Susan Stewart states it more boldly in writing about the activities of antiquarians: "[the antiquarian's] search is primarily an aesthetic one, an attempt to erase the actual past in order to create an imagined past which is available for consumption. In order to awaken the dead, the antiquarian must first manage to kill them."[18]

Although the concept of museological "cannibalism" pertains most directly to anthropological exhibits, it may also be applied to musical instrument collections because these mute bodies were once animated by sound. Jacques Drillon, in an article that appeared in the *Nouvel observateur* on the occasion of the opening of the Museum of Music, even attributes human emotions and aspirations to the museum's artifacts: "The musical instrument is a pacifist by nature. He is friendly, fraternal. He aspires only to age, to acquire a patina, to grow a white beard like an old sage. Instruments like to enjoy long years of intimacy with their masters."[19] Drillon's comments highlight a key facet of music-making that the Museum of Music tends to overlook, which is the interaction between players, instruments, and spectators. In this regard, the museum's performance spaces—simple, raised platforms, where Conservatory students can test out their repertoire in an informal setting—are its most successful feature. They allow visitors to experience the human aspects of musical performance: the sight of the performer holding the instrument and collaborating with it to produce sound. What does this suggest, then, about the museum's other spaces, its non-performing smorgasbord of musical fare? Does the Museum of Music really serve up *music* or an audiovisual substitute? Like the remarkably life-like representations of sushi displayed in restaurant windows, do the museum's interpretive technologies take the place of food itself, triggering the appetite through the imagination without delivering real pleasure to the palate?[20] How is one to distinguish between plastic sushi—or plastic music—and the "real thing"?

Music Mapped

The architect for the City of Music was Christian de Portzamparc who, for his contribution to La Villette, utilized his favorite technique of fragmentation.[21] In this structure, he sought to replicate the small-town character of La Villette itself: squares, streets, stairways, and alleys, many small interlocking spatial units assembled as in a puzzle.[22] In explaining his conception, Portzamparc emphasizes his desire to create a work of architecture that would resemble a musical suite: "an ensemble which discloses itself in the sequences of an itinerary, over a stretch of time. It is here in this experience of movement, linkages, surprises, that architecture meets up with music."[23]

Within the City, the Museum of Music's own spaces replicate this frag-mentary musical structure. The museum's itinerary leads visitors from one gallery to the next via narrow passageways and staircases, at first steadily upward, then downward again to the point of departure. No two galleries are the same. Some are cavernous, with very high ceilings, others are narrow or box-like. Some have one concave wall and one flat one. Occasional win-dows afford glimpses of other parts of the City, equally varied and capri-cious. At the end of each gallery a list, painted on the wall, reminds visitors of the spaces they have already traversed and directs them to the next one.

Franck Hammoutène was the architect for the galleries themselves. His challenge was to devise a means of displaying some nine hundred musical instruments without overcrowding them. His clever solution was to mount the instruments at varying levels in the cases, with very light supports, so that they seem almost suspended in the air. Many of the cases are freestanding, allowing visitors to view the instruments from all sides. As Hammoutène explains, "I was concerned with creating depths of field, with multiplying the levels of reading," and also, "I wanted to give the impression that the instruments inhabit the museum."[24]

However, the way in which the instruments are grouped—largely according to types, in spare metal and glass cases, like utensils in a laboratory—counteracts this effect to some extent. This classification by species overlooks the fact that while some of the museum's artifacts were evidently intended to be *objets d'art*, others clearly were not. Drillon was not pleased with the uniformity of the installation:

> Possessed by the demon of coherence, Hammoutène has designed three or four types of cases, conceived according to one model, with holes drilled in the same places; he has designed identical pedestals and labels which are all the same (uniformly illegible). The musical instruments, with their rather over-ornate forms, for they were not designed by conceptual architects, do their best to adapt to the situation: they suck in their stomachs.[25]

Drillon would have preferred to turn the museum space over to an interior decorator, who "would have placed pretty lamps throughout, would have gone to buy lovely fabrics at the Saint Pierre market, and would have placed bouquets of buttercups next to the Stradivariuses."[26] This would certainly have created a more comfortable habitat for these objects, many of which, in their original homes, would have been accustomed to rub elbows with other species of objects rather than finding themselves only in each others' company. Drillon's criticism highlights the ultimate artificiality of the enterprise of devoting an entire museum to the display of musical instruments. Like souvenirs purchased by tourists and carted away from their place of origin to become part of the possessor's own history, the instruments are destined (in Stewart's words) to "remain impoverished and partial," silent, awaiting the application of a narrative that will make them part of the museumgoer's world.[27]

Music Produced

Recorded sound has long provided a means of giving a voice to mute musical instrument collections. The "self-guided walking-tour" system, in which visitors rent a headset with a cassette, permits individuals to move through a facility at their own pace, and portable headsets have the advantage of being non-intrusive to other visitors.[28] The technology deployed in the Museum of Music differs from this older technology in that it creates the illusion that the instruments in the cases are actually producing the sound. With the old technology, visitors carry the source of the music themselves; with the new, that source is located elsewhere: in fact, it is virtually undetectable to the eye. There are no cassettes, and the headsets have no cords. They work automatically (one can only control the volume). As one approaches a display case, the headset picks up a signal from a sensor, allowing one to hear a recording. The recordings run on continuous loops, with each segment lasting several minutes. When visitors step into a particular sound zone, they pick up the segment wherever it happens to be in its course, and they may listen for as long as they like, even hearing the entire segment several times if they wish, until they step away again. There is no sound interference between exhibits because the headsets can pick up only one set of signals at a time. The audio tour is quite extensive, offering more than forty segments.

Unfortunately, the instruments in the Museum of Music are at times as much eclipsed as enhanced by this audio technology: not just by its wonders but its flaws too. Between sound fields, visitors are treated to bursts of static. Occasionally one picks up a recording unexpectedly, in a place where there are no exhibit cases at all, such as halfway down the staircase between two galleries. Within sound fields, it is sometimes difficult to position yourself correctly to pick up the recording. If you're not in the right spot and you turn your head slightly, you stop receiving the signal.

Whereas Portzamparc's architecture and Hammoutène's display cases delineate visible boundaries between the museum's galleries, different types of musical instruments, and the visitors and the artifacts, the museum's sound system creates invisible frontiers. The physical boundaries between the different audio zones are generated by sound alone. As you walk about the museum, you cannot see where one audio segment will end and another begin. As a result, you sometimes find yourself crossing borders unexpectedly, passing from one musical territory into another without warning. The fragmentary techniques employed by Portzamparc in the building's structure are thus mirrored in its audio system, which packages sound into multiple and varied units. But unlike the architectural units, these are not visibly identifiable.

Richard Leppert has pointed out that the sense of sight tends to distance us from the world because it provides a means by which we measure and classify, whereas hearing, by its enveloping character, brings us closer to everything alive.[29] But in the Museum of Music the audio system, rather than bringing us closer to the musical instruments or bringing them to life, seems to falsify them. For Jean Baudrillard, historical objects are always false, in the sense that they present themselves as authentic within the context of a system that is actually structured by the calculation of relations between them.[30] Stewart, glossing Baudrillard's point, notes that historical collections do not draw attention to the past; rather, the past lends authenticity to collections.[31] Yet this is a secondhand authenticity, one in which history—that is, the context in which objects were once active—is replaced with classification. Whereas a tiny *pochette-violon* may have spent its life shuttling between different Parisian *hôtels particuliers* in the pocket of a dancing master, in the museum it finds itself juxtaposed with other objects similar to itself, such as the *pochette-bateau* and *pochette-viole*. Thus classification uses history as its justification, but history structured according to principles of chronology and taxonomy. Each *pochette* "belongs" with the others because collectively they represent a species, known to have been produced and to have circulated in the same period. This system of classification is like the anatomical categorizations traditionally applied to natural history collections, where insects (for instance) appear out of context, with no visible reference to their geographical origins, so as to be juxtaposed with similar-looking specimens.

In the Museum of Music, the use of recorded musical selections underscores the limitations of classification as a historicizing principle. The recordings attempt to create sensual immediacy, but they come into conflict with the concrete presence of the instruments themselves and with the fact that they no longer inhabit the world of live music-making.[32] The musical mimesis generated by the audio system is illusory and fragmentary. The instruments heard in the recordings are not the very ones being viewed in the cases. Many of the recorded excerpts are indeed excerpts: clips lifted from larger works, which simply fade out after a few minutes, often before the end of the musical section. Moreover, the narrator on the recordings identifies the musical works but not the performers, a practice that disavows the role of human beings in the music's production and implies that the technology itself generates the sound.[33] In the audio tour, the instruments are without masters.

Music Contextualized

The Museum of Music seeks to redress the loss of social context for its artifacts by incorporating them into a linear historical narrative. Henri Loyrette, who is now director of the Musée d'Orsay in Paris, designed the museological program for the Museum of Music, which reflects his particular interest in the nineteenth century. In describing his conception, Loyrette has stressed the desire to transform the Conservatory's former musical instrument museum into a "museum of music": a space devoted to instrument collections, but one that would incorporate attention to iconography, musical practice, and conditions of performance.[34] To this end, the museum's displays are organized around a series of key musical events that have had an impact on France's classical music tradition. Each exhibit space features a particular musical work (with nods to others of the period), illustrated by a display of instruments necessary to its performance, an excerpt of the score, a scale model of the hall where it was first performed, and paintings and other visual materials related to it. The tour leads visitors from Monteverdi's *Orfeo*, past works by Lully, Rameau, Mozart, Berlioz, Meyerbeer, Wagner, Saint-Saëns, Stravinsky, and Varèse, to conclude with Kagel's *Ex-Position*. These works are, with only two exceptions, resolutely French in nature; even the Mozart selection is his *Paris Symphony*. Loyrette treats them as representative of nine overarching phases of musical activity, beginning with "Baroque Italy" in the seventeenth century and concluding with "Instrumental ruptures" in the twentieth (Table 13.1).[35] Within each phase, the displays of instruments are organized according to instrumental types: lutes, clarinets, pianos, and so on, instruments that came into use or were popular during the period. A preliminary exhibit titled "Resonances" presents information on ancient instrumental forms and symbols; an ancillary exhibit located between the sixth and seventh galleries surveys the evolution of Western musical notation (Table 13.2).

Hence, although Marie-France Calas, the museum director, calls it "The museum of all musics,"[36] the objective of the museological program is not to narrate a history of different musical styles (classical, folk, sacred, jazz), or even the history of music-making in France, but rather to extract several large themes from the French collections, with a particular emphasis on the birth of the orchestra.[37] As a result, the museum's narrative is propelled by

Table 13.1: General Plan of the Museum of Music

Phase of Musical Activity	Date(s)	Site(s)	Composer(s)	Work(s)
Gallery 1: 17th century, "Baroque Italy"	1607	Imperial hall of ducal palace in Mantua	Claudio Monteverdi	*Orfeo*
Gallery 2: 17th century, "Music at Versailles"	1674	Marble courtyard of château of Versailles	Jean-Baptiste Lully	*Alceste*
Gallery 3: 18th century, "Opera and the Paris salons"	1739	Hall of Palais-Royal	Jean-Philippe Rameau	*Dardanus*
Gallery 4: 18th century, "Public concerts"	1778	Hall of Tuileries palace	Wolfgang Amadeus Mozart	*Paris Symphony*
Gallery 5: 19th century, "The Romantic orchestra"	1830	Concert hall of Paris Conservatory	Hector Berlioz	*Fantastic symphony*
Gallery 6: 19th century, "Grand opera and lyric drama"	1831	Le Peletier opera hall	Giacomo Meyerbeer	*Robert le Diable*
	1882	Festspielhaus in Beyreuth	Richard Wagner	*Parsifal*
Gallery 7: 19th century, "Outdoor music"		Military orchestras		
Gallery 8: 19th century, "Universal expositions"	1889	Festival hall of Trocadero palace	Camille Saint-Saëns	*Organ symphony*
Gallery 9: 20th century, "Instrumental ruptures"	1913	Champs-Élysées theater	Igor Stravinsky	*Rite of Spring*
	1933	Carnegie Hall	Edgar Varèse	*Ionisation*
	1978	IRCAM	Mauricio Kagel	*Ex-Position*

a "great composers" approach to music history. Like the "great rulers" approach that views the past in terms of political regimes, the "great composers" approach has the advantage of lending a kind of totality to the period in question. But when applied to the formal presentation of a collection of musical instruments, it suggests that individual composers have largely been responsible for organological innovation when in fact they have often been inspired by it.[38] In representing music history as composer-centered, the museum further separates its inhabitants from their "masters": the builders and players with whom they would have interacted most regularly and intimately.

The musical story told in the Museum of Music is one that Lydia Goehr, as it happens, has used museological terms to describe. She has adopted the expression "the imaginary museum of musical works" to designate the aesthetic practice that views its activities and goals "as conceptualized in

Table 13.2: Detailed Plan of the Museum of Music
(*indicates audio segments)

A. RESONANCES

I. 17th century, "Baroque Italy"
  Monteverdi, *Orfeo**
  Cornetti*
  Lutes*
  Citterns*
  Italian keyboards*

II. 17th century, "Music at Versailles"
  Lully, *Alceste**
  The dancing master
  The vogue for the guitar
  The hunt
  The *Grande Écurie*
  Viols*
  Oboes*
  Recorders*
  Transverse flutes*
  Bassoons*
  Flemish keyboards*
  French keyboards*

III. 18th century, "Opera and the Paris salons"
  Rameau, *Dardanus**
  Monsieur de la Pouplinière's salon*
  Pastoral music*
  Mandolins
  French harpsichords*
  Clavichords*

IV. 18th century, "Public concerts"
  Mozart, *Paris Symphony**
  Clarinets*
  Harpsichord and forte-piano*
  Harps*
  Guitars*
  Stradivarius
  Mechanical music and glass instruments*
  Builders under the *ancien régime*

V. 19th century, "The Romantic orchestra"
  Berlioz, *Fantastic symphony**
  The Romantic musician
  Virtuosity and playing technique
  Romantic piano*
  Violins*

VI. 19th century, "Grand opera and lyric drama"
  Meyerbeer, *Robert le Diable**
  Wagner, *Parsifal**

B. MUSICAL NOTATION IN THE WEST

VII. 19th century, "Outdoor music"
  Military parades
  The kiosk*
  Serpents and *ophicléides*
  Trombones and bugles* Horns
  Trumpets and *cornets à pistons**

VIII. 19th century, "Universal expositions"
  Saint-Saëns, *Organ Symphony**
  Jean-Baptiste Vuillaume
  Adolphe Sax*
  The discovery of other musics*
  The revival of early music
  The memory of sounds*

IX. 20th century, "Instrumental ruptures"
  Varèse, *Ionisation**
  Stravinsky, *Rite of Spring*
  Jazz made in France*
  Reproduction and diffusion*
  Acoustic and electric guitars*
  Kagel, *Ex-Position*
  From electricity to electronics*
  The electro-acoustic studio

terms of, and directed toward, the production and interpretation of musical works of fine art."[39] Underlying this aesthetic practice, which was essentially founded at the end of the eighteenth century, Goehr has identified a fundamental shift in Western thinking about music and what it does. As she explains, before 1800 the pivotal question in philosophical thought about music was, "What is music?" Those who sought to describe the nature of music looked mostly at its ritualistic and pedagogical value in order to specify its extramusical function and significance: Should music serve religious or secular ends? How does it convey, represent, or affect human and social qualities? What should be its relationship to speech? In what ways does it mirror natural phenomena? But later, toward the end of the eighteenth century, the basic question "what is music?" began to be treated less in connection with extramusical functions than with specifically musical ideals. The question about the nature of music was gradually subsumed by the question: What is a musical work? The emergence of the concept of a musical work of fine art came to involve all aspects of musical practice: aesthetic theory; the music produced; the social status of musicians; the rules, manners, codes, and mores.[40]

The new practice assumes that to be a serious musician one either creates or performs musical works. However, this assumption overlooks the fact that in earlier periods (from the troubadours, through the Renaissance, right up to and including Handel and J.S. Bach) musical production was not perceived as generating "works." Prior to the nineteenth century, as Goehr demonstrates, the task of musicians was not to create musical works, but to produce music: at the behest of their employers, as time and occasion demanded, for the here and now. Music was not always produced to outlast its performance or survive more than a few performances. When it did, it was treated as adaptable: to the available ensemble, to the occasion, to temporal constraints.[41] Early music-making was therefore much more oriented toward the art of improvisation than the interpretation of a composer's score. Indeed, because the circumstances of musical performance were understood to be contingent and transient in nature, fully specifying systems of notation were not perceived to be necessary. Renaissance scores, for instance, typically provide one or more lines of music and nothing more: no instrumentation is indicated, no scoring, no dynamics, no articulation, no ornamentation. These decisions were left to the musicians who were trained in the conventions of the time. Prior to the nineteenth century, whatever types of music-making a musician engaged in, whether vocal, instrumental, or mixed, they were generally more like those of jazz or folk musicians today than classical musicians. Consequently, musical instruments, the tools of the trade, would have played a more active role in determining the nature of musical production.

Music Colonized

Museums have often been criticized for their imperial propensies, for appropriating other people's material and then confining their representation of it to glass boxes.[42] Much recent museology seeks to respond to the sociopolitical demands this critique has prompted, including the expectation that museums will strive for parity of representation for all groups and cultures within their collecting, exhibition, and conservation activities.[43] In keeping with this trend, the Museum of Music's guidebook states that "non-Western instruments are displayed throughout the museum space," suggesting a desire to integrate the foreign and indigenous collections.[44] Yet in fact the non-European instruments are concentrated in a gallery titled "The discovery of other musics" (*La découverte des musiques d'ailleurs*), which chronicles the acquisition of musical instruments in Africa and Asia by French missionaries and travelers beginning in the eighteenth century and documents the presence of these instruments—as exotica— in the universal expositions of the nineteenth century. The museum's permanent exhibition therefore fails completely to consider these objects outside of the imperial context.[45] Further, the museological narrative considers their primary importance to be the influence they had on French orchestral composers such as Claude Debussy, who first heard the gamelan at one of the expositions. This gallery also fails to distinguish between different cultures: instruments from India, Iran, Afghanistan, and so on, are juxtaposed indiscriminately. Unified collections of non-Western instruments are relegated to the museum's temporary exhibit space, a policy that no doubt aims to spotlight them, but also perpetuates their classification as "exotic," "primitive," and "other."

The Museum of Music's historical narrative colonizes the internal collections, the objects of domestic manufacture, as well. The notion that "serious" music consists of musical works of fine art, created by renowned composers, and interpreted by professional performers working together in large ensembles, effectively marginalizes many of the museum's artifacts. It deprives them of a measure of their agency by ignoring their role as catalysts in the numerous types of musical production and social interaction around music-making that did not directly contribute to the "birth of the orchestra": for instance, amateur music-making, chamber music, and musical idioms and practices that combine instruments and voices.

The colonization of objects is an inevitable by-product of any museological enterprise. Museums need systems of classification if they are to be coherent institutions. Tony Bennett observes in *The Birth of the Museum* that artifacts, placed in these institutions, automatically become rhetorical objects to which multiple layers of interpretation adhere:

No matter how strong the illusion to the contrary, the museum visitor is never in a relation of direct, unmediated contact with the "reality of the artefact" and, hence, with the "real stuff" of the past. . . . For the seeming concreteness of the museum artefact derives from its *verisimilitude*; that is, from the familiarity which results from its being placed in an interpretative context in which it is conformed to a tradition and thus made to resonate with representations of the past which enjoy a broader social circulation. As educative institutions, museums function largely as repositories of the *already known*. They are places for telling, and telling again, the stories of our time.[46]

The Museum of Music's particular mission—the interpretation of the French national collection of musical instruments—of necessity dictates to some extent the stories it may tell. Yet one wonders whether, in the context of an institution that so clearly aspires to democratization and innovation, some measure of decolonization of the museum's artifacts might not be possible. Are there ways in which they could be allowed to speak from their own experience?

Toward a Museology of *Metissage*

The process of decolonizing the museum's collections might well generate a multiplicity of stories. The question is whether this would simply impose fragmentation as yet another type of classification. Ania Loomba has evoked this problem in her discussion of the relationship between postmodernism and postcolonial studies: more specifically, in the context of the debate over whether the modern world should be understood as fundamentally capitalist in nature or fundamentally splintered. Loomba questions the usefulness of replacing overly simplistic foundational narratives—the old "reality"—with an equally simplistic connection between multiplicities of histories and a celebration of fragmentation as the new reality. "Surely," she posits, "there should be another way of rethinking the relationship between the local and marginalized, on the one hand, and the larger structures in which they are housed, on the other."[47]

Musical instruments are played by amateurs as well as professionals; they speak from the margin as well as the center. It should be possible to locate that margin and negotiate it, to use it to challenge and revise the types of narrative systems that silence these objects. Decolonization would not necessarily result in the destruction of musical-instrument museums as institutions or in the complete restoration of their artifacts to some prior, purer cultural state, any more than political/theoretical postcolonialism, in contesting the domination of colonialism, and its legacies, necessarily signifies its demise.[48] In the opinion of many theorists, including

Gayatri Spivak, the pre-colonial is in any case unrecoverable; always reworked by the history of colonialism, it is not available to us in a pristine form.[49] The "post" in postcolonialism is therefore less a temporal term than a spatial one, less a reference to something that comes "after" and allows us to regain what came "before" than to something that emerges in apposition to the here and now: something that contests without supplanting.[50] Debussy's orchestral writing was in fact influenced by the sound of the gamelan. Debussy's story has therefore been grafted onto the gamelan's and cannot be removed. What the gamelan can do, however, is to tell stories about the lives it has led and continues to lead, apart from—or even in opposition to—the one it has shared with Debussy and the European orchestra.

Two notions derived from postcolonial studies suggest potential avenues of inquiry for musical-instrument museums. One is the overarching postcolonial project of provincialization of dominant cultures. What subaltern voices might emerge from the Museum of Music's artifacts if its narrative opted to provincialize the great composers and the large-scale institutions (ecclesiastical, noble, civil, and educational) that supported them? This would allow visitors' attention to be drawn, for instance, to types of music-making in which they might well have participated themselves, as amateurs, in earlier times.

Further, embracing another postcolonial concept, that of *metissage*, would give the museum license to envision an encounter or dialogue between objects across time or without time. One of the salient characteristics of *metissage* is its absence of historicity, its eternal presentness. The structure of the term reflects this quality in its pejorative sense: *mé-tissé, mal tissé*, poorly woven. Yet its application can be beneficial, for *metissage* permits the bringing together of disparate elements that tell stories from the margins, the stories that are overlooked by foundational narratives. Valorizing *metissage* would allow the museum to consider, for example, creating an exhibit that would juxtapose European lutes with non-European *rabâbs*, as instruments that share common ancestors and fulfill or have fulfilled similar functions in their societies of origin.

For France's Museum of Music, Lompech would have preferred a museological narrative focusing on the circumstances of production of the museum's artifacts: "It would undoubtedly have been more pertinent to construct a museum of the art and craft of instrument making. It could have illustrated the practice of fabricating instruments from the beginning of time and the ways in which composers and instrument makers collaborated."[51] Other potential interpretive frameworks are proposed by the authors of "Voices for the Silenced: Guidelines for Interpreting Musical Instruments in Museum Collections," an on-line publication of the International Committee of Musical Instrument Museums and Collections. They suggest directing attention to such topics as: the place of instruments in the cycle of human life (daily life, social life, political life, religious life); the status conferred on individuals through the ownership of different types of instruments; the association of instruments with religious or other types of ritual when they are played or made; the use of musical instruments as media for communication; the use of musical instruments for imitating animals and birds; the symbolism of instruments; musical instruments as *objets d'art;* and (a more self-reflexive approach) the ways in which instruments are cared for within the museum.[52] Any of these narrative techniques, or a combination of them, would help to place the objects themselves on center stage, restoring some of the agency they lose when subordinated to a presentation that privileges the "center" over the "margins."

Dissonance and Resolution

Despite the Museum of Music's reliance on a highly imperial narrative, the effects of decolonization are in fact manifested in the museum's final gallery. Overall, a visit to this museum is like taking a walk through a musical suite (as Portzamparc wished it) in which all of the earlier movements, those devoted to tonal idioms (Baroque, Classical, Romantic), create more "dissonance" than the final one, in which tonality is abandoned but resolution nonetheless achieved. The incongruity evidenced by the earlier galleries, in which early musical instruments (spinets, crumhorns, and so on) confront a high-tech presentation, dissolves in the museum's final cluster of exhibits, gathered under the rubric of "Instrumental ruptures." Here the disparate components of the institution suddenly join forces: the exhibition technology, the objects, and the sounds they actually produce. In "Instrumental ruptures" the modernist museological narrative breaks apart, becoming as fractured as the postmodern architectural environment. The last major work featured in the museum's itinerary is Kagel's *Ex-Position*, a composition that is not so much performed as created anew, each time it is programmed. Strikingly, Kagel's description of his piece evokes the functional and provisional circumstances of production typical of much music composed before 1800. Reconfigured by the composer himself according to the capacities of the modulating halls where it is presented, dedicated to the "impossible marriage between serious and popular music," *Ex-Position* consists of a series of "sonorous actions for athletes," encompassing the "simultaneous execution of two independent scores."[53]

Yet in the museum's final spaces, rupture on one level is counterbalanced by fusion on another because, in the galleries that present "Instrumental ruptures," the voice of the museum's audio technology actually becomes the voice of its objects. Here the museum is actually about its technologies: those that record sound, those that manipulate it, and those that create it.

Here plastic music and "real" music are one and the same thing. On display are guitars whose tones are produced by vibrating strings but whose volume is generated by electricity. Also exhibited are instruments that can no longer be classified according to the four traditional categories of chordophones (vibrating strings), aerophones (vibrating air columns), membranophones (vibrating membranes), and idiophones or autophones (matter vibrating without the aid of strings, air, or membranes). The *éthérophone*, for instance, translates manual gestures into musical sounds, and the *piano Bechstein-Nerst-Siemens* is both an electric piano and an appliance for diffusion (radio or phonograph).[54] Finally, in this last section of the museum's itinerary, the orchestra itself is rendered obsolete. With the advent of the electronic studio, one musician can now simultaneously "play" numerous instruments, singlehandedly producing an orchestral performance.

When Lompech compared the Museum of Music to a giant CD-ROM, he was criticizing the institution's reliance on hyperaesthetics. With his proposed revision of the museum's narrative from a "great-composers" story to one of production and collaboration, he was lobbying for a return to an aesthetics somewhat more bound by natural constraints. An aesthetics of this type, while apparently more limited, might in fact counteract the "plasticizing" effect of the museum's technologies. The resulting itinerary might well have greater sensual impact because the institution would then be offering "real" music for consumption.

Notes

1. This essay has benefited from my discussions with Jeanice Brooks and Laurier Turgeon who have also visited the Museum of Music and shared their observations with me.
2. Alain Lompech, "Les instruments prisonniers du Musée de la musique," *Le Monde* (Paris), Sunday, January 19–Monday, January 20, 1997, "Culture," 21. All translations from French are mine unless noted otherwise.
3. Kate Arnold-Forster and Hélène La Rue identify four broad types of presentation that cover the vast majority of contemporary displays dedicated to musical instrument collections: (1) essentially mute collections, displayed primarily for study of the physical appearance and design of instruments and related material, usually within conventional secure museum cases; (2) those that combine conventional displays with additional methods of interpretation, such as the use of different types of audio systems; (3) those that are intended for playing and so are organized to be accessible to the student, performer, or demonstrator; and (4) contextual or theme displays in which musical instruments and material form part of a historic reconstruction, such as in a birthplace museum. See their *Museums of Music: A Review of Musical Collections in the United Kingdom* (London: HMSO, 1993), 43. France's Museum of Music has characteristics typical of both the second and fourth categories.
4. Philippe Bray, ed., *Guide du musée de la Musique* (Paris: Éditions de la Réunion des musées nationaux, 1997), 35.
5. Michael M. Ames, *Cannibal Tours and Glass Boxes: The Anthropology of Museums* (Vancouver: University of British Columbia Press, 1992), 23.
6. La Villette, constructed between 1982 and 1997, includes the City of Science and Industry, the Geode, the Great Hall and Zenith concert spaces, and an outdoor park.

The City of Music was the last of the La Villette structures to be completed, and within it, the museum section was the last to open. Far from the most popular of French president François Mitterrand's immense building projects, the City of Music nearly succumbed to political infighting on several occasions in the 1980s. Jack Lang, Mitterrand's culture minister, envisioned a "Beaubourg of music"—which was precisely what many feared it would be. On the history of the City of Music project, see Francis Rambert, "Une architecture plurielle," *Cité de la Musique*, a special number of *Connaissance des Arts* 101 (1996), 6–23.

7. Brigitte Marger, "Préface," *Cité de la Musique*, 4.
8. Jean Vilar, *Manifeste du T.N.P.*, November 1951, cited in Philippa Wehle, *Le théâtre populaire selon Jean Vilar*, trans. Denis Gontard (Avignon: Alain Barthélemy, and Le Paradou: Actes Sud, 1981), 55. Vilar used the term "popular" to indicate that this would be a theater for all of the French people and "national" to indicate the theater's responsibility to conserve the national cultural heritage. The repertoire of the *T.N.P.* was the French "classics": Corneille, Racine, and so on.
9. The web site, whose chief editor is Patrice Verrier, is found at www.cité-musique.fr.
10. Bray, 9.
11. Denis Picard, "Le musée de la Musique," *Cité de la Musique*, 44–47 and 53.
12. On the transition from early modern cabinets of curiosities to public museums, see Oliver Impey and Arthur MacGregor, eds., *The Origins of Museums: The Cabinet of Curiosities in Sixteenth- and Seventeenth-Century Europe* (Oxford: Clarendon, 1985). On museums and nineteenth-century imperialism see Tony Bennett, *The Birth of the Museum: History, Theory, Politics* (London: Routledge, 1995).
13. Ames, 11–12.
14. Brigitte Marger, "Préface," *Musée de la Musique*, a special number of *Beaux Arts Magazine* 135 (1996), 5.
15. Here I cite the English version of the brochure.
16. Ames, 3.
17. Ron Scapp and Brian Seitz, "Introduction," in *Eating Culture*, ed. Scapp and Seitz (Albany: State University of New York Press, 1998), 2.
18. Susan Stewart, *On Longing: Narratives of the Miniature, the Gigantic, the Souvenir, the Collection* (Baltimore: Johns Hopkins University Press, 1984; reprint, Durham: Duke University Press, 1993), 143.
19. Jacques Drillon, "Sonnez vièles et pianos girafes," *Le nouvel observateur* 16–22 (January 1997), 52.
20. Scapp and Seitz, 2.
21. Portzamparc was the first French architect to win the Pritzker prize, in 1994, for the ensemble of his work (in which the City of Music figures prominently).
22. Gilles de Bure, "La cité de la Musique et la parc de la Villette," *Musée de la Musique*, 13. The City of Music's web site offers an architectural tour, with photographs. For additional views, especially of the interior of the museum, see the special numbers of *Beaux Arts Magazine* and *Connaissance des Arts*.
23. Cited in the web site.
24. Odile Fillion, "Entretien avec Franck Hammoutène," *Musée de la Musique*, 30; Francis Rambert, "Un monde à part," *Cité de la Musique*, 50.
25. The labels are indeed sometimes hard to read, because of the museum's (necessarily) dim lighting, because of the shadows cast by the instruments and the cases, and because they are printed white on a dark background.
26. Drillon, 53.
27. Stewart, 136.
28. Arnold-Forster and La Rue, 45.
29. Richard Leppert, *The Sight of Sound: Music, Representation, and the History of the Body* (Berkeley: University of California Press, 1993), 28–29.
30. Jean Baudrillard, *Le système des objets: La consommation des signes* (Paris: Gallimard, 1968), 90.
31. Stewart, 151.

32. Ludmilla Jordanova observes that a common museological technique for making his-
    tory "come alive" is to create a sense of traveling back in time. But in seeking to efface
    the distance of time, and in drawing on intuitive rather than analytical responses to the
    artifacts, museums "ignore the abstract elements necessary for historical under-
    standing. . . . What is lost in the process is precisely what makes historical under-
    standing distinctive and important." See Jordanova, "History, 'Otherness' and Display,"
    in *Cultural Encounters: Representing Otherness*, eds. Elizabeth Hallam and Brian V.
    Street (London: Routledge, 2000), 249.
33. The commentary includes brief descriptions of instruments and their sound qualities
    and information about how different composers have used them, either alone or in
    combinations. Neither the recordings nor the guidebook identify the performances. To
    find out what they were, I visited the museum's documentation center, where I was
    given a booklet that lists the recordings used for the audio tour.
34. Myriam Boutoulle, "Entretien avec Henri Loyrette," *Musée de la Musique*, 24.
35. In sum, the museum's guidebook cites Monteverdi's *Orfeo* for its innovative instrumen-
    tation, Lully's *Alceste* for its five-part "orchestra" (strings, winds, two harpsichords,
    trumpets, and drums), Rameau's *Dardanus* for the increased size of the orchestra
    (45–50 players), Mozart's *Paris Symphony* for being his first symphony with clarinet,
    Berlioz's *Fantastic Symphony* for its literary program (a largely biographical "life of the
    artist"), Meyerbeer's *Robert le Diable* for being the first great Romantic opera, Wagner's
    Parsifal as representative of German lyric drama, the *Organ Symphony* of Saint-Saëns
    for its emotion and scope, Stravinsky's *Rite of Spring* for the scandal caused by its
    primitivism, Varèse's *Ionisation* for its use of an orchestra comprised entirely of percus-
    sion instruments, and Kagel's *Ex-Position* for its incorporation of multiple genres and
    artistic mediums.
36. This is the title of her communication in the special issue of *Beaux Arts Magazine*
    devoted to the new museum.
37. Boutolle, 24.
38. In our separate visits to the museum, Jeanice Brooks and I both noted fairly frequent
    errors and omissions in the music historical commentary. For example, in the com-
    mentary for the display of French harpsichords, in introducing an excerpt from an
    unmeasured prelude by François Couperin, the narrator on the recording refers to the
    "absence of rhythmic indication" in the scores for these pieces; but in fact there is
    rhythmic indication, although the pieces are not "measured" in the same way as others
    of the period. In the display on "La vogue de la guitare" the label notes that the guitar
    was very popular in Spain in the sixteenth century and also in Italy in the first half of
    the seventeenth century. No mention is made of the vogue for the guitar in France,
    although the instrument flourished there in both the mid-sixteenth and early-seven-
    teenth centuries (this seems a particularly surprising omission in the context of a
    museum dedicated to bringing the French art music heritage to the public). In this
    respect, the Museum of Music exemplifies the separation between history as leisure
    industry and history as academic production that characterizes recent trends in muse-
    ology. As Jordanova points out, in recent years "commercial and ideological forces out-
    side the historical profession have been the prime movers in processes of
    commodification of the past" ("History, 'Otherness' and Display," 249).
39. Lydia Goehr, *The Imaginary Museum of Musical Works: An Essay in the Philosophy of
    Music* (Oxford: Clarendon, 1992), 8.
40. Goehr, 122–23.
41. Goehr, 178–79, 186, and 181.
42. Ames, 3.
43. Bennett, 9.
44. Bray, 9.
45. For a series of reflections on the representation of "other" cultures in European
    museums, see the essays in part two of *Cultural Encounters*, eds. Hallam and Street
    ("Displaying Cultures," 149–283). See also Anna Laura Jones, "Exploding Canons:
    The Anthropology of Museums," *Annual Review of Anthropology* 22 (1993), 201–20.

46. Bennett, 146–47; emphasis in original.

47. Ania Loomba, *Colonialism/Postcolonialism* (New York: Routledge, 1998), 248–49.

48. Loomba, 12.

49. Loomba, 18.

50. I draw here on Jean-François Lyotard's definition of the term "postmodern." For Lyotard the postmodern is a cyclical moment, a moment of future anteriority, outside the modern, but not necessarily after it, in time: an expression of "what will have been done" that may surface at any number of different historical moments. Indeed, Lyotard maintains that the "idea of a linear chronology is itself perfectly 'modern'." In his view, the "post" of "postmodernism" alludes to the various procedures related to "ana-" (analysis, anamnesis, anagogy, and anamorphosis) that can be employed to elaborate or redress "an initial forgetting." See Lyotard, "Note on the Meaning of 'Post,' " in *Post-modernism: A Reader*, ed. Thomas Docherty (New York: Columbia University Press, 1993), 47–50.

51. Lompech, 21.

52. I have borrowed these examples from the guidelines that the International Committee of Musical Instrument Museums and Collections has produced for the use of museum educators and guides who interpret collections of musical instruments for groups of visitors. See Margaret Birley, Heidrun Eichler, and Arnold Myers, with the CIMCIM Working Group for Education and Exhibitions (co-ordinator Jos Gansemans), "Voices for the Silenced: Guidelines for Interpreting Musical Instruments in Museum Collections," www.music.ed.ac.uk/euchmi/cimcim/iwte.html#Introduction, April 6, 1999.

53. Commissioned and presented in 1978 by the Art Center Henie Onstad in Oslo, *Ex-Position* was re-created later in the same year in the modulable projection space at IRCAM (the "Institut de recherche et de coordination acoustique/musique" [Institute for research and acoustical / musical coordination], located near the Pompidou Center in Paris). For excerpts from the program notes that Kagel provided for the Paris presentation, see Bray, 256–57.

54. On these and other twentieth-century inventions, see Bray, 258 ff.

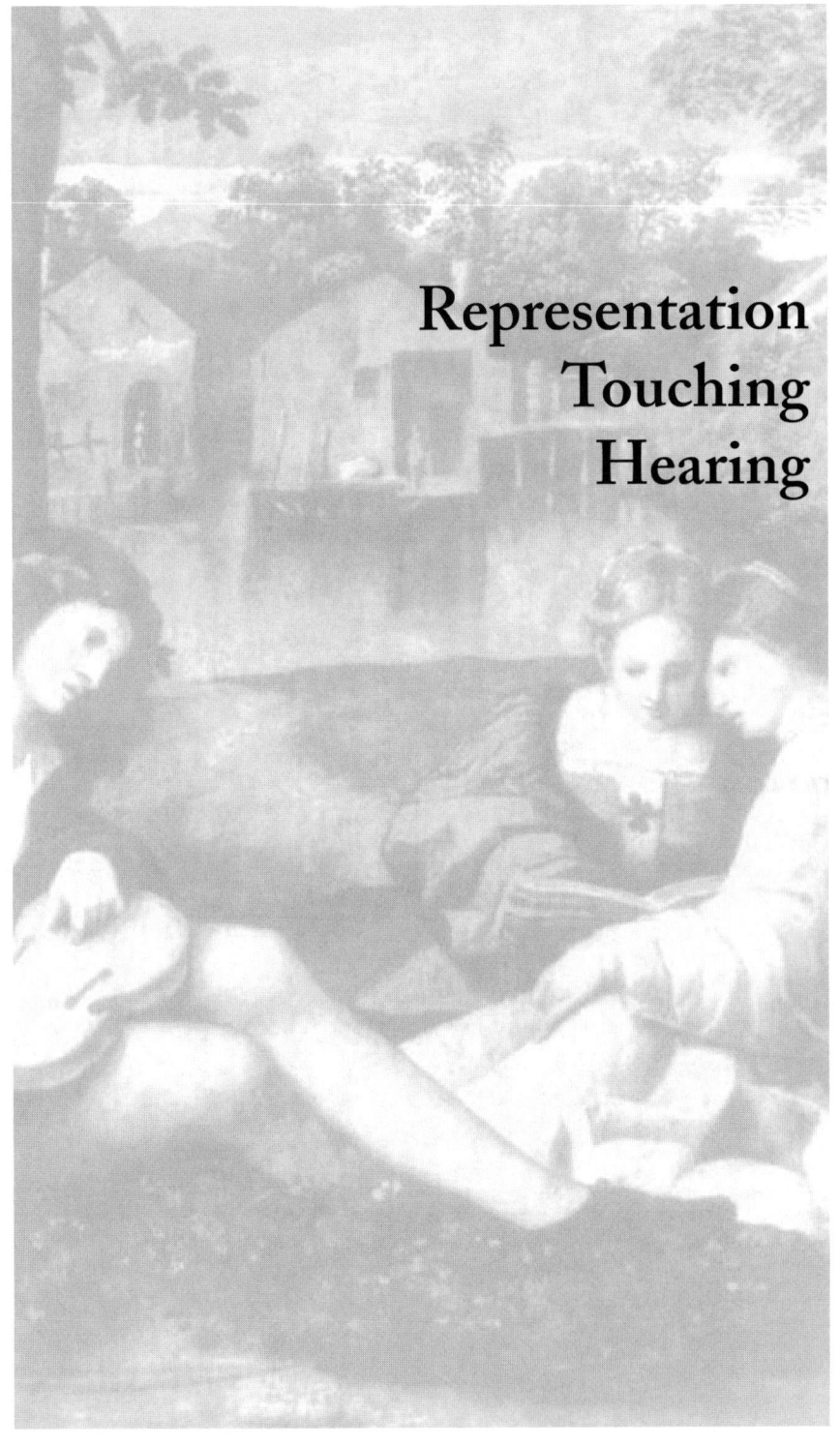

Representation
Touching
Hearing

14

Village Noise and Bruegel's Parables

Hiroyuki Minamino

Life in a medieval village brings familiarity with many sounds and noises. The wind breezes gently in summer but whistles in winter. The rain drops softly in spring but pours in fall. A clap of thunder suddenly invites a storm, and the sun comes out warmly as if nothing has happened. The leaves rustle and dance down to the ground. The brook murmurs, and the snow falls silently. A lone wolf howls in the night, the cocks crow at dawn, and the birds chirp in the morning. The water mill turns slowly and steadily. The boat's rudder chops the water, and the waves lap against the shore. On a distant hill, a shepherd blows his horn to herd his flocks that dangle jingling bells around their necks. The woodcutter cuts a tree, making echoes all over the forest. The hunter's arrow whizzes toward a leaping hare. Men plow the field with lumbering oxen. The lunch crowd joyously gathers under a tree after the morning's hard work. Women drop a bucket into a well, talking and laughing. Children play clamorously, blowing handmade pipes and beating clappers. The dog barks at a meowing cat. A hay wagon rattles on the stony road. A man rushes through the village on a neighing horse. The ice skaters make merry noises on the frozen lake. And the church bells toll, joyously, sadly, alarmingly, or proudly. On some days, the villagers hear unfamiliar sounds that draw their attention and seduce them to stop whatever they are doing. The new sounds come from the outsiders. They travel from town to town, village to village, bringing merchandise, news, entertainment, disease, and trouble.

Sing, Dance, and Be Merry

Wars, famines, and storms are some of the disasters and calamities, either natural or man-made, which befell villages in medieval times. Baptisms, weddings, and funerals were some of the everyday events of village life. Each villager went through the cycle of life, constantly accompanied by music.

Perhaps the merriest events in a villager's life in which music played a central role were weddings. Pieter Bruegel the Elder's painting known as *The Bridal Procession* depicts such an occasion.[1] The title procession takes place in a hamlet on a nice sunny day. The bride is flanked by two men, perhaps her father and brother, followed by some women, perhaps her mother and sisters, and finally by other relatives and neighbors. The procession may have started from one of the three houses at the righthand corner, and now the group is passing in front of a windmill, heading toward a church with a tall bell tower. They will attend a service with an invocation, a sermon, singing, and organ-playing. The focus of this painting is no doubt the bride. But a musician also takes a prominent place. He leads the procession, walking in front of the bride, as if to scare evil spirits away from this happy occasion by the raucous sound of his bagpipe.

Once the wedding ceremony is over, it is time for a feast. A barn is now a makeshift banquet hall, and a strong smell of the hay on the floor gives the peasants satisfaction for their good harvest. People gather around a long table, merrily talking to their neighbors with animated gestures. The bride sits quietly at the center, flanked by her female relatives along with a man of importance in front of a green cloth with a hanging crown, as the uninvited villagers look on through the open doorway. Food and wine are served to the eager guests, who are seated on rough-hewn benches. Bowls of pudding are brought around on a door taken off its hinges, and wine is served in small jugs. Musicians are often at the center of this commotion. Bruegel's painting known as *Peasant Wedding* depicts such a scene.[2] Although the wedding banquet is a good excuse to be carefree, the painting includes a moral message. Bruegel has clearly warned against the deadly sin of Gluttony, symbolically depicted in the guise of a musician. The bagpiper in red jacket forgets his function as the provider of entertainment, instead looking longingly and with parted lips at the servers and greedy eaters, as if wishing the food would go into his empty stomach.

Any celebration invites merrymaking, and dancing is a favorite of the peasants. Many sorts of dancing cost nothing. It can be warming, joyous, and gives an opportunity to get physically closer to members of the opposite sex. Such dancing is the model for Bruegel's painting known as *Peasant Dance*.[3] The feast is held outside for a celebration of a saint's birthday. People eat, drink, talk, sing, dance, and make love, ignoring the church in the background and the image of the Virgin and Child hanging to the tree. A man in a bulging red codpiece dances with a woman. The old man with a spoon in his hat drags a woman to join the dancing, and two children dance as the adults do. One couple is kissing in public. Another couple sits at the table and mimes the action behind them. The woman at the door invites a man to come inside. A fool stands next to a man who frowns and raises his arm as if to proclaim a victory. The painting warns against Lust, and dancing is a part of this sin. Dancing cannot be done without music. Indeed, there is a bagpiper at the center of the painting. An ambitious youth with a stylishly cocked hat and peacock's feather offers wine to persuade the musician to teach him how to play the bagpipe. But the music played by Bruegel's gluttonous bagpiper is not unambiguous. Bruegel depicts music as an instrument that helps seduce innocents and not-so-innocents to satisfy the lust of the flesh.

Once the merrymaking is over, the entertainer is no longer wanted. He goes back to his daily routine of begging for alms. But the situation may not be favorable. The villagers' generosity wanes after the good time, and they may even turn hostile toward such an unwelcome guest. An engraving made after Bruegel, called *The Fat Kitchen*, depicts such a scene.[4] The less-than-benevolent cooks shove and kick an impoverished bagpiper out from the well-stocked kitchen of an inn. Even their faithful dog assists its masters by biting his rival's skinny, bare leg.

The Parable of the Blind

Pieter Bruegel's painting known as *The Parable of the Blind* depicts six blind men who link themselves together by tugging with sticks or with their hands on the shoulder of the person ahead.[5] As the leader of the group tumbles backward into the swamp, the second man spills onto his lap. The third man is jerked closer to these two, and the rest will also go over the brink. Bruegel's inspiration for this painting comes from a story in the Bible. When seeing his disciples agitated by those who criticize them, Jesus explained thus: "Let them alone, they be blind leaders of the blind. And if the blind lead the blind, both shall fall into the ditch" (Matthew, 15:14). This is not to disdain the deprivation of sight but to condemn the spiritual blindness that robs a person of salvation and eternal life. The leader of the group is a musician. Half of the instrument that he carries on his back is under water, but its shape suggests that it is a hurdy-gurdy.

As we "see" from Bruegel's blind musician, music is an auditory, not a visual, experience. This is not unlike the riddle in a musical composition from the same era. The Cathedral of Segovia now preserves a manuscript of polyphonic vocal music of the Renaissance. Most of the compositions were copied in Toledo around 1502 for use at the court of Queen Isabella of Castile, but some may have been brought to Spain when the Burgundian duke, Philip the Fair, made a tour there in 1502.[6] One composition is attributed to *"Fernandis et frater ejus"* (Fernandez and his brother) and has this inscription: *"Cecus non judicat de coloribus"* (The blind cannot judge color).[7] This seems more likely to be a sort of commentary or epithet rather than the title of a piece, or the incipit of a text. The blind, of course, cannot distinguish any color. What then is the meaning of emphasizing the obvious?

It has its origin in antiquity. It appears in Aristotle's *Physics*, 2.1, which can be paraphrased as *"Caecus natus non potest disputare de coloribus quantum ad rem, sed quantum ad nomen."*[8] It became a commonplace expression in the Renaissance. Giovanni Spataro, for instance, used a similar phrase, *"cecus non iudicat de colore,"* in his letter of 1528 to his fellow music theorist Giovanni del Lago.[9] Here "blind" refers to an ignoramus. It conveys the idea of the novice's incapacity to find and appreciate the subtleties that are apparent to the learned or initiated. What kind of subtleties does the Fernandez brothers' composition hide? A hint may be the "color."[10]

The Fernandez brothers' composition lacks any texts and appears in the section of the Segovia manuscript that seems to be devoted to a collection of compositions either composed for instruments or conceived as suitable for instrumental performance.[11] The instrumental character of the music may be seen in the extensive use of sequences with continuous motion, scale fragments dispersed over wide musical ranges, and stretto-like imitations. Renaissance instrumentalists customarily applied ornaments to the music they played. Virtuosi pushed the limits of adding ornaments to the vocal compositions so far that they often obscured the original composition (a practice that dismayed its composer) in order to show off their finger dexterity. The instrumentalists who followed this performance practice were called colorists. Is the inscription a mockery of the practice of instrumentalists who were "blindly" infatuated with the extravagant use of ornaments in small note values? If so, who is mocking whom? Are the Fernandez brothers mocking themselves?

This raises the question of whether it is the blind man who is to be blamed for his ignorance. The musical term "coloration" refers to the notational convention according to which the note loses one-third of its value when daubed with black, and is therefore considered imperfect.[12] In medieval and Renaissance music theory, ternary meter was considered perfect because of the significance of the number three, the Holy Trinity, while binary meter was regarded as imperfect. The mensuration in the Fernandez brothers' composition is *tempus imperfectum*, and some pitches are written in black notes. Does the deprivation of note value refer to the deprivation of sight, therefore suggesting that the Fernandez brothers were "blind"?

The Fernandez brothers' composition is not a unique source for the use of coloration, imperfect mensuration, and ornamentation, but an example of a widely spread practice of the late fifteenth and early sixteenth centuries. Why then is the inscription attached to this particular piece? If subtlety is not in the "color," where else do we see it? A clue may be the one who sees (or cannot see) the color.

The Segovia manuscript had a strong association with Philip the Fair, and the composition is attributed to "Fernandis et frater ejus." Johannes Tinctoris described his encounter with the brothers Carolus and Johannes Orbus at Bruges, an event that might have occurred between 1476 and 1480.[13] Tinctoris expressed his admiration for their musicianship, particularly the brothers' mastery on the *"viola cum arculo"* (the four-stringed medieval fiddle).[14] Tinctoris may have used the Latin word *"Orbus"* to refer to the physical characteristics of the brothers: *"Orbus"* means either blind or orphan in Latin.[15] Johannes was "nearly blind," and his blindness was an inheritance. The father of Johannes and Carolus was the legendary Spanish blind instrumentalist Jehan Ferrandez (or Fernandez) who, together with his blind companion Jehan de Cordoval, was employed for many years at the court of Burgundy.[16] By the time the Segovia manuscript was compiled and the inscription was attached, both Johannes and Carolus Fernandez were most likely no longer alive; Johannes died in 1496 and Carolus certainly before 1506 when Jodocus Badius Ascensis published a homage for him.[17] If the deprivation of sight refers to the deprivation of life, the blind who does not see the "color" must refer to Johannes or Carolus or both. And yet, if this interpretation is correct, is it not strange that Johannes and Carolus could not find the subtleties they created in their own composition?

Much as Bruegel's blind hurdy-gurdy player tried to see his way to salvation, I tried to see the "color" in the Fernandez brothers' composition. Instead, we both fell into the ditch.

The Wandering Musician

Merchants, run-away monks, artisans, student drop-outs, minstrels, prostitutes, gypsies, and beggars are the outsiders who come to medieval villages. They are jacks-of-all-trades who hope their entertainment draws the attention of the villagers, help increase the sales of their merchandise, and provide them with better alms. They play various musical instruments, sing songs, recite tales, throw knives into the air, jump rope, balance chairs, somersault, and do walking handstands.[18] Bruegel's musicians were not the kind of musicians who frequented the courts of kings and princes, but wandering minstrels who earned their living by singing popular songs and accompanying themselves on instruments.

In Medieval and Renaissance societies, occupational specialization most often arose from hereditary calling. Birth and inheritance often determined one's occupation. Family members strove to continue their family vocation so that the skill of their trade could be passed from father to son.

We do not know whether Bruegel's blind musician followed this tradition. He may not have had any other choice. Because of their visually challenged physical condition, blind people had to select occupations that emphasized their other senses. Many blind men and women therefore turned to music as their profession. Music depends more on ears than on eyes.[19] Singing and playing instruments require mouths and hands. A well-trained musician does not have to see the keyboard, fingerboard, or fingerholes when playing the instrument. He can feel the keys, frets, holes, and strings with his hands. Moreover, the blind person's sense of hearing was perhaps sharper than that of their sighted counterparts because of a greater concentration on hearing. In fact, some blind musicians became internationally renowned composers or instrumentalists.[20]

In Bruegel's time, one or another subject of music was taught in universities, ecclesiastical institutions, courts, music-schools, academies, and by private teachers. The object of learning music and the subjects taught at these institutions differed. The student's social status and his future occupation determined the kind of education he was to receive. The university curriculum focused on music theory. Princely courts and the choir schools belonging to the major churches educated the composers and singers of polyphonic music. The master-apprenticeship system provided the training for the would-be professional instrumentalists that concerned the practical side of music making.[21] Bruegel's beggar musician was likely to have learned music with little formal training, instead picking up the trade from a friend or two, or being self-taught, using whatever talent he possessed.

Even those who had little talent in music had no choice but to become musicians. The donkey, the hound, the cat, and the cock in the Grimm brothers' folk tale "The Bremen Town-Musicians" are good examples of such an ambitious career move. Having grown too old to do the tasks that have been entrusted to them to serve their masters, the four castoffs decide to become town-musicians in Bremen. The donkey plays the lute, the hound wants to learn the drum, the cock has a good voice, and the cat knows night-music. The four of them set out to Bremen and reach a forest where they find some robbers having a feast. The musicians perform together to drive the robbers away: the donkey brays, the hound barks, the cock crows, and the cat meows. Surprised and scared, the robbers hastily take flight. The four musicians happily satisfy their empty stomachs with what is left of the feast. They never make it to Bremen.[22]

What kind of night-music did the cat know? Perhaps it was a serenade. The donkey must have been happy to assist the cat, for the elegant shape and delicate sound made the lute a suitable instrument for lovers' courting.

One Bonifazio Uberti, for instance, serenaded a lady with his song and lute accompaniment, no doubt expecting to receive her favor, platonically or carnally.[23] The donkey-lutenist did not have to know the intricacies of the finger-plucking technique that was the standard in the sixteenth century.[24] Strumming chords could provide exciting rhythms. In fact, serenading became so extravagant and noisy that musicians often disturbed the order of a town. The Florentine statutes of 1325, for instance, sought to regulate the practice by laying down the penalty of confiscation for instruments played at night.[25] No wonder serenading was considered a fool's pastime in Sebastian Brandt's *Das Narrenschiff.*[26]

The Instrument of Seduction

Bruegel's peasants march and dance to the sound of the bagpipes. The simplest bagpipe comprises a bag, a short blowpipe, and one or more reed pipes. One pipe is called the chanter, fitted with several fingerholes that permit the player to produce different pitches. The other one, usually larger and longer, has no fingerholes, and is only capable of producing one pitch (therefore called the drone). The player holds the blowpipe in his mouth, blows air through it to inflate the bag, fingers the chanter in front of him, and squeezes the bag held under one of his arms, thus regulating the air pressure and forcing the air through the reed pipes.[27]

The bagpipe produces raucous sound, audible even at a far distance. It is indeed the volume of sound that makes the bagpipe a suitable instrument for accompanying dancing. The noisy footsteps, singing, and shouting do not even muffle the sound of a lone bagpiper. Beggars, servants, and peasants played the bagpipe. Boccaccio in the *Decameron*, for instance, created a scene in which a servant plays the bagpipe while his masters and ladies dance to forget about the deadly plagues that were ravaging their hometown of Florence.[28] It was a scene from the real world. In the midst of life lurks death, and music offers momentous joy in a fleeting time.[29]

Bruegel may have depicted his country scenes from real life, or he may have added hidden meanings.[30] In Renaissance iconography, musical instruments had various meanings, sometimes opposing and contradictory. They may have been depicted as symbols of love, mostly appearing in astrological drawings, because musicians of all kinds were among the "children of Venus."[31] In Christian art, musical instruments are the allegorical representations of the passage in Psalm 150, "Laudate eum in sono tubae, laudate eum in psalterio." All kinds of instruments are depicted as means to praise God. This may be the symbolism of the bagpipe in *The Bridal Procession*, the notion strengthened by the church in the background.[32] The bagpipe was, on the other hand, depicted as a favorite instrument of a Phyrigian satyr Marsyas, a symbol of Bacchanalian frivolities. Because of its shape, the bagpipe also had phallic significance, a suitable attribute in wedding scenes.

The blind musician in *The Parable of the Blind* is a hurdy-gurdy player. The hurdy-gurdy is a sort of mechanized fiddle. The performer produces sound by turning a crank at the tail of the instrument's body, which makes a wooden wheel in the middle of the sound box revolve, and consequently vibrate the strings. There are two to four stopped strings and one or two unstopped strings. The melody strings are stopped by a primitive key mechanism, a set of stopping rods, equipped with little projections that press inwardly against the strings when the rods are pushed in. The vibrating strings of the hurdy-gurdy produce a nasal sound.[33]

Like the bagpipe, the hurdy-gurdy had a long history by the time Bruegel painted this image. The hurdy-gurdy first began to appear in the Gothic period and was called *organistrum* or *symphonia*. When the *organistrum* was first invented and cultivated, it was an instrument of some importance. Musicians and theorists used it as a tool to teach musical intervals because music education required students to know the fundamental of mathematics. It was also used in many cloisters and monastic schools to perform religious polyphony and provide correct intonation for singers. We do not know when the *organistrum* became an instrument of wandering musicians and beggars. By the time Bruegel depicted the hurdy-gurdy in the hands of a blind beggar, its negative connotations had been firmly established. The learned considered the hurdy-gurdy a lowly instrument. Michael Praetorius called the hurdy-gurdy "the peasants' and vagabond women's lyra," and Marin Mersenne testified that "it is played only by the poor, and especially the blind."[34]

Bruegel's musicians are one-man bands. It is therefore fitting for them to choose the bagpipe or hurdy-gurdy, which are equipped with mechanisms to produce more than one voice. Also important is these instruments' capacity to produce loud, penetrating sound. The musicians' business cannot begin until they attract people's attention in a wide, open area. But the villagers are suspicious of the outsiders. The legend of the Pied Piper of Hamelin is still fresh in their mind. A minstrel who wore a varicolored dress came to Hamelin to help drive the rats, which were plaguing the villagers, out of town. By playing music on his pipe, he successfully led the rats to the river where they drowned. When the town officials refused to pay the reward money promised for the deed, the piper became angry and planned revenge. Through the power of his music he lured the children of the town to the nearby mountain and made them disappear forever. The date was June 26, 1284.

It was the enchanting music that seduced the rats and the children. Does music have such a power? Ancient philosophers such as Plato and Aristotle discussed how the power of music affected the human psyche, but it was the legend of Orpheus that was especially popular in Bruegel's time. A Thracian poet, Orpheus's skill in lyre playing was such that with his music he was said to tame the wild beasts and move the trees and rocks. But his life was tragic. While fleeing from an unwelcome suitor, Orpheus's wife Eurydice trod on a snake and died from its bite. Orpheus, learning of his wife's tragic death, descended into Hades where Eurydice had gone. By the power of his music, Orpheus succeeded in persuading the god of the dead to allow Eurydice to follow him back to earth, on one condition: Orpheus should not look back at her until they reach the upper world. But, at the last moment, Orpheus could not contain himself, and Eurydice vanished forever to the underworld.[35]

In the Renaissance, the story of Orpheus was made widely known through Ovid's *Metamorphoses.* It became a favorite of poets, composers, and painters, partially due to the fact that the main character was a musician-poet.[36] The painters depicted Orpheus in musical scenes (mythological or contemporary), and several lute and vihuela books included drawings of Orpheus playing an instrument, alluding to their association with the musician.[37] It was the highest honor for the musician, particularly the instrumentalist, of the Renaissance to be equated with Orpheus; among those who won this praise were Pietrobono de Burzellis, Francesco da Milano, and John Dowland.[38]

"Is it not strange that sheep's guts should hale souls out of men's bodies?" Thus Benedick, a young Paduan lord, in Shakespeare's *Much Ado about Nothing* (2.3) wonders about the magical power of music. In the Renaissance, the ancient lyre was equated with various stringed instruments of the time, but most frequently with the lute. Shakespeare may have been thinking of the Orpheus legend and superimposed the ancient lyre on contemporary lute playing. However impressed Shakespeare was by the sound of gut strings, these very intestines caused pain to the lutenists. Until the invention of nylon strings, the gut of the ram was the standard material used for lute strings. Gut strings were notoriously easy to slacken and break, the more so if the humidity was high. Some gut strings were certainly not satisfactory due to the underdeveloped technology of the time. Shakespeare's wonder at the marvelous effects created by some lutenists despite their use of vulgar material was indeed legitimate.[39]

The Invisible Sound

Paintings and woodcuts often show beggar minstrels singing and playing musical instruments in towns and villages. We see their music making, but we do not hear their sound. Reconstructions of medieval and Renaissance instruments based on the descriptions, paintings, and a few surviving specimens give us an idea about the kind of sound the beggar minstrels' instruments produced. But we achieve this only through our imagination.

Numerous extant manuscripts and prints offer us a glimpse into the musical activities of performers and listeners of the Middle Ages and the Renaissance. They show us how churches, princely courts, and wealthy amateurs patronized music and what kind of music upper-class societies favored. In Bruegel's time, musical notation belonged to a small number of highly educated professional musicians who worked at princely courts or churches, as well as to a small number of amateur dilettantes who had the financial means to afford the luxury of spending time and money to cultivate such an expensive pastime. The kind of music they favored, polyphonic music, needed notation so that several vocal or instrumental parts could be viewed simultaneously or separately and could be recorded for future performance.[40]

Surviving music, however, does not give us the complete picture of music making from the Middle Ages and the Renaissance. There is a lost layer of music that was not written down.[41] Beggar minstrels of towns and villages did not record their music. They were ignorant of music theory and did not know any music notation. In fact, there was no need for beggar musicians to be musically literate (and Bruegel's blind musician could not have seen notation, anyway).[42] Wandering minstrels memorized popular tunes by rote and improvised upon them or even "composed" new melodies in order to please their audience. The street songs of catchy melodies with topical, comical, satirical, or erotic lyrics may have sufficed to satisfy the appetite and taste of the townspeople and villagers. And because Bruegel's musicians lived before the age of electronically operated recording systems, there is no way of recovering the music and sound of wandering minstrels and street musicians. Is there?

The printed collections of "art music" seem to be the last place to look for the kind of music Bruegel's beggar musicians played. A sixteenth-century Nuremberg lutenist Hans Newsidler published a lute piece called *Der Bethler Tantz* in his lute book of 1540.[43] The word "Bethler" (or "Bettler") means "beggar." *The Beggar's Dance* is a short piece. In keeping with the custom of Newsidler's time for dance arrangements, the piece consists of two sections (Example 14.1).[44] The main section is in duple meter, followed by the section, called *Hupff auff*, in triple meter. The melody is a catchy one, and the rhythm is lively. It is tempting to imagine that *The Beggar's Dance* was quite attractive to villagers and townspeople when played and danced to it by a beggar entertainer.

What made Newsidler name this piece *The Beggar's Dance*? Was he familiar with the popular melody sung or played by beggar musicians in the streets of Nuremberg, and so impressed that he made a lute arrangement? Did Newsidler compose the entire piece based on his impression of the music of beggar musicians, therefore offering an early example of "program music"?

Example 14.1. Hans Newsidler, *Ein newes Lautenbüchlein* (Nuremberg, 1540), ff. D1–D1v, "Der Bethler tantz" and "Hupff auff."

Newsidler was certainly familiar with the songs popular among the common people of Nuremberg; indeed he was one of them. He published several lute pieces called *Gassenhauer*, meaning "street (or popular) song."[45] What makes this piece a "street song"? One of Newsidler's *Gassenhauers*, published in his lute book of 1536, shows some unusual musical characteristics, with a melodic style not compatible with the vocabulary of sixteenth-century vocal counterpoint (see Example 14.2).[46] It is definitely instrumental in character and, in this case, plebeian. The melody lacks any significant contour; it hardly moves more than the interval of a third (the first phrase uses only two pitches). Moreover, each main note is repeated four times, giving the effect of a tremolo, a trademark of stringed instruments.[47] The alternating motion of fingers or a bow on one note is easily produced on them.

Another nonvocal style in the *Gassenhauer* is the use of the "strumming style" (Newsidler called it *"durch straichen"*). This style best applies to the situation in which all the chordal notes appear on the adjacent strings of an instrument, thereby creating pseudo-polyphony. The player plucks the strings with a plectrum, a finger or fingers, from the lowest string to the highest or vice versa.[48] This produces chords in arpeggio, either fast or slow depending on the speed of the strumming. If the chords are repeated rapidly, a drone effect and lively rhythm are created. In Newsidler's *Gassenhauer*, the chords occur on the first and third beats, creating a bouncy triple meter.

The basic musical structure in Newsidler's *Gassenhauer* is a combination of simple melody and chordal accompaniment. The chordal notes are added

Example 14.2. Hans Newsidler, *Ein newgeordent küntslich Lautenbüch* (Nuremberg, 1536), ff. x1–x1v, "Gassenhauer."

to strengthen the sound on the lute. If we simplify this lute arrangement by omitting the chordal notes, the result is the combination of a melody and a single-voice bass pattern.[49] The hurdy-gurdy and bagpipes are equipped with a melody-producing device and a drone-producing device, the chanter and a drone pipe for the bagpipes and the keyboard and drone string(s) for the hurdy-gurdy. We may not be so far-fetched in imagining Bruegel's beggar minstrels playing music such as Newsidler's *Gassenhauer* on his hurdy-gurdy or bagpipes.

Time is Semibrevely Money

Hans Newsilder was a lute player, lute instructor, maker of instruments, and published several books of lute compositions and arrangements with extensive instructions on how to play the instrument and how to read tablature. He was an educated man. But his life was not much better than that of Bruegel's beggar musicians. Newsidler's struggle with his financial situation is best exemplified by his instruction on how to count time. He instructed his students that the rhythmic sign for the semibreve (the basic *tactus* in lute compositions and intabulations) should be played in the same tempo as the striking of the hour or bells on a tower, or the sound of counting money "nice and gently" while saying "one, two, three, four."[50]

A miser may count money slowly. A spendthrift may count money quickly. Newsilder had to count money "nice and gently" for good reasons. He lived in a city that was struggling for its economic growth and had an occupation that offered no financial stability or prosperity. As Keith Moxey has written, during the first half of the sixteenth century "more than half the inhabitants [of Nuremberg] were artisans who lived a more or less precarious existence, continually threatened by unemployment and inflation."[51] Newsidler indeed complained about his financial difficulties. He had to raise thirteen children (plus an additional four children after his second marriage). At one time Newsidler had to sell his house after his appeal to the Nuremberg city council for help failed.[52] When he wrote the instruction on how to count time, he may have been thinking of his own purse emptying too quickly.

Gone with the Wind

Everything must end. The musicians who entertained the villagers must move on. Only those who have lands to cultivate and those who have occupations that cater to the everyday needs of the villagers remain. Wandering minstrels and beggar musicians are not allowed to stay in the same village for long. They come and go like the wind.[53] Once the musicians leave, only the more familiar sounds will fill the villagers' ears.

Notes

I am indebted to April Parkins and Guy Johnson for their help.

1. Brussels, Musée Communal de la Ville de Bruxelles. Reproduced in Bob Claessens and Jeanne Rousseau, *Bruegel*, reprint ed. (New York: Portland House, 1987), pl. 92. The painting is now attributed to Jan Bruegel the Elder. For a summary of the biography and works of Pieter Bruegel the Elder, see Alexander Wied, "Bruegel, (1) Pieter Bruegel I," *The Dictionary of Art* (London: Macmillan; New York: Grove's Dictionaries, 1996), vol. 4, 894–910; and F. Grossmann, *Pieter Bruegel Complete Edition of the Paintings* (London: Phaidon Press, 1973). Bruegel's paintings with peasant subjects are discussed in Margaret A. Sullivan, *Bruegel's Peasants: Art and Audience in the Northern Renaissance* (Cambridge: Cambridge University Press, 1994); and Ethan Matt Kavaler, *Pieter Bruegel: Parables of Order and Enterprise* (Cambridge: Cambridge University Press, 1999), esp. 149–62, 184–200. See also Claude-Henri Rocquet, *Bruegel or the Workshop of Dreams*, translated by Nora Scott (Chicago and London: University of Chicago Press, 1991).

2. Vienna, Kunsthistorisches Museum. Reproduced in Wilfried Seipel, ed., *Pieter Bruegel the Elder at the Kunsthistorisches Museum in Vienna* (Milan: Skira Editore, 1998), 131; and Claessens and Rousseau, *Bruegel*, pls. 127, 128–29 (details). Gustav Glück, *Pieter Bruegel the Elder*, trans. Eveline Byam Shaw (London: The Hyperion Press), 34, points out that the "guests do not exceed twenty, the number prescribed by Charles V in a proclamation as the limit for participators in country weddings such as this."

3. Vienna, Kunsthistorisches Museum. Reproduced in Seipel, *Pieter Bruegel the Elder*, 141; and Claessens and Rousseau, *Bruegel*, pls. 125, 126 (detail).

4. Reproduced in Emanuel Winternitz, *Musical Instruments and Their Symbolism in Western Art: Studies in Musical Iconology* (New Haven and London: Yale University Press, 1967), Plate 28b.

5. Naples, Museo e Gallerie Nazionali di Capodimonte. Reproduced in Claessens and Rousseau, *Bruegel*, pls. 109, 110–15 (details).

6. For the manuscript, see Higini Angles, "Un manuscrit inconnu avec polyphonie du XVe siècle conservé à la cathedrale de Ségovie," *Acta musicologica* 8 (1936): 6–17; idem, *La musica en la corte de los reyes catolicos*, Monumentos de la musica española, 1 (Madrid: Consejo Superior de Investigaciones Cientificas, Instituto Diego Velazquez, 1960), 106–12; Herbert Kellman, *Census-Catalogue of Manuscript Sources of Polyphonic Music 1400–1550*, Renaissance Manuscript Studies, 1 (N.p.: American Institute of Musicology/Neuhaussen-Stuttgart: Hanssler-Verlag, 1984), vol. 3, 137–38; and Norma Klein Baker, "An Unnumbered Manuscript of Polyphony in the Archives of the Cathedral of Segovia: Its Provenance and History" (Ph.D. diss., University of Maryland, 1978).

7. Segovia Cathedral, Archivio Musical, no shelf number, ff. 195v-97. It is also attributed to Alexander Agricola in St. Gall, Stiftsbibliothek, MS 462, and to Heinrich Isaac in Hradec Králové, Museum, Codex Speciálník. A modern transcription of the piece may be found in Edward R. Lerner, ed., *Alexandri Agricola: Opera Omnia*, Corpus mensurabilis musicae, 22 (N.p.: American Institute of Musicology, 1970), vol. 5, 102–5.

8. The paraphrase is taken from Bonnie J. Blackburn, Edward E. Lowinsky, and Clement A. Miller, eds., *A Correspondence of Renaissance Musicians* (Oxford: Clarendon Press, 1991), 330, n. 3.

9. Ibid., 330–34.

10. The symbolism of visibility or invisibility in a composition was presented differently in the sixteenth century. Allusion to vision was a well-known compositional technique among madrigal composers. If a text refers to eyes, for instance, the composer may present the physical feature of the eyes in musical notation. A row of two breves or semibreves on the staff may look like eyes, but the symbolism can be noticed only on paper, not by sound. On "eye-music," see Alfred Einstein, *The Italian Madrigal*, trans. Alexander H. Krappe, Roger H. Sessions, and Oliver Strunk, 2nd ed. (Princeton: Princeton University Press, 1971), vol. 1, 234–44.

11. See Jon Banks, "A Piece of Fifteenth-Century Lute Music in the Segovia Codex," *The Lute: The Journal of the Lute Society* 34 (1994): 3–10; Hiroyuki Minamino, "Johannes and Carolus Fernandez, Fifteenth-Century Composers of Music for Lute," *The Lute: The Journal of the Lute Society* 37 (1997): 5–8; and Jon Banks, "Performing the Instrumental Music in the Segovia Codex," *Early Music* 27 (1999), 295–309.

12. On coloration, see Willi Apel, *The Notation of Polyphonic Music, 900–1600*, 5th and rev. ed. (Cambridge, Mass.: The Mediaeval Academy of America, 1953), 126–44.

13. Johannes Tinctoris, *De inventione et usu musicae* (Naples, 1481–1483), libro quarto. For the relevant passages, see Karl Weinmann, *Johannes Tinctoris (1445–1511) und sein unbekannter Traktat "De inventione et usu musicae,"* 2nd ed. (Tutzing: Hans Schneider, 1961), 45; and Anthony Baines, "Fifteenth-Century Instruments in Tinctoris's *De inventione et usu musicae*," *The Galpin Society Journal* 3 (1950), 24. For the date of compilation of the treatise, see Ronald Woodley, "The Printing and Scope of Tinctoris's Fragmentary Treatise *De inventione et vsv mvsice*," *Early Music History* 5 (1985): 241–45. For Tinctoris's trip north, see idem, "Iohannes Tinctoris: A Review of the Documentary Biographical Evidence," *Journal of the American Musicological Society* 34 (1981): 235–36.

14. Johannes and Carolus Orbus worked as organists at Bruges; see Reinhard Strohm, *Music in Late Medieval Bruges* (Oxford: Oxford University Press, 1985), 32, 88, 143. Tinctoris regarded the bowed "viola" as an instrument suitable for the recitation of epic poems as well as for sacred music.

15. Indeed, Tinctoris called the blind German instrumentalist Conrad Paumann "Orbus ille germanus" in the same treatise. For the identification of "Orbus ille germanus," see Hiroyuki Minamino, "Conrad Paumann and the Evolution of Solo Lute Practice in the Fifteenth Century," *Journal of Musicological Research* 6 (1986): 291–310.

16. See Paula Higgins, review of Reinhard Strohm, *Music in Late Medieval Bruges*, in *Journal of the American Musicological Society* 42 (1989): 159, n. 20. For the biography of Cordoval and Fernandez, see Jeanne Marix, *Histoire de la musique et des musiciens de la cour de Bourgogne sous le règne de Philippe le Bon (1420–1467)*, Sammlung musikwissenschaftlicher Abhandlungen, vol. 29 (Baden-Baden: V. Koerner, 1974), 117–18; and Albert Van der Linden, "Les aveugles de la cour de Bourgogne," *Revue belge de musicologie* 4 (1950): 74–76. In some documents Johannes and Carolus were called "Brugensis" or "Normannus." It may not have been improper to regard them as such, if they were born after their father came to Burgundy in 1433.

17. Tinctoris praised both Carolus and Johannes not only as excellent musicians but also for their knowledge of literature. This makes it likely that Johannes is one and the same person as the "Johannes Citharoedi" or "Le Harpeur" who became a rector at the University of Paris in 1485 and retired from the chair of ethics in 1491, and that Carolus is identical with the rector who taught literature at the same university; see Strohm, *Music in Late Medieval Bruges*, 88. Both Johannes and Carolus are further recorded as instrumentalists to Charles VIII in 1488 and 1490; see André Pirro, "L'Enseignement de la musique aux universités françaises," *Acta musicologica* 2 (1930): 46–47.

18. One such account can be found in Edmund Bowles, "Haut and Bas: The Grouping of Musical Instruments in the Middle Ages," *Musica disciplina* 8 (1954), 116, n. 3. On medieval minstrels, see Christopher Page, *The Owl and the Nightingale: Musical Life and Ideas in France, 1100–1300* (Berkeley and Los Angeles: University of California Press, 1989); John Southworth, *The English Medieval Minstrel* (Woodbridge, Suffolk: The Boydell Press, 1989); Zoltán Falvy, *Mediterranean Culture and Troubadour Music*, Studies in Central and Eastern European Music, 1 (Budapest: Akadémiai Kiadó, 1986).

19. Only exceptionally talented and strong-willed persons such as Beethoven conquer this devastating handicap for musicians.

20. Francesco Landini and Conrad Paumann to name a few.

21. This is necessarily a simplification. Some musicians crossed the lines discussed here. An Elizabethan composer and instrumentalist, John Dowland, for instance, was trained in the master-apprentice system, attained the bachelor's degree in music from

Cambridge and Oxford, and was employed at aristocrats' households. On music education in the Renaissance, see Paul Oskar Kristeller, "Music and Learning in the Early Italian Renaissance," *Journal of Renaissance and Baroque Music* 1 (1947), 255–74, reprinted idem, *Renaissance Thought and the Arts*, expanded edition (Princeton: Princeton University Press, 1990), 142–62; Nan Cook Carpenter, *Music in the Medieval and Renaissance Universities* (Oklahoma, 1958); Nan Cook Carpenter and Iain Fenlon, "Education in Music: III. Renaissance," *The New Grove Dictionary of Music and Musicians* (London: Macmillan; Washington D.C.: Grove's Dictionary of Music, 1980), vol. 6, 8–12; and Hiroyuki Minamino, *Sixteenth-Century Lute Instruction* (The Lute Society in preparation).

22. The musicians in this tale could have been contemporaries of Bruegel's musicians. The hint is the lute. The lute was developed from the Arabic *'ud*, most likely in thirteenth-century Spain. During the fourteenth and fifteenth centuries, the lute was an "aristocratic" instrument, expensive to buy and to maintain. In the sixteenth century, the lute became the most popular among secular instruments. Unlike the organ or harpsichord, the lute was easy to carry, and according to one lute enthusiast's account, could be hidden in an overcoat. In the seventeenth and eighteenth centuries, the lute had more bass strings, sometimes with two peg-boxes. We should, of course, take into consideration the fact that the term "lute" (*"laute"* in German) was loosely applied and could mean any plucked stringed instrument.

23. Bonifazio's story, told by Giovanni da Prato, is discussed in Howard Mayer Brown, "The Trecento Harp," in *Studies in the Performance of Late Medieval Music*, ed. Stanley Boorman (Cambridge: Cambridge University Press, 1983), 59. See also Albert Pomme de Mirimonde, "Le musique dans allégories de l'amour," *Gazette des beaux-arts* 68 (1966), 265–90.

24. See Hiroyuki Minamino, "Sixteenth-Century Lute Treatises with Emphasis on Process and Techniques of Intabulation" (Ph.D. diss., University of Chicago, 1988).

25. On this Florentine statute, see John Larner, *Culture and Society in Italy 1290–1420* (New York: Scribner, 1971), 172.

26. The drawings of serenaders in *Das Narrenschiff* are reproduced and discussed in Edmund A. Bowles, *Musikleben im 15. Jahrhundert*, Musikgeschichte in Bildern, Band III: Musik des Mittelalters und der Renaissance, Lfg. 8 (Leipzig: Deutscher Verlag für Musik, 1977), 106–7.

27. William A. Cocks, Anthony C. Baines, and Roderick D. Cannon, "Bagpipe," *The New Grove Dictionary of Music and Musicians*, vol. 1, 19–32; and R. D. Cannon, "Bagpipes in English Works of Art," *The Galpin Society Journal* 42 (1989): 10–31.

28. Angelo Ottolini, ed., *Il Decamerone* (Milan, 1932), 20. For the performance of music in the *Decameron*, see Howard Mayer Brown, "Fantasia on a Theme by Boccaccio," *Early Music* 5 (1977): 324–39. One of the gentlemen plays the lute, while one of the ladies plays the viola.

29. Lorenzo the Magnificent, who underwent a number of fortunes and misfortunes, is alleged to have composed a song with lyrics of such a sentiment. See Walter H. Rubsamen, "The Music for 'Quant'è bella giovinezza' and Other Carnival Songs by Lorenzo de' Medici," in *Art, Science, and History in the Renaissance*, ed. Charles S. Singleton (Baltimore: Johns Hopkins University Press, 1967), 163–84.

30. *The Parable of the Blind* is a pictorial manifestation of a famous biblical story, but Bruegel's execution of it superimposed past and present. The church, village, and landscape were those of the sixteenth century. Indeed, the place has been identified as being the church village of Pede-Sainte-Anne in Brabant. On this point, see Claessens and Rousseau, *Bruegel*, pl. 115.

31. See Albert P. de Mirimonde, *Astrologie et Musique* (Geneva: Minkoff, 1977).

32. The bagpipe was also depicted in the hands of shepherds, a symbol of Christ.

33. See Francis Baines and Edmund A. Bowles, "Hurdy-gurdy," *The New Grove Dictionary of Music and Musicians*, vol. 8, 814–18; Christopher Page, "The Medieval *Organistrum* and *Symphonia* I: A Legacy from the East?" *The Galpin Society Journal* 35 (1982): 37–44.

34. The quotation is taken from Winternitz, *Musical Instruments*, 75. The engravings depicting street musicians of eighteenth-century Paris offer abundant evidence of the hurdy-gurdy as their chosen instrument; see Florence Gétreau, "Street Musicians of Paris: Evolution of an Image," *Music in Art: International Journal for Music Iconography*, 23, nos. 1–2 (1998): 62–78.

35. Another instance of music being a vehicle for tragedy is the musical contest between Apollo and Marsyas. According to Ovid's *Metamorphoses*, Marsyas found a double-flute floating in a stream, not knowing that the instrument was enchanted by the magic spell, a curse of Pallas Athena. The divine music so pleased Marsyas's compatriots that they cried out that Apollo himself could not have made better music. Marsyas foolishly challenged Apollo and was flayed after he lost the contest. For the pictorial presentation of this contest in the Renaissance, see Edith Wyss, *The Myth of Apollo and Marsyas in the Art of the Italian Renaissance: An Inquiry into the Meaning of Images* (Newark: University of Delaware Press/London: Associated University Presses, 1996); Edgar Wind, *Pagan Mysteries in the Renaissance*, revised and enlarged ed. (New York: Norton, 1968), 171–76; and Winternitz, *Musical Instruments*, 150–65. There is a story of a blind Buddhist monk from medieval Japan whose talent in reciting *Heike-monogatari* (The tale of the Taira clan) with biwa accompaniment was such that the ghosts of the Taira Clan came to ask him for his performance, which nearly cost the musician's life. I am preparing a study of this subject, tentatively entitled "Earless Hoh-ichi and the Art of Narrative Singing."

36. For the popularity of Orpheus's life as a subject for dramas and operas in the Renaissance and the Baroque, see Nino Pirrotta and Elena Povoledo, *Music and Theatre from Poliziano to Monteverdi* (Cambridge: Cambridge University Press, 1982), originally published with the title *Li due Orfei* (Torino: Eri, 1969).

37. See Jack W. Sage, "A New Look at Humanism in Sixteenth-Century Lute and Vihuela Books," *Early Music* 20 (1992): 633–41. The significant resemblance between the drawing of a lutenist and two listeners on the title page of Francesco Marcolini's *Intabolatura di liuto* (Venice, 1536) and an account of one Monsieur de Ventemille [Jacques Descartes de Vintimille?] about Francesco da Milano's performance in Milan, which was printed in Pontus de Tyard, *Solitaire second ou prose de la musique* (Lyons, 1555), may have been based on the Orpheus legend. I am preparing a study of the Marcolini drawing, tentatively entitled "Orpheus in the Renaissance and the Power of Music."

38. On the medal made in 1457 by Giovanni Boldù, the inscription reads "PETRVS. BONNVS . . . ORPHEVM. SVP[ER]ANS"; reproduced in George F. Hill, *A Corpus of Italian Medals of the Renaissance before Cellini* (London: British Museum, 1930), Pl. 79, no. 416. Moritz, Landgrave of Hessen-Kassel, called Dowland the "English Orpheus" ("Anglorum Orphei"). The epithet is printed in Robert Dowland, ed., *Varietie of Lute-lessons* (London, 1610), f. H2v; see the facsimile edition by Schott (London, 1958).

39. See Hiroyuki Minamino, "Harping on a Lute String," *Discoveries: South-Central Renaissance Conference News and Notes* 16, no. 2 (1999): 5–6. Giambattista della Porta in his *Magiae naturalis libri viginti* of 1589 discusses musical magic of sheep-gut and wolf-gut strings. I am indebted to Linda Austern for this information. On Renaissance musical magic, see Gary Tomlinson, *Music in Renaissance Magic: Toward a Historiography of Others* (Chicago and London: University of Chicago Press, 1993).

40. It should be reminded here that polyphonic music could be improvised with written parts.

41. See Nino Pirrotta's essays "New Glimpses of an Unwritten Tradition," "The Oral and Written Traditions of Music," and "Music and Cultural Tendencies in Fifteenth-Century Italy," all reprinted in his *Music and Culture in Italy from the Middle Ages to the Baroque: A Collection of Essays*, Studies in the History of Music, 1 (Cambridge and London: Harvard University Press, 1984), 51–71, 72–79, and 80–112, respectively.

42. A blind German musician Conrad Paumann is alleged to have invented German lute tablature, possibly for dictation purposes. Paumann, an organist, lutenist, and composer, mainly dealt with the polyphonic music. On Paumann's alleged involvement in

inventing German lute tablature and the critics who denounced the credibility of the story, see Minamino, "Conrad Paumann," 291–310. On the literacy of musicians, see Christopher Page, "Musicus and Cantor," in *Companion to Medieval and Renaissance Music*, eds. Tess Knighton and David Fallows (New York: Schirmer Books, 1992), 74–78.

43. Hans Newsidler, *Ein newes Lautenbüchlein* (Nuremberg, 1540), ff. D1-D1v. The volume is listed and described in Howard Mayer Brown, *Instrumental Music Printed before 1600: A Bibliography* (Cambridge: Harvard University Press, 1967), as item 1540-1.

44. It is transcribed in Adolf Koczirz, ed., *Österreichische Lautenmusik im 16. Jahrhundert*, Denkmäler der Tonkunst in Österreich, XVIII/Bd. 37 (Vienna: Universal, 1911/ reprint, Graz: Akademische Druck- und Verlagsanstalt, 1959), 38 (transcribed in the nominal A tuning). My transcription reproduced here uses the nominal G tuning.

45. On *Gassenhauer*, see Peter Branscombe, "Gassenhauer," *The New Grove Dictionary of Music and Musicians*, vol. 7, 177–78. On the sixteenth-century German lute dance, see Jenny Dieckmann, *Die in deutscher Lautentabulatur überlieferten Tänze des 16. Jahrhunderts* (Kassel: Bärenreiter-Verlag, 1931).

46. Hans Newsidler, *Ein newgeordent künstlich Lautenbuch* (Nuremberg, 1536), ff. x1-x1v. The volume is listed and described in Brown, *Instrumental Music*, as item 1536-6. A facsimile edition by Institute pro arte testudinis (Neuss am Rhein: Junghänel, Päffgen, Schäffer, 1974). The piece is transcribed in Koczirz, *Österreichische Lautenmusik im 16. Jahrhundert*, 35. My transcription reproduced here uses the nominal A tuning.

47. An earlier instance of the tremolo style in lute compositions may be found in Joan Ambrosio Dalza's *Intabolatura di liuto libro quarto* (The fourth book of lute tablature), which Ottaviano Petrucci published in Venice in 1508. The section called "Piva" of a dance suite "Pavana alla venetiana" has a three-note tremolo figure throughout the section: it also uses the strumming style.

48. Hans Judenkünig, *Ain schone kunstliche Underweisung* (Vienna, 1523), f. C1v, recommended that the strumming technique should especially be used for dance arrangements. The strumming technique may have originated in the plectrum-plucking technique of the fifteenth century. Some of the "ricercars" in the late-fifteenth-century Italian manuscript Pesaro, Biblioteca Oliveriana, MS 1144 are made of passages in single notes and chords that are played on adjacent courses. On this manuscript, see Vladimir Ivanoff, *Das Pesaro-Manuskript: Ein Beitrag zur Frühgeschichte der Lautentabulatur* (Tutzing: Hans Schneider, 1988); and idem, ed., *Ein zentrale Quelle der frühen italienischen Lautenpraxis: Edition der Handschrift Pesaro, Biblioteca Oliveriana, MS 1144* (Tutzing: Hans Schneider, 1988).

49. Newsidler's *Gassenhauer* of 1536 is based on an Italian *ostinato* bass known as *passamezzo moderno*. This dance formula may be found in Gustave Reese, *Music in the Renaissance*, revised ed. (New York: W. W. Norton, 1959), 524.

50. Newsidler, *Ein newgeordent künstlich Lautenbuch*, f. b3v. See Ephraim Segerman, "A Re-examination of the Evidence on Absolute Tempo before 1700—I," *Early Music* 24 (1996), 227–48, esp. 232; Minamino, "Sixteenth-Century Lute Treatises," 58–63; and idem,. "On the Semibreve: Time Is Money," *Lute Society of America Quarterly* 33, nos. 1 and 2 (1998): 29–30.

51. The quotation is taken from Keith Moxey, *Peasants, Warriors, and Wives: Popular Imagery in the Reformation* (Chicago and London: University of Chicago Press, 1989), 1.

52. See Hans Radke, "Neusidler," *The New Grove Dictionary of Music and Musicians*, vol. 13, 156.

53. Schubert's song cycle "Winterreise" ends with a song "Der Leiermann" (The organ-grinder). Wilhelm Müller's poem describes an old beggar musician playing his tunes with frozen fingers on a frosty street in a village and a young wanderer's wish to make a journey with the musician.

15

Pastoral Pleasures, Sensual Sounds

Paintings of Love, Music, and Morality in Sixteenth-Century Italy

Katherine A. McIver

The perfect moments of music itself, the making or hearing of music or its accompaniment, are themselves prominent as subjects ... music at the poolside ... mingled with the sound of the pitcher in the well, or heard across running water, or among the flock; the tuning of instruments; people with intense faces, as if listening ... detect the smallest interval of musical sound ... a momentary touch of an instrument in the twilight ...[1]

So goes Walter Pater's description of the enigmatic and provocative painting, *Pastoral Concert* (Paris, Musée du Louvre, c. 1510), attributed to both Giorgione and Titian. Pater's words, as poetic as the painting itself, capture the essence of the image and, at the same time and like the painting, send the mind wandering into another world. Clearly associated with the classical pastoral genre as well as sixteenth-century poetry, this work tells no exact story and, consequently, appears to have no precise meaning—it is a painted poem, and as Paul Barolsky so eloquently states, "... its lush, verdant landscape evokes the conventional 'locus amoenus' or 'pleasance,' and the nymphs are woodland creatures who populate sylvan realms. As the courtier seated at the very center plays his lute and a rustic herdsman inclines his head to listen, the viewer recalls those bowers of bucolic poetry where friends rendezvous for the sheer pleasure of each other's company and in the background sits a herdsman, whose bagpipes distinctly echo the song of the poet...."[2] As visual poetry, this painting, which defies traditional analysis, has provided inspiration for artists from the time of its creation.[3] Images like Cariani's *Pastoral Concert* (Paris, Seve Collection, c. 1515), his other *Pastoral Concert* (Warsaw, Muzeum Narodowe w Warszawie, c. 1515), Palma Vecchio's *Concert* (Ardencraig, Lady Colum Crichton-Stuart Collection, c. 1515–20), as well as Titian's series of paintings depicting Venus with a musician all show some allegiance to the Louvre *Concert*.[4] And while the pastoral imagery is idyllic, evoking the rarified world of shepherds, poets, and the like, Titian's series is more overtly sensual, more worldly.

Like the Giorgionesque *Concert*, Titian's "Venus with a Musician" series has been the subject of much discussion; most often the paintings are interpreted as Neoplatonic allegories of perceived beauty through the spiritual senses of hearing and sight—the higher senses rather than with the lower ones of touch, smell, and taste.[5] However, according to Rona Goffen, in Titian's musician series, "sensory experience, embracing all the senses, though privileging sight, is . . . Titian's subtext, in keeping with Neoplatonic tradition and indeed his own beliefs."[6] She speculates further that "the goddess whom men worship with their music and adore with their eyes" is neither a bridal Venus nor a courtesan; rather, she is "the epitome of all beauty and the embodiment of all sensuous pleasure, including sexual pleasures of the flesh."[7] Thus Goffen suggests that Titian's images reflect the best of both worlds: spiritual and profane. It is not my intention here to debunk any of the theories proposed for this series, but rather to explore other avenues of interpretation, considering literary sources, the social milieu in Venice, and the artist himself.[8] This paper will focus on three of Titian's images: *Venus with the Organ Player* (Madrid, Museo del Prado, 1540s, Figure 15.1), *Venus with the Organ Player* (Berlin, Staatliche Gemaldegalerie, 1540s, Figure 15.2), and *Venus with the Lute Player* (New York, Metropolitan Museum of Art, 1560s, Figure 15.3), as well as considering the two paintings by Cariani (Figures 15.4 and 15.5), and the one by Palma Vecchio (Figure 15.6) mentioned above.

In all of Titian's paintings in this series, Venus reclines in a chamber in essentially the same manner as in his *Venus with Cupid* (Florence, Galleria degli Uffizi, c. 1540s), but now she is joined by a musician, an organist or lutenist. The musician serenading Venus sits at the end of her bed, at her feet, as she reclines; youth or mature gentleman, his hands always make music, while his gaze lingers on the woman. In some versions of the painting, another instrument is included and is sometimes considered to be a reference to a third music-maker or the viewer himself. Sometimes Cupid attends the woman, while in others a dog shares her bed. In all versions, Venus ignores her lover.[9] The viewer, like the musician, is indulged in every regard: he is permitted to look at Venus and invited to hear the music and other, distant sounds made by background figures, and to smell the perfume of the goddess's flowers and the fragrant air of the park visible through the windows. One factor remains constant: Venus never acknowledges the musician who worships her with his glance and his music. As in the *Pastoral Concert*, the woman is nude and the man clothed. While the nude women in the Louvre *Concert* are often considered to be invisible to the two clothed men, in the Venus paintings it is the musician who seems to be unseen and unheard; Venus, by choice, neither looks his way nor responds to his serenade.[10] Reclining on her side, Venus turns her body to the beholder, her head always turned away from the musician. Although naked, she is bejeweled with bracelets, rings, and necklaces, and her hair is formally styled, sometimes adorned with pearls. Her right arm always lies by her side, hand on thigh, while with her left hand she may pat her dog or hold her flute or let her fingers rest idly on the surface of her velvet bed clothes. Each of these casual actions or inactions is a visual stimulus to the tactile sense for the benefit and gentle torment of the beholder who can only imagine her touch—much as Titian must have done as he used his brush to caress the imagined flesh as he painted. Here, the paragone of the senses (higher vs. lower) is represented by the rivalry between sight (the musician's gaze) and touch—not only must the fingers touch the instrument in order to produce music, but the gaze itself replaces the lover's hands in "touching" (caressing) the nude woman's flesh as it wanders over the contours of her body reading every curve. Metaphorically speaking, as the eyes linger, so do the fingers, implying the sensation of touch through the gaze. By association, the viewer/voyeur, re-creates in his imagination the sensuous feel of the flesh which is only enhanced by the perceived sensuous sounds of the music and fragrant perfumes of the flowers—thus, once again, implying touch.[11]

In the formal Renaissance garden background of the Prado *Venus with the Organ Player* (see Figure 15.1), a couple strolls along a tree-lined path (at left, to the side of the organ); a stag reclines nearby. At the right, a peacock perches on the edge of a fountain, the upper portion of which is a statue of

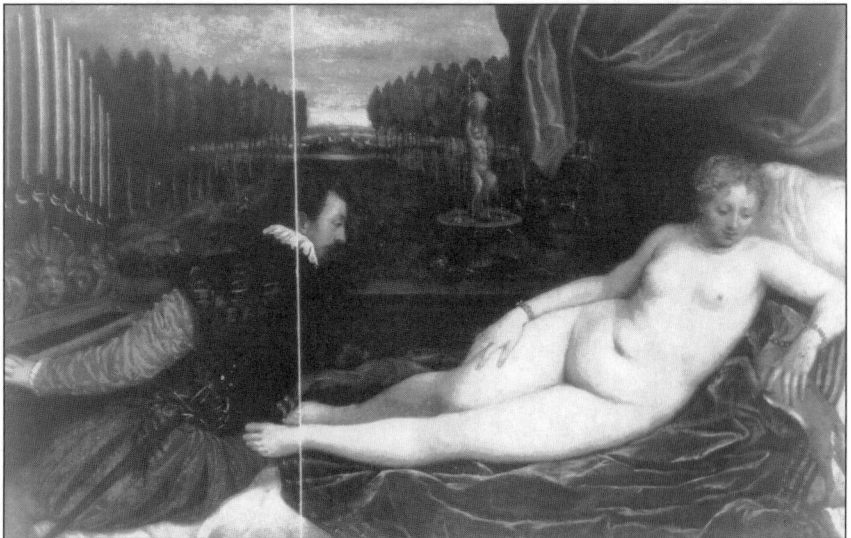

Figure 15.1. Titian, *Venus with the Organ Player* (Madrid, Museo del Prado, 1540s).

a satyr; to its left is another deer. The musician's gaze is focused on the woman's pudenda. In order to look at this object of his desire, the musician must turn away from the organ, twisting at the waist while his hands remain on the keyboard. His backward torsion is stopped visually by Venus's feet pressing against his waist. Specifying his interest in her sex, his targeted glance also delimits his interest in Venus; his wooing through music, the painting's exquisite evocation of the senses of sound and smell, the tenderness of the elegant couple who stroll arm-in-arm through the park— all this sweetness is belied by that downward gaze. The thrust of his staring is echoed by the line of his sword and the organ's shining, phallic pipes.

In other versions of this painting like the one in Berlin (see Figure 15.2), Titian juxtaposed rustic background details in contradistinction to the foreground action. He made one more fundamental adjustment: the musician's eyes now turn toward Venus's face, and a sheer, white drapery lays across her lap, almost shielding her sex from his view and from ours as well. In the Berlin painting, moreover, the organ is now parallel to the picture plane and the musician sits on a bench before it, not directly on her bed. The lower part of his body conceals the lower part of the instrument, so that we no longer see the pipes coming from its carved base. The pipes are also cropped somewhat at the top, a modification that curtails their phallic energy. Other modifications include: a small dagger instead of a sword; her feet no longer touch his waist, so that the tactile sense is restrained; and her body is closer to the picture plane, the contour of which is elongated into a unifying curve. It is a psychological rather than a physical relationship. In both the Prado and Berlin painting, dogs are included; a yapping white Maltese confronts the viewer in the latter, while in the former

Figure 15.2. Titian, *Venus with the Organ Player* (Berlin, Staatliche Gemaldegalerie, 1540s).

a small brown dog is caressed by Venus. The alterations and modifications continue in the paintings of *Venus with a Lute Player* (see Figure 15.3). In the Metropolitan version, for instance, Titian adds a viola da gamba and partbooks, makes the musicians young, and eliminates the dogs. Venus holds a flute and is being crowned by Cupid. In contrast to the lutenist's refined music, rustic nude satyrs dance in a circle to raucous bagpipes in the background. The landscape, with golden fields and a lake with swans, is mountainous. Presumably, the viola is for the viewer who is invited to join in with the music making. Venus's flute has been associated with the *flauto d'amore* as seen in Titian's *Three Ages* (Edinburgh, National Gallery of Scotland).[12]

Why has Titian apparently cleaned up the Berlin painting and made further refinements to the lutenist series? We can only speculate. Generally speaking, both Prado versions of the organist are akin to Aretino's writings in their overt sensuality,[13] while the Berlin organist and the lutenist series seem to share a greater affinity with the Petrarchan poets. It has been suggested, moreover, that the organist in the first Prado version (Figure 15.1) is none other than the Italian composer Girolamo Parabosco (1524–57), who was first organist at St. Mark's in Venice in the 1550s and who had a passion for the ladies;[14] on the other hand, the Berlin organist (Figure 15.2)

Figure 15.3. Titian, *Venus with a Lute Player* (New York, Metropolitan Musem of Art, 1560s).

has been associated with Philip II of Spain, who was noted for his piety.[15] While neither identification can be substantiated, the suggestions are provocative since the modifications between the two paintings can be interpreted as a reflection of the demands of the clientele for whom the work was made—one patron whose interests were, obviously, more openly sensual than the other. The refinements evident throughout the lutenist series suggest, once again, the demands of the market for which they were produced. In some ways, the additions to the lutenist paintings—the part-books, the third instrument for an unspecified musician, the pastoral, almost bucolic, landscape background—evoke the more idyllic and rarified world of the Louvre *Pastoral Concert* and the higher senses of sight and sound, in contrast to the organist series with its emphasis on the lower senses of touch and smell.

Focusing once again on the Prado (Figure 15.1) and the Berlin (Figure 15.2) organist paintings, it has been suggested that rather than reflecting the Neoplatonic tradition, these paintings may derive from the poetic and musical tradition of Petrarch and the Petrarchans and the madrigals they inspired.[16] Following this tradition the suitor in each painting implores his lady through his music to take pity on him and to return his love. Titian's lady, like Laura, is the cause of the lover's passion, misery, and frustration; she is the ideal beauty adored by the love-sick courtier. Goodman postulates further that "If Titian's lady is not an actual Venus, she can be said to be at least a metaphorical one—the Petrarchan mistress who embodies the ideal, beautiful woman, the object of man's affection."[17]

Titian, a noted admirer of women, may simply have painted a beautiful woman not only for his own pleasure but for that of his patron as well, a point many scholars overlook. We can assume that he derived a sensual pleasure by merely creating the image, as is evidenced by his passionate brushstroke, the warm, alluring colors, and so on.[18] The sheer number of copies and variants suggests that they were popular images much in demand.[19] Eroticism, humor, and sensual pleasure seem, by our modern standards, too base for the Renaissance mind. Paul Barolsky, on the other hand, in his usual illuminating manner, has suggested that the two Prado versions of *Venus and the Organ Player* are satires rather than Neoplatonic allegories.[20] "There has been a tendency in the scholarly literature, as in the case in the interpretation of Titian's two paintings, to find Neoplatonic intentions in works of art where there is no firm evidence to justify such interpretations."[21]

Contrary to Goffen and others who see sight (the musician's gaze) as triumphing over the other senses, it is quite the opposite case; the lower one of touch is stressed. Not only do Venus's feet touch or appear to touch the music-making courtier in both Prado paintings, but also in one version Cupid touches Venus, and in the other she touches a dog.[22] The emphasis

on touch is found, as well, in literary sources; in Ludovico Domenichi's
La nobilita delle donne (Venice, 1555), for instance, Francesco Grasso speaks
of the female body as appealing to the sense of touch as well as sight, and
his observations, as Barolsky notes, closely parallel Titian's image of Venus.[23]
Grasso states, "From this, it follows that the female body is very delicate to
see and touch; the very tender flesh, the fine pale neck, the luminous and
fine hair, the beautiful head . . . the full breasts, dressed abundantly in flesh
to form solid mounds . . . the very fleshy thighs."[24] It is as if Grasso had
one of Titian's Venus paintings in front of him while he was speaking.

The sense of sight, moreover, need not be related to the Neoplatonic
philosophy of love; rather as Coppina instructs in Bartolomeo Gottifredi's
Specchio d'amore (published in the 1550s),[25] the sight of any part of a woman's
body will inflame her lover, a point surely emphasized by the gaze of the
Prado musician (Figure 15.1)! More to the point, Titian's Venus paintings
can be tied to the strong and pervasive tradition in Venice of humorous anti-
Neoplatonism found in the writings of Francesco Sansovino, Alessandro
Piccolomini, Pietro Aretino, and others who satirized the Neoplatonic
idea of love.[26] As Paul Barolsky writes, "The spirit of the two Prado
paintings does not relate simply to the serious neoplatonizing texts of Ficino,
Bembo, Leon Ebreo and Castiglione, but to a playful treatment of
neoplatonism that one finds in the humorous, if vulgar, writings of Aretino
and his circle. After all, the aperture of Venus's body at which Titian's
musicians are looking in the two paintings is clearly not the Neoplatonic
'window' to the soul."[27] One cannot overlook the satyr on the fountain in
the background of both paintings; he surely speaks not only to the lascivious
nature of the painting's content, but also refers to the painter's satirical
intention. More importantly, the ambience of both Prado paintings recalls
that of the Venetian courtesan of whom both Titian and Aretino had
intimate knowledge, and may, therefore, reflect the comic and erotic aspect
of an evening spent by the two men visiting their favorite courtesan, Angela
Zaffetta as they did one December night in 1547.[28] And one should keep in
mind, too, that this type of painting often hung in a bedroom or *studiolo*,
and was viewed by a select and limited audience that would have appreciated
the provocative nature of the subject matter.

On another level, these paintings (Figures 15.1, 15.2, 15.3) can be read in
terms of Titian's dual passions: one for women and the other for painting.
The ancient and Renaissance conception of the beautiful woman as the
archetypal image of beautiful art forms the subtext of both the organist
and the lutenist series. More to the point, Titian's relationship to these
paintings is intimate because his subject is himself; and Titian's identification
with his subject, particularly in terms of the Prado organist (Figure 15.1), is
comparable in a sense to Aretino's speaking with a female voice as he does
in his *Ragionamenti*, a dialogue between women.[29] This analogy between

the artist and his subject can be taken further in relation to this series. In accord with Renaissance aesthetic ideas, painters and musicians create *armonia* and *concordia*, and are identified with each other since painting and music are considered "sister arts," much like music and poetry.[30] And what about the Louvre *Pastoral Concert* with which we began this discussion? Is it not a visualization of these very ideas? Once again we turn to Paul Barolsky for illumination: "Picturing this courtly musician poet [the lutenist in the center of the painting] the artist (Titian) renders his own persona, since the painter is himself a poet—the poet-painter does not simply paint a poem but fictively projects the imaginative image of himself as poet. . . . Painting a poet at the center of his idyll, Titian renders the idealized image of the very poet with whom he identifies himself as the poetical author of his own pictorial poem."[31]

And what about those paintings like Cariani's two concert scenes (Figures 15.4 and 15.5) and Palma Vecchio's Ardencraig *Concert* (Figure 15.6)? How are we to read such paintings whose point of departure is certainly the Louvre *Concert*? Do they appeal to the senses in the same manner as Titian's Venus series, or are they merely poor imitations of popular pastoral imagery? Certainly, Palma Vecchio's painting, like the Louvre *Concert*, is about poetry. In Palma's painting, a young man, crowned with a laurel wreath, sits on the ground tuning a lira da braccio; the bow lies beside him. Across from him, two women sit together holding music books; one leans on the other and gazes toward the young man who seems oblivious of them. Behind them a river flows, probably to the sea. On its banks are houses; trees and mountains

Figure 15.4. Giovanni Cariani, *Pastoral Concert* (Paris, Seve Collection, c. 1515s).

Figure 15.5. Giovanni Cariani, *Pastoral Concert* (Warsaw, Muzeum Narodowe w Warszawie, c. 1515).

lie in the distance. Rather than the idyllic world of poets, shepherds, and the like, this setting is a contemporary one, anchored in reality, and recalls northern Italy as well as the setting for Pietro Bembo's *Gli Asolani* (published in Venice, 1515), in which a young man sings his poetry to young women.[32] The laurel wreath identifies the young man as a poet; the tuning of the lira, perhaps to the young women's voices, suggests musical harmony and functions as a prelude "all'accordo d'amore."[33] Harmony, coupled with the emphasis on the higher senses of hearing and sight, would seem to support a Neoplatonic reading of this painting. Unlike Titian's musician series (Figures 15.1, 15.2, 15.3), however, here the gender roles have been reversed. It is the young woman who does the looking. She is all but ignored by the musician-poet, who is intent on the tuning of his instrument, and the senses of hearing and touch (higher/lower, spiritual/profane) are intertwined in the process.

Cariani's Paris *Concert* (Figure 15.4), similar in format to Palma's painting, depicts a young man playing a lira da braccio to two young women. Yet, the subject of Cariani's painting is distinctly different, as is its setting. The young man, in an Orpheus-like costume, plays his instrument while a bird, on a branch to the left above his head, sings—perhaps in competition with the musician. The young women sit opposite listening; one holds a recorder and the other a lute. At the top center of the painting, a cupid, with blindfold removed, shoots arrows in their direction. Thus, the general theme of this painting is about love, and it is often considered to be a pendant to

Figure 15.6. Palma Vecchio, *Concert* (Ardencraig, Lady Colum Crichton-Stuart Collection, c. 1515–20).

Cariani's Warsaw *Concert* (Figure 15.5),[34] where Titian's reclining nude woman has been taken out of doors into a wooded setting.[35] The woman, partially draped, wears sandals, but no jewelry, and is accompanied by a small dog begging for her attention. Ignoring the dog and propping her head up with her hand, she appears either introspective or bored. Across from this figure sits a young man who pauses in his flute playing to confront the viewer with an open gaze, as if to say that by his music making he has conjured up her image. His gaze and position in the painting recalls that of the Maltese dog in Titian's Berlin *Organist* (Figure 15.2). Behind this couple and nearly in the center of the composition, another young man, accompanied by a nun, sits playing his flute while she rests her hand on the back of his shoulder, perhaps keeping time to the music. Neither figure seems aware of the nude woman; they gaze in the opposite direction. As in the Louvre *Concert*, one youth is simply dressed, while the other's costume is more refined: shepherd and courtier. In terms of the background, both of Cariani's paintings show the impact of the Louvre *Concert*.

The two women in Cariani's Paris *Concert* (Figure 15.4) are opposites. The dark-haired recorder-player wears the sleeveless, loose fitting garment often associated with courtesans, and her instrument is one associated with that of shepherds and bucolic poetry. The blond lutenist, on the other hand, is dressed in a red and green garment with long sleeves, clearly reflecting a higher social status, perhaps nobility. The dilemma here is one of choice. Like Hercules at the crossroads, the young man must choose between sacred and profane love. Described as "clear and joyous,"[36] the higher senses of hearing and sight seem to be emphasized. As in Palma's painting (Figure 15.6), it is the women who do the looking while the musician is absorbed in singing and playing, the women must await his decision. Conversely, in the Warsaw *Concert* (Figure 15.5), the choices have, apparently, already been made. Described both as "a night concert"[37] and as "dark and melancholic,"[38] it seems to parody the theme of sacred and profane love. The nun, whose gesture of keeping time suggests harmony, represents sacred love where hearing and touch are once again intertwined: while she listens, she taps his shoulder. Profane love and the sense of sight are recalled here by the image of the nude woman, yet, if she is the ideal of beauty, she could also personify the Neoplatonic idea of sacred love. She seems to play a dual role. The dog's position, opposite the young man yet paralleling it, speaks of his desires for the woman; the dog is his representative, begging to be touched, to be loved. Read together, Cariani's two paintings take the idyllic world of the Louvre *Concert*, with its shepherds and poets, out of the pastoral and into a contemporary, more mundane world of choice and conflict.

Certainly, all the paintings discussed in this paper derive their inspiration from the Titian/Giorgione Louvre *Pastoral Concert*; however, not one of them evokes the idyllic, rarified world of shepherds, poets, and the like, which few painters could achieve. Rather, the themes in all the paintings discussed here are more worldly, rooted in reality. And while paintings like Titian's musician series have generally been interpreted as Neoplatonic in nature with an emphasis on sight and hearing, it is the sense of touch— sensual and implied through the gaze, the playing of an instrument, the painter's brushstroke, and the viewer's imagination—that, at the very least, forms the subtext that runs through all of these paintings.

Notes

1. Walter Pater, *The Renaissance* (New York: New York University Press, 1980), 118–19.

2. Paul Barolsky, *The Faun in the Garden: Michelangelo and the Poetic Tradition in the Renaissance* (University Park, Pa.: Pennsylvania State University Press, 1994), 49.

3. Questions of attribution and iconography will not be addressed here; rather the author refers the reader to the vast literature on this painting such as: Patricia Egan, "Poesia and the *Fete Champetre*," *Art Bulletin* 41 (1959), 303–13; Patricia Emison, "The *Concert Champetre* and Gilding the Lily," *Burlington Magazine* 133 (1991), 195–96; Tamara Fomiciova, "Giorgione e la formazione della pittura di genre nell'arte Veneziana del XVI secolo," in *Giorgione: Atti del convegno internazionale di studio* (Castelfranco: Banca Popolare di Asolo e Montebelluna, 1979), 159–70; Francis Haskills," Giorgione's *Concert Champetre* and Its Admirers," in *Past and Present in Art and Taste: Selected Essays* (London: Oxford University Press, 1987), 141–52; Elhanan Motzkin, "The Meaning of Titian's *Concert Champetre* in the Louvre," *Burlington Magazine* 132 (1990), 51–65; Terisio Pignatti, *Giorgione* (Milan: Electa, 1969, 1971, 1978); and Marie Tanner, "*Ubi Sunt*: An Elegiac Topos in the *Fete Champetre*," in *Giorgione: Atti di convegno*, 61–66. This is by no means a complete bibliography on this painting.

4. There are at least eight variations in this series, four of the musicians are organists and predate the remaining four, which depict a lutenist with the reclining Venus figure. For the most current bibliography on these paintings see Rona Goffen, *Titian's Women* (New Haven and London: Yale University Press, 1997). See also: Roberta Giorgi, *Tiziano, Venere, Amore e il musicista in cinque dipinti* (Rome: Gangemi Editore, 1990), in which the author summarizes the literature on these paintings.

5. In addition to Goffen, *Titian's Women*, cited in note 4, see: David Rosand, "*Ermeneutica Amorosa:* Observation of Titian's Venuses," in *Tiziano e Venezia*, ed. Nino Pozza (Venice: Fondazione Cini, 1976), 125–31; "So and So Reclining on a Couch," in *Titian 500*, ed. Joseph Manca (Washington: National Gallery of Art, 1993), 101–15, W. G. Studdert-Kennedy, "Titian's Metaphor's of Love and Renewal," *Word and Image* 3 (1987), 27–40; Carlo Ginzburg, "Titian, Ovid and Sixteenth-Century Codes for Erotic Illustration," in *Clues, Myths and the Historical Method*, trans. John and Anne C. Tedeschi (Baltimore and London: John Hopkins University Press, 1989), 77–95; and David Summers, *The Judgement of Sense* (Cambridge: Cambridge University Press, 1987), particularly Chapter 4.

6. Goffen, *Titian's Women*, 169.

7. Ibid.

8. For those who see the Neoplatonic association improbable, see Paul Barolsky, *Infinite Jest: Wit and Humor in Italian Renaissance Art* (Columbia and London: University of Missouri Press, 1978), 165–70; Charles Hope, "Problems of Interpretation in Titian's Erotic Paintings," in *Tiziano e Venezia*, 111–24; Elise Goodman, "Petrarchism in Titian's *The Lady and the Musician*," *Storia dell'arte* 49 (1983), 179–86; and Paola Tingli, *Women in Italian Renaissance Art* (Manchester and New York: Manchester University Press, 1997), 142–44. Tingli notes that there is no evidence directly related to this series of paintings that supports the Neoplatonic/ideal of beauty reading; rather she states that the number of copies and variants suggests quite the opposite (143).

9. For specific references to Titian's Venus paintings see notes 5 and 8.

10. This is the case in all the variations and variants whether the musician is an organist or lutenist.

11. Carol M. Schuler ("The Courtesan in Art: Historical Fact or Modern Fiction," *Women's Studies* 19 [1991], 219–20) suggest that it is a modern reading and a modern male fantasy to suggests that these women are all courtesans; on the other hand, Susan Gubar ("Representing Pornography: Feminism, Criticism and Depictions of Female Violation," *Critical Inquiry* 13 (1987)) queries, "Does a genre produced primarily by

and for men necessarily demean women and alienate or exclude the female spectator/reader?" (715). Both provocative observations are pertinent to Titian's paintings. See also Richard Leppert, *Art and the Committed Eye* (Minnesota: Westview Press, 1996), Chapter 9, "The Female Nude: Surfaces of Desire," 211–16.

12. Goffen, *Titian's Women*, 28 and 166.

13. See particularly, Pietro Aretino, *Ragionamenti. Sei giornate*, ed. Romualdo Marrone (Rome: Tascabili Economici Newton, 1993).

14. H. C. Slim, "Girolamo Parabosco," in *The New Grove Dictionary of Music and Musicians*, ed. Stanley Sadie (London and New York: Norton Publishers, 1980), vol. 14, 173. Parabosco was active in the literary and musical academies in Venice. He knew Antonfrancesco Doni, Andrea Calmo, Pietro Aretino, and Titian. The suggestion that this was a portrait of the composer was first made by Molmenti and accepted by others; it is probably incorrect (Slim, 173). H. E. Wethey, *The Paintings of Titian* (London: Phaidon, 1971), vol. III, no. 50, 199, states that the organist has also been identified as Ottavio Farnese; see also Giorgi, *Tiziano*, 103–12.

15. *Catalogue of Paintings: Thirteenth—Eighteenth Century in the Picture Gallery* (Berlin: Gemaldegalerie, 1978) #1849, 447–48. For the identification as Philip II, see Erwin Panofsky, *Problems in Titian, Mostly Iconographic* (New York: New York University Press, 1969), 119–25, Wethey, *The Paintings*, vol. II, 42–43 and vol. III, 63–68, 197–99, and Giogri, *Tiziano*, 113–17.

16. Goodman, "Petrarchism," 181.

17. Ibid., 181–82.

18. Rona Goffen's book, *Titian's Women* cited in note 4, makes this an obvious point. It is amazing to consider the number and variety of women Titian painted.

19. For those who see the women in Titian's paintings as more earthly, see Charles Hope, "Problems of Interpretation," David Rosand, *"Ermeneutic Amorosa,"* and "So and So," and Paul Barolsky, *Infinite Jest.*

20. Barolsky, *Infinite Jest*, 165.

21. Ibid., 166.

22. Ibid., 167.

23. Ibid., 167.

24. For Grasso's remarks quoted here, see Ibid., 167.

25. This text is reprinted in Giuseppe Zonta, ed., *Trattati d'amore* (Bari: np, 1913), 250–302.

26. Barolsky, *Infinite Jest*, 168.

27. Ibid., 169.

28. Ibid., 170.

29. See note 12 for the complete citation of this work; see also Rona Goffen, "Introduction," *Titian's Venus of Urbino* (Cambridge: Cambridge University Press, 1998), 16.

30. Barolsky, *Faun*, 49. Titian is presumed to have been a musician and is thought to be portrayed as such in Veronese's *Marriage at Cana* in the Louvre where the artist is usually identified as the viola da gamba player. We do know that he had musical interests and that he even purchased an organ. See also Clark Hulse, *The Rule of Art: Literature and Painting in the Renaissance* (Chicago: University of Chicago Press, 1990) and Moshe Barasch, *Theories of Art: From Plato to Winkelmann* (New York and London: New York University Press, 1985).

31. Barolsky, *Faun*, 49–50. See also David Rosand, *Places of Delight: The Pastoral Landscape* (Washington, D.C.: National Gallery of Art, 1989), 30–45.

32. Pietro Bembo, *Gli Asolani*, trans. Rudolf B. Gottfried (Bloomington: Indiana University Press, 1954).

33. Augusto Gentili, *Da Tiziano a Tiziano: Mito e allegoria nella cultura veneziana del cinquecento* (Milan: Electa, 1980), 27, and "Savaldo, il ritratto e l'allelgoria musicale," in *Giovanni Gerolamo Savaldo: tra Foppa, Giorgione e Caravaggio*, eds. Bruno Passamani Elena Lucchesi-Ragni and Renata Stradiotti (Milan: Electa, 1990), 68.

34. Rodolfo Pallucchini and Francesco Rossi, *Giovanni Cariani* (Bergamo: Silvana Editoriale, 1983), 136.

35. A more likely model for Cariani's nude reclining out of doors is Giorgione's *Sleeping Venus* (c. 1510, Dresdan, Gemaldegalerie), which was well known in the period; it is generally assumed that this paiinting was adapted by Titian for his many reclining Venus figures. See Goffen, *Titian's Women* for current bibliography on this topic.
36. Pallucchini and Rossi, *Giovanni Cariani*, 136.
37. Paul Holberton, "The Pastorale or Fete Champetre in the Early Sixteenth Century," in *Titian 500*, 247.
38. Palluchini and Rossi, *Giovanni Caviani*, 136.

16

The Signifying Serpent

Seduction by Cultural Stereotype
in Seventeenth-Century England

Julia Craig-McFeely

Music has been shown to bridge many boundaries: language, culture, the natural and the supernatural, and, to some extent, also gender. In the sixteenth century professional musicians were generally considered members of the servant classes, though occasionally on a par with a baker or shoemaker. Italian Humanism saw the rise of the gentleman musician, but that cultural change only reached England much later and never to the same extent.[1] However, English musicians had found effective ways of circumventing the rigid social hierarchy by using their profession.

Most "artisan" musicians were apprenticed to family members, or simply thrust into the job because they had agile fingers. Some household servants were taught to play simply because another body was required to make up a consort. There was certainly no culture of the inborn "gift" that has pervaded Western musical thought since the nineteenth century. However, playing as a member of a noble household meant that musicians were often privy to much that was kept private from other servants, circumstances in which a musician could become a highly trusted and valued family member. Some were taught to read and write, and even entrusted with the education of the children. A skillful performer who came to the notice of a visiting dignitary could find himself gifted to a nobler household, and even end up at court. The lutenist Daniel Bacheler was one such who, from lowly beginnings apprenticed to his uncle in a minor country household, became a musician of the Queen's bedchamber, entrusted with letters between Elizabeth and Essex, and was the only royal musician known to have been granted arms.

In gentle and noble circles, musical accomplishment was considered an appropriate skill, as based on the humanist model. However, there was always a fine line between playing well enough to be considered cultured, and playing so proficiently that one could be thought vulgar. The practice of music was believed to heighten all of the senses; thus one became a more cultured and sensitive person though its practice. However, those whose skill was professional were only rarely admitted to have more gentlemanly qualities.

Music comes to mind less frequently when examining the boundary between the visual and the aural, even though musical instruments are featured prominently in a great deal of Western art. At no time had this been more true than during the sixteenth and seventeenth centuries. Especially in the modern world with its privileging of sight, we tend to consider music as *sound* dissociated from the visual and social space that it occupied, and hence overlook vital aspects of its meaning and purpose.[2] Musical notation supplies the sound, but not the context.

In England, the lute enjoyed a period of immense popularity between about 1570 and 1630, after which it declined gradually until 1700, when it had almost fallen from use completely. The lute's decline in Italy a century earlier has been linked by Victor Coelho to the rise of humanism,[3] but the impact of that philosophy in England was not so dramatic, and in particular the decline of the lute in England seems to stem more from the symbolism that had grown up around it. By the middle of the seventeenth century, it had become both an instrument of immense expressive power and a metaphor for sex.[4] Very few early-modern sources discuss this symbolism, and none directly, but images of the instrument pervade art and literature, supplying an indirect but nevertheless detailed portrait of the lute in secular life. The picture that emerges is one of increasing power—both natural and supernatural—wielded by an inanimate object, an object that progresses from being a simple emblem meaning "sex" to a living, breathing, feeling entity in its own right.

From its origins, the lute had been allegorically associated with fertility; its rounded back reminding the observer of the pregnant belly of a woman.[5] It is a short step from fertility and pregnancy to an association with sex, and in particular with women's sexuality; Thomas Coryat's *Crudities* of 1611 describes the practice of Venetian courtesans carrying the lute as a badge of their trade, and also comments that the courtesans were often independently famous for their skill as players.[6] Beginning in the sixteenth century, painters from the Low Countries had begun to employ an emblematic technique using objects inscriptively in portraits to describe the sitter and his or her attributes as vividly as if verbalized. This is a hallmark of the Dutch style that became popular throughout Europe. Dutch genre painting, with its increasingly naturalistic style, was immensely influential in England: it drew on a code of imagery that was far more geographically widespread than the Low Countries, and related to the popular, and often crudely simplistic, metaphorical interpretation of the world. What did the lute mean in this language of images? In the simplest terms, the Flemish for lute, *luit*, was also the word for vagina, explaining a host of pictures involving prostitutes. Among these are three paintings titled *The Procuress:* one from 1625 by Honthorst (1590–1656); a second from 1635 by Baburen (owned by Vermeer; see Figure 16.1); and a third from 1656 by Vermeer (1632–75).

The three *Procuress* paintings show negotiations between a procuress and a prospective client for the favors of a courtesan. In the first, all the characters are gesturing at the lute, and appear to be bargaining over *it* rather than the courtesan; the message is less explicit in the Baburen, although the lute is still very prominent. Vermeer's own *Procuress*, undeniably sexual in tone, hides the lute (in this case a cittern) but suggestively uses the position of the neck and the way it is held. Vermeer's apparently chaste *Young Lady Seated at the Virginals* (1673–75) is paradoxically accompanied not only by the phallic viol, but also by Baburen's *Procuress*, hung prominently behind her.

There are literally hundreds of paintings from the late sixteenth and early seventeenth centuries on subjects such as Van Mieris's *Brothel Scene* (1658), in which the nature of convivial tavern gatherings is defined by a lute hung on the wall or in the hands of one of the female subjects. However, the image extends beyond the genre study to allegories on themes like *The Five Senses*, in which the lute represents hearing, but transforms the whole picture to lust and vanity as the results of indulging the senses.[7]

These images are among the many in which the lute appears crudely as a sexual metaphor from the fifteenth through to the late seventeenth century. There is another and more subtle use of the lute emblem, however, one that made it not only possible but appropriate for gentlewomen to play the instrument: the lute was a vehicle for the socially acceptable expression of subtle emotions and feelings.

From classical antiquity well into the eighteenth century, music held a unique position in Western thought as the bridge between the tangible and magical worlds. The very fact that music could affect the passions solidified its association with occult phenomena and with humoral medicine. According to Aristotelian and Galenic thought and the early modern medical practices founded on them, health relied on a balance of humors, which, in turn were inexplicably affected by music. That music could affect these humors, or the passions that were linked to them, was ultimately beyond the scope of scientific medicine to explain, and gave tremendous occult power to the musician-magician who could control them. Love, the most powerful passion and the one most difficult to understand, was especially associated with music.[8]

Figure 16.1. Barburen, *The Procuress.* Courtesy, Museum of Fine Arts, Boston. Reproduced with permission. Copyright 2000 Museum of Fine Arts, Boston. All Rights Reserved.

Of all musical instruments, the lute in particular seemed capable of curing any ill, decreasing or increasing terrestrial vapors, opening or closing the heart, and generally setting aright the faculties of the soul. Why should the lute have been so spectacularly effective? The sixteenth century had seen the rise of the lute and the keyboard as two instruments that could produce a "consort of music" by themselves. Harmony dramatically increased the emotive and affective power of simple melody, and these instruments allowed a single player control of all aspects of the music, thereby intensifying its powers of communication. By the standards of European courtly poetry of the preceding century, Mary Burwell's manuscript *Lute Tutor*,[9] now known as *The Burwell Lute Tutor*, is decidedly restrained. Probably written in the late 1660s, when the lute was a long way down the slope of its decline, it is nevertheless rich in the praise of her instrument:

... we doubt not of that truth, that will help us to believe that the lute is fit to assuage the passions as choler sorrow and the pains that we suffer from distastes and hurts[,] impatience and hunger itself when the bilious humour pricketh the stomach and causeth its peevishness and displeasure.

This heavenly harmony, rising unto the brain as an intellectual dew, does moisten gently the heat and dryness of it and if there be too much moisture and terrestrial vapours it dissipates and dries them by the melodious activity that produces a subtle fire[.] So that rarifying the spirits in purging them of these fulginous vapours and fixing their extraordinary motion it followeth that this harmony set aright the faculties of the soul and perfect them.

If the heart be closed it openeth it and if it be too much opened, it gently shutteth it to embrace and keep in the sweetness that the lute inspires into its sensible concavities ... it is fed there with so favourable a nourishment that it loseth all bitterness and casts out all her venom.

This harmony softens stony hearts and banishes the cruelty from it to give room to compassion[;] it turneth out hatred to lodge in love.[10]

The lute became preeminent because it was the only instrument capable of considerable dynamic range as well as harmonic subtlety. Given its power as a communicator, it became an ideal tool for the expression of feelings and sensibilities that might otherwise be beyond the power of the player to communicate. This aspect of the lute's capabilities is explored widely in early modern European literature.

The lute was associated with sensibility and sex and also came to symbolize marriageability because emblematically it represented harmony. Theodor van Thulden's allegory, *Harmony and Marriage*, gives the lute pride of place in the hands of "harmony." It is easy to view early modern woman's life as one of silence, humility, and passivity, but it is abundantly clear that women were not only far from passive, but actively manipulated their silence to further their needs. Marriage was essential if a comfortable life was to be assured, and those whose lot was uncertain could take steps to provide themselves with a voice to inform their listeners that they could offer something more enduring than physical beauty. Mary Burwell's praise of the lute constantly returns to the ability of the instrument to express feelings, and her paean is emphatic about the importance of playing well to exploit that faculty.

Added to this are the undoubted visual enticements of a woman "stroking" her lute, physical aspects to lute-playing that Mary Burwell is quick to advance:

All the actions that one does in playing of the lute are handsome, the posture is modest free and gallant. . . . The shape of the lute . . . sets [the body] in an advantageous posture.

The beauty of the arm, of the hands and of the neck are advantageously
displayed in playing of the lute. The eyes are employed only in looking upon
the company. . . . Nothing represents so well the consort of angelical choirs
and give[s] more foretastes of heavenly joys and of everlasting happiness.
For the advantages of marriage, how many bachelors and maids have we seen
advanced by this agreeing harmony. When persons of both sexes have neither
considered wealth nor beauty of the person, but suffering themselves to be
drawn by the charms of this sweet melody.

Some hath believed that they should possess an angel incarnate, if they
could unite themselves by a marriage to a person that enjoys this rare
quality. . . . Of all the arts that I know there is none that engages more the
inclination of men than the lute. For ravishing the soul by the ear and the
eyes by the swiftness and neatness of all the fingers.[11]

This is the crux of the matter for Mary Burwell: the lute was an ideal
tool for the seduction of men. Having gained attention with your first few
notes, you then captivate with the elegance of your poise and grace of
movements—even the most graceless person appears elegant when
playing—and follow this with an assault on the sensibilities that could not
fail to move any true gentleman.

The presence of the lute as an expression of marital harmony (or
disharmony) has been discussed by Leslie Dunn in relation to Thomas
Heywood's play, *A Woman Killed with Kindness* (1603).[12] Anne Frankford,
the principal female character, is renowned as an excellent lutenist (one
whose sensibilites are finely communicated and appreciated), in itself a
rather risky level of skill to have attained. When she refers to her fall from
grace following adultery, she calls on the image of the woman with her lute,
describing her predicament thus: "We are both out of tune, both out of time"
(XVI, 19). When she is banished from her husband's house, she leaves her
lute behind, itself a symbolic act, suggesting that although finer feelings
are betrayed with the marital breakdown, she leaves the body of those
feelings within her marriage. Her husband, however, discovering the lute
"flung in a corner" declares:

> Her lute! O God, upon this instrument
> Her fingers have run quick division,
> Sweeter than that which now divides our hearts.
> These frets have made me pleasant, that have now
> Frets of my heartstrings made. (XV, 13–17)

He sends his manservant after Anne with the lute, banishing even her
memory from him and rejecting all her finer sensibilities. When the lute is
returned to its owner, Anne takes it up to play, "My lute shall groan;/It

cannot weep, but shall lament my moan," and even the rude servants are moved to pity and compassion by her playing. However, having played her swansong, she bids the servant break the lute against the wheel of the coach, effectively silencing her feelings forever, and destroying the cause of her infidelity. The lute becomes the receptacle for Anne's wrongdoing, and is blamed for her actions, relieving Anne of that responsibility. The breaking of the lute is closely followed by Anne's death, presumably from a broken heart, reinforcing the nature of the bond.

In France, Louise Labé, a Lyonnais poet writing around the year 1555, uses the lute metaphorically in several of her sonnets, always inspired by the absence of a lover.[13] The content of Labé's poetry is unashamedly erotic. She was a lady, not a courtesan, but she is not discussing chaste, appropriate love within marriage: she is eulogizing lust and the power of sex. However, there is more to Labé's imagery than this. By 1550, the image of the lute in France and Italy had progressed further. In her Sonnet XII, she endows the lute with an anthropomorphic existence: not only does it express the subject's feelings, being transformed by the writer's mood, but it also fulfills the role of both a compassionate friend and a protagonist in the argument.

Sonnet XII

Lut, compagnon de ma calamité,	Lute, my companion in adversity,
De mes soupirs témoin irreprochable,	Blameless witness of my sighs,
De mes ennuis controlleur véritable,	Moderator of my troubles,
Tu as souvent avec moy lamenté:	How often have you lamented with me:
Et tant le pleur piteus t'a molesté,	My piteous tears have vexed you so much,
Que commençant quelque son délectable,	That starting some delightful air,
Tu le rendois tout soudein lamentable,	You changed your tone at once to a lament,
Feignant le ton que plein avoit chanté.	As though it were a plaint you had begun.
Et si te veus efforcer au contraire,	And if I force you to a different vein,
Tu te destens et si me contreins taire:	Your strings relax, force me to be silent;
Mais me voyant tendrement soupirer,	But seeing that I sigh so tenderly,
Donnant faveur à ma tant triste pleinte:	Giving preference to my sad lament;
En mes ennuis me plaire suis contreinte	I am forced to find my pleasure in grief,
Et d'un dous mal douce fin espérer.	And hope for sweet endings to so sweet a pain.

Labé endows the lute with the power to make decisions, to offer comfort in its own right as well as to act as a vehicle for the expression of the players' anguish. In her works, the lute is always melancholy and an outlet for pent emotion. For her, the lute represents and expresses the inexpressible: the passions and sensibilities. In Sonnet XII, she uses the idea of singing to the lute to express the conflict between expression of the private and internal (the lute) and the public externalized convention verbally or vocally expressed (singing).

The lute is divorced from the body but is able to express the body's inner conflicts, while the voice as an instrument betrays the emotions by refusing to perform under stress. The distance of the lute from the lover enables it to express passion freely. In Labé's Sonnet XII, the lute refuses to play when asked to express false emotions: thus forcing the lover to be silent rather than lie. In contrast, Sonnet II progresses through physical and emotional description of the loved one, until finally his lute is introduced in the same breath as a whole host of body parts. Labé blames the lover's lute just as much as his looks and moods for her state, while, significantly, as the lute player, he remains unmoved.

SONNET II

Ô beaus yeus bruns, ô regars destournez,	O beautiful brown eyes, O averted looks,
Ô chaus soupirs, ô larmes espandues,	O warm sighs, O spilt tears,
Ô noires nuits vainement atendues,	O blackest nights for which I vainly wait,
Ô jours luisans vainement retournez:	O shining days that vainly return.
Ô tristes pleins, ô desirs obstinez,	O sad laments, O persistent desires,
Ô tems perdu, ô peines despendues,	O time that's lost, O cares I have suffered,
Ô mile morts en mile rets tendues,	O thousand deaths in a thousand snares,
Ô pires maus contre moi destinez.	O worse ills destined to be against me.
Ô ris, ô front, cheveux, bras, mains et doits:	O smile, O brow, hair, arms, hands and fingers,
Ô lut pleintif, viole, archet et vois:	O plaintive lute, viol, bow, and voice:
Tant de flambeaus pour ardre une femmelle!	So many torches, one woman to enflame!
De toy me plein, que tant de feus portant,	I complain of you that, carrying so many fires,
En tant d'endrois d'iceus mon cœur tatant,	And touching my heart in so many places with them;
N'en est sur toy volé quelque estincelle.	Not one spark of them has flown onto you.

Labé also refers to the tuning of the lute, although in terms that involve playing in minor keys when she would rather be trying to cheer herself with a major tonality. The lute is thus truthful in its expression of the player's feelings, unable to take part in any artificiality. The corollary is that the truth of a lover's feelings can only be heard if he (or she) plays the lute because words alone are untrustworthy, and even singing can falsify expression.

The English poet Thomas Wyatt (1503–42) had been using this sort of imagery for the lute nearly a quarter of a century before Labé. It appears in a number of his courtly poems (such as "My lute awake," "Blame not my lute," "Since you will needs," and "All heavy minds"). "Blame not my lute" in particular anticipates Labé's problem of the lute betraying feelings that the player would rather remain hidden. It is a complex exploration of the instrument that begins with a statement that the lute lacks the wit to express anything other than that which it is told to, and so what it speaks of must come from the poet's heart. Wyatt is denying the independent will of the instrument, but not its power to express his torment, and constructs the lute as a figure for the poet himself.

BLAME NOT MY LUTE

Blame not my lute for he must sound
   Of these or that as liketh me;
For lack of wit the lute is bound
   To give such tunes as pleaseth me:
Though my songs be somewhat strange,
And speaks such words as touch thy change,
    Blame not my lute.

My lute, alas, doth not offend,
   Though that perforce he must agree
To sound such tunes as I intend
   To sing to thee that hearest me;
Then though my songs be somewhat plain,
And toucheth some that use to feign,
    Blame not my lute.

My lute and strings may not deny,
   But as I strike they must obey;
Break not them then so wrongfully,
   But wreck thy self some wiser way:
And though the songs which I indite
Do quit thy change with rightful spite,
    Blame not my lute.

Spite asketh spite and changing change,
   And falsèd faith must needs be known;
Thy fault so great, the case so strange,
   O right it must abroad be blown:
Then since that by thine own desert
My songs do tell how true thou art,
    Blame not my lute.

Blame but the self that hast misdone
    And well deservèd to have blame;
Change thou thy way, so evil begun,
    And then my lute shall sound the same:
But if till then my fingers play
By thy desert their wonted way,
      Blame not my lute.

Farewell, unknown, for though thou break
    My strings in spite with great disdain,
Yet have I found out for thy sake
    Strings for to string my lute again;
And if perchance this foolish Rhyme
Do make thee blush at any time
      Blame not my lute.[14]

Just as the lute was the symbol of feelings and inner sensibilities, so the lute-case symbolized the outward appearance or superficial presentation of emotions. This is famously evident in Holbein's *Ambassadors*, in which the open lute-case refers to the willingness of the ambassadors to treat the English monarch honestly and openly. The lute is prominently displayed while the lute case is hidden beneath the table, reinforcing the message that the ambassadors' intent is one of open and honest discourse, having set aside their superficial ambassadorial rhetoric. In *Much Ado about Nothing* (II: i) Shakespeare employs the lute and its case to symbolize the conflict between the inner person and the public image, as is the case with Labé, Wyatt, and Holbein:

> ACT II, SCENE i: A hall in LEONATO'S house.
> . . . .
> {Enter Leonato, Antonio, Hero, Beatrice, and others.}
> {Enter Don Pedro, Claudio, Benedick, Balthasar,
> Don John, Borachio, Margaret, Ursula and others, masked.}
> DON PEDRO: Lady, will you walk about with your friend?
> HERO: So you walk softly and look sweetly and say nothing,
>   I am yours for the walk; and especially when I walk away.
> DON PEDRO: With me in your company?
> HERO: I may say so, when I please.
> DON PEDRO: And when please you to say so?
> HERO: When I like your favour; for God defend the LUTE should
>   be like the case!

Shakespeare's many references to music are usually independent of those that he makes specifically to the lute, in which he refers to the capabilities of the instrument to alter mood or arouse passion. There are definite signs, however, that this power was dangerous, and even frightening because its effects were too profound to be natural. In *Richard III* (I: i, 1–13), the King is seduced by a lady playing a lute (he "capers nimbly in a lady's chamber / To the lascivious pleasing of a lute")—although, as we have seen, this may simply be a metaphor for sex. The implication, however, is that the playing ensnares and bewitches him more than the lady herself: he is literally dancing to her tune. The sexually manipulative interpretation is a direct descendant of the teaching of the Church that women were evil and dangerous, that they could ensnare men and force them to perform sinful acts against their will. In *Titus Andronicus* (II: iv, 38–51) the lute tames the beast before bewitching the man to love the player, particularly if "she" also sings, while in *Pericles, Prince of Tyre* (IV, 1–33) nature itself is silenced by the lady's playing. Here, there is also the suggestion of pain in hearing her play, as she pierces to the heart.

> GOWER: . . . Be't when she weaved the sleided silk
> With fingers long, small, white as milk;
> Or when she would with sharp needle wound
> The cambric, which she made more sound
> By hurting it; or when to the Lute
> She sung, and made the night-bird mute,
> That still records with moan; or when
> She would with rich and constant pen
> Vail to her mistress Dian; still
> This Philoten contends in skill
> With absolute Marina. . . .

This dangerous image of the lute did not disappear as the century progressed, and is still present in works like the frontispiece of Adrianus Poirter's *Lady World* (1670), an allegorical depiction of women's deceit and manipulation of the physical world in which the lute is the dominant symbol.

A subtler message is conveyed in *The Taming of the Shrew* (II: i, 56–163). Hortensio enters disguised as a music teacher bearing a lute. His encounter with Katherine is disastrous: Katherine breaks the lute over his head, thus breaking the symbol of love, lovers, and finer feelings over the disguised suitor's seat of reason. This is an image that must have had a multiple impact for those watching. Hortensio chose the lute because of its associations with love and marriage, and the unavoidable conclusion arising from Katherine's actions is that his suit is rejected—before he has even had a chance to offer it. Katherine's willful nature was known, so Hortensio made a serious mistake in trying to insinuate himself by *teaching* her the lute ("I did but tell her she mistook her frets," 150). In so doing, he was telling her how and what to *feel* because the lute is the window to the heart. He fails because he is trying to manipulate her emotions instead of expressing his own, or even just attending to her feelings. He should have heeded the advice given in *Two Gentlemen of Verona* (III: ii, 73–88). Proteus refers to Orpheus's lute, which could melt hard hearts and tame wildness, making the vicious gentle. It can be employed therefore to turn the heart of a woman to look well upon a man, which is what Hortensio had hoped to achieve by teaching it. He should simply have played to her.

Mary Burwell's discussion of the magical and affective properties of the instrument recall the lost golden age of the lute and expound its qualities with an almost desperate intensity. Her terminology and subject matter show an attitude toward the instrument that was evident in earlier literature, and is clearly still immediate for her. She describes it as:

> ... the king of instruments. It maketh alone a consort of music[,] it speaks without any origin and out of dead and dumb things it draws a soul that seems reasonable by the several thoughts and expression that the skilful master makes of his lute upon all kinds of matters and subjects. It is a faithful & commodious companion that watcheth amidst darkness[,] and when the whole nature is in silence it banisheth from it horror and unquietness by pleasing sounds.[15]

The naive symbolism of her lute as a noble companion, endowed with an emotional life of its own, pervades Mary Burwell's language. It is always gendered as male, often praised as a Prince or King and at times seems to hold the importance of a lover in her life.[16]

Clearly, the lute has a special association with and for women in England, but there is undoubtedly a paradox between the lute as a symbol of the lascivious and of venal love, and the lute in its far subtler guise of a vehicle for the expression of higher sensibilities. How was it that the hard-worked image of the lute as the badge of the courtesan could coexist with its nobler counterpart?

The key must surely lie in the play of the two senses: the visual and the aural. In visual terms, we have the venal images of the genre paintings. Even Mary Burwell can see that the lute serves as a mold around which a woman can drape her physical, sexual attractions. On the more esoteric plane of the aural, the ability of sound to penetrate within and affect the humors allows it to express something more delicate, but the paradox is still there. The reference to the lute in Richard III (he "capers nimbly in a lady's chamber / To the lascivious pleasing of a lute") refers more to the visual and physical aspect of playing than to the aural side.

This paradox is apparent in Jan Steen's *The Morning Toilet* (1663; see Figure 16.2). At first glance, this is a simple comment on venal love: the

Figure 16.2. Jan Sten. *The Morning Toilet*. Copyright The Royal Collection, Her Majesty Queen Elizabeth II.

still life of the arch showing conventional symbols of vanity introduces the moral content, but the erotic matter is defined both by the emblems and in reference to linguistic usage. The woman's state of undress and the setting of a bedchamber is added to the carelessly abandoned lute, implying both a recent sexual encounter and venal love; while the shoes, usually a symbol of domestic harmony, are kicked awry, implying adultery. The woman is conspicuously pulling on a stocking: the Dutch word (*kous*) was slang for vagina. The unlighted candle usually referred to ephemerality, but in this case it accompanies an open jewel box on the side table, which is probably referring to a popular saying: "Neither does one buy pearls in the dark, nor does one look for love at night." The lute is in the foreground, but its message is qualified as it is accompanied by a book of music—a visual representation of the *sound* of the instrument—and a rarity in this context. The notated music adds a further layer to the tale. The lute signals the woman's profession, but the music implies that she not only employed her physical attributes to entice her lover to her bed, but also the mystical and manipulative powers of the instrument, perhaps giving the absent male protagonist an excuse for his infidelity. That conflict between the erotic and the delicate must have confused and inflamed generations of suitors and contributed to the downfall of the instrument in modern time. Playing the lute was analogous to playing ball with a live grenade.

The richness and power of lute emblems rendered the instrument a volatile symbol for the private and supposedly chaste player, but one with enormous power.[17] Given its charms, it is surprising that not more women played it despite its dangerous nature. Looking at the age of the women who took up the lute, apparently to snare a husband, it may easily have been a weapon of last resort for the girl who was in danger of spinsterhood.

Mary Burwell is too coy when she tells us that any man beholding a woman playing the lute will be instantly captivated by the grace of her body and hands. The message conveyed, even privately, must have been an unmistakable promise of passion, deliberately reinforced by the emotive affect of the music being played. To play the lute to a potential suitor was many things: a form of self-expression, a semi-magical exercise of power, and a deliberate and outspoken erotic invitation. In other words, a woman playing a lute is promising sex. Add to this Mary Burwell's assertion of the elegance of the body and the simple beauty of the sound; if you remained unmoved you were coarse, if you were moved you were lost. Many men clearly took up the invitation (seen by some as entrapment through emotional manipulation). The ladies, however, abandoned the lute once they were married and had achieved their goal, perhaps because continuing to play could be a cause for infidelity; Anne Frankford's troubles began when she played her lute to guests at her wedding.

There is something unexpected in such consciously manipulative behavior of an overtly sexual nature. Why should this be surprising? Our experience of early modern poetry and the madrigal should lead us to expect an open attitude to eroticism. That this is being expressed by women is no more surprising than that it is being expressed at all. Women were clearly far from passive or impotent in expressing both their feelings and their desires. The lute performed the specific social function in this context of advertising their willingness to have sex, and therefore bear children: it was worn as a badge of fertility.

Throughout the sixteenth and seventeenth centuries, society was increasingly coming to recognize the worth of a woman who could provide intelligent conversation as well as heirs, and perform useful functions in the household.[18] How, then, could a woman demonstrate that she possessed higher sensibilities and emotions in an environment where it would have been immodest to take any lead in these matters? The answer lay in the lute, and as women's exploitation of the corpus of expressive and emotive music grew, so also did their ability to communicate their feelings in an appropriate and acceptable way. A woman could attract attention to herself by surrounding herself with silence while she played, and into that silence she could "speak" volumes.

Playing the lute was recognized as one of the great accomplishments of the young lady, and many seventeenth-century noblewomen were painted in close association with their instruments.[19] According to Aubrey's memoir of him, old Dr. Kettle, the President of Balliol College, was utterly captivated by Lady Isabella Rich who wandered about Balliol gardens twangling in full view of the desiccated dons (see Figure 16.3).[20] She was renowned for her skill at the lute and her portrait reeks of seductive desirability. Edmund Waller's poem about her betrays another helplessly enraptured listener. He also recognizes the power and danger of the woman playing the lute. His picture of Lady Isabella is of a Siren, and among his images of power and danger listeners become no more than animals:

OF MY LADY ISABELLA PLAYING ON THE LUTE

Such moving sounds, from such a careless touch!
So un-concern'd her self, and we so much!
What art is this, that with so little pains
Transports us thus, and o'er our spirits reigns?
The trembling strings about her fingers crowd,
And tell their joy for ev'ry kiss aloud:
Small force there needs to make them tremble so:
Touched by that hand, who would not tremble too?
Here Love takes stand, and while she charms the ear,
Empties his quiver on the list'ning deer:
Music so softens, and disarms, the mind,
That not an arrow does resistance find.
Thus the fair tyrant celebrates the prize,
And acts herself the triumph of her eyes:
So Nero once, with harp in hand, survey'd
His flaming Rome, and as it burn'd he play'd.[21]

Figure 16.3. Dirk van Baburen, *Lady Isabella Rich*. Reproduced by permission of the Marquis of Bath, Longleat House, Warminster, Wiltshire, Great Britain.

Lady Mary Wroth (niece of Sir Philip Sidney) was celebrated for her intelligence and subtlety. She was known among her contemporaries as a poetess, but is depicted in her portrait with a more powerful instrument than the pen. Nor is the archlute leaning negligently to one side, or turned coyly away from the viewer as in the naturalistic view of Lady Isabella. Lady Mary's lute is as prominently posed as she is herself, and undoubtedly significant. Its presence tells us that this is a woman of great sensibility and expressive emotional power, just as clearly as her clothing and stance advertise her station, confidence, and nobility. Lady Anne Clifford similarly poses with her lute, holding it like a lance, troping one of Hilliard's miniatures of a nobleman. This is a public recognition of the symbolic role of the lute that is just as direct as Mary Burwell's text or Labé's sonnets. None of these depictions are of ladies *playing* the lute, but all are portraits that feature the lute prominently as a symbol of the personality, sexuality, sensitivity, and *power* of the subject. Clearly, the emphasis of the message depends on whether the lute is being played or is only a prop, which explains why portraits of noblewomen rarely, if ever, show them in the act of playing the instrument, although Lady Isabella's pose is highly suggestive even so.[21]

Although the two stereotypes seem to be clearly defined (the visual lute as a metaphor for sex and sensuality or the aural lute as a metonymic substitution for the expression of complex feelings that could not be adequately or appropriately verbalized), these stereotypes merge seamlessly in many situations. The basic erotically charged image overlaps with the artful manipulation and expression of emotions seen in Labé's poetry and pictures such as *Lady World*, created over a century apart.

That stereotype of female manipulation and sexuality was hardly new, nor was the idea of a woman's power unusual: what is surprising is that such a charged and complex image should have survived so long attached to the lute. The steady rationalization of the early modern world tried to devolve magical influence from persons to objects, so within a framework of humanistic rejection of superstition it would be natural to try to divorce supernatural control from a person and instead look to some external mechanism for explanation.

The keyboard lacked emotive strength, had no overt sexual imagery, playing technique resulted in a virtually motionless stance, and also required the player to turn modestly away while performing. Its ascendancy during the seventeenth century may have been due in large part to its safety as a symbol and its inability to sway the emotions. It was increasingly found in images like Vermeer's *Young Lady Standing at the Virginals* (1673–75), where Cupid holding the single playing card of fidelity dominates the scene both spatially and symmetrically. The lute was already set up as a scapegoat for the "dangerous" woman by the sixteenth century. By the middle of the seventeenth, because magic was still the only explanation for many events, the metaphorical transfer of power was so complete that the lute had become invested with a life of its own. The logical outcome of that progression was that the lute should decline in popularity and eventually become obsolete, its place in domestic life being taken by the keyboard.

Notes

1. See Penelope Gouk, *Music, Science, and Natural Magic in Seventeenth-Century England* (New Haven and London: Yale University Press, 1999), 24–28.
2. Richard Leppert has begun to remedy this lack by suggesting some of the many ways in which painting suggests the culturally determined meaning and purpose of music; see *The Sight of Sound: Music, Representation, and the History of the Body* (Berkeley and Los Angeles: University of California Press, 1993), 1–14.
3. Victor Coelho: '*L'ultima parte:* Some Perspectives on the Decline of the Lute in Seventeenth-Century Italy' in *Music and Science in the Age of Galileo* (London, 1992)
4. See, for example, the material given in Linda Phyllis Austern, "The Siren, the Muse, and the God of Love: Music and Gender in Seventeenth-Century English Emblem Books," *Journal of Musicological Research* 18 (1999), 113–15.
5. Francesco del Cossa in the detail of *April* (1465), shows the triumph of Venus, where the lute is held pendant before the womb. In Baldung's *Ages of Womankind* (1540), the lute signals the fertile part of the woman's life [See also *The Four Ages of Man* (1625), Moise Valentin (1591/4–1632)] and Valentin's *Four Ages of Man which* conveys a similar message, where the lute symbolizes the age of love and sexual dalliance.
6. Thomas Coryat, *Coryat's Crudities* (London, 1611), 267.
7. In Metsu's *Tête-à-tête: Lady Lute Player and Cavalier* (1655), even the pretense of playing the instrument is abandoned, and it lies suggestively in the lap of the player. Although scenes in which *men* play the lute publicly are more ambiguous, the lute could hold sway in the hands of either sex. There are often pointers to the intent of the characters, such as can be seen in Vermeer's *Concert* (1665–66), where the viol and Baburen's *Procuress* are again in evidence. There are less obvious images that nevertheless draw on the genre tradition to reinforce ideas stated in the title of the work. Isaac Oliver's Love theme, *Allegory of Virtuous and Vicious Love* (c1595), places the lute among the "vicious" and unchaste participants; Buytewech's *Tavern Scene* (1617–20) implies something of the conversation of the men without actually giving a lute to the man whose hands are held as if playing, while Steen's *Life of Man* (1665) employs a wealth of devices to depict man's lust and vanity, including the suggestion that the old woman with the fiddle is a procuress because she is holding it sideways as if it is a lute.
8. See Linda Phyllis Austern, " 'For, Love's a Good Musician': Performance, Audition, and Erotic Disorders in Early Modern Europe," *Musical Quarterly* 82 (1998), 614–53; Peregrine Horden, ed., *Music as Medicine: The History of Music Therapy since Antiquity* (Aldershot: Ashgate, 2000), 147–248; and Gary Tomlinson, *Music in Renaissance Magic: Toward a Historiography of Others* (Chicago: University of Chicago Press, 1993), 173–77.
9. In the private collection of Robert Spencer, Woodford Green, Essex, England; also available in facsimile as *The Burwell Lute Tutor*, introduction by Robert Spencer (Leeds: Boethius Press, 1974). There is some question as to its date of compilation and its original owner; Spencer cites evidence that it may have belonged to Mary's mother, Elizabeth Burwell (1613–78), rather than to Mary, as I believe it did. Mary was born in 1654 and married in 1672; see Spencer, Introduction to *The Burwell Lute Tutor*, p. 1.

10. *The Burwell Lute Tutor* (1668–71), ff. 43–43v. Spelling, punctuation, and capitalization are standardized. Commas are only added to the original text where essential, as their placement can alter the intended meaning. Those that have been added are enclosed in square brackets to differentiate from original punctuation.

11. *The Burwell Lute Tutor* (1668–71), ff.43v-45.

12. I am indebted to Leslie Dunn for bringing this source to my attention, and for her discussion of it at a seminar of the Shakespeare Association of America, Chicago, March 25, 1995.

13. Labé's dialogue with her lute is discussed in Line Pouchard, "Louise Labé in Dialogue with Her Lute: Silence Constructs a Poetic Subject," *History of European Ideas* 792 (1993), 126, where the author constructs an entirely phallic and erotic framework for the poetry. This seems a rather narrow view, given the wealth of imagery that Labé is using. Her poetry is taken from Enzo Giudici, ed.: *Ôeuvres Completes de Louise Labé* (Geneva: Droz, 1981). English translations are available in versified form in Edith Farrell, *Louise Labé's Complete Works* (Troy, N.Y.: Whitson Publishing, 1986), those used in this paper were made by Louise Locock.

14. E.M.W. Tillyard, ed., *The Poetry of Sir Thomas Wyatt* (London: The Scholar Press, 1929), 101–2.

15. *The Burwell Lute Tutor*, f.43.

16. "As the lute is the king of instruments so hath it few things that are common with other instruments. Its music and its manner of composing is special to itself[,] and as the human body[,] is like a little microcosm that gathereth and comprehends in itself all that is[,] and all that is fine and rare in music." *The Burwell Lute Tutor* (1668–71), f.68v.

17. For further information about the English paradox of female chastity and erotic musical power, see Linda Phyllis Austern, "'Sing Again Siren': The Female Musician and Sexual Enchantment in Elizabethan Life and Literature," *Renaissance Quarterly* 42 (1989), 420–48.

18. Castiglione's *Book of the Courtyer* states that women are only useful for child-bearing: "the world hath no profit by women, but for getting children". This attitude and the other ideas of the worthlessness of women unless they could bear children is discussed by Nanette Salomon in "Positioning Women in Visual Convention: The Case of Elizabeth I," *Attending to Women in Early Modern England*, eds. Betty S. Travitsky and Adele F. Seeff (Cranbury, N.J., 1994).

19. The Countess of Pembroke, Lady Anne Clifford, and Lady Margaret Hoby are also depicted with a lute.

20. Daughter of the Earl of Holland, born 1623, who married Sir James Thynne some time in the late 1630s. Aubrey states that "Our Grove was the Daphne for the Ladies and their gallants to walke in, and many times my Lady Isabella Thynne (who lay at Balliol College) would make her entry with a Theorbo or Lute played before her. I have heard her play on it in the Grove myself, which she did rarely [i.e., unusually well]; for which Mr. Edmund Waller hath in his Poems for ever made her famous." Quoted from Oliver Lawson Dick, ed., *Aubrey's Brief Lives* (London, 1949), 186.

21. *The Works of Edmund Waller . . . published by Mr. Fenton* (London, 1729), 105–6.

22. Hilliard painted Elizabeth I in the act of playing the lute, but the queen was outside social norms when it came to her accomplishments and representations: Elizabeth I was an overtly manipulative ruler, and Hilliard's miniature merely comments on her use of her womanly virtues as part of her arsenal.

Noise and Science

17

Musicology and the Problem
of Sonic Abuse

Jamie C. Kassler

Thirty years ago a Canadian composer and music educator by the name of
R. Murray Schafer began publishing a series of pamphlets with the titles
Ear Cleaning (1967), *The New Soundscape* (1968), *The Book of Noise* (1970),
and *The Music of the Environment* (1973). Then, in *The Tuning of the World*,
he argued for the establishment of two new studies: acoustic ecology and
acoustic design.[1] Acoustic ecology would focus on the relations of living
organisms, particularly humans, to their sonic surroundings, sonic habits,
and sonic modes of life; acoustic design would formulate soundscape
policy through the interdisciplinary efforts of artists, scientists, and
environmentalists. These studies, however, were conceived as instruments
for Schafer's main project: to eliminate the corrupt present-day soundscape
by recovering positive silence as a precondition of all creative human life.

In the same year that Schafer's book appeared, a French economist,
Jacques Attali, published his book *Noise*, in which he called for a new
historiography that would anticipate future developments.[2] Believing that
music exemplifies the prophetic role required of a new historiography, Attali
undertook an ideological criticism based on the idea that the relationship
between noise and order in a single piece or in a collection of music reveals
how the society that produced this music channels violence. His critique,
therefore, was conceived not merely as an instrument for producing a new
historiography but also for achieving his main project: to eliminate the
corrupt present-day form of social organization (order) by recovering noise
(disorder) as a precondition for all creative human life.

Despite the difference in subject matter and argumentation, both authors
sought to return to some imagined prior state as a precondition for their

utopian aim of transforming the world into an artform. For Schafer, that artform would result from soundscape studies, whereas for Attali, it would result from historiography. In this short essay, I eschew utopias and ideological projects. Instead, I will focus on a problem that Schafer recognized but that Attali ignored. This is the problem of sonic abuse, a term I define as the abuse people suffer either voluntarily through self-inflicted noise or involuntarily from noise imposed by others.[3]

Noise versus "Noise"

The meaning of the term "noise" has changed over time, as the reader may discover by consulting Volume 7 of *The Oxford English Dictionary*, where only one entry is currently in use: noise as a loud or harsh sound of any kind. Other entries are either rare or obsolete: for example, noise as the attainment of notoriety, an outcry, a rumor, a company of musicians. In the eighteenth century the lexicographer Samuel Johnson classed all these different meanings into one general definition: noise is "Any kind of sound,"[4] a definition that has been repeated many times.[5] From the second half of the nineteenth century, some investigators sought to give a more precise definition of noise within the field of so-called tone psychology. These attempts were reviewed by Edwin G. Boring,[6] who identified two problems confronting the older tone psychologists: (1) Does the continuity from an indefinite pitch of noise to a definite pitch of tone mean that the noise and the tone belong to the same class; and (2) Are there different sense organs for noise and tone? Answers to these questions were given by a number of different investigators.

In 1863, for example, Hermann von Helmholtz thought that aperiodic wave-forms gave rise to noise and periodic ones gave rise to tone; hence, there were two different acoustic end-organs, one for noise and one for tone. But in 1875 an experiment showed that when the speed of a sound producer increases, tone begins to come in before noise completely disappears. As a result, Helmholtz concluded that noise, like tone, is mediated by only one end-organ, the cochlea; and he stressed that aperiodic vibrations of noise are more or less indeterminate in pitch, whereas the periodic ones, no matter how complex, are determinate. But in 1890 Carl Stumpf, relying on introspection, argued that noise is not pitch even though one of the two may enter into a perception as the other passes out, and that their perceptual disparity indicates the existence of separate acoustic end-organs. In 1913, E. R. Jaensch developed this notion into a "duplicity" theory of hearing: periodic vibration excites the cochlea and gives tone; aperiodic vibration excites some other organ, perhaps in the vestibule of the ear, and gives rise to noise; and intermediate sounds excite both organs in varying degrees.

With the work of Georg von Békésy the duplicity theory disappeared because there was no physiological evidence for it.[7] But the physical problem remained: how to define noise. In 1928, for example, Harvey Fletcher, the first president of the Acoustical Society of America, defined noise as "sound with no definite pitch,"[8] whereas Boring himself believed the opposite: "that a noise is a complex fusion of tones, often brief or rapidly varying, with the indefiniteness of its pitch depending upon the range, equivocality, and brevity of the determinant frequencies."[9] About the same time, a more fruitful definition of noise began to emerge with the work of telephone engineers who found that the presence of other sounds interfered with telephone reception. But one telephone engineer, Claude E. Shannon, developed a precise theory by giving the terms "information" and "noise" a technical meaning: information was defined as a measure of the decrease in uncertainty; noise was any random interference in information, not merely a crackle on the telephone line.[10] Unlike the older approach that attempted to define tone or noise in isolation, an information-theoretic approach attempts to understand how signals can mask more regular patterns that convey information.[11] From that time, noise took on its modern definition as unwanted background signals, whether in acoustics, electricity, radio, or optics.

When the background signals are sonic events, noise means unwanted sound. But even when this modern definition is utilized, the assumption, often tacit, is that the unwanted sounds are loud sounds. In a recent dictionary of physics, for example, we find the following definition:

> **noise 1.** (general) Sound that is undesired by the recipient, usually a discordant sound such as that produced by a low overflying aircraft or a pneumatic drill. The loudness of a noise is expressed in decibels or phons and is measured with an audiometer or noise-level meter.[12]

This definition of noise as "undesired sound" brings out the physical aspect denoted by "sound," as well as the subjective aspect (the reaction of the hearer) denoted by "undesired." But the assumption that noise also is a loud sound seems to have determined the focus of early investigations, where most attention was paid to the recording of noise levels and to the materials that might absorb noise or keep it from various locations (residences, concert halls, etc.). In the 1950s, investigators began to take new directions with studies into the sources of noise, paths followed by noise, noise reduction at the source, noise reduction along the path of the sound, and noise reduction at the ear.[13] Most importantly for our problem, in the 1960s we find the first attempts to understand, quantitatively, the effect of noise on living creatures.[14]

Noise Effects as Harmful

Initially, most studies of the effects of noise were concerned with risks to hearing from occupational activities. It has been known for some time that professional musicians, including piano tuners, sustain hearing damage at roughly twice the rate of the rest of the community. Studies of hearing risks from recreational activities have been relatively recent, even though some twenty-eight years ago the composer Otto Luening warned that "unless the general level of rock and roll is reduced, we will have a generation with a severely damaged hearing capacity."[15] Luening's warning was not heeded: audiologists and other hearing researchers now report that some 78 percent of men and some 25 percent of women will suffer hearing damage by the 2010s, much of it self-inflicted through loud sonic events via radio, CD-player headphones, rock concerts, discos, and the like.[16] Nevertheless, the organizers of a recent "scientific" colloquium, "Noise: Musical Language, and Technological Innovation," tell us that:

> noise is understood nowadays to be a complicated phenomenon whose analysis allows us to approach the complexity of our perception. Noise can be seen as a state of constant interaction between languages. It can also be viewed as a preliminary condition of compositional inspiration, within which the activity of choosing and allowing expressive paths to emerge becomes the deterministic order upon which the rules of musical composition rest.[17]

The colloquium organizers seem totally unaware of the statistics concerning damage to hearing, even though Luening had already spelled out the implications when he queried: "What is the use of writing certain kinds of music, if people have become so deaf that they cannot hear them?"[18]

Loudness, however, is not the only factor involved in hearing loss because all senses tend to become less responsive to stimuli after a particular duration of stimulation. In 1928, this phenomenon was studied by the neuro-physiologist Edgar D. Adrian, who used the term "adaptation" to describe the gradual settling down of neural activity as the stimulus of the end-organ is continued.[19] But if a sense organ is stimulated excessively, the period of rest required before the maximum sensitivity can be achieved becomes prolonged, so that the sense organ is fatigued. In the case of hearing, fatigue denotes reduced sensitivity, either temporary or permanent, which also may be accompanied by other effects (e.g., tinnitus, headache, and tiredness). In short, two types of stimuli produce auditory fatigue: sonic events that are impulsive at high dynamic levels, and sonic events that are steady-state in nature regardless of dynamic levels.[20] With the first type of stimuli, the reduced sensitivity is due to loudness levels, but with the second type, it is due to time of exposure. In the 1950s and '60s, an interest in learning the safe limits of auditory exposure and in discovering how the ear operates at various levels of stimulation led to the investigation of the effects of these and other types of sensitivity-reducing stimuli on auditory function. The main aim was to determine quantitatively the point at which stimulation exceeds critical limits.[21]

For the cochlea (the acoustic end-organ), the critical limits are elastic limits of the tissues, especially the two sets of hair cells in the so-called organ of Corti.[22] One set, the outer hair cells, amplifies low intensity sounds, whereas the other set, the inner hair cells, analyses frequencies, splitting one signal that spreads across several frequencies into a number of discrete signals of varying strengths at individual frequencies. Because of its tapering, spiral form, different points along the cochlea resonate at different frequencies. When a complex sound wave enters the ear, the inner hair cells in places that are resonating convert the mechanical resonance to an electrical impulse, which in turn triggers the nerve leading to the brain. It seems that the stiffness of the hair cells increases toward the basal end of the cochlea, where elastic limits become more and more restricted.[23] Hence, these stiffer portions are more subject to permanent damage from excessive stimulation either from exposure to a continuous stretching force (steady-state stimuli) or to an intermittent but intense stretching force (high-intensity impulse stimuli).[24]

Although the ear itself is structured to minimize damage from loud sounds, modern electronics introduces a new factor in the history of humankind. It makes readily available the technology for reproducing steady-state and high-intensity impulse stimuli, thus increasing the risks to hearing not only of individuals but of large groups of people. If, from the irresponsible use of electronic (or other) technology, hearing sensitivity is reduced at birth or in infancy, a child will have developmental difficulties that result in speech and other behavioral deficits. If reduced sensitivity occurs in adolescence or in adulthood, the listener will no longer perceive some of the sonic clues previously used, so that judgments will be based on a set of imperfect clues and distorted auditory patterns. Of course, reduced sensitivity is not just a loss of sensation. It also is a loss of the ability to select what one wishes to listen to, as well as a loss of facility in communicating and, hence, in maintaining relationships with others. For the professional musician, deficits in receptive and expressive function will terminate, involuntarily, a life in music; and this may lead to depression severe enough to undermine the will to live.[25]

Noise Effects as Annoying

Reduced auditory function is not the only deficit due to the two types of sonic stimuli already described. Other bodily functions are affected, including the general electrical conductivity of tissues, the action of certain reflexes, and the sense of vibration (touch).[26] When there is an invasion of the private spaces in which individuals and groups pursue a range of day-to-day activities, other effects take place that reflect the derivation of the term "noise" from the Latin *nausea:* seasickness, disgust, and hence, annoyance.[27] Although annoyance may be associated with loudness, it also depends on other factors that may be of a personal nature.[28] These personal factors, which vary with the individual, include heightened sensitivities to sounds and vibrations. In some individuals, the heightened sensitivities are inherited, whereas in others they are acquired through practice. For example, Evelyn Glennie, who slowly lost her hearing from the age of eight, discovered she could "hear" music by feeling the vibrations. She then developed this complex ability into a highly specialized skill that now enables her to perform internationally as a percussionist.[29]

Musicology is another profession that requires a specialized skill called "auditory discrimination."[30] This skill, which is limited by the sensitivity of the ear, involves more than mere sensitivity because it requires taking advantage of all four attributes of sound (pitch, loudness, timbre, duration) as clues for discriminating one auditory experience from another. Although gross auditory discrimination begins in infancy, more refined discrimination is taught in classes called "ear training," whereby an aspiring musicologist learns to distinguish correctly musical events either as discrete pitches or as patterns in relation. After formal training ceases, the now professional musicologist continues to refine the skill through practice of musicology's core activities: listening to, composing, or performing music; transcribing sounds heard (mentally or actually); reading a score and related texts; and thinking, discussing with others, and writing about what has been listened to, composed, performed, transcribed, or read.

When considered in relation to these core activities, musicology may be said to explore—and to engage in discourse about—different ways of hearing music, whether that music is one's own, or from one's own culture and era, or from other cultures and other eras. The broader tasks of musicology draw on this expertise: the enhancement through practice of the natural discriminatory powers of the auditory system, a system that includes not only peripheral but also central processors.[31] When this enhanced power has been acquired, consciousness is changed irretrievably. The philosopher Daniel Dennett provided an example of this change in the training of an apprentice piano tuner.[32] Before training, the apprentice hears sounds as "bad" or out of tune. After training, the same apprentice has learned to isolate in auditory experience the interference beats as the source of out-of-tuneness and to tune the piano by tuning out the beats. Although prior to training, the beats contributed to the apprentice's auditory experience, they were not themselves present in that experience. After training, however, the tuner detects and also recognizes the beats and their patterns. Hence, training results not merely in an augmentation but also in a change of conscious experience.[33]

From Dennett's example we might draw the inference that our biological heritage—in this instance, the auditory system—is the base upon which culture builds. We might then ask: what is the biological importance of hearing? Answers to this question tend to stress that hearing is our danger sense.[34] But the philosopher John Dewey provided a deeper analysis of the biological importance of hearing.[35] Starting with the premise that sounds are always effects of the forces in nature and that hearing is the experience of these effects, he made the following points:

1. Hearing, taking for granted the background that vision provides (a scene in which things happen and on which changes are projected), "brings home to us changes as changes."

2. Sounds come from outside the body, but sound itself is intimate because it is an excitation of the entire organism: we feel the clash of vibrations throughout our whole body.[36] It is sound that makes us jump or turn our heads (that is, results in a startle reflex).

3. Because of the connections of hearing with all parts of the organism, sound affects us with more reverberations and resonances than any other sense; indeed, sound stimulates directly, not indirectly, immediate change because it reports a change.

4. Sound is the conveyor of what impends, of "what is happening as an indication of what is likely to happen." Hence, sound is fraught with a sense of issues: about the impending there is always indeterminateness and uncertainty, conditions favorable to intense emotional stir.

5. The intellectual range of hearing, though enormous, is acquired; in itself the ear is the emotional sense; and its intellectual scope and depth come from connection with speech.

In its biological function, then, the auditory system is both the danger sense as well as a portent of the future ("what is happening as an indication of what is likely to happen"). Hearing warns us of changes behind us or at a distance, that is to say, in places we cannot see, and in this way prompts us to action. Nature, of course, provides a rich sonic environment; but most natural sounds are background events to humans, coming to the foreground only insofar as they stir us emotionally to respond to reports of change. By means of language (and, I would add, music), the natural auditory system becomes increasingly fine-tuned to the needs of human communication. Thus develops analytic judgment, which, for Dewey, is a test of the mind of a person, because "mind, as organization into perceptions of meanings derived from past intercourse with objects, is the organ of discrimination."[37]

With analytic judgment, sonic events become foreground events because they are the object of one's attentive activities. In the case of our musicologist, therefore, even a trace of noise interferes with fruitful work and, hence, causes annoyance.

Noise Measurement

From about the 1930s, there have been increasing attempts to measure noise for its loudness level, and more recently, for its annoyance. In the latter case what is measured is noise quality, not annoyance itself, for annoyance is a behavioral (emotional) parameter that does not lend itself to precise quantification.[38] Hence, when legislation is involved, it is deemed desirable to use a physically measurable scale of loudness that shows some degree of conformity with physiological experience. The physical correlate that underlies loudness is intensity, usually expressed in decibels as sound pressure level (a relative, not an absolute measure). Although there are several different types of loudness scales, none of these can be applied fully satisfactorily in all conditions. As Rudolf Rasch and Reinier Plomp pointed out:

> Judgment of musical loudness cannot have the degree of reliability and preciseness that is possible with the judgment of (relative) pitch, duration, tempo, etc. This is a consequence of the fact that the underlying physical dimension, intensity, is hard to control precisely. Sources of variation are encountered in sound production, in the fixed acoustic conditions of a room (absorption and thus attenuation by walls, floor, ceiling, etc.), in variable acoustic conditions (like . . . the relative positions of sound source and listener, disturbing external noises), and in the audiograms of the listeners. In all the stages on the road from sound production to sound perception, sound pressure level is liable to be altered whereas frequency is not.[39]

There are, however, numerous other difficulties besides the control of the physical dimension, only a few of which can be mentioned here. First of all, there is the difficulty of exactness. Measurement involves (1) an object upon which an operation is to be performed; (2) an observable whose value is to be determined; and (3) some apparatus by means of which the operation can be carried out. These three aspects—object, observable, and apparatus—are essential to the performance of a measurement, but they are not by themselves sufficient to constitute one, because a measurement must culminate in the emergence of a numerical value. Because the numerical outcome of a measurement characterizes the state of the observed object at the time at which the observation was made, a single measurement never provides the maximum information desirable concerning an observable.

Instead, a set of measurements, statistically treated to supply one optimum value, is required and placed over against a theoretical prediction for confirmation.[40] This is the ideal, which may or may not be followed in laboratory experiments; but, unfortunately, officials involved in enforcing noise legislation tend to avoid repeated noise quality evaluations, in part because they are costly and time consuming.[41]

Second, when scales are utilized for measuring industrial or recreational noise, it often is assumed (sometimes tacitly, sometimes not) that the practice of measuring by using a sound level meter is given. This assumption is equivalent to operationalism, the doctrine that theoretical concepts are defined in terms of measuring operations. Against this doctrine, the philosopher Karl Popper argued that measurements presuppose theories: there is no measurement without a theory and no operation that can be satisfactorily described in non-theoretical terms. For him, a general theory of measurement explains measurement by analyzing its function in the testing of scientific hypotheses.[42] Such hypotheses—for example, models as theories of the cochlea—are formulated in the experimental laboratory, where testing takes place. But, with steady-state and high-intensity impulse stimuli, testing on humans is limited. Instead, tests are performed on guinea pigs, cats, and other creatures. However, these tests may confirm false hypotheses because creatures smaller or larger than humans have different time constants and, hence, hear sonic events differently from the human standpoint.[43]

Third, in classical physical theory (Newtonian), the interaction between object and observer was negligible: the measurement process was fully analyzable in terms of the equations of motion alone. Indeed, measurement constituted a branch of applied physics, so that physical theory and the analysis of measurement employed the same category of concepts. Hence, an isomorphism was supposed that every attribute of a sensation would correspond to some dimension of variation of the stimulus. But in the new physics (quantum and relativity), it seemed that the relation between elements of the physical theory and human experience was not so simple because in every measuring process there is an unanalyzable element due to the intervention of the observer on the object. On this approach, the observer can no longer be regarded as an innocent registrar of his or her objective observations, so that predictions can never be exact, and only probability values can be established.[44]

Is Anyone Listening?

The ubiquitous and frequent broadcasting of sonic events in public or private spaces performs a similar role to what psychologists call "operant conditioning," whereby people's habits are altered voluntarily or involuntarily by reinforcement.[45] At least two alterations are occurring as a result of the reinforcement of steady-state or high-intensity impulse stimuli. First, auditory fatigue, either temporary or permanent, results in loss of auditory sensitivity so that loudness levels are increased, thereby decreasing the quality of life for those who cannot turn off the interfering and unwanted noise. Second, people's preferences are changed, for example, by reinforcing certain styles of music over other styles or, more importantly for our problem, by reinforcing ever-present man-made noise over nature's "quiet" noise. The first alteration is supported by hard evidence in the form of statistics compiled by audiologists and other hearing researchers; but the second alteration is supported only by anecdotal evidence chiefly in the form of newspaper reports. Two such reports will suffice to make my point. First, the British composer, Peter Maxwell Davies, lamented that young people might now be afraid of quiet, that it is something alien and forces them to face up to emptiness within.[46] More recently, the British Broadcasting Corporation announced that it would introduce a noise machine to play "mutter" after employees complained that their new office was much too quiet.[47]

Of course, it is not at all clear that people actually listen to the steady-state and high-intensity impulse stimuli of the man-made variety that increasingly constitute the background noise of daily life. Perhaps this is the central challenge for musicologists, who spend their lives cultivating auditory discrimination as ways of listening but have yet to convince the wider community of the importance of developing this skill. Whatever the challenge, I hope this essay has convinced you that sonic abuse is a problem with a history, that this problem requires urgent investigation by musicologists as well as by crossdisciplinary teams of researchers, and that its solution will not be a simple affair of returning to some imagined pristine state as Schafer and Attali previously supposed.

Notes

1. R. M. Schafer, *The Tuning of the World* (New York: Alfred A. Knopf, 1977). Perhaps because of Schafer's connection with Simon Fraser University, Vancouver now has an action group, Right to Quiet, that maintains a web site with useful data (www.quiet.org).
2. J. Attali, *Bruits: Essai sur l'économie politique de la musique* (Paris: Presses Universitaires de France, 1977); *Noise: The Political Economy of Music*, trans. B. Massumi (Minneapolis: University of Minnesota Press, 1985).
3. For a different use of the term "sonic abuse," see M. Bayles, *Hole in Our Soul: The Loss of Beauty and Meaning in American Popular Music* (New York: Free Press, 1994). The problem of sonic abuse, as I conceive it, dates from the twentieth century (a number of my citations are now historical documents), although no doubt there are historical antecedents.
4. S. Johnson, *A Dictionary of the English Language* (London: Dodsley, 1755).
5. It is the sole definition in J. Walker in *A Critical Pronouncing Dictionary and Expositor*

of the English Language (19th ed., London: T. Cadell and W. Davies, 1818): noise is "Any kind of sound; outcry, clamour, boasting or importunate talk, occasion of talk," and it is one of the definitions in A. Delbridge et al., *The Macquarie Dictionary* (McMahons Point, New South Wales: Macquarie Library, 1981).

6. E. G. Boring, *Sensation and Perception in the History of Experimental Psychology* (New York: D. Appleton-Century, 1942), 363–64.

7. For a summary of his work, see G. von Békésy, *Experiments in Hearing* (New York: McGraw-Hill, 1960) and *Sensory Inhibition* (Princeton: Princeton University Press, 1967). The ear does contain two end-organs: the cochlea for the sense of hearing, and the semicircular canals for the vestibular sense, i.e., the sense of turning in space (including, besides rotation, also acceleration).

8. R. T. Beyer, *Sounds of Our Times: Two Hundred Years of Acoustics* (New York: AIP Press, 1999), 206.

9. Boring, *Sensation and Perception*, 365.

10. For the collected articles, see C. E. Shannon and W. Weaver, *The Mathematical Theory of Communication* (Urbana: University of Illinois Press, 1949). For brief historical background to Shannon's theory, see Weaver's note, 95. See also N. Wiener, *Cybernetics or Control and Communication in the Animal and the Machine*, 2d ed. (New York: M.I.T. Press and John Wiley and Sons, 1961).

11. For an early application of information theory to music, see F. Winckel, *Phänomene des musikalischen Hörens* (Berlin: Max Hesses Verlag, 1960), revised as *Music, Sound and Sensation: A Modern Exposition*, trans. T. Binkley (New York: Dover, 1967). For background to some of Winckel's concepts, see J. R. Pierce, *Electrons, Waves, and Messages: The Art and Science of Modern Electronics* (Garden City, N.J.: Hanover House, 1956), 275–306.

12. V. Illingworth, *Dictionary of Physics* (Harmondsworth: Penguin Books, 1991), 321–22.

13. Beyer, *Sounds of Our Times*, 327.

14. According to Beyer, ibid., 331–32, the first experiments predicting precise quantitative effects of noise on humans were conducted in the 1960s. Not until the 1970s, however, was the effect of noise on animals studied in detail.

15. O. Luening, "Musicology and the Composer," *Current Musicology* 15 (1973), 92–94. Earlier, J. Backus, *The Acoustical Foundations of Music* (New York: W. W. Norton, 1969), 92 wrote: "the recent practice of performing certain forms of popular music at high sound levels runs the serious risk of producing a permanent hearing loss in the listeners."

16. That electronically amplified music, rock bands, and boom boxes all contribute to hearing loss appears in many studies, too numerous to cite here. Many were carried out under the auspices of various organizations; in Australia, the Australian Hearing Services (formerly National Acoustic Laboratory); in the United States, the American Speech-Language-Hearing Association, the Council for Accreditation in Occupational Hearing Conservation, the National Hearing Conservation Association, the National Institutes of Health; and in the United Kingdom, the Institute of Hearing Research. Some of these organizations have their own journal; others maintain a web site.

17. For a report of the colloquium, organized by Centro Ricerche Musicali, Rome, see *Computer Music Journal* 22 (1998), 15–16.

18. Luening, "Musicology and the Composer," 93–94.

19. T. S. Litler, *The Physics of the Ear* (Oxford: Pergamon Press, 1965), 226.

20. On adaptation and fatigue, see Litler, ibid., 226–38; Winckel, *Music, Sound, and Sensation*, 103–7 et passim; D. N. Elliott and W. R. Fraser, "Fatigue and Adaptation," *Foundations of Modern Auditory Theory*, ed. J. C. Tobias (New York: Academic Press, 1970), 117–55.

21. According to Elliott and Fraser, ibid., 130, "the search for the critical level of intensity that clearly separates damaging from nondamaging stimulation is a futile one." See also the same authors, 136, whose conclusion may have been influenced by the findings of W. Dixon Ward and his colleagues that certain types of fatiguing effects are unmeasurable because they involve anatomical units so sensitive that their responses are masked by physiological noise (i.e., noise produced by the human body itself).

22. The important cytological elements in the organ of Corti are the hair cells, the supporting cells (the pillars of Corti, Deiters' cells, Hensen's cells, sulcus cells), the tectorial membrane, and the basilar membrane. The basilar membrane vibrates more like a stiff plate (Békésy) than a taut string (Helmholtz), so that a variation of the law formulated in the seventeenth century by Robert Hooke is involved. See F. Winckel, *Music, Sound, and Sensation*, 87–95; see also J. C. Kassler, *Inner Music: Hobbes, Hooke, and North on Internal Character* (London: Athlone, 1995).

23. The first investigator to observe the difference in tension between the short basilar fibers and the longer ones may have been A. A. Gray, "On a Modification of the Helmholtz Theory of Hearing," *Journal of Anatomy and Physiology* 34 (1900), 324–50.

24. When damaged by such stretching forces, the hair cells react incorrectly, or not at all, to sound waves. When hair cells are lost throughout the cochlea, there is total deafness, because the nerve endings in the cochlea cannot be excited acoustically. See H. F. Schuknecht, "Functional Manifestations of Lesions of the Sensorineural Structures," *Foundations of Modern Auditory Theory*, ed. J. C. Tobias (New York: Academic Press, 1970), vol. 1, 383–404.

25. For an instance, see the poignant last statements of the pianist, Sviatoslav Richter, captured at the conclusion of the video, *Richter, The Enigma* (NVC Arts, 1998).

26. T. H. Fay, ed., *Noise and Health* (New York: New York Academy of Medicine, 1991).

27. W. W. Skeat, *A Concise Etymological Dictionary of the English Language* (1882, reprinted, New York: Capricorn Books, 1963).

28. See B. L. Clarkson, "Effects of Noise on Structures and Human Beings," *Technical Aspects of Sound*, eds. E. G. Richardson and E. Meyer (Amsterdam: Elsevier, 1962), vol. 3, 178–220.

29. E. Glennie, *Good Vibrations* (London: Hutchinson, 1990).

30. Auditory discrimination is not to be confused with acuity of hearing, which is the capacity of a listener to hear faint sounds.

31. For the structure of the auditory system, see F. Blair Simmons, "Monaural Processing," *Foundations of Modern Auditory Theory*, ed. J. C. Tobias (New York: Academic Press, 1970), vol. 1, 345–79. The enhancement of its powers for pitch discrimination is sometimes called "musical ear," see J. C. Kassler, "Musicology and the Problem of Musical Ear," *Musicology Australia* 22 (1999), 18–30, and Chapter 10 in *Music, Science, Philosophy* (Aldershot: Ashgate, 2001), 265–94.

32. D. C. Dennett, *Consciousness Explained* (Harmondsworth: Penguin Books, 1993), 337. The example is a variant of the theory of Helmholtz—not mentioned by Dennett—that in synthetic perception the upper partial tones (for example), corresponding to the simple vibrations of a compound motion of the air, fuse into the whole mass of musical sound; but in analytic perception those partials can be recognized without any other help than a proper direction of attention. For details, see Boring, *Sensation and Perception*, 308–11, 315.

33. Some philosophers claim that in addition to training, consciousness is widened through evolution. These philosophers rely on Darwin's mechanism of natural selection to argue that art (taken generically to include music) is merely an accidental manifestation of a physiological change in cognitive processing—Homo sapiens hear the world differently from their predecessors. This explanation, however, does not explain why a different way of hearing leads to the origin of music. Equally unsatisfactory is the competing theory that relies on Darwin's mechanism of sexual selection to argue that art (taken generically to include music) has the specific function of showing off to and, hence, attracting the opposite sex. For some early variants of these theories, see J. C. Kassler, "Edmund Gurney's The Power of Sound (1880)," *Musicology Australia* 17 (1994), 31–42, 18 (1995), 13–24. For Stumpf's response to the sexual selection theory, see J. C. Kassler (book review), *Musicology Australia* 10 (1987), 79–81.

34. E.g., H. Davis, "Physics and Psychology of Hearing," *Hearing and Deafness: A Guide for Laymen*, ed. H. Davis (New York: Murray Hill Books, 1947), 36: "Sound is one of nature's surest signs of activity, and therein lies its primitive biological significance. Hearing keeps us informed of activities going on at some distance from us and gives us warning if that activity becomes more powerful or approaches very close."

35. J. Dewey, *Art as Experience* (1st ed. 1934, New York: Capricorn Books, 1953), 236–44.

36. The sense of vibration is the sense of touch. But, as Davis, in "Physics and Psychology of Hearing," 28, observed, the sense of hearing itself is a highly specialized organ of touch—specialized to be "touched" only by vibrations of the air. Hence, the senses of hearing and touch merge imperceptibly. For example, when listening to the lowest notes of a pipe organ or an amplified instrument, we feel the vibration as much as we hear it. As the tones get lower in frequency, the ear is less sensitive to them and the tones must be stronger, with larger vibrations, in order to be heard. And when a certain level of intensity is reached, the pressure waves begin to stimulate the skin, the linings of our noses and throats, the hairs of our heads, and even our bones, joints, and inner organs.

37. Dewey, *Art as Experience*, 310.

38. For the early attempts to scale loudness, see H. Fletcher and W. A. Munson, "Loudness, Its Definition, Measurement, and Calculation," *Journal of the Acoustical Society of America* 5 (1933), 82–108; S. S. Stevens, "Measurement of Loudness" and "Calculation of the Loudness of Complex Noise," *Journal of the Acoustical Society of America* 27 (1955), 815–29; 28 (1956), 807–32. For work done in the 1950s to assess both loudness and annoyance of broadband noise, see Clarkson, "Effects of Noise," 215–19. For a recent attempt to find a single number index to measure the annoyance of engine and vehicle sounds that can be utilized in a similar way to the decibel (dBA) scale employed for measuring loudness levels, see W. Stucklschwaiger, "Application of the AVL-annoyance Index for Engine Noise Quality Development," *Acoustica* 83 (1997), 789–95.

39. R. A. Rasch and R. Plomp, "The Perception of Musical Tones," in *The Psychology of Music*, ed. D. Deutsch (New York: Academic Press, 1982), 12. These authors also summarize the different types of loudness scales—sone scale, phone scale, sensation-level scale, physical-level scale.

40. See H. Margenau, *The Nature of Physical Reality* (New York: McGraw-Hill, 1950), 369–83, to whom I am indebted for this summary statement about measurement. See also T. S. Kuhn, "The Function of Measurement in Modern Physical Science," *Isis* 52 (1961), 161–90.

41. For measuring techniques and instruments prior to the 1950s, see A. J. King, "Noise Measurement," *Technical Aspects of Sound*, ed. E. G. Richardson (Amsterdam: Elsevier, 1953), 159–77.

42. K. Popper, *Conjectures and Refutations* (London: Routledge and Kegan Paul, 1978), 62.

43. According to J. Tonndorf, ed., *Physiological Acoustics* (Stroudsburg: Hutchinson Ross, 1981), 2, structural differences among members of the mammalian class are "rather small so that the ears and the central auditory systems of the guinea pig, cat, monkey, and so on may serve as suitable models of their human counterparts." But mammalian structures differ in size, so that, as Robert Hooke pointed out in the seventeenth century, the vibrations or sensible motions of creatures are proportioned to their bulk. See Kassler, *Inner Music*, 133–34; see also Winckel, *Music, Sound, and Sensation*, 53.

44. For the relation of the "new" psychophysics to quantum physics, see J. G. Roederer, *Introduction to the Physics and Psychophysics of Music*, 2d ed. (New York: Springer-Verlag, 1975), 8–11. For a discussion of some of the problems of measurement in the experimental laboratory (e.g., absolute *versus* fluctuating thresholds), as well as a critical examination of one auditory theory based on statistical decision theory, see J. C. R. Licklider, "Three Auditory Theories," *Psychology: A Study of a Science*, ed. S. Koch (New York: McGraw-Hill, 1959), vol. 1, 41–144.

45. For operant conditioning, see B. F. Skinner, *Science and Human Behavior* (New York: Macmillan, 1953). For a study of one type of ubiquitous background noise, see J. Lanza, *Elevator Music: A Surreal History of Muzak, Easy-listening and Other Moodsong* (New York: Quartet, 1994).

46. *Daily Mail* (London) quoted in *Sunday Telegraph* (Sydney, April 14, 1994), 11.

47. *The Guardian* (London) quoted in *Sydney Morning Herald* (October 15, 1999), 12.

18

An Historical Perspective on the Study of Music Perception

Amy B. Graziano

Music is one of the most complex of human activities. It has played a role in human culture since before recorded history, serving ritual, functional, and entertainment purposes. But music has also been studied as a product of human perception and cognition. It is considered both perceptual and cognitive because it involves sensory processing on two levels: the progress of sound through our auditory physiological system (perception); and the processing of that sound into higher-order conceptual thinking about music (cognition). During the late twentieth century, the study of music sensation and cognition developed into a fairly unified field of intellectual inquiry, one in which psychologists, neuroscientists, music theorists, and musicologists participate. This field is the largest and most significant research area in music psychology, and is generally referred to as "music perception."

The academic discipline of music perception is distinguished by its experimental research methodologies and its interest in auditory sensory mechanisms. Well-defined research topics in the field cover a broad range that can be roughly categorized as:

1. Psychoacoustic factors that affect the perception of basic musical elements such as pitch, intervals, time, volume, and timbre.
2. The perception and cognitive organization of complex musical elements such as rhythm, melody, chords, mode, harmony, tonality, tuning and temperament, consonance and dissonance, form, and style.
3. The qualitative development of musical cognitive processes in children. Most research in this area centers on identifying cognitive stages for

listening to, performing, and composing music that parallel processes in other domains of cognition.

4. The relationship between musical structures and non-musical structures, such as the linguistic aspects of music, semiotics, or group theory.[1]

Understanding the physiological sense of hearing lies at the basis of music perception. For scholars and researchers in the field, the German physicist and physiologist Hermann von Helmholtz (1821–94) is considered the first to have emphasized that in order to understand acoustical issues, it is necessary to understand how the ear works. John G. McKendrick, writing just a few years after Helmholtz's death, claims that, before Helmholtz, questions about perception were not of interest to musicians. According to McKendrick, musicians were only "occupied with the consideration of [music's] aesthetic relations."[2] Helmholtz's work generated a renewed interest in sensation and perception among both scientists and musicians, giving them a practical basis through which to address important questions, such as, why is an octave more satisfying to the ear than a minor sixth? Or, what is the physiological basis of dissonance? Because of this, there is a consensus among contemporary practitioners of music perception that the roots of the field lie in the nineteenth century with the work of Helmholtz.

The modern academic discipline of music perception blossomed in the 1960s and 1970s when, as pioneering practitioner Diana Deutsch puts it, there was a "sudden flowering of interest in the empirical study of music."[3] This sense-based empirical approach was a deliberate contrast to the earlier rationalistic approach to musical understanding, which, in Deutsch's view, had dominated musical thinking from antiquity through the first part of the twentieth century. This latter approach, by no means universally practiced during the era, had been characterized by a distrust of the evidence of the senses in favor of a reliance on the mathematical basis of music.[4] The roots of musical empiricism—as well as an interest in auditory sensory mechanisms and the physiological processing of sense-data in sound and music—can actually be traced to the late sixteenth and early seventeenth centuries, particularly to the pioneering work of such influential thinkers as Vincenzo and Galileo Galilei, Johannes Kepler, René Descartes, and Robert Hooke.[5]

The scientific study of music remained close to music theory for most of the seventeenth century, but eventually moved away from a musical context and developed into a new branch of the recently formed experimental sciences. By the early eighteenth century, this new field had been named "acoustics" by Joseph Sauveur, who described it as the science of sound.[6] Acoustics is concerned with empirical research into the physical phenomena of sound, generally with no deep bond to practical music or to perception.[7] From the late seventeenth through nineteenth centuries, most researchers in acoustics were experimental scientists and mathematicians who were interested in confirming mathematical laws through experimentation rather than human reception and response to music.

A great deal of acoustical research during the Enlightenment focused on calculating the fundamental and overtones for different pitches. Except for "occasional remarks about the nature of the ear,"[8] researchers were not concerned at all with the actual sense of hearing or with human sensory response to musical stimuli. Instead, for approximately 150 years, most acoustic scientists limited themselves to studying the physical properties of sound. It was not until the second half of the nineteenth century that research returned to sensation and perception.

Modern interest in the sensation and perception of auditory stimuli came about most directly through interdisciplinary work in acoustics and physiology, as conducted principally by Helmholtz. As mentioned, he particularly emphasized that in order to understand consonance, dissonance, and other acoustical issues, it was necessary to understand how the ear receives and processes sensory data. The field of psychoacoustics—the experimental study of how physical mechanisms in the ear and auditory centers of the brain allow us to perceive auditory stimuli—traces its most immediate origins to Helmholtz's work. The great physicist and physiologist conducted research relating the structures of the inner ear to pitch perception, but remained unconcerned with practical music and its connection to the body and its senses. Nonetheless, his work is seen as the starting point for all subsequent psychoacoustical research.

Helmholtz originated the place theory of pitch perception, which states that different areas of the basilar membrane in the inner ear vibrate in response to different sound frequencies. Pitch is determined by the particular area of the membrane that vibrates in response to the sound stimulus. As von Békésy demonstrated in the 1920s,[9] this claim was not entirely correct, but it was enough to initiate a whole line of psychophysical and pitch-perception research. This ultimately led to the work of Diana Deutsch, W. Jay Dowling, and others in the 1960s and 1970s.

Helmholtz was also the first to discuss consonance and dissonance perception in terms of beats.[10] Beating occurs when two pure tones of only slightly different frequencies are heard simultaneously and combine into a complex wave form. The two component waves go in and out of phase with each other; when they are in phase, their amplitudes match and they rise and fall together. This reinforces the perception of the sound, heard as an increase in the level of loudness, rather than as two different tones. The perceived fluctuation in loudness is usually described as a dissonant roughness or beating.[11] According to Helmholtz, intervals composed of two complex tones (which contain upper partials as well as the pure fundamental) are perceived as dissonant when the upper partials of the two tones produce beats. Intervals are perceived as consonant when the upper partials of the two complex tones "coincide to a high degree and therefore do not produce beats."[13] Some twentieth-century ideas about consonance can be traced back to this nineteenth-century research on beating.

While Helmholtz and his German contemporaries Stumpf, Mach, and Fechner contributed to the developing field of psychoacoustics, other late-nineteenth-century German scientists were becoming interested in more immediately musical issues. Neurologists, especially concerned with brain physiology and function, showed a significant interest in documenting aspects of music functioning in neurologically impaired individuals. This interest stemmed from describing music abilities in individuals with aphasia, a neurological disorder characterized by the breakdown of language functioning after brain damage. The observation that words could be produced in the context of singing but not in spontaneous speech caught the attention of several notable neurologists. The study of music abilities initially reflected an interest in comparing language with other cognitive abilities (for example, music, calculation, and memory) and studying language in other contexts (for example, song texts). The investigators were interested in demonstrating that language could be impaired independently from other cognitive abilities, and also that language could remain preserved in other contexts, such as while singing the text of a song. In 1888 the German neurologist Knoblauch coined the term "amusia" to refer to musical impairment.[13]

Knoblauch and other neurologists were especially interested in how language and music systems were organized in the brain, that is, cognitively. Studying impaired systems helped them decipher this structure, and they were able to develop some initial models of musical cognitive structure.[14] Yet the nineteenth-century combination of music and neurology does not appear to have influenced subsequent research in music perception.

After psychoacoustics became an established field, research in music perception developed fairly rapidly. In the early twentieth century, theoretical music, divorced from science since the late seventeenth century, once again became a topic of scientific research. The combination of music theoretical topics, psychoacoustic measurements, and the developing field of psychology led to experimental research in the sensation and cognitive organization of music. One of the first to bring these fields together was American psychologist Carl Seashore, who became interested in measuring levels of musical ability. He developed an assessment tool that used psychoacoustical measures, in particular judgments of pitch discrimination, which he believed measured innate musicality. Four of these measures involve discrimination judgments between paired tones in order to measure the ability to perceive pitch, loudness, timbre, and time.[15] The remaining two measures involve discrimination judgments between paired sequences of tones, that is, pattern comparisons, in order to measure the more musically complex elements of rhythmic and tonal memory.

By the mid-twentieth century, psychologists began conducting empirical studies using psychoacoustical measures similar to Seashore's discrimination tasks to investigate the perceptual and cognitive organization of music. Through the 1970s, much of this research remained psychoacoustical in nature, useful for understanding auditory processing, but not offering much for an understanding of music. These music perception studies were often "reductionistic," a term used to describe research that breaks a larger stimulus into smaller parts, for example, music into individual pitches, intervals, chords, and so forth. It is difficult to gauge how far results from such research can be generalized because stimuli like these are far removed from an actual musical context.

However, the interest Seashore displayed in more complex musical elements, such as rhythm, influenced subsequent research. The focus on music as a complex phenomenon was indicative of a shift in emphasis from psychoacoustic to more cognitive factors. Gradually, psychologists became interested in studying music as a complex perceptual and cognitive system, in order to learn about higher-level cognitive structure, rather than about individual perceptual processes such as how sound travels through the inner ear. Researchers began to investigate the perception and understanding of melody, harmony, and rhythm, each of which is made up of several psychoacoustical factors.

One direction for a more cognitive approach came from Gestalt psychology. In the first half of the twentieth century, Gestalt psychologists held that our understanding of the world is based on the way we cognitively organize our perceptions into patterns that are unified wholes rather than individual parts. Gestalt principles of visual perception were applied to music, especially to the perception of temporal (rhythmic) patterns. Based on perceptual experiments, it was found that both rhythmic and melodic patterns were perceived as units if they followed Gestalt laws of visual perception. For example, the Gestalt law of proximity held that music-notes grouped close together in auditory space will tend to be perceived as a unit. Also, the law of similarity applied to music: People tend to hear a series of notes with some element in common as a unit.[16]

Although by the 1980s the Gestalt School was no longer considered a separate branch of psychology, the cognitive approach had permeated music-perception research. Researchers began to recognize that results obtained from reduced stimuli may not always "engage other perceptual or cognitive processes normally operating during listening to actual music."[17] However, as late as 1985, Sloboda described a gap between knowledge gained from psychological research on music and knowledge gained from music history and theory. In his view, music-perception research was not addressing questions of musical importance.[18] Because of Sloboda and like-minded researchers, the late 1980s and early 1990s saw an increase in the role that music theory played in music-perception research. This helped to shape research in musically meaningful ways, by directing attention "to more interesting and subtle musical questions," and by providing "a context for interpreting empirical results."[19]

One example of musically meaningful research focused on the sensation of consonance. Psychoacoustic factors, such as beating, were still studied. The traditional consonances (octave, fifth, and so forth) were described as having certain acoustical properties that influence how they are coded by the sensory system.[20] However, these psychoacoustic factors were found to be only one factor in the overall perception of musical consonance. Other factors also contribute to the sensation of consonance, for example, cultural norms and musical experience. Indeed, Lundin argued in the 1940s that consonance is mainly a matter of cultural conditioning.[21]

A distinction is now made between musical consonance (a sensation of consonance based on musical context) and psychoacoustic consonance (a sensation of consonance based on psychoacoustic factors). Krumhansl found that the summary statistics of the use of intervals in actual music, rather than psychoacoustic judgments, played the main role in determining a sensation of musical consonance.[22] Another area that used a cognitive approach to complex music focused on relating aspects of music theory directly to aspects of cognition. Serafine suggested that musical cognitions can be understood as the psychological manifestations of different musical aspects and vice versa. Agmon suggested something similar: that one can map certain formal, structural theories of music directly onto cognitive processes. Christensen took this one step further by offering a perceptual view of Rameau's theory of tonality, and by looking at Mattheson's views on the sensory basis of music as a theory of perception.[23]

By the mid-1990s, the relationship between music sensation and actual, practical music was at the center of a large proportion of research in music perception. In 1992, Butler pointed out that music perception research had become "musically more realistic and therefore better related to actual musical listening."[24] The field of music perception and cognition gradually evolved as a function of increasing interest in two things: The sensation of sound and the cognitive processing of that sound, and how auditory sensation relates to practical music. Both interests began in the seventeenth century, were sidetracked into the physical properties of sound (divorced from sensation) during the eighteenth century, then renewed and developed during the late nineteenth and twentieth centuries. Today, music perception has become part of mainstream scholarly and educational institutions, with a large and growing literature of scientific research and a number of in-depth textbooks on the topic. Many colleges and universities now offer interdisciplinary music-perception courses in both music and psychology departments, and there is an international scholarly society devoted to this topic (the Society for Music Perception and Cognition) with its own scholarly journal, *Music Perception.*

And what does the future hold for the study of music perception? During the last five years there has been an increase in the empirical investigation of complex musical stimuli, and of various non-Western musical stimuli. This trend seems likely to continue. In addition, there is an increasing interest in the neurophysiological mechanisms of sensation and cognition. It seems likely that neuroscientific research, as well as psychological, behavioral research, will become a standard part of the study of music perception.

Notes

1. David Butler, *The Musician's Guide to Perception and Cognition* (New York: Schirmer Books, 1992), 2.
2. John G. McKendrick, *Hermann von Helmholtz* (New York: Longmans, Green, 1899), 137. More recent historical research has, of course, shown this view to be incorrect; see, for example, Penelope Gouk, *Music, Science and Natural Magic in Seventeenth-Century England* (New Haven: Yale University Press, 1999), 66–114, 157–92, and 261–76.
3. Diana Deutsch, *The Psychology of Music* (New York: Academic Press, 1982), xiii.
4. Deutsch, xiii.
5. For further information, see, in particular, H. F. Cohen, *Quantifying Music: The Science of Music and the First Stage of the Scientific Revolution, 1580–1650* (Dordrecht: Dreidel, 1984); Stillman Drake, "Music and Philosophy in Early Modern Science," in *Music and Science in the Age of Galileo*, ed. Victor Coelho (Dordrecht: Kluwer, 1992), 10; Penelope Gouk, "The Role of Acoustics and Music Theory in the Scientific Work of Robert Hooke," *Annals of Science 37* (1980), 573–605; Claude V. Palisca, *Humanism in Italian Renaissance Musical Thought* (New Haven: Yale University Press, 1985), 265–79; Claude V. Palisca, "Scientific Empiricism in Musical Thought," in *Studies in the History of Italian Music and Music Theory*, ed. Claude Palisca (Oxford: Clarendon Press, 1994), 204; Bruce Stephenson, *Music of the Heavens* (Princeton: Princeton University Press, 1994).
6. S. Dostrovsky, James Bell, and C. Truesdell, "Physics of Music," in *The New Grove Dictionary of Music and Musicians* 14 (London: Macmillan, 1980), 665.
7. Thomas Kuhn, *The Essential Tension: Selected Studies in Scientific Tradition and Change* (Chicago: University of Chicago Press, 1977).
8. S. Dostrovsky, James Bell, and C. Truesdell, 669.
9. James O. Pickles, *An Introduction to the Physiology of Hearing*, 2nd ed. (San Diego, Calif.: Academic Press, 1988), 26–77.
10. However, the phenomenon of beating has been discussed since at least the early sixteenth century in relation to organ tuning practices (see H. F. Cohen).
11. W. Jay Dowling and Dane L. Harwood, *Music Cognition* (San Diego, Calif.: Academic Press, 1986), 35.
12. John Booth Davies, *The Psychology of Music* (Stanford, Calif.: Stanford University Press, 1978), 159.
13. A. Knoblauch, "Ueber Stärungender musikalischen Leistungs fähigkeit infolge von Gehirnläsionen," *Deutsches Archiv für klinische Medizin 43* (1888), 331–52.
14. Julene Johnson and Amy B. Graziano, *Amusia: Nineteenth-Century Perspectives on Music and the Brain* (manuscript in preparation).

15. Rudolf E. Radocy and David Boyle, *Psychological Foundations of Musical Behavior*, 2nd. ed. (Springfield, Ill.: Thomas, 1988), 306–7.
16. See Leonard B. Meyer, *Emotion and Meaning in Music* (Chicago: University of Chicago Press, 1956).
17. Carol L. Krumhansl, "Perceptual Structures for Tonal Music," *Music Perception 1* (1983), 31.
18. Sloboda, *p.v.*
19. Carol L. Krumhansl, "Music Psychology: Tonal Structures in Perception and Memory," *Annual. Review of Psychology* 42 (1991), 278.
20. Carol L. Krumhansl, *Cognitive Foundations of Musical Pitch* (Oxford: Oxford University Press, 1990), 51.
21. R. W. Lundin, "Toward a Cultural Theory of Consonance," *Journal of Psychology* 23 (1947), 45–49.
22. Krumhansl, 1990, 76.
23. See Mary Louise Serafine, *Music as Cognition* (New York: Columbia University Press, 1988); E. Agmon, "Music Theory as Cognitive Science," *Music Perception* 7 (1990); Thomas Christensen, "An Eighteenth-Century Model of Musical Perception," paper presented at the Second International Conference on Music Perception and Cognition (1992); and Thomas Christensen, "Sensus and Ratio: Mattheson's Critique of Mathematics in Music," Paper presented at the annual Meeting of the AMS (1993).
24. Butler, ix.

INDEX